Richard D. Taylor

BEHIND
YESTERDAY

BOOKS BY THE AUTHOR

THE GENEVA INTRUSION
Kate Adler thriller #1
Iran attacks the world's financial markets to start a war.

PRIMARY PROTOCOL
Kate Adler thriller #2
Kate and the cartel uncover a terrorist plot on French soil.

ISLANDS OF PEACE
Kate Adler thriller #3
Things are never what they seem.

BRIMSTONE OFFENSIVE
Kate Adler thriller #4
Never underestimate your enemy.

AT RANDOM
"Thoughts From a Marginal Mind."

BEHIND YESTERDAY

History, romance and intrigue
in a time of war.

Richard D. Taylor

Pacific Grove Press

Behind Yesterday

Pacific Grove Press

Printed in the United States of America

For more information on this and other books by Mr. Taylor:

RichardDtaylor@gmail.com

I would love to hear from you.

Version V2024.6

To my father, Harold Taylor, who fought in the Pacific,
and to all those who fought for today's freedom in WWII.

FREE OFFER
BEHIND YESTERDAY'S
COMPANION PIECE

A great deal of research goes into any historical novel. Sometimes it's nice to know more than what made it into the book. So I've compiled a 17-page booklet containing additional information offering more history and insight into the story. It includes descriptions of items relevant to the story and period and individual chapter comments. Sign up for my email list, and you'll get this booklet at no cost. You'll also get upcoming release dates and purchase information on my other books, Geneva Intrusion, Primary Protocol, Islands of Peace and Brimstone Offensive, and the sequel to Behind Yesterday, Target London. Your email won't be shared.

ACCESS THE FOLLOWING LINK FOR YOUR COMPANION PIECE.

https://landing.mailerlite.com/webforms/landing/i4l4f6

History 'tis but bottom sand in the hourglass,
Turned only at the will of the master,
Aloft for now, and beneath for then,
Save for the point of passing,
When at once there is neither and ...

-- Richard D. Taylor

"I don't understand the mystery of my being here, but just because we don't know how or why doesn't mean there isn't a significant reason it occurred.

Thomas Watson

Chapter One

Caribbean Sea
Cruise Liner: Voyager of the Sea
11:15 pm New Year's Eve, 1989

Thomas Watson stopped at the mirror and caught the reflection of his reddened eyes. He put his drink down on the marble counter of the men's room and leaned in for a closer look. Indeed his eyes were in a deplorable state from days in the sun. Good thing the New Year's Eve party upstairs was in a darkened ballroom.

Thomas wasn't sure what caused him to keep staring at his face but he ended up peering directly into his pupils for a short time. He attributed the peculiar feeling emerging from within to the alcohol. He'd done this staring a few times before and found, if prolonged, it created unusual effects on his perception. After a time, the reflection of his face changed. Truth be known, he thought the staring was an old parlor game.

As he was ready to turn around, the feeling went from peculiar to alarming. Suddenly, the mirror seemed to have a depth and softness, as if it had disappeared. He extended his right hand upward and watched his reflection do the same. He placed a finger on the glass, thinking he could touch not his reflection but what looked like an actual person on the other side. The image did almost the same thing but instead placed two fingers against the other side of the glass.

"Whoa," he thought. It startled him back to reality. He dropped his hand, and, to his relief, all returned to normal. Starting over, he returned to his weary eyes. His gaze drifted from his face to an almost imperceptible movement in the room reflected behind him. He blinked; no, it wasn't a movement; it was change. Something was different—very different. Thomas turned and found himself in a completely different bathroom. His hand knocked his drink off the discoloured counter—

wait, it was now a bottle—not a drink. He watched it descend towards an old hardware floor. At the sound of shattering glass, he froze.

Chapter Two

Twenty Minutes Earlier On The Ship

The ocean spray lifted to Thomas Watson's face as turbulent water parted from the cruise ship sailing in the balmy Caribbean. Tall and fit, the professor of history presented the image of a handsome, confident man. The wind rearranged his light brown hair as he leaned on the railing.

Thomas had excused himself from the party inside, coming out on the deck for some air and a secluded moment. He needed a break from the chaos and commotion of the New Year's Eve party in the Explorer Lounge directly behind him. Another strong gust pressed the left lapel of his tuxedo jacket against his face. Thomas took a deep breath and made his way back inside.

Only recently, he realized the need to stop avoiding any serious relationship, as the repeated behavior would result in him being alone for the rest of his life. He was now determined to find what appeared an impossible find, a true lifetime soul mate. The cruise, with a few friends, was an excellent way to start anew. Throughout the week-long cruise, the constant socializing was precisely what he needed.

Thomas realized another problem required immediate attention and decided to find a restroom. He weaved through the crowd, making his way toward the sizeable formal entrance of the ballroom. He saw the ship's captain holding court, kissing the women, and shaking hands.

"What a great job," Thomas thought as he worked his way through the frantic social mass toward his general destination. Squeezing into a slight opening, he ducked a particularly hearty descriptive gesture and ran straight into a woman. His belated attempt failed to catch her drink as it tumbled onto the carpet.

"I'm so very sorry," he said, embarrassed but at the same time immediately taken at how attractive she was; more than that, she was utterly beautiful.

"Wow, where has *she* been all week?" Thomas thought.

He said, "Oh, God, that was clumsy of me. Did I spill any on you?"

Looking down at her dress, she said in a British accent, "No… no, you didn't, and it's quite all right." Looking back up, she pulled her hair back behind an ear.

She said, "What's a party without running into a few people…literally?" she laughed as she withdrew her hand, expecting him to acknowledge her witty remark.

Instead of replying, Thomas remained captivated by the picture that stood before him. She appeared to be in her late twenties, a little taller than medium height, with an above-average figure. Her wavy, shoulder-length hair had a WWII victory wave on the left. When she moved, its red-auburn colour reflected the lights in the room. Her greenish-blue eyes sparkled as she spoke directly to him amid the surrounding clamor and bedlam. She had a small, delicate nose and high cheekbones with a light, even skin tone, suggesting an Irish heritage. Around her neck was a delicate gold necklace. "It didn't matter who or what she was." Thomas thought. He couldn't overcome her striking, evocative Avedon/Vogue manner and appearance.

Thomas just stared at her, smitten like a schoolboy, as the prolonged silence begged him to say something. He started with a weak "Then… why didn't I see you earlier in the week?" It wasn't Shakespeare, but it was the first thing that came to him.

"Well, now, that's an interesting question. Perhaps it wasn't time for our paths to cross. On the other hand, but much less mysterious, I generally avoid areas with masses of people. But how could I say no to tonight? So," she said, striking a pose with both hands on her hips and a turned knee, "here I am."

"Oh," Thomas said. "Well, either way, I'm glad they did… cross. Our paths, I mean."

She looked, almost stared, right at him, evaluating not just the outside but his whole person. Thomas didn't mind. "How rude of me," he said, "I'm Thomas Watson."

"Pleased to meet you, Thomas Watson. My name is Margaret…"

Before she could finish, the band started again, and someone who was obviously a friend came rushing over in full top hat, bright blue cummerbund, and flowing tails.

4

"This is the one you promised me, dearie," he said, gently pulling her onto the dance floor by the hand. "Everyone watch us now," he shouted over the band at the rest of her group. "The master will now demonstrate the finer arts of dancing with a beautiful woman." She giggled, and while looking directly at Thomas, she addressed her friend, saying, "Okay, a promise is a promise, but you have to return me to where this very interesting man is standing."

"Agreed, my lady," he said with an over-the-top feigned bow, one hand holding his hat at his waist, the other high in the air. He just missed the nearest elegantly dressed couple, who responded with an icy stare.

Remembering his previous agenda, and while she was still looking at him, Thomas said, "I'll be back when the song is over," and pointed straight down to a spot on the floor. "I'll be right here."

She let go of Mr. Top Hat's hand about ten feet onto the dance floor. She put that hand at her waist and, with an extended right arm, bent wrist, and sassy finger pointed down at the same spot, "Right there then!" She said, laughing. "Promise, will you?"

Thomas managed but a pathetic speechless nod.

As she went spinning away, her long satin dress flared out parallel to the floor, catching the light and giving the impression she was floating away. A sultry and confident smile accompanied one last look over her shoulder as their eyes met, and then she was lost in the dancing crowd.

"So," Thomas thought, "that's what they mean by instant attraction." Emerging from deep within was a desire to know more about this woman.

Realizing his brief time until the dance was over, he quickly turned, aiming for the restroom one deck down. He grabbed Margaret's empty glass off the floor and tossed it into an overflowing bin. Given how hard cocktails were to come by, he decided to keep his.

Chapter Three

In a strange new bathroom.

Thomas was deeply confused after staring at the mirror and seeing his reflection react in such an unusual way. Having hit the bottle, he watched what used to be his drink fall in slow motion to the dark hardwood floor. He stared at the broken glass next to his feet. For whatever reason, he thought he was in a strange and small bathroom. Behind him, an oversized, old-fashioned claw-foot tub dominated the room. Wide-mouth brass taps had replaced the sink's chrome faucets, and on a small shelf to his right, two bottles of bath oil sat beside a glass bowl filled with talcum powder. Busy wallpaper covered the walls, and various plants hung from the ceiling. In the corner was a toilet, a toilet with a pull chain.

Thomas stood absolutely still as if the slightest movement might knock him over. He took a deep breath and held it. Shock was holding him rigid, and fear was beginning to take over when a feminine voice called out from beyond the closed door.

"Thomas, what was that? Are you all right, love? What on earth are you doing in there?"

She had a wonderfully smooth, upper-class British accent. Thomas could see movement through the door's mottled glass and then a gradually darkening shadow. The doorknob turned, and a woman in her late twenties, dressed in a bra and garter belt under an opaque slip, appeared. The slip was high enough to see she'd one nylon stocking attached to the fasteners; the other stocking was loose in her hand. She noticed his glance and quickly pulled down the slip. She pointed an angry finger at him and said, "We've discussed this, Thomas. Stop staring. It won't do you any good."

However, it wasn't her exposed leg that had caught his attention; it was the fantastic white skin of her face, framed by beautiful red hair.

The long waves pulled back behind her ear on one side fell to bare shoulders. Her face's delicate features and light skin enhanced her greenish eyes. A gold necklace hung from her neck, and as he took it all in, he thought for a brief second he recognized her. Even in this out-of-this-world moment, Thomas registered that she was strikingly attractive. However—who was she?

She ran her hands down her hips, smoothing the fabric, still concerned with the length of her slip when she looked down at the floor. Looking back up, she said good-naturedly, "Good thing it was almost empty. Otherwise, it couldn't been no supper for you."

She bent down, picking up the biggest piece of the broken bottle. While holding it up between them, she said, laughing, "You brute, this was my favorite face cream, and you just destroyed it. I can't buy this anymore. It was supposed to last me until the end of the" She stopped mid-sentence.

Thomas, still leaning against the counter, just looked at her. She sensed something, and her smile disappeared. "Thomas ah… are you all right?" Despite her previous admonishment, her manner and voice showed genuine tenderness and concern. She leaned up against him, placing one hand gently on his chest.

"What's wrong?" she asked, looking up at him. He didn't move or say anything.

She waited a few seconds before grabbing his hand and slowly pulling him out of the bathroom and into the next room. She dropped the piece of glass into a dustbin and sat him down on a bed. Sitting right next to him, she put her arm around his waist. She was looking for a response.

It was a small bedroom with two windows and several large wardrobes. On a nightstand was a small wind-up clock. It said it was 11:15. Thomas guessed p.m. but didn't know as the windows were covered in dark paper. Looking out the bedroom's open door, he could see a short hallway leading to other rooms. It was a house, but what house—whose house?

"Thomas?" she said.

He turned and looked at her. "I'm not sure," he managed to say. "Just a little confused."

He didn't know what else to say. What could he say? "What am I doing here? Who are you?" The tenderness in her voice intimated an obvious affection. But she was certainly shy about her state of dress. His mind searched for answers. His first memory was of looking in the mirror. What was I doing before that? Focused thinking came to nothing. Now he was utterly confused. The most obvious explanation was a dream. Yes, that's it.

The sound of sirens from outside abruptly interrupted his search for an answer. They weren't police sirens but those that take a few seconds to get up to speed and then have a constant deafening steady sound.

"Oh, no, it's another drill," the woman said, standing up. "Thomas, grab your coat."

He sensed the urgency in her voice.

"Thomas, quickly!" she said, pulling a dress over her head.

He stood up, catching her eye as her head emerged. "The wardrobe," she pointed across the room. He pulled open the cabinet doors and saw it was full of coats, including a long black men's overcoat, which he grabbed.

"Get mine," she ordered.

"I don't see it," he said, looking for something like a woman's coat.

"Thomas! Not there. Look in my wardrobe, love. We need to hurry."

He rushed over to the other cabinet, and a dark green coat was hanging on the inside of the door. He handed it to the woman, as she grabbed his hand and quickly led him out of the room and into the hall.

She threw the coat around her shoulders and grabbed a silk headscarf. It was when she was reaching down for two boxes with handles sitting on the bottom of a hall tree he said, "Where are we going?"

She slowly turned, staring right through him. He thought she was starting to feel uneasy. "Thomas, just come with me. We can talk later."

Chapter Four

London Suburbs 1940
Town of Amersham—Amersham Tube Shelter
11:20 p.m. Saturday

They stepped out the brick home's front door, down a short walkway, and out the front gate. Thomas looked up and down the street at the identical brick row houses. It was a black night and slightly cool. He looked around, still uncertain in his thoughts, as the distinctive silhouette of a British cab flew by with small slots for headlights. He thought, "A British cab?" He paused, but the fact didn't provide anything of value.

Groups of people were walking and running, all in the same direction. The sirens were still going off, and a dull roar was in the background. Thomas and Margaret moved briskly for a few minutes and traveled three blocks before turning right at a corner. Passing the enormous doorway to a pub, he could see groups of people from several directions walking into an opening leading below street level. Across the street, he saw an elderly couple quickly locking the door to their bakery shop. The roar was getting louder and presumably closer. Children rushed with jackets over their nightclothes, accompanied by the unmistakable sights and sounds of concerned mothers protecting their young. It wasn't a feeling of panic but more of genuine concern.

Suddenly, the sky lit up like a summer night at an amusement park, but it wasn't fireworks—it was gunfire. A tracer round followed every sixth bullet in the night sky. They could be seen in crossing patterns from about a mile away. Columns of interlaced light pierced straight into the blackness, lighting up the undersides of the high clouds. The dull roar was now deafening as the crowd broke into a slow run.

"Oh, God, it's not a drill," Margaret yelled. "Thomas, follow me. We can sort this out later if we're still alive."

"If we are still alive?" Thomas thought.

They ran faster, approaching the stairway to the shelter's opening. They were among the last ones in sight as Thomas helped her take the wide concrete steps down to the entrance. At the second step, Thomas looked up and saw "Amersham Station" painted on a sign above the opening and stopped as Margaret continued forward. To the right was the unmistakable tri-colour logo of the London Underground, and underneath was a round yellow and black metal placard that said "Air Raid Shelter, Night Only, Max. Persons 125." Weathered sandbags around the entrance were efficiently stacked in a neat matrix as if their effectiveness depended on a precise pattern.

A thunderous boom followed by a crushing wall of hot air two blocks away caused the street to erupt in a fireball. The noise and wall of hot air stunned him as he placed both hands over his ears. In a half-second, he realized it was the bomb's pressure wave. The blast had also slammed his teeth together, which fortunately missed his tongue. He ended up against the sandbags on the opposite wall. "Thomas," she screamed, running back up the steps. She grabbed his coat sleeve and pulled him down toward the doors of the station below. "Get in the shelter—now."

They both looked up when they heard low moans from an older, heavyset man wearing what looked like a police uniform. He was the ARP (Air Raid Precaution) warden of the shelter. The man had been standing at the top of the stairs and thrown down by the blast. The warden continued to moan as Thomas slowly rolled him over onto his back.

Thomas turned to Margaret, "You go on down; I'm coming."

Margaret shouted over the increasing sound from above. "Thomas, there isn't time."

"Please do it now. *Please*," Thomas said firmly. Margaret paused, her glance lingering over Thomas, before continuing down. Thomas rushed back up the steps to the warden. Debris, strewn everywhere, also covered the warden. Small shards of roofing tile, bricks, dirt, and burning wood had rained down with a good share landing on the man. Thomas threw off a larger piece of what looked like furniture and bent on one knee over the man, looking for any serious injuries.

"Sir, can you get up?" Thomas asked.

The man rolled over again and rose onto all fours.

"Can you walk?" Thomas asked.

The warden looked at him, aware that Thomas was there but didn't respond. It wasn't long before his head started to clear, and he reached for his tin hat lying on the ground next to him.

The man's face was covered in dirt. He looked at Thomas and said, "Obliged, Son, just an arm, if ya' please." Thomas doubted the man could hear himself speak. Unlike Thomas, he'd taken the full force of the bomb's pressure wave without the protection of the sandbags and stairwell.

Thomas helped the man to stand. He didn't appear to be seriously injured, but he was going to need help walking. Thomas pulled the man's arm over his shoulder and, with the other hand at his waist, they started down into the stairwell. Thomas could feel the man getting steadier as they approached the station door, but he was breathing heavily. Someone stood aside and opened the door for them, and once inside, Thomas helped the man lean against a wall. Slowly the warden slid down to a seated position.

"The doors, someone close the doors," the warden said. The tall man who had opened the door for them was already closing one, and Thomas started with the other one. When the two steel doors slammed shut, the tall man rotated the locking arm, as he'd no doubt done before.

She was right there. "Thomas, darling, were you hurt?"

"Me?" Thomas replied. "No, I think I'm fine."

With that, Margaret dropped down to attend to the warden and, in a second, started working his collar loose. She pulled the scarf off her head and started wiping his face to remove what dirt she could.

"I'm fine, Margaret," the warden said slowly. "Jus' need a bit ter gather me thoughts."

The man reached out an arm, waving her back, and ordered, "Take places, everyone, jus' like the drills. There's no need ter getting in a fret now. You too Margaret."

Not completely satisfied, Margaret rose and turned toward Thomas. She placed her arm inside his and proceeded deeper into the rail station. "Are you sure you're okay? Weren't you thrown against the side?"

"Yes, a bit dizzy like the officer, but okay."

After a few more steps, she turned, "Did you hit your head?" She asked again in a normal tone of voice while looking at her soiled scarf. "You mean from the blast?" Thomas said.

"No, Thomas, before the blast. It's the same question."

His ears were still ringing, but he said, "I don't think so."

They made their way past groups of people laying out items on the floor. Families gathered around one another. Mothers were settling toddlers and tending to crying babies. It was evident that some had been there for a while. In fact, some were sleeping on metal-framed cots and looked as if they had permanently moved in. Under each cot, every inch of space contained boxes and bags of belongings.

"Over here is our place," Margaret said, directing him to a spot on the floor next to the now-unoccupied ticket counter. "Here, sit here, on the floor. After all this practice of heading for shelters, it's finally paying off. I can't believe they're actually doing it."

"Doing what?" he said.

"Bombing civilians. It's against the Geneva Convention, but when did they ever give a bloomin' wit about conventions?"

Thomas thought about asking, "Who are 'they'?" but decided it wasn't a good idea as other, more pressing, questions needed answers.

"Evening, Professor," an elderly woman said to him as she spread a blanket on the concrete floor right next to them. "Margaret, didn't you bring your blanket?"

"No, Mrs. Somerville," Margaret replied, still holding Thomas's arm." We got a bit of a late start and just managed our coats, but we'll be fine."

Mrs. Somerville just smiled and noted that Margaret had buttoned her coat wrong and was missing a stocking. Thomas took Mrs. Somerville's hand and elbow and gently helped her get seated on her blanket.

"Well, Professor," she said, surprised, "this is most kind and unexpected of you."

As soon as she was seated, she looked up at him with an expression that gave him pause, and for a brief second, she continued to hold his hand.

Upon releasing it, she added, "As to you, young lady, I quite understand your tardiness. Wish I were young again. In our younger days, when Charles and I were courtin'," she said with a wink his way, "we were late for everything." She laughed, obviously enjoying the memory.

Thomas had walked away, confused and trying to make sense of his surroundings. "What's going on here?" He said to himself. "It looks like a London Underground used as a bomb shelter?" The British cab, beams of lights in the night sky, the air raid shelter, the accents. "It's England." He thought, "—but how?" On the far wall of the station, he saw a billboard advertisement for American-made Chesterfield cigarettes. Right next to it was a similar one for the competing French Gauloises. The art looked vintage, as if taken from the pages of an old Life magazine.

He walked over to a newsstand about twenty feet away. He first saw a display for The Tattler, a social gossip rag, and another for The Sketch, which covered the theater and ballet. He picked up a copy of The Illustrated London News and looked for a date. There it was: Saturday, 24 August 1940.

Thomas stared at it with a detached sense of reality. He said to himself, "1940? What happened to 1998? What am I doing here? I don't belong here. Is this a trick? Is it a movie or a dream?" Running out of explanations, he seized onto the dream theory for a moment. But the ringing in his ears was hardly a dream.

A hand gently touched him from behind. In a soft voice, Margaret said, "Thomas, can you tell me what's going on and why you're acting like this? It's not like you at all."

He turned and faced Margaret. "I'm not sure. For reasons I can't explain, I'm in a place where I'm not supposed to be and don't recognize anything. Perhaps it's amnesia. I'm sorry, I don't know."

The faraway sounds of bombing crept into the shelter, and he looked up from her face. All around them, kids ran and played with the joy of being allowed up past their bedtime.

He turned back to her. "Margaret?" he said slowly, "is that your name?"

"What?" she said, backing away.

"Look, I'm very sorry. I don't mean to be rude, but I'm very disoriented and confused, and it has nothing to do with the blast."

She put her arms around his waist and hugged him. "Thomas, love, I'm scared. This isn't funny," she said.

"Well, it's not like it has happened before. At least, I don't think so. I need to try and figure out who I am and why I'm here."

"Why you're here?" she said.

He could hear the impatience starting to creep into her voice. "It's easier for me to understand that you don't know who you are, but why are you here?"

"I'm sorry," he said. "I need time to think a bit. I need a little walk. None of this makes sense. I'll be right back, okay?"

Margaret nodded, released him from her embrace, and sat next to Mrs. Somerville. "Where's he going?" the lady asked.

"I don't know, Mrs. Somerville. Thomas is acting very strange. Says he doesn't know who he is and wants to know why he's here," Margaret said. "He looks like my Thomas, but he isn't acting like my Thomas."

Mrs. Somerville looked over to Margaret. "Well, of course he looks like your Thomas. However, those are interesting questions from the

Professor, don't you think? Well, he's not going to wander very far down here, that's for sure," Mrs. Somerville said. "None of us is."

Chapter Five

The Secret Cabinet War Rooms
Whitehall, London
12:15 a.m. Sunday

John (Jock) Colville, the prime minister's private secretary, impatiently paced outside the closed door of the Telephone Room. He tucked a message folder under his arm, pulled up the sleeve of his uniform, and checked the time. It was well past midnight and almost twenty minutes since he'd received the message. He knew not to bother Mr. Churchill when he was on the phone with the States but knew his message was important.

Given the prime minister's renowned girth, the space inside the Transatlantic Telephone Room was small, barely measuring more than one by two meters. Entering the area through a simple wooden door, two wooden bookshelves painted a dull industrial green sat against the left wall. Beneath them was an old two-drawer table that fit snugly along the meter-and-a-half width of the space. Directly in front of the table sat a government-issued oak chair that looked as if it had bravely survived several narrow escapes in the previous war.

A lone desk lamp with a brass base and a green glass shade sat atop the table. The lamp cast its light directly onto the only other item on the table, a standard black telephone whose humble origins were said to have been in an upstairs office. Doubtless, the installer hadn't the slightest notion that this telephone was to remain exactly where the technician installed it for the next sixty years. Save for these items, the room looked as it had in its previous role, as a storeroom for brooms and domestic cleaning items.

The sole purpose of this solitary telephone was to allow Sir Winston Churchill, the prime minister of England, and Franklin Delano

Roosevelt, the president of a still-neutral United States, to conduct their vital strategic discussions in complete secrecy. Some of the most important decisions of the war would travel over this most unimpressive device.

Their conversations traveled via cable from the Transatlantic Telephone Room into a particular London telephone terminal located in an annex basement of the Selfridges department store on Oxford Street. This highly classified facility was a secret and assigned the code name "X System." Inside was Sigsaly, a large piece of equipment developed by the American Bell Telephone Laboratories. It was a new type of telephone scrambler that encrypted conversations before they were transmitted, by cable, to Scotland and then by radio to Washington, D.C.

The room was part of a secret maze of temporary facilities buried deep beneath Whitehall called the Cabinet War Rooms. Whitehall, a collection of public buildings, had been constructed during the Edwardian era when they administered the Commonwealth and were the center of a worldwide empire. They included the Law Courts, the Whitehall government buildings, and the British Museum. However, unknown to the general public until many years later, many rooms, quarters, and facilities were secretly used to conduct the affairs of World War II. After Germany invaded Poland and Britain officially declared war, priority construction began transforming the Whitehall into the physical center of the war effort. They located the headquarters in the humble basement chambers of the Office of Works building which faced St. James's Park on one side and Great George Street on the other. The Works building was the first structure constructed with steel-reinforced concrete in 1932 and offered the strongest structure of any in Whitehall. In communication cables, the location's secret code name was No. 1 Storey's Gate, the site's actual address, so obvious they hoped no one could think it true.

The Cabinet War Rooms, conveniently located between Parliament and the prime minister's official residence at No. 10 Downing Street, connected to the bunker via underground tunnels. These 'temporary' facilities included a Central Map Room, a Cabinet Room, Churchill's office bedroom, a collection of administrative offices, a mess, and spartan sleeping quarters for other personnel. The intention was to occupy them for only a few months to a year. They eventually served as the central shelter for London's government and its military strategists for the next five years. The day Germany surrendered, Churchill ordered the lights turned off and the doors locked; he wanted the site available for what he believed to be an imminent war with Russia.

Finally, Colville heard the heavy, muffled scrape of the chair across the floor as Churchill pushed back from the table. The door opened quickly, hitting Colville square in the back, as he'd stopped right in front of the door to check the time.

"Mr. Colville," Churchill said gruffly and a bit loudly.

"Yes, Mr. Prime Minister?"

"Of all the available space allotted to this administration to wage war against the enemy, why, in God's name, would you choose to stand right where you could become a casualty?

"Dreadfully sorry, sir, you caught me off guard."

"And who was the authority that added this new responsibility?"

"Sir? Ah, what new responsibility?"

"Guarding Mr. Colville, guarding. You said I caught you off guard."

"Ah, no, sir, I meant…"

"Let it pass, Mr. Colville, let it pass. It was an attempt at a bit of levity that, I can see, has been lost. You must be distracted, as you usually allow me the benefit when I venture into humor."

"Well, yes, sir, I am. I mean, distracted. I just received this from Avery Doyle of the Home Guard." Colville presented Mr. Churchill with a pen and the message folder.

Churchill initialed the transfer slip and opened the cover. He stood silent for a moment as he read the message, then dropped the folder down to his side. He needlessly adjusted his spectacles, shifted his considerable weight, and then brought the folder up as if starting all over.

After a brief time, he told Colville, "It's hard to imagine the experience as will presently befall our London citizens and that such a dark warning could arrive on a single slip of paper."

"Sir?"

"Hitler, Mr. Colville, in a spate of bad judgment, has changed the rules. He bombed Amersham this evening, but we shall not be put off. Summon Air Marshal Harris, I believe he is in town, and Major-General Ismay at once. Tell them to meet me in the Map Room as soon as possible. I'll be in my office."

The prime minister turned to walk away and stopped. Turning back, he said, "Ah… Mr. Colville, I see no need to bother Lord Halifax. We can perform this duty without his contrary rancor."

"Yes, sir."

Chapter Six

London Suburbs
Amersham Tube Shelter
12:35 a.m. Sunday

Sometime later, a pensive Thomas Watson returned to where the women were sitting. The' all clear' siren sounded just as he met Margaret's eyes. Everyone rustled and started picking up belongings, except those who stayed the night on the cots. Margaret looked up as if waiting for him to say everything was back to normal. He said nothing as he helped Margaret and Mrs. Somerville to their feet. Margaret turned toward the same stairway leading out of the station and into the night. He followed her in silence.

Thomas looked down the other street in the direction of the explosion. A fire company with trucks and emergency rescue crews were frantically at work. Flames came from what looked like three houses in a row. It was hard to tell as dust, smoke, and rubble fell into the street, and the intense flames hid anything behind them. Thomas could feel the heat where he stood.

"It's the National Fire Service," he thought, a collection of volunteers and professionals in splendid uniforms. Their legacy in the history of the war would be saving hundreds of lives from burning buildings. After the war, people would remember that just the sight of them racing down a street on their way to an emergency had been a significant factor in keeping morale up during the blitz.

"The Blitz? In history? Where did that information come from?" he thought.

Before he could start the reasoning process, Margaret said, "Are you coming, or don't you remember where you were before the shelter?"

Thomas turned to follow her. Neither spoke a word as they made their way back to the house.

Margaret opened the door and threw her coat on the couch in the small living room. In the darkness, he could hear her say, "The power is out again, and we shall have to make do with the lamps." She turned around and, gently guiding him in the right direction, said, "There's a divan directly to your left. Mind the throw rug on the floor."

She opened a drawer in a light-coloured chest not far from the entry door. She grabbed some matches and the candle lying alongside them in well-practiced motions. Lifting the glass chimneys, she touched the wick of three lamps, and the room acquired the radiated glow only flame can provide. She placed the lamps around the room in their assigned places.

Thomas looked around for the first time. They had hurriedly passed through the room on their way to the shelter. It was warm, simple, and orderly, and everything looked precisely in place except for a single painting. The painting looked original, with a massive frame seemingly out of scale, given the size of the room. He was sure it was Henri Matisse's "Femme au manteau violet" ("Woman in a Purple Coat"), an impressionistic study of a woman lying on a couch in a brilliantly coloured room. At that time in his career, Matisse and his style weren't popular, collected mainly by independently minded people who made their own way against the flow of society. The very interest in one of his pieces made a statement about its owner.

Thomas looked at Margaret as she backed away from the last lamp and the light brought her into full view. As she moved around the room, she demonstrated a natural grace. He'd already noticed that her hands became wildly expressive when she became excited or impatient. He couldn't tell the colour of her eyes, but her complexion tended toward that of the Irish. However, by far, the strongest impression he received from her was her simple but striking beauty. Despite the incoherence and confusion, it was his first thought when she walked into the bathroom.

She nervously refolded her coat, bending over and placing it on an empty chair. Coming upright, she unconsciously tucked her hair behind an ear and sat at the other end of the divan with her arms and legs crossed. "Okay," she said, "where do we start? Do you know who I am?"

Thomas realized he didn't know how to handle trying to make this right. What was right? He tried to sort things out in his mind. "I'm in the middle of World War II," he thought, then corrected himself. "Actually, more like the beginning, as it wouldn't end until 1945—but how could I know this and not know who I am?"

"It's not just amnesia," he thought. "It's the distinct feeling I don't belong here. It feels like I'm a visitor, but none of that makes sense. Life may present us with things we don't understand, but most of it makes physical sense. My current situation doesn't come close."

"Thomas," Margaret said, "are you going to participate in this? Because it will be very difficult to do it by myself."

"Margaret," he said. "I mean, your name is Margaret, and it seems you love me or feel strongly about me. I could feel your voice's concern when the blast knocked me down. There is also, given the circumstances of…well," he looked down at her legs, which were still one nylon short.

She followed his line of sight and saw the same thing, then, with two clenched fists on her hips, looked up and said very distinctly, "We're married, you bloke. That's the first thing I want you to remember. The fact that I'm your wife," she threw a pointed finger first in his direction, then back at herself.

"Got it," Thomas responded.

"Margaret?" he said.

"What?" she said tersely. She looked at him and, in an exaggerated motion, re-crossed her arms.

"I didn't mean to do this. I'm bewildered right now. It's not just the memory loss, but the fact that I don't know things I should, and I know things I shouldn't."

"Like what sorts of things?" she said.

"Like I don't know who I am."

"Thomas, your lack of memory couldn't a simple medical explanation."

"But there are other things I shouldn't know," he said, gesturing to the outside world.

"Like what?"

"Like the art world will eventually revere Matisse, your radio will turn into a small cinema screen, and," he paused, "we will win the war."

"*This war?*" Her eyebrows shot straight up, causing her eyes to widen. "The one we're in?" She was utterly confused.

He nodded.

"How could you know that?"

"That's the very confusing part. I'm not guessing but absolutely positive. History appears to be something I'm interested in."

"Thomas, my love, this war is not history. The last war is history. The outcome of this war is still very much in doubt. There's talk of Germany invading England; if that happens, things will get very bad very fast. They increased the Home Guard, and the bombing inland is heavier every night. Tonight, they bombed civilians. I think it's the first time. I can assure you we haven't won *this* war."

She stood up as if ending the current discussion and walked to a low cabinet below one of the paintings. Leaning down, she opened the solid wood doors and, moving some things around, pulled out a bottle of liqueur.

"May I interest you?" she said, holding a bottle of Orange Corona. "Let's have a drink to winning this war and start over."

He looked at her with the bottle in her hand and smiled at her. "I'm not such a bad guy, Margaret," he said.

"From what I've heard, how would you know?" she said and broke into a smile for the first time since telling him off in the bathroom. "Yes or no?" she said, waving the bottle.

"Definitely," he said. "Margaret, there won't be an invasion. Hitler invades Russia instead. He'll make a stupid decision to follow Napoleon into the gates of hell and freeze to death. I think it would be wise not to tell anybody. They won't believe you, but you must promise not to tell anyone."

"Thomas?" she whispered. He looked up. She came over, handed him one of two tiny glasses filled nearly to the brim, and sat on his lap, extending her arm around his shoulders. They touched glasses, and she said, "Cheers."

The first sip was surprising, very sweet and fizzy, but good. While looking at her glass, Margaret didn't take a drink and said, "Do you love me?"

"I don't know, Margaret. I want to, but I've only known you for a matter of hours."

She turned her head and looked directly into his eyes. A long time passed. She turned her head back to her glass and said, quietly and ever so slowly, to herself, "Well, life doesn't provide many second chances; we'll just have to start over."

It was a curious statement.

She then got up from his lap, perhaps realizing it wasn't the same place she'd expected it to be and she didn't belong there. She walked to one of the windows and fussed with the blackout shade behind the curtains. "Can't let the light out," she said to someone; it wasn't him.

Margaret was overwhelmed. She couldn't take in everything and keep it orderly. She needed events to slow down and allow her to catch up.

She said, "Now, I don't know about you, but between the train trip and the stress of the bombing, everything has tired me out. Sleep sounds wonderful right now." Margaret stopped, realizing that Thomas probably didn't remember their train trip earlier in the day to see Mother, even though he was the one who had wanted to go.

Thomas thought, "She doesn't know I wasn't there."

"Perhaps if we hadn't gone, this wouldn't have happened," she said.

Thomas didn't follow the logic and remained quiet.

Without waiting for a response, she picked up one lamp, walked over to the other two, and blew them out. Thomas followed her into the bedroom, and she showed him where all his things were kept, then disappeared to undress. After an extended period, she emerged from the bathroom dressed head to toe, almost wearing more than she'd taken off. He remembered the full slip he'd seen earlier and her great modesty. He stood up. She passed him, saying something about being done and that it was his turn.

He hesitated and hoped his uneasiness wasn't apparent as he stepped into the bathroom and slowly closed the door behind him. Looking around the room, he noticed that faint light filtered in from the bedroom through the glass in the door. He couldn't help but lean over the counter toward the mirror and look into his eyes. He closed them for a second, receptive to even the slightest explanation his mind might provide; he opened his eyes. He was still here—or there. Somewhere.

It was more than uncomfortable when Thomas came out. At the bed, he lifted the corner of the blanket on his side. It was a strange situation, and he didn't know how he was supposed to act. Margaret came over and put her head on his shoulder.

"It will be okay, Thomas," she said. "It will be okay because we have each other. This situation just adds to what we had to work on."

She leaned over and blew out the lamp on the nightstand. There was a long pause in the dark.

"What's tomorrow?" he asked.

"Monday, but school is out on summer break. Why?"

"Then it will give us time to talk? I have lots of questions."

"Yes, it will," she said. "And so do I."

Chapter Seven

London, Whitehall
Secret Cabinet War Rooms
1:30 a.m. Sunday

The vice air marshal was the first to arrive and was none too pleased with the hour. Sir Arthur Harris had insisted on being at the debriefing of the last flight of Wellington's arriving back from France at 23:30 hours. He was gathering information to make his case against what he felt was a disastrous strategy of indiscriminate bombing, promoted and insisted on by his chief of bomber command. He'd barely had a chance to warm his sheets after returning home when Colville had called.

He knew the prime minister worked late into the night every night, but calling everyone to assemble at this hour was an exception. Harris wondered if Halifax would attend; it would be a better meeting without him. It would eliminate the automatic and strenuous arguing that permeated the strained relationship between Halifax and the prime minister. Halifax couldn't put aside the fact that he'd almost been named prime minister instead of Churchill. Although lacking the title, he considered himself an equal in political power. He also felt he knew precisely how to defend the island nation and properly take the war to the Germans.

"The Map Room, is it?" Harris said to Colville.

Colville turned and withheld the reflex to salute and just stood at attention. Mr. Churchill had insisted that the Cabinet War Rooms be an 'at ease' environment.

"Yes, indeed," Colville replied. "Given the hour, I presume some tea is also invited to the meeting? I can have Elizabeth prepare some straightaway."

"Mrs. Nel? Doesn't she ever go home?"

"It's the end of her week on the late shift. Mr. Churchill now has three shifts of secretaries to keep up with his correspondence. Go in and have a seat, and I'll send the tea in."

Sir Hastings Ismay had just crossed Great George Street and noticed a new wall of sandbags, creating an artificial blast corner to protect the underground entrance to the war rooms. He was looking forward to getting out of the cold air, as he'd chosen to walk the two blocks from the Home Secretary's office. He took one last look at the now-quiet sky before ducking into the complex's entrance. The network of rooms that he oversaw was his destination. He searched for his military ID inside his overcoat and presented it to the security detail on the first level. Before him were three flights of stairs leading downward to the meeting with the prime minister.

Ismay, an Army man, was mostly educated at Charterhouse and the Royal Military Academy, Sandhurst. He'd worked hard at each of his assignments. His first mission had been with the 21st Cavalry Frontier Force in India. Soon after, in Somaliland, he suffered significant wounds in an ill-advised action ordered without proper intelligence. Since then, he steadily rose through the ranks of the British Army, with numerous political victories and a heartbreaking marital defeat. The latter had been almost five years ago, but it was like yesterday. He chalked it up to the price one paid, winning the trust of the prime minister who appointed him chief of staff. He had a good idea why he'd received the message to attend the meeting. The chief of staff's job was to know the critical issues. He'd just met with Avery Doyle, and the news was nothing less than a change in the entire tenor of the war.

Coming off the last stair and entering the main hall, he stepped down directly into the path of Elizabeth Nel, balancing a full tray of tea. Reacting quickly, he reached forward to place a hand on each side of the tray, thinking something was sure to fall off. Elizabeth Nel was a soft, patient soul whose demeanor effectively concealed an extremely disciplined administrator at the rock center of Churchill's staff and secretaries. She was in her late forties, the mother of three, and the only person who could eloquently tell the prime minister to settle down and stop scaring the clerks without being shot at sunrise.

"Why, Major, that was a startle," she said in her usual upbeat and supple voice.

"I'm so sorry," said Ismay. "I should have been looking instead of mentally wandering about like that."

"No harm to the tea, and that's what's important," she said. "Air Marshal Harris is waiting in the Map Room, and I understand Mr. Colville has the PM on his way."

"Yes, thank you. May I take that in for you?"

She waited for just a second and said, "That would be very kind of you, as I must finish preparing a paper for Mr. Churchill." She revealed a knowing smile. "Right away, if you know what I mean?"

Ismay laughed, knowing the PM's notorious impatience, and reached for the tray. "In that case, I believe I'm obligated, don't you think?"

"In that case, Major, off you go."

He grabbed the tray and started walking the short distance to the Map Room. Almost from the first day that he'd declared the room ready for use, it had become the centre point of the underground site. Given its name, it was no surprise that maps of the Atlantic, the Far East, and Europe covered every available inch of wall space. Multiple phone lines and radios were available to communicate with the outside. It was in the Map Room where they monitored the conflict's progress and devised war strategies. At this hour, the usual daytime assemblage was empty, and the resulting calm was noticeable.

Stepping in, he found Marshal Harris, pipe in hand, staring intensely at a map of southern England, where most of his fighters were stationed.

"Marshal Harris, I see you've been keeping the same late hours as the prime minister."

"Not by choice, my dear man. I see you've been at your regular job as Mrs. Nel's assistant," he said, pointing his pipe toward the tray.

"Well, Arthur, we all qualify for something now, don't we?" Ismay said, putting down the tray and extending a hand.

"How have you been, my friend?" Ismay said.

"Well, now, let's see, other than I can't replace bomber pilots and planes as quickly as I'm losing them, it could be worse. In addition, we get intelligence about the same time it's being played out across the sky. Can't those chaps at Bletchley press on through a tea break and get us something a bit more timely?"

"It's coming, Arthur. It's a tough project. We need a breakthrough, as well as a little luck. I know it's on the prime minister's mind, and he thinks the information is essential to winning the war. I also know additional funding, everything requested, is being approved this week."

"I know, Hastings, but things are getting a bit tight. My young boys give more than they have and then give it again. When this is over, we should knight them all."

"Welcome, gentlemen," Churchill said as he entered the room. "Thank you for interrupting your busy schedules. Arthur, you were booked through the night, I understand," at which point Harris laughed.

"An accurate assessment, Mr. Prime Minister. At your bid nonetheless."

"We've an urgent matter that demands immediate attention or, should I say, a response. Avery Doyle and his group at Home Office sent over an urgent message. He reports German planes deliberately bombed and destroyed several residential homes near the Amersham tube shelter."

"An aerial bombing? I should ruddy well think not. That's almost London proper," Harris said. "I've seen the reports of a stray hit now and then, mostly scaring cattle and strafing trees inland. Moreover, if true, this is an attack directly on London or at least on the outskirts. Why would he do that?" Harris started pacing with his pipe, looking at the floor.

"I'm afraid it's all too true," Ismay said. "I've just come from Avery's office, and he confirmed the information. Thankfully, there were no injuries, as the Home Guard sector had most people in the shelters. It'll be the last time they moan about the drills. First reports say it took out about a half block."

"But what's it mean?" Harris said. "Is he sending a signal? I thought we'd intercepted traffic that established Hitler's orders to the contrary. To not attack civilian targets." He was in disbelief and becoming agitated. "It wouldn't surprise me that intercepted messages ordering this raid are still in a cavern at Bletchley."

Churchill put the message folder he was carrying down on the conference table. "Well, gents, I think the task at hand isn't an interpretation of what it means, as much as what we propose as our response. There's not a single military target within miles of Amersham aside from a few broom factories and 14th-century buildings lacking the proper plumbing. It means he has directed attacks against civilian targets, and we cannot be the lamb on this," Churchill said as he pulled out a cigar, yanked the wrapper off, and put it on the table.

Harris stood up and leaned over the table toward the tray. "I think I'm in need of some of that tea."

"I as well," said Ismay.

There was silence for a moment as Harris filled the second cup. Without finishing, he put the cup and teapot down, looked across the table, and said, "We've no choice but to strike back."

"Bloody hell, we ought to level Berlin," Churchill almost yelled as he hit the table with his fist, causing the cups to collide. "That bastard Hitler or Göring or whoever ordered this will pay, and quickly."

The outburst startled Ismay. He'd seen the PM irritated but hadn't not seen him use more than his sharp tongue to express it. Colville rushed into the room at the noise, not knowing what to do. He found all three men staring at him.

Standing at attention, Colville said, "M… Mr. Prime Minister, is there anything I can do?"

"Yes, Mr. Colville, you can tell Mrs. Nel that this is no time for a holiday, and if she would be so kind as to find her typewriter, we would all be in her debt."

"Yes, sir," he said and left as quickly as he'd entered.

Churchill said, "I've prepared a response to be carried out at once. I, of course, would like your input, but I dare say I've made up my mind, and you would do well to agree. We will dispatch a mission to bomb a military target just outside Berlin to let him know we won't be assuaged in any way. Air Marshal Harris, you'll carry this out tomorrow night. No later."

Thinking of the inescapable repercussions he would receive from Halifax, Harris said, "Mr. Prime Minister, shouldn't we get a broader consensus on an escalation this radical …?"

"I'll take care of the political battle," the prime minister interrupted, "you take care of the Germans."

"Very well, sir, but the cost will be high. The maximum range of both the Hurricane and the Spitfire is well short of being able to provide air cover for the bomber squadrons much past the French coast. The boys will be dealing with considerable fighter resistance. It's going to be a very rough ride."

Churchill's tone softened. "I'm aware of the costs, Arthur, but we cannot leave it unanswered. A tepid response could affect their future decisions and opinions as to our resolve. Obviously, the rough ride that awaits these boys shall be shared in whole and not in part by their country." Churchill turned to Ismay.

Ismay knew he was looking for his consensus. There was no doubt that these were tense days—dark days. England faced invasion for the first time since 1066 with the Norman incursion onto British soil by

William the Conqueror. This war, barely a year old, had been going Hitler's way. The German army had rolled up a series of very successful campaigns, having conquered France and come very close to defeating the only other major power in the world. Ismay thought of their responsibility to future generations of Europeans, who would face learning the dark art of living in a totalitarian state. These were dismal days indeed.

Ismay reached for his cup on the tray. "Mr. Prime Minister, even though I have no choice, as you've made up your mind, I fully support your position as though you hadn't. The long-term strategic cost could be higher. If we were to let it pass without a response, it might lead to the bombing of London. However, I'm most perplexed by the strategic issues. What does he have to gain by changing the front to civilians?" Ismay got up and walked over to the map of southern England and the Channel. "Their targeting of the southern airbases has put us in a perilous situation."

"To say the least," Harris followed. "The southern shore attacks on 15 August between London and Croydon stopped production in four aircraft factories. In addition, they damaged five of my fighter airfields. My boys are scrambling to repair several runways and three aircraft maintenance facilities. The attack on the 12th knocked one radar station out completely, and five are under repair. We should have four of them fully functional by tomorrow afternoon. Perhaps I should say this afternoon. It's an unpleasant situation as we're not keeping pace with the losses."

"That about puts it in perspective," Ismay added. "All he needs to do is to keep to his plan. It's why this doesn't make sense. Has the Ultra team picked anything up at Bletchley?"

Churchill looked uneasy. "I'm afraid that they're woefully behind in deciphering messages. It's a truly complicated affair requiring untold man-hours. They're working on a new machine to aid in the deciphering that utilizes quite sophisticated electrical works. I've been led to believe it's faster, but we shall see."

"Arthur, as you'll be more than busy with these orders for the next twenty-four hours, do you mind if I have Mr. Ismay have a look at the fifth station's repair schedule? He's most effective at cutting red tape and getting at the heart of it."

"Not at all," the air marshal looked at Ismay. "I appreciate the help. We're now blind above Suffolk, running constant patrols off the coast with PBYs."

Churchill turned to Ismay. "Find out if we can be of help with anything that will return it to full operation as soon as possible."

"Yes, sir," Ismay said.

The prime minister was quiet and still, looking at the maps on the far wall. "I'm receiving inconsistent reports regarding the southern air defenses. They're right along the lines of what Arthur is saying, but they're not specific. Mr. Ismay, can you put together some information for me on our situation? It's obvious that filling out reporting forms comes in second compared to running for your life out of a bombed building. However, knowing where we stand at readiness is critical information. I'll give you what reports I've received and then venture out into the southern field and fill in the missing parts. See if you can get me a complete picture by week's end or sooner."

"Yes, will I be making a presentation?"

"You might. I don't know right now." Churchill felt he might need the information soon, as someone was certain to question him on the subject.

Colville entered the room with a folder and placed it in front of the prime minister, who quickly glanced at the one-page document. Then, with a fountain pen from his pocket, he scrawled at the bottom, blotted the signature, and handed it to the air marshal.

"Here are your orders, Arthur. I want to hit them in a night raid tomorrow evening with as many airplanes as you can spare. I take it you're in line with this?"

"Yes, without reservation."

"Again, I agree," said Ismay. "Reluctantly, but I agree. We've no alternative, but I would like to be in Göring's pocket when he must explain away his broken promise to the people of Berlin. It looks like his impenetrable defense, provided by his beloved Luftwaffe, is about to have a big hole punched right through it. He'll have an angry, stunned population, will have soiled his family's name, and he'll be more than angry," he said, smiling.

"War, Mr. Ismay," Churchill added, addressing the end of his unlit cigar, "is a burden to the souls of all that partake. To it then, shall we?"

They rose as one and left to their duties.

Chapter Eight

Sunday
Amersham
Mrs. Somerville's Home
6:30 a.m.

It was early morning as Mrs. Somerville stared at the faded photo in the album she'd pulled from its place in the top drawer of the dining room credenza. The steam from the train obscured his polished boots but didn't obscure the cut of his tall, thin frame in that dashing uniform. It was the day he shipped out and the start of the rest of her life. Since their marriage in 1910, she and Charles had seven years of pure joy, living life like a taximeter gone over. He'd been a spirited adventurer, suddenly storming into the life of Miss Bethany Leeds, age 25, filling out every part of her existence with surprises. He left just as suddenly, fighting alongside Canadian troops and dying at Vimy Ridge on 9 April 1917, leaving every aspect of her empty.

His death came during a similar time with the country threatened, and what was to be an easy war quickly changed to the country needing every man. Because of his age, they had assigned Charles civil duties, but he soon found himself transferred to the front. Before he left, they had made a solemn pact. She promised to maintain the spirit for them both if he failed to return. Of course, as with every wife, she'd firmly believed it would be someone else's husband not returning.

She grabbed the loose edge of one photo and tucked it back into its black corner tab, pressing the picture flat. Closing the album's velvet cover, she left her hand on top as if the story told by the images within radiated into her hand. Now and then, she could almost feel the strength of Charles, not in the room, but in her life. He found her in a sea of women and created those happy years now mounted in the album. It's just not fair that her generation had to live through two wars when the first one was the war to end all wars.

There, she'd done it, dipping into feeling sorry for herself. It didn't happen often, and she couldn't remember the last time she'd taken the album out of the drawer in the sideboard. She kept true to their pact, living a good life, and was seldom anything but upbeat and positive. She paused a bit to determine what had caused her to revisit a time so given to affection and devotion, and the image of Margaret's professor drifted into her thoughts. Why had he unexpectedly noticed she was there, let alone offered the slightest hint of kindness? Last night, something different about him had touched something sleeping within her, bringing it out into the daylight. Something other than his story of not knowing where or who he was.

There was a look in his eye. The last time they spoke over the fence, it hadn't been there. Instead, a distinct, lost look in his eyes made the back of her neck tingle. It was the same look Charles had when she was standing on the platform, waving her handkerchief in the air like a thousand other wives and girlfriends. Charles was hanging out the window of the moving train. Over the whistle, train noise, shouting, and the band playing, he said, "I love you … I won't be back."

She only saw the words; she didn't hear them. Her arm stopped waving and remained suspended in the air. She was stunned and started running after the train, but the crowd kept her from keeping up, and Charles faded into the distance. That was the last time they had any contact, as he went directly into battle to liberate a piece of ground someone was now farming.

Her first indication that the Professor was different was his helping her down to the floor. It was a small act that wouldn't have entered his mind before last night. True, he would move the odd bit of furniture on request, but until last night in the shelter, he'd never paid her any mind. Nor, up to now, had she really cared. However, his wife was a different story.

"Margaret, my dear Margaret," she said aloud. The beautiful, spoiled little rich girl who threw it all away to spite her mother. She married a chap the exact opposite of Charles and the opposite of what Margaret's character needed. She remembered the day Margaret came by with the news advert in her hand, inquiring as to the availability of the house she owned next door. Margaret arrived after she'd been turning people down. Since then, she'd become very fond of Margaret but found Thomas very inconsistent. He would go from 'life is a lark' to generally devoid of personality, sullen at times, usually when Margaret wasn't around. It almost appeared Margaret had made a hasty decision and was surprised at who she got after the wedding.

Nonetheless, she was going to make a go of it to spite her mother, who was a powerful force. Oh, he was a charmer when he had to be, but it wasn't inside him; it was something he put on like a coat. However, last night he was different, walking with purpose and conviction, although sounding very confused.

Chapter Nine

Amersham - Margaret's Home
6:40 a.m. Sunday

The morning sun was bright on what should have been a typical day. Thomas had gotten up before Margaret, who appeared to be still sleeping. Perhaps she was thinking of yesterday's events crashing into her life, not wanting to be disturbed. An equal possibility was she didn't want to get out of bed with him still in the room. Margaret was obviously not yet comfortable with certain aspects of her new life, and who could find fault?

On his way to the kitchen, he passed a narrow hall table below a wooden framed mirror. In the centre of the table was a Chinese porcelain bowl filled with potpourri. Photos of the old Thomas and Margaret in various poses and places around England were carefully arranged in silver and brass frames. He didn't recognize any of the locales. He picked one up and looked at it more carefully. The photo in his hand had both of them on a bridge. Margaret was holding onto his folded arm, and her face was utterly radiant, with a beautiful smile. Her other arm was victoriously raised in the air, the fingers in a V sign, while kicking her leg forward as far as the long skirt would allow.

Looking at the picture and then the mirror verified he looked like the man in the photo. Placing the frame carefully back in its place, he glanced at the other images from her life. For all he could tell, old Thomas and Margaret enjoyed each other's company and were hopelessly in love.

With three more steps, he entered the small kitchen he'd seen the night before. At first, it appeared very cluttered but, upon closer inspection, looked disorderly in a purposeful way. The room contained the contented emotions of an owner who loved to cook and who collected all the various gadgets required. He could see neat stacks of

Rockingham China, Lalique crystal glassware, and an ornate silver tea set through the glass cupboard doors. On the small table sat an overly large and very impressive Philco wireless, a single round speaker above its three dials.

In deep contrast to this array of items that appeared to exceed one's station were the cooking pans that hung from a small wooden ceiling rack. In short, they looked like the invasion had already occurred, and Margaret had single-handedly fought off a mechanized Panzer division, with heaving swings of her sauté pans and boiling pots. Then, in a strange way he didn't understand, he remembered that people donated every available aluminum pot and pan. After melting and manufacturing, the pots reappeared as diving Spitfires or Hurricanes flying high in the sky. Consequently, the owner had to settle for decidedly inferior enameled substitutes that tended to chip and apparently came in very interesting colours.

He heard sounds coming from the back room.

Continued searching failed to reveal the object that had brought him to the kitchen in the first place. He wanted to surprise Margaret with something small and meaningful, but it appeared he would need her help.

With the last two cabinet doors open, he said, "Margaret, where's the coffee pot?"

She was instantly at the kitchen entry, pulling at the fabric belt of yet another dressing robe.

"Coffee? You want coffee? Who drinks coffee? Not you, that's for sure. If you're going to start drinking that stuff, we've some serious talking to do. If you want my support through whatever this … situation …is. Ah, anyway, bub, you'll drink tea. Unless, of course, you're going to act like those precocious Americans," she said with a laugh.

"Now," she said, with a straight arm and finger pointing toward the space outside in the hall, "if you would please remove yourself from my kitchen."

"Good morning, Margaret," he said, feeling the tenseness ease. "I'm just trying to share the chores, so you'll think I'm a nice person." It had been an apprehensive, silent time since they went to bed last night, and he thoroughly enjoyed this light interchange.

"Sharing chores and drinking coffee? You're not making me like you—you're scaring the hell out of me. When was the last time you helped around the house? The answer to that question is never. In fact, when was the last time *any* man helped around the house? I think it's more than your memory we're dealing with here.

"If you want to do something nice for me, I'm very fond of cream cheese turnovers with fresh fruit. Of course, a million pounds sterling would also be nice," she said with a quick, phony grin before opening a lower cupboard door.

She turned to the teakettle and said, "Now, go get your trousers on, and I'll bring our tea out to the garden."

Thomas looked down curiously, as she obviously hadn't noticed— he already had his pants on. Walking toward the back of the house, he noticed in another room what looked like a metal cage about the size of a kitchen table with a flat top, metal tubing, and wire mesh on the sides. It had a metal tag riveted to the top that said "Morrison." It was up against the wall with books and paper on top and looked entirely out of place. After a few seconds, he realized it was a Morrison Cage, produced and supplied to families as a type of shelter from falling debris during the expected bombing preceding an invasion. It would protect two people by supporting most falling walls and ceilings. The design wasn't to avoid injury but save lives. Churchill directed them to be made and distributed, knowing they were of limited help but would contribute to home morale.

"Thomas, of course, would know this," he thought. "However, why did he know it?"

Perhaps he really was Thomas.

Chapter Ten

The Embassy of the Union of Soviet Socialist Republics
5 Kensington Palace Gardens, London
6:50 a.m. Sunday

It was very early in the morning for Yuri Stakova as he walked out the front gate of the Russian Embassy. Passing the British guards outside the compound, he nodded and raised a hand slightly as he continued. It was an odd time to be called to attend a very peculiar meeting with the ambassador. Yuri was still mulling over all the hidden and unwritten meanings that clouded the truth. In Russian affairs, you had to learn to read between the lines *and* the pages. In Soviet matters, there were always alternative ways to interpret the same information. It sometimes made it hard to do the right thing. However, if you knew the system, it made it hard to say you failed and—Yuri knew the system.

The ambassador and Yuri had a long history. Earlier in their careers, when they were both assigned to the Italian Embassy, they had taken different paths to the London station, one of the premium posts in the Foreign Service. When Yuri, head of embassy security, entered the Ambassador's office, he found the chief counsel for legal affairs, a pitifully precise man devoid of emotion. He'd already taken a chair and was sitting with a notebook on his knee. Yuri took a seat.

At first, the Ambassador took a very official stance, reminding Yuri of foreign policy directive SVD435.9 that Yuri was not to involve the embassy directly or indirectly concerning NKVD affairs. Yuri found the ambassador's approach awkwardly formal and, glancing at the note-taking counselor to his left, chose to listen now and talk later.

Sitting uncomfortably upright at his desk, the ambassador continued, "I'm to officially inform you that an agent or courier, I'm not sure which, is on his way from Moscow Centre. He's delivering a message about the embassy's security affairs, a division you currently head. The message contains orders stipulating your travels back to Moscow and your new duties at Moscow Centre. In accordance with the stated directive, I've scheduled the courier to meet with you sometime today at your flat. This meeting isn't to take place on embassy grounds. Is that clear?"

Yuri nodded, "Of course, Comrade Ambassador."

The ambassador was reading a prepared statement and glanced up from the paper in his hand. Yuri detected a pause before his next statement. "You'll report back to me the results of that meeting. Is that also clear, Comrade Stakova?"

Yuri took a minute to look at the ambassador, who was now looking at the counselor taking notes. As soon as the man finished, he turned to Yuri and, with a questionable look on his face, waited for Yuri's answer.

"Yes, I understand," Yuri responded.

With a final flurry of his pen, the counselor dutifully memorialized Yuri's response and waited for the following words from the ambassador.

The Ambassador rose behind his desk and said, "That's all for this morning. You're both dismissed."

Yuri nodded as he rose from his chair. The counselor tucked the ruled notepad under his arm and, with Yuri leading, headed for the door. As they each deferred to the other, the ambassador said, "Oh, one more thing. Comrade Stakova, I've noticed one of your staff has failed to report to the London authority, resulting in a denial of the renewal of his residency papers. I'm not pleased and have further business with you. Thank you for your time, counselor. That will be all for now."

As the counselor was about to close the door, the ambassador said rather loudly, "You'll remain standing, Comrade Stakova, as this will be brief and to the point."

The door closed, and Yuri took tentative steps toward the man's desk.

The ambassador exhaled, unbuttoned his suit coat, and smiled at Yuri. "The games we must play," he said. The ambassador pointed to the chair Yuri had just vacated and said softly, "Yuri, sit down. I must be brief. We've shared our interests and careers for many years, so I must tell you to be careful. There's something in the air, and it's not the invasion.

"I wanted to let you know as quickly as possible, thus the early hour. Now, unofficially, my sources say that shortly you're to be relieved as station chief. Someone, who I've never heard of, by the name of Joseph Alexikov, will replace you. Is there something I should know?"

"No, there are the usual problems, but nothing that could foretell them replacing me," Yuri said. "Certainly nothing that could remotely affect your standing on this, I'm sure. Is the replacement the courier?"

"I'm not sure, Yuri. They haven't said. My uncertainty is why the spy counselor was here, to protect my arse. He reports everything, and I needed the record of my actions to be clear in the confusion."

"As always, Comrade Ambassador," Yuri said with a smile, "your arse appears to be well-documented."

The ambassador chuckled as he blew out the smoke of a new cigarette.

"Our old friend Ivan sent a sealed and coded message in the last diplomatic pouch for my eyes only. He indicated his NKVD sources had very little information. They knew the person who had worked himself into this assignment. He's rising fast in the company and, as we shall say, does not excel in compassion. His Foreign Service contacts also say the swords are out back home. Every opportunist wants to use the inevitable confusion the Germans will create to work themselves or their departments into something that will further their cause. Yuri, I must cut this short."

"Of course," Yuri said. "As always, I'm indebted."

"As always, I'm honored to work with you," the ambassador said, extending his hand. "Good luck. I'm not sure if I can be of more help."

Yuri took long, thoughtful strides to the office door and, with his hand on the doorknob, he gave the ambassador a nod. The ambassador nodded and smiled with a concern only years of mutual respect could engender. Yuri opened the door and said loudly back into the room, "As you wish, Comrade Ambassador. I'll take care of this immediately."

Chapter Eleven

Amersham - Margaret's Home
7:00 a.m.

Leaving Margaret in the kitchen, Thomas proceeded back down the corridor, locating the door that opened into the enclosed glass conservatory at the rear of the house. From inside he could see a small patch of ground outside, where neat rows of plants and vegetables thoroughly used all available space.

"So, she likes to cook, and she likes to garden. She's beautiful and has a great sense of humor. It could be worse," Thomas thought.

It's too bad that he'd to put her through this. It's too bad he had to go through whatever it is. He stepped outside, kneeled, and mindlessly ran a small twig through the loose dirt. He sighed deeply and could see the mist of his breath. "That sounds like the big question," he thought. "What is 'it'? "

He heard the rattle of china and turned to see her put the tray on the table inside the conservatory. He stood up and moved back inside.

"It's cold out there," he said, shoving his hands into his pockets and trying to act normal. He hoped she was in the same humorous mood that had chased him out of the kitchen. She was pouring tea and didn't reply. She finished and went back inside the house.

"This won't be easy," he thought. How could he explain walking right into this person's life and that he was sorry? Her previous husband was gone and now he was here. He'd spent most of the night trying to come up with something that made even a little sense. He'd chanced another trip to the bathroom mirror in the middle of the night, but it only made him feel foolish rather than providing anything of value.

She came back out with a small bowl. "I brought sugar; I'm not sure how you take yours, do you know?" Then, in a completely different, more strident tone, she said, "Thomas, I'm having a real hard time with this. How can you just forget who you are? We spent a marvelous day together, well, except for the time at Mother's; we came back, you walked into the bathroom, and suddenly—bang—you were gone. I mean, you were still here, but most of you was gone, or at least your memory. Oh, bloody hell. I don't know what's going on," she finished in frustration, her hands in the air.

Thomas looked at her. Her eyes were wet and red. It was apparent reality was setting in right on top of the confusion. She grabbed a napkin off the tray and turned as if wiping a tear was suddenly a private act. He wanted to go over to her to satisfy his growing desire to hold her, to make things better. He wanted to show some compassion for upsetting her life, but he wasn't sure she would let him. He should have tried but didn't and, in those few seconds, already regretted it.

"I'm usually stronger than this," she said, looking at him over her shoulder.

"That was my second chance," he thought. "Yes, she will let me." He gently reached out and turned her around as he wrapped his arms around her.

She looked at him and said surprised, "Thomas?"

He waited a moment. "Yes."

"…Nothing," she said.

She drew in close, folded her arms inside his embrace like a child, and then placed her head on his chest.

"Thanks," she said. Then after a pause, she followed with, "Whoever you are."

He stood there holding her. Deep inside, there was this marvelous feeling, and he pulled her closer. "I don't know who I am. Are you okay?"

The top of her head rested on his cheek and he moved his face slightly, feeling the smoothness of her hair.

"Sure," she said. "Wouldn't you be okay? Tell me this is going to be all right. Lie if you have to."

Still holding her, he said, "Margaret, I don't know what it is, but I don't think we're dealing with something easily explained."

She didn't look up but moved, so he lowered his arms and said, "It's not just amnesia, although it seems my memory only goes back to the incident in the bathroom. The thoughts and emotions circling in my mind don't come anywhere near providing a clear picture."

After reaching for her teacup, she moved to the window. She thought about it and put her finger on the windowpane as if testing it. She was thinking about more than just a new Thomas; she was thinking about her previous situation with the old one. It was strange; it was almost as if she was relieved.

Thomas tried again. "The issue isn't about how far my memories go back or how many I have. The part that could be trouble concerns the timing and content." He shook his head. "Do we want to go into this right now?"

"Well, Thomas, what else are we going to talk about? Mother's attitude toward you yesterday?"

"You're right. Okay," he said, "but be patient. It's not as if I'm accustomed to having to explain this every day. Or at least I don't think I am... I mean"

She gave him an impatient look and said, "Thomas!"

He put his hands in his pockets and looked at her. "It's about memories and knowledge. In our past, we have memories and knowledge of what has occurred in a thousand yesterdays. The memories result from things we've directly experienced, like weddings or birthdays. Knowledge, however, comes from other sources, like books. They tell us something we haven't experienced, like the reign of the pharaohs in Egypt. Together, memories and knowledge blend into our daily lives.

"With me, something is wrong with that system, as I know the past, but I have no memories of anything in which I took part. I can't recall our wedding, your birthday, or the trip to see your mother."

With a hopeful look and smile, she put her cup down and said, "That's easy. It sounds like amnesia to me. If we can cure that, we're home free. We have our lives back, we fix the war, and we live together for the rest of eternity."

They both smiled. Margaret was one very special, although a tad unrealistic, woman.

"That would be nice. There isn't anything I want more for you or us. No, it's not that easy," he said. "There's another part. The problem is that not all of my yesterdays have occurred yet. Margaret, for some reason, my knowledge appears to contain the future. It's as if I'm looking at the past from the future. However, for some reason, the past hasn't occurred yet."

"That's as clear as mud," she interrupted as her energy rose. "Are you doing this on purpose just to confuse me? It sounds like the next thing I'll hear is some mumbo jumbo about how they found you in an Egyptian reed basket at Stonehenge," she said, actually managing a laugh. "Thomas, we're trying to sort this out, and I feel you're not helping. I don't know about you, but I have or had a life, although slightly broken, and would like to resume it at some point. We were discussing ways to cure your amnesia, not sitting around a campfire with a bunch of gypsies or playing word games to see who can twist a sentence so badly it's not a sentence. We're educated people, and we can get to the bottom of this, but it'll take a little seriousness on your part."

"Margaret, please be patient. I'm deadly serious, but give me some time to get to an explanation. I'm trying to educate you while trying to understand myself."

"Okay," she said. "You've all the time you need. However, I'd prefer you start now and be completed by lunch." She leaned forward, crossed her legs, and looked at him, resting her chin on the palm of her hand.

Okay, so she didn't exactly excel at patience. He tried again. "My brain is struggling that there are few nice places to put most of what I'm thinking right now. There are clear images and feelings, like waking up and wanting coffee. I know that in the past, I drank coffee and really liked it. Yet, you tell me I never did. When we started talking last night about the war, the information about there not being an invasion was just there, but it was in the past. In fact, if yesterday was… ah, today is the 25th of August?"

She just looked at him. "And…," she whispered.

"I think this is a monumental day in history. You were right last night when you said it was the first time Germany bombed London or civilians. It was, but it appears to have been a mistake. A tremendous mistake, against Hitler's orders, and it sets in motion a series of events and a clash of egos bringing civilians from both sides into the war."

She looked at him, giving nothing away, so he kept talking.

"On the 24th… yesterday, Göring directed his bombers inland to destroy factories and facilities that supplied the RAF. The path took some German bombers close to London as they headed north toward some oil refineries. In the night, twelve Heinkel 111 twin-engine bombers became disoriented and lost their way. Navigation at night is always problematic, and errors are common on both sides. Up to now, they just hadn't resulted in bombing any civilians. For unknown reasons, one of those bombers either dropped its bombs in a panic or jettisoned them to increase speed in returning to base because they thought they were over the Channel. Either way, they violated a direct order from Hitler that no one could bomb a civilian target without his written permission. As punishment, those pilots would become part of the infantry and sent directly to the front.

"As a result, Mr. Churchill will be mad as hell. In retaliation, he'll order 80 RAF bombers to hit munitions factories outside Berlin."

"Thomas, how can you be sure? You're so sure," she said. "How do you know this will happen? How *can* you know this will happen?"

"That's the point, Margaret. I don't know how I know. I just know I know."

"There you go again."

"I'm sorry, Margaret; this is hard for me too."

"Well, I guess with tomorrow's *News*, we'll have the answer, won't we?

He was sure she didn't believe him.

She rose and approached the window, holding her cup between two hands. She was staring at the rows in her garden, hoping it was all a dream.

Without turning to look at him, she said, "Where's my other Thomas?"

"I'm sorry, I don't know. I might ask where's the other 'I,' but I don't know that either," he said.

"You look the same, but you're very, very different."

He didn't want to get into whether he was better or worse, so, trying to change the subject, he said, "The woman last night called me 'Professor.'"

Ignoring the question, Margaret turned around and looked at him. She was still unwilling to believe this turmoil had entered her life, which she usually completely controlled. "As if the war wasn't enough," she said slowly and sadly.

"Will you help me?" he said.

"And how am I supposed to do that? We don't even know what's wrong. How do I explain this to Mother?"

"Tell her the truth. Tell her that Thomas has suffered amnesia, and it might take some time for his memory to come back," he said.

"Do you think it will?" she said with a noticeable tone of hope.

"I've no idea, but it would be nice to be normal. With the war and all, I'm not exactly excited by putting you through more than I already have."

She managed a smile. She came over, sat on Thomas's lap, and placed her arm around his neck. She put her head right up against his and didn't say a thing.

Chapter Twelve

London
Silvertown
London Docks

Yuri stepped out of the underground transit car and looked in wonder at all the people coming and going to work. He wasn't sure how the British people maintained an everyday life under these circumstances, but to their credit, they were keeping on with the day-to-day. Toward the far end of the station area stood rows of cots used during air raids, which just re-asked the question.

Yuri trudged up the tube station's tile steps and out the entrance of the Silvertown Station into the sunlight. Yuri was a burley fifty-five and saw those steps as a challenge he conquered daily. He stopped by the newsstand, read the headlines, "Bismarck Enters Service," and purchased a Times newspaper. He folded the paper, placed it under his arm, and turned toward the outlines of multiple gigantic ships drawn up along the quayside.

He was heading home to a nice flat by the docks and wharves in London's East End. The flat was larger than usual for a single person because it also served as a place for Russian 'visitors' to stay when they came into town. The flat was in the poorest section of the largest city in the world. Being this close to the docks allowed Yuri to observe shipping traffic. The Victoria and Albert Royal Docks, with their towering cranes and grain elevators, were the commercial center of the most significant trading empire the world had ever seen. The flat was also removed from any military bases, which were the targets of the nightly bombing raids. At least the targets were military until last night.

Yuri's official job at the embassy was military liaison to the British First Sea Lord. The First Sea Lord was the highest military position in the British armed forces and was held by Winston Churchill until last May. During that time, Yuri had gotten to know well the man now leading his nation to war. However, in truth, Yuri was the London station chief for the NKGB, the People's Commissariat for State Security, the Soviet intelligence service. Yuri Ivanovich Stakova was a spy.

For seven years in London and twelve years in various countries before that, he'd lived in the shadow world of intelligence, counter-intelligence, and double counterintelligence. It was an insane job, requiring complete concentration as he tried to sort out the real from the surreal. The gathering years of constantly remaining one step ahead had, of course, taken its toll, but he was still one of the best.

Being a spy meant his actual function was to complete anything the higher-ups in Moscow felt was necessary. As a spy, some section chief in a crisp uniform, medals to his waist, who had never left the home country, always told you exactly what needed to be done and how to do it. They were always wrong—always. He'd survived these many years by learning the art of delicately balancing the literal directive with what he knew to be the operation's actual requirements for success and then delivering that in a manner that made the dim minds in Red Square look like bright shining lights. Quickly and without warning, this morning's meeting had set up his retirement from the field with a desk job at home.

By this time, Yuri wasn't sure where home was, as his years in the field had made him a man of the world. He admired the British for their tenacious resolve, the Germans for their machine mentality, the Italians for their women and food, and the Americans. Well, what can you say? They're Americans.

He enjoyed his freedom and wasn't looking forward to returning home. Enduring the secretive games was an integral part of his beautiful homeland. He struggled to understand how a government full of bureaucrats, all half as smart as a bottle of vodka, could have all the answers for all the people. The system appeared to work from the outside. However, inside, Stalin brutally crushed an entire nation's will.

Today, he was to meet his replacement, Joseph Alexikov, a young rising star in the company. It had come as a shock to Yuri that someone from the home office was already in town, and he hadn't known. Yuri usually knew everything. The official reason for the change was to have a new man in place for the coming German invasion. There had been no previous sign that Moscow was thinking in that direction.

Yuri, a big man, was walking very lightly now through things he couldn't see.

Chapter Thirteen

Margaret's House
Amersham

For Thomas, the next couple of hours were a challenge as he tried to unravel the story and learn about his life with Margaret. They started to establish an understanding. She wasn't hard to like; it wasn't hard at all. In fact, one of the strangest things in all of this was that the moment she stood in front of him in the bathroom, he felt attracted to her.

It was easy to see what appealed to Thomas. Her humor, intelligence, and self-confidence were out of place for a woman of this time. She was a professor in the English department at the local college. He held some research positions at Cambridge and did most of his work at home. They were both off for the summer. Her father died about five years ago, and her mother lived in the family mansion in the exclusive Fernhurst area outside London.

During the day's conversation, it became apparent they enjoyed each other's company. Everything would go along splendidly, then one of them would remember their predicament—and silence would follow. She listened to his assertions regarding what was to come of this or that. However, Thomas thought she was reserving judgment until tomorrow morning.

Fixing dinner, she turned on the oven and said it would take time to heat, so he had to be patient. Thomas indicated there would eventually be ovens that would heat food in minutes using radar waves. "It's the same basic electrical technology used by the RAF to track German planes coming over the Channel," he explained. He talked of things he could remember from the future that might interest her, like the tunnels under the English Channel, and she wouldn't believe it.

"Why not?" he asked.

"It's simple—the French wouldn't allow it. Their poodles might breed with our beagles."

"How about the British?" he asked. "Would they allow it?"

"Of course," she said. "We don't have a distorted view of ourselves and haven't favorably rewritten the world's history to revolve around ourselves like Frawnce!" She drawled out the final word with her chin up, hand extended, and a pinkie in the air.

Thomas wanted to return to learning about this person, a charming woman who was bringing him slowly into her world. Trying to move to a subject that hopefully would result in her revealing more about herself, he remembered the oversized painting by Matisse in the living room. "I'm fascinated by the painting in the front room. When did you get it?"

"Oh, that's quite a story, that one," she said.

"Well, I would very much like to hear it."

"I keep the painting as a reminder of how much I have to learn about myself and the world."

She told him the story of being at a private showing at the Mersinet Galleries when she was about nineteen. Her father allowed her to have the run of the place while she was still living at home. She'd left in a huff after some silly argument with her mother and wanted to stay away long enough to make her worry. Margaret could have easily asked the chauffeur to take her anywhere, as she'd known all the drivers since she was a child. Instead, she opted to catch a ride to the nearest station for a bus into the city. During the ride, Margaret enjoyed just looking out the window and being free.

Closer to London, she passed the gallery. It was pretty busy, with people queued outside, all waiting to get in, and others milling about. They were all very formal, as was she, having previously dressed to go to a party with a group that didn't meet with her mother's approval. That was the basis of their argument. Margaret decided the gallery was the perfect place to spend some time. Running to the front of the bus, she asked to get off at the next stand, and the driver smiled and pulled over at an unscheduled stop right then and there.

She thanked him, giggled, and turned back to address everyone else on the bus, saying, "thank you. Sorry for the delay." A scruffy man in the back said, "Oh, it's all right, miss. If I looked like you, he'd be stoppin' for me too, but then I don't, do I?" Everyone laughed, and she bounced down the steps, waving vigorously at everyone through the windows as the bus drove off.

Once inside the gallery, she wandered about, not really interested in anything and aware that everyone was much older. Margaret liked art and enjoyed reading about the artists and listening to the comments people offered and the opinions they argued.

Eventually, one piece took her fancy. The Mersinet was three stories, and in a corner on the third floor, she found a painting that spoke to her. She stood for a long while looking at the only Matisse on display and found herself alone almost the entire time.

She knew of Henri Matisse from conversations among Mother's guests during the afternoon teas Mother insisted she attend. Mother said the teas were training, so she could observe firsthand how proper women spent the afternoon. The women never spoke of Matisse in a tone that would have been reassuring to a developing artist's career. This small talk had far-reaching effects, as polite society tended to move, as a whole, with little tolerance for the freethinker. Person after person at the teas ridiculed Matisse's painting and his approach to life. The subject of his painting wasn't what captured Margaret. Instead, it was the spirit the artist put into the colour, as well as his method of application. Behind every stroke was a stout heart that persistently presented his vision of the world, in his own style, against a chorus of lesser minds who didn't consider Matisse's efforts real painting but a faint attempt at real art by an untalented ruse.

At the gallery Margaret had tried to explain to people walking by that the artist presented the observer with an impression, intending for the viewer to take part in the ultimate image. It was to no avail; she talked until she was blue in the face, and London's proper Society would have none of it.

From behind her in the gallery came a voice. "Get the man a proper brush and let the starving sod try again," said a man with pipe and bowler, tapping his umbrella on the hardwood floor to emphasize each of the last three syllables.

Later, arm in arm, a grand old couple was walking by the spot that Margaret was starting to defend. He was a perfect portrait of old money, with a bright white beard and hair, in a summer gray pinstripe suit and a dark wool derby with a gray faille band. A substantial gold pocket watch chain curved under his sizable girth to a ticking bulge in his silk waistcoat. With an apparent engagement later in the evening, the woman had dressed in a cream-coloured taffeta ball gown that glistened. Her matching round profile-style hat and veil presented the perfect semblance of the opera-gloved elite. She was much younger than her husband, although she appeared over sixty. They paused behind Margaret, observing the painting, and then her husband, resetting his pince-nez, said with unfiltered disdain, "It would appear my spectacles require adjustment."

"I rather like it," the wife said. "Besides, one can't appreciate art with a simple observation. One must appreciate an artistic piece through one's heart. If you stand back, Charles, the whole becomes known; his style requires participation," the woman elegantly said.

"I'll stand back, alright. It shouldn't be in the building. If it's your fancy, you had better inquire now. At the rate his paintings sell, he'll be the literal ghost of a starving artist," he said.

At that exact moment, Margaret decided to buy the painting and, with a gallant tilt of her head, called the owner over in a loud voice that all in the building surely heard.

"Good for you, young lady," the wife said with a knowing smile derived from her years. The husband moved on, but she asked him to wait. She dropped his arm and walked back over to Margaret. She looked at young Margaret standing there, with her chin up a little too high, then at the painting, and then at Margaret. Moving forward a step, she placed a soft hand on Margaret's arm and, in the tone of a caring mother and with courteous deference, said, "It's admirable to meld your independent thinking to action. However, I would mind your true reaction to this purchase when considering life's larger decisions. You must not be swayed solely to embrace the contrary over what could be the superior path." She smiled. "If I may offer advice, of course, to someone so young and noble."

"Yes, mum. Thank you, mum," Margaret said with a quick curtsey. The well-meaning, experienced advice fell on young, obstinate ears.

Listening to the story, Thomas became more engaged by the minute and concentrated on her every word. Time took flight as conversations continued over drinks into the night.

"Tell me about your mother," Thomas said.

"What's to tell?" Margaret said, lifting her voice at the end of the sentence. "She doesn't like you."

"Well, that's to the point. Would you be so kind as to elaborate on that, Miss?"

"I told you, Thomas Watson, we're married. I'm a Mrs. *Your* Mrs."

"Okay, sorry. You're *my* Mrs.," he said with equal emphasis.

"On second thought, I'm *not* your woman—I'm my *own* woman!"
They both fell into much-needed laughter.

The story of her mother started with her father. Margaret had decided at a very young age her father was special, and she related to his no-nonsense approach to life. He taught her straight away that her mind, not her lineage, would determine her station in life. As a direct reflection of his family's exemplary record of service to the Royal Court and his business success, Sir Ian Everett Hatcher II had entered peerage as a knight. He had been placed on the 'watch list' by Sir Winston Churchill for noble acts of skill and courage. This vague honor referred to a somewhat mysterious business agreement between the government and his company. There was quite the pomp and circumstance, with no one ever knowing exactly why he received the honor. However, she knew it was important and it wouldn't be the last time.

Sir Hatcher's close ties extended into the inner circles of the English government. He produced many fabrics and materials in several stone-walled textile factories in Northern England and Scotland. Since the war, the bulk of the company's sales came from custom bolts of cloth used by the military for their uniforms. He would always revel in doing his bit to promote inter-service rivalry, keeping each department insisting on a unique texture and weave. Custom fabrics required unique designs, requiring each bureau to place orders separately.

Margaret recalled how late one evening, her father had said, "It's in the tank, my dear, if those blokes ever sober up and order the same lot across the board." He then spun his finger in a corkscrew from above his head to the floor while making obnoxious airplane sounds, laughing, and spilling his brandy on his shoes.

His most significant contract was with the Royal Navy, and during his best years, Sir Winston Churchill had been First Sea Lord. Being an island nation, England rightfully regarded its Navy with almost religious reverence. The men's relationship started with Margaret's father and Mr. Churchill, discovering a mutual absence of patience for the obliqueness and lack of transparency of high society and an affection for the same brandy. It turned into a full-blown friendship when they quickly discovered they also liked their brandy in the same quantities.

With these common bonds, they spent years spoiling scores of fancy dinner parties, with footmen in livery behind each guest, telling ribald stories more appropriate for paneled rooms where only the men would retire for liqueurs and cigars. Many times, bored with the boorish attempts by guests to curry favor, and before the main course, Mr.

Churchill would crow above the dinner conversation: "Why, Mr. Hatcher, brandy and cigars appear to be missing from the menu."

Looking at the card next to his place, Mr. Hatcher would reply, "My Gawd, Mr. Churchill, an observation with chilling consequences." They'd then excuse themselves for an excursion to locate the missing ingredients essential to a civilized evening. Their actions were, of course, to the ashen shock of the hostess, who invariably had worked years to get Mr. Churchill to her much-publicized dinner.

Young Margaret Hatcher loved her father. He taught her to be independent and follow her feelings when "girls" were still supposed to retire to the parlor. Her father would say, "Don't ever let a man see you gossiping in a parlor, my dear, or in his mind, he'll never see you out of it." Mr. Hatcher had died in a plane crash on a trip to a factory about five years before.

She hadn't known what to do with her life. Instead of becoming closer, his death caused her and her mother to grow apart. Her mother wanted Margaret to finish college and marry any of the six young men she'd picked. Her comment, "Should I try them all, mother, or do you have a favorite in mind?" just added fuel to the fire.

In frustration, Margaret moved out of the family mansion, taking only a few special things, like the Matisse. She also left behind the monthly allotment, which created immediate problems, like finding work and a place to live. Alastair, her father's manservant and head of household, just happened to know of a small house up for let at week's end. It saved her the embarrassment of having to put up at a hotel. Shortly thereafter, she applied for a position as a teacher's assistant at a local middle school. It wasn't easy, as Margaret refused to produce any letters of recommendation and wouldn't divulge her previous address. The headmaster took a chance on something he saw in the young woman, and the decision bore fruit for both the school and the students.

It was a needless exercise to say that her mother didn't approve of these actions. Upon discovering that Margaret was seeing someone, she insisted on meeting him, which created more strife, as she dismissed him as an opportunistic nobody unworthy of their time.

She *really* didn't approve and was more than a bit out of sorts when, days later, on a Saturday afternoon, Margaret announced she'd gotten married to one Thomas J. Watson, an aspiring educator at the university. It was the great war all over again, but it was particularly wretched this time. They didn't speak for months as Mother had insisted that their kind arranged marriages with proper regard to position, fortune, and community of circumstances. Margaret's opinion was that the underlying cause of her mother's extreme anger was her presiding at centre stage in a Chanel gown at a glittering high-society wedding. Certainly, the pinnacle event in the life of a mother who was first a socialite and, therefore, saw it as an obligation. In that regard, Margaret was definitely her father's daughter.

Eventually, mother and daughter connected on this and that; conversations turned into overnight stays, and things smoothed into an all-new relationship. Nevertheless, her mother's contempt for Thomas was hard to ignore. She perceived him as a man entering into a world far above his station and using Margaret to enable his advances toward the family estate. Margaret conceded her husband was mysterious at times but, with head held high, quickly added that they were working on it and making grand progress.

Margaret recounted how Mother had never made a slight or even a 'polite' effort to inquire about Thomas's work at yesterday's visit. She always believed real men run businesses and don't spend time researching historical minutia.

She once said, "It's a useless endeavor. The past cannot change, and documenting it won't increase its chances." Shortly after that, Margaret started postgraduate work in history.

Thomas looked across the table, completely taken by this Margaret, having no desire for the day to end. He suggested a walk, and the conversation continued uninterrupted through tea at a café. They then sat on a bench surrounded by a green and took a long way home. However, it was getting late, and after tidying things up, they went into the bedroom. Then the free flow of the evening came to a halt as a certain tenseness entered into what had been two people enjoying each other's company.

Margaret went to the bathroom to change. When she emerged, she wore an assemblage of clothing that was good to minus 20 degrees centigrade.

Thomas looked at the layers of flannel. Moving toward her armoire he said, "Surely you've something that doesn't double as medieval armor."

Margaret said, "I'd leave it be if you were a bright man, mister. You've spent the better part of a fine afternoon with your stories of being uncomfortable with your situation. Well, it may surprise you, I'm not quite comfortable with this either and feel like a little tart cheating on her husband."

"Are you going to cheat?" he asked with an irrepressible smile.

"*I AM NOT!* Moreover, you'd better find another way to be funny, if you want to live. Get the lamp, be quick about it, and stop staring at me."

For the second night, they were in a new world neither understood. He was exhausted from lack of sleep the night before. Apparently, so was she, for as soon as her head found the pillow, there was telltale deep breathing. After an extended period spent trying to quiet the thoughts racing through his head, he slowly reached over and quietly turned on the light. She didn't move. He rose on an elbow, leaned over, and looked at her sleeping face. Observing someone as they're sleeping reveals much to the observer, and he deeply admired everything he saw in Miss Margaret.

Chapter Fourteen

London
Whitehall
Air Ministry

Upon arriving at his office in the morning, Air Marshal Harris settled into the average day, filled with intelligence briefings, damage assessments, and combat readiness reports. However, this day would belong to Bomber Command as they prepared to penetrate Nazi Germany farther than ever before, at the PM's directive. Throughout the day, until it was time for Harris to make his way to the airfield, he monitored preparations closer than normal.

It was a military target but deep inland and next to a civilian zone outside Berlin. Although the Germans had bombed Amersham at Chiltern, the mission wasn't to create civilian casualties but to make a point. The message: If the war were to take a new direction, the British would strike at the heart of Germany. This mission would be the first attempt at bombing Berlin. The pilots knew they'd be over the most heavily defended city on Earth, without fighter support and with a lower chance than usual of returning.

When the pilots saw their names listed on the alert board, the briefing officer knew the heightened risk of not returning would be on everyone's minds. They left letters to families written earlier in the day with those not scheduled on the mission. All around, the air was thick with apprehension.

The officer ended the preflight presentation, saying, "Gentlemen, we didn't start this war, and I, for one, don't give a bloody hell if we get over there and destroy the entire city. Last night, they hit Amersham at Chiltern and destroyed the homes of families just like yer mum and dad.

Now, let's show the Jerries tonight by waking them up to the sounds of bombs in *their* backyards. *Tally ho, lads.*"

Everyone cheered and headed out to their planes. Two made it to the door and rushed back into the men's loo, giving up on keeping dinner down. Everyone was mentally moving into that altered state of being— scared but brave simultaneously.

Harris left his office, stepping into his staff car as the corporal took the door. The 1938 Ford, painted the traditional dull British green, worn well beyond its two years of service, stood ready. He sat in the back and thought about tonight, but more about how the war was going. From the amount of information the PM received, he was sure that Churchill could glean that Fighter Command was in a sorry state. The country was losing the battle of production. They couldn't indefinitely sustain the number of pilots and fighter planes lost daily. Even with Canadian, Polish, and a few American pilots, all the available planes were often not taking to the air. Everyone was doing a fabulous job, but the critical essentials needed to sustain the resistance were becoming scarce. The instances became more frequent when the radar stations would pick up an incoming attack and couldn't scramble sufficient squadrons to respond. How long would it be before the Germans accurately estimated the actual order of Britain's airpower?

In his heart, he knew it wasn't a hopeless situation. What the RAF needed right now was time. More time to get additional fighter planes from the factories to the field. More time to repair airfield facilities, and most of all, more time for those young fighter pilots to back up from the daily grind of scrambling at a moment's notice. It would be best if they had their wits about them, which means rest.

"It's the officers' quarters, sir?" the driver asked.

"No, son," Harris said, slipping into a rare informality, "take me to the field control tower."

"Right, sir. Be just a bit, sir."

Reaching behind the steering wheel, the driver pulled the column shift lever back down into first and headed off.

"Where're you from, soldier?"

"Pennington, sir. Still live with me mum and sister."

"Your father?"

"Lost him in the last war, sir, but we're makin' it fine and all. Me sister works and keeps watch on Mum."

The car fell silent. Everyone had a story, and each reflected the intimate moments of ordinary people doing their best in a ruddy situation.

By 2210 hours, Harris was in 11 Group's Uxbridge Flight Control Centre. He wanted to see the Group take to the air, as they were off to delete from history the Edwardian concept of a 'proper' war. He was also there because he was the one who had asked them to fly into a world of uncertainty. Harris took a long breath, knowing deep in his heart the immense sadness that might befall their families was his responsibility. A young orderly appeared before Harris, holding up a cup.

"A minute for tea, sir?"

"Just the thing, lad," Harris said, placing his hands around the hot cup as he watched plane after plane lift off into the night sky. The Bristol Blenheim IV bombers, outstanding in their day, growing old but they were all that was available. "If America gets into the war, we might get a new fleet," he thought, "but for now, we're taking the fight to Germany with what we have."

"Message, sir."

Harris set down his cup and signed the acknowledgment offered by the young lieutenant, who saluted smartly and returned to duty. "Can't we draft men?" Harris thought. "These boys should all be in classes complaining about the night's studies."

Melville in repair was reporting seventy-eight planes would take to the air comprising fifty-seven returning fit, nineteen repairs from last night, and two new deliveries.

That's all the sector could muster, as all the remaining equipment was in repair or flagged as a top priority for pilot training. Only twenty-eight Spitfire fighters were available from 11 Group to accompany the bombers to their maximum range. He'd twenty-nine planes but only twenty-eight pilots fit to fly. It was another fantastic job by the repair crews considering the bombing of the Northolt repair facility during the day. Repair crews had just finished filling in the damage to the airstrip barely thirty minutes before the bombers were due to lift off.

Harris thought, "Where are the medals for those sitting atop those tractors? In the last raid, the construction crew lost three pieces of heavy equipment used to repair the runway. It was getting harder to complete repairs before the next wave of bombers took off. At morning's light, they'd touch up the painting of the hedges and trees on the runway, used as camouflage to fool the German bombers, and hope it was effective.

In his preflight executive summary, Harris had learned that Paddy Hemingway, one among the dwindling number of squadron leaders, had engaged and had taken to his chute over the Channel early this morning. An RAF speedboat sent from the Clacton Lightship, used to rescue downed pilots, had picked him up. Dry clothes, a hot cup of tea, and some Navy food on the way back made it not half bad. Upon returning, he'd volunteered for tonight's fighter escort group, but they denied his request. Dickey Lee, his wingman and closest friend had also gone down, but no one had reported seeing a chute. Everyone would sorely miss Dickey's irreverent sense of humor in the officers' club.

"They'd raise pints as yet another of their own left them," Harris thought. That's the most challenging part, losing friends. Paddy wouldn't let anyone touch Dickey's things. He wanted to be the one to prepare the package and letter to his parents.

Harris left the warmth of the radio tower and walked out onto the observation deck. He looked up at the sky as the last squadrons lifted into the air. Only their landing lights were visible, accompanied by the deafening roar of their engines.

"These are *my* boys, not England's," he said to himself.

The PM might have given the order, but it had fallen to him to decide who would ride into an uncertain future. Mere boys asked to be men before they finished being boys. They did it not so much for king and country as for their parents and families. War was personal, not fought with machines, but with those lads protecting the country's future.

Coming after 'the war to end all wars,' this conflict shouldn't have come at all. They'd fought and won the last Great War. That war was one of history's defining moments as the country prepared for what the generals promised would be a quick victory.

"Over by Christmas" had been the rallying cry. With a grim face and anger in her voice, his mother had repeatedly told him the stories. She and other mothers had watched the marching parade of soldiers in their brand-new uniforms, with brass bands and the citizenry lining the streets. Finely dressed women were waving their hankies and throwing flowers and kisses; men waved bowler hats, their chests puffed, yelling, "Bravo, lads!" and "Empire!"

The end of chivalry, gallantry, and innocence was when the world woke up to the smell of mustard gas and the cries of a generation dying.

Yet again, he reached into his back pocket and pulled out a curved wallet, worn at the corners. He opened it, removing the page his mother had cut from a book of poems. He carefully unfolded the paper, which he promised to keep as long as he was in uniform. The creases and folds obscured some of the letters, but it was of no consequence, as he'd memorized the verse long ago. As the last plane headed toward the horizon and its running lights faded away to an uncertain fate, he once again read the words:

> You smug-faced crowds with kindling eye,
> Who cheer when soldier lads march by,
> Sneak home and pray you'll never know,
> The hell where youth and laughter go.

>   –   Siegfried Sasson

Chapter Fifteen

Margaret's House
Amersham

Thomas woke up lying on his back, staring straight up at the ceiling. The ceiling was blank, like his memory, and just as ineffective at explaining his unique existence. Nevertheless, he *did* recognize the ceiling and remembered it being there yesterday. In the vacuum created by not knowing what's customary, the brain seized upon anything familiar, and the ceiling was the barest example of normal. He could feel the weight of the covers on his toes and up by his neck.

He thought, "This is supposed to be my bed, but it's missing the bond that you usually feel with something that's a component of your everyday environment." If the bed lacked his imprint, the ceiling was at least, a familiar and fresh memory.

A faint shadow cast itself across the cabinets and the wall as his thoughts drifted back to things more productive. Warm thoughts and scenes from yesterday filtered in as he replayed the time spent with Margaret as they discussed subject after subject at lightning speed. A playful happiness accompanied the vision of Margaret spinning in circles, holding her hand high in the air and flying it down to knee level as she imitated her father. Yesterday, setting aside all the negatives, exceeded the finest first date anyone could dare hope to experience. From his inward emotional center came the realization that Margaret was quickly becoming something big in his short life.

Smiling at the memories, he turned, hoping she was awake, and discovered only the space she'd occupied. Concurrently, he heard disturbing sounds from somewhere outside the bedroom. Quickly, he jumped out of bed and grabbed his robe from the wardrobe. He walked while slipping his arms into the robe and headed toward the sounds. Rounding the corner into the living room, he found Margaret sitting on the couch, her face hidden behind her hands, her elbows resting upon her legs; she was crying. The sight of her sadness created a deep sorrow within him, and he realized he wanted nothing but joy for this person and never to be the source of distress.

He quickly walked over and kneeled in front of her. She didn't look up.

"Margaret, what's wrong? Are you alright?" he said.

She didn't respond. On impulse, Thomas got up and, sitting beside her, put his arm around her shoulder. She drew back just slightly, barely perceptibly, and he let go.

"Thomas," she said slowly, "I just want things to be as they were, and things are so very wrong." She lifted her head, turning to look at him. Her eyes were deep, sad, and heavy.

"I'm scared," she said as she stood up, tossing the morning paper onto the couch behind her. "Where's this leading? I feel like there's a big end to this because it doesn't fit into this world. It's not natural. How can you know this about the war—about the future?"

Thomas turned and looked at the paper and read the headline. It was a decisive moment for them both, for very different reasons. Across the country, newsagents' placards would be black with the news, "RAF Bombs Berlin—Munitions factory targeted near civilians." On this tear-stained newsprint was proof that he knew what the future held, at least the parts he could remember. It also dimmed any hope that this day and any in the immediate future would dawn and present this lovely person with what she wanted, an everyday life. It was yet more evidence of something different, strange, and, like a flame, at once good and evil.

It also confirmed that, however vague, he'd some knowledge of certain future events. Obviously, this knowledge would be of great use and critical to those prosecuting the conflict. His first reaction was to be of service in any way possible. A more reasoned second reaction faced the fact: it would be difficult, if not impossible, without exposing Margaret or himself to any unwanted attention. He would have to be very cautious in this regard. How could he go about presenting the future without causing animosity and fear? The question could be, should it be presented at all?

He recalled stories about the witches in Salem and the inability of the population to handle information that challenged existing beliefs and standards. A common thread between human beings was the desire to feel comfortable in our world. Wise advice would be to avoid any situation that would expose them to forces he couldn't control. Yet, given the potential consequences of silence, did he have a choice? Hitler and his elite were on a path to world domination and come uncomfortably close to succeeding. He realized, with a heavy heart, the moral obligation to those giving their lives prevented inaction. Although its origin and clarity eluded him, it inalterably committed him to share the information.

Accepting his strange knowledge and the obligation to share it created a world without acceptable codes or disciplines. The physical universe where we placed our trust had decided to take a proverbial leap right out the window.

Thomas felt angry as he contemplated what or who decided he was the one to bear this responsibility. "What forces or people are aware of what was fast becoming a burdensome 'gift'? What part, if any, will they play?"

His thoughts searched for the conventional spaces in his brain that stored normal information. Unfortunately, they remained suspended … somewhere.

Chapter Sixteen

Croydon Satellite Airbase
11 Group Kenley Sector

The morning sun created a beautiful painting as it moved up from the horizon and threw its light through the scattered clouds and into the new day. It was a blatant contradiction that such beauty could coexist with such violence in the same heaven. Such thoughts were far away for Lt. Paddy Hemingway, as he thought about never seeing his friend Dickey again. They'd scrambled early to support the bombers returning from the Berlin run, but the Germans didn't follow the bombers past the French coast.

He adjusted the flight stick slightly to the left, and the plane responded by banking over, lining up with the runway still several miles out. His squadron flew toward Croydon, their alternate field. Kenley, their home field, had suffered considerable damage from a German bomber attack while they were gone. Crews were still working on both runways, but it would be another four hours before they could return. Luckily the bomb drop had been off target at Croydon, and the facility had gotten just the tail end of the bomb pattern. He could still see smoke rising from several enormous bomb craters in the surrounding field and from one of the dispatch huts near the woods.

The rest of his squadron had already landed, and he was the last to come down. He was cold, and his mind blunted. His vision was blurring, all effects of being up two nights in a row. He should have taken a shift off and gotten some rest. However, he didn't, so now he was using all the energy he could muster to focus on landing.

Last night, when the escort force turned around and headed back to base, the bomber pilots knew they'd see German Me 109s within minutes. The Supermarine Spitfire Mk IIA had a range of 497 miles, much shorter than the bombers. The Germans knew precisely when the Spitfires had to turn back. It wasn't a pleasant feeling for a fighter pilot, knowing they couldn't protect the Blenheim IV bombers beyond that range, but it was worse knowing the bombers couldn't protect themselves. With a top speed of 260 miles per hour, a single rear-facing dorsal, 7.6mm tail guns, and no fighter escort, they were flying coffins. They were no match when fighting against the 347-mph German Messerschmitts. It was one thing putting your life on the line, but a grave injustice to courage not having a fighting chance to save it.

It took extraordinary bravery, risking your life every day, but you came through because you loved your wife, family, or friends. In Paddy's case, it came down to Edith Bristo, a girl he'd seen for a long while, or at least a long time in his book. Just recently, he started to understand how serious he was becoming. Edith was, as far as he was concerned, perfect in every way. They spent most of their available time together, and when he was with her, he felt a deep, warm happiness, and he wanted that feeling to stay. Invited several times to her parent's home, he'd got on quite well with her family. She somehow could understand his need to fly and encouraged him to pursue those things that made him happy.

Glancing down, he tried to move his stiff icy fingers. They acted as if they formed into the shape of the stick. He couldn't feel his toes as his feet worked the trim pedals. He needed all his wits about him as things were getting sticky. Having traveled as far out as they could last night, getting back to the English coast required firing all the ammunition in the magazines into the channel to lighten the planes. Despite that, ten minutes ago, the needle on his petrol gauge was resting on the empty peg. If he were going to land this plane, he would have to do it with his instincts as one of the best pilots in his group.

Paddy brought the stick back and started to level off. He took his left hand from under his leg, where it was trying to stay warm, and put the glove on the throttle controls to his left, just under the canopy latch.

"Slow it down just a little," he said to himself. "Keep the nose up; that's good."

The cockpit was tight, with his head so close that his breath fogged the canopy when he looked toward the ground. Churchill kept saying the key was America entering the war. The problem was the Americans didn't want to enter the war. They thought Britain was merely an imperial overlord trying to keep a fragile world empire together. Let them have the world was the attitude of the isolationists. There hadn't been an ounce of sympathy in America until their journalists started covering the battle that was taking place in the skies over Britain. Ed Murrow had interviewed some boys in No. 14 Squadron when he came in several weeks ago to do a broadcast for CBS. Right in the middle of the broadcast, the Germans decided it was a cracking good spot to open the bomb bay doors. The attack was carried live via undersea cable directly into the homes of America and caused quite a stir. Paddy hoped it was enough to get America involved because they were already involved, whether they liked it or not.

His head jerked up to the shouting coming in over his radio. "R23, what in bloody hell are you doing? You're too low. *Pull up now.*"

Startled, Paddy looked through the windscreen and could make out sunlight breaking over a massive dark shadow dead ahead. Instinctively, he pushed forward on the throttle and back on the stick and felt the thrust as the plane gained altitude and cleared the bank of trees.

The plane had drifted badly out of the approach path, and the lapse scared him. He brought the plane back in line and leveled out. That was entirely too close, and he knew he had to focus intently.

The voice said, "R23, put your undercarriage down. Release your undercarriage. Can you hear me?"

Reaching to his right, he pushed the pump lever forward; an enormous thump followed as the gear started dropping because of its own weight. Paddy compensated for the drag as the plane yawed left and right as the gears descended one at a time.

The voice in the tower said, "Confirmed, undercarriage down. Paddy, can you hear me? Talk to me."

"R23 here. Sorry boys guess I took a little nap. Landing clear, R23?"

"Yes, you're clear. Get her down, man; you're late on approach."

Paddy eased back on the throttle and adjusted the stick, keeping the nose up. His drifting off had used up too much of his approach path, and he was very high.

He thought, "If you really know how to fly this thing, mate, now is the time to prove it, as there isn't enough petrol for another pass."

He turned the wheel that set full flaps, which would allow him minimum stall speed.

"There," he said, "that's going to have to do."

He was still too high. The ground was coming up fast, but he needed to lose altitude, so he aggressively pushed the stick forward, bringing the nose down. He caught sight of the leading edge of the runway and knew it would be over in a few seconds, one way or another. He waited until the last possible second and threw the throttle so far forward that it reached the restraint the ground chiefs installed to protect their engines. At the same time, he pulled the nose up just enough, catching the heavy morning air underneath, creating a controlled drop but avoiding the stall. He succeeded in losing the altitude and somehow avoided hitting the ground, but now his airspeed was too high.

In a few seconds, the wheels hit hard, and he could feel the compression impact his spine, and his chin went into his chest. On impact, the plane bounced high, and the wheels not being on the runway delayed when he could apply the brakes. Coming back down, he cut the power. Now the problem was if he hit the brakes too hard, he would cause the plane's nose to drop and its tail to rise. To keep from flipping the plane right over the nose, Paddy feathered the brakes, 'flying' the nose back up gently until his tail wheel hit. Only then did he press down on the brake lever with all his might. Now, it was just a matter of his speed and the runway length. To his right, about 300 feet away, he could see the ground crew standing in the back of an open truck, speeding alongside to the end of the runway. Behind the truck was the fire crew. Everyone knew it would be close, and Paddy was now running on pure adrenaline.

The smoke from burning tires and the smell of burning brake pads filled the cockpit. Paddy cut the engine entirely and feathered the prop so the flat blades would push against the air as a kind of air brake. The smoke was thick, so he flipped the canopy release lever and tried to slide it back, but it stuck just an inch or so open. Fumbling around, Paddy found the oxygen mask and held it over his face while turning the control valve next to the throttle. The smoke and fumes were so thick he couldn't see a thing, but at least he could breathe. Still feeling the sensation of speed, he knew buildings were close enough to be a problem, as he was losing a sense of direction. Paddy no longer controlled the airplane except for the trim pedals, and he tried to keep them straight, hoping he was going down the middle of the runway.

Just as he was being thankful he was at least on the ground, the plane headed off the runway with a tremendous thump. Paddy jerked in the cockpit, feeling the rough ride on the uneven surface of the grass field, which wasn't good news. However, it meant he was away from the hangars and hardened shelters on the other side of the runway. Still blind, Paddy and the plane were careening uncontrollably over the grass field when the aircraft hit a bomb crater, and the left gear collapsed. As the forward force of the plane sheared the landing gear, it pulled the plane around. He lost consciousness as his head slammed sideways against the glass. The high velocity propelled the aircraft farther, spinning it in several slow circles surrounded by smoke and dust. It came to rest about a thousand feet from the runway, the front part on its nose with its tail about ten feet off the ground. The deformed left wing was flat on the ground, and the right-wing was pointing to the sky, supported by the remaining landing gear.

Smoke billowed off the remaining wheel and out of the small opening in the cockpit. The speeding truck carrying the ground crew came off the concrete and churned to a halt next to the plane. Someone yelled about being careful of the orange 'unexploded bomb' markers as two workers jumped out with fire extinguishers, shooting clouds of white powder at the burning tires and wheels.

Denis Legget, Paddy's commanding officer and friend, who had landed earlier, climbed up on the right wing, and Diggins, the best mechanic in the country, stepped up on the left. Diggins released the outside canopy lock and tried to slide it back. Diggins looked up at Legget when it wouldn't move. They could see it was already open enough to get a grip.

Legget said, "All right, on three." He counted off, and both threw their weight at the canopy and felt it slide back to the stops.

Smoke and fumes rose from inside, and they saw Paddy strapped in with his head slumped down, holding the oxygen mask against his face. Diggins pulled the exit door down and started pulling at the safety harness. He could hear the ambulance in the distance; then Paddy moved his head slightly.

"Don't move," Diggins said to Paddy.

Paddy coughed twice, and it caused a spike of pain to the side of his head. He put his hand up to his head and said slowly, "… think I'm okay."

"Well, you don't sound okay. You were out cold, so how would you know anyway?" Legget said.

"Because I know I'm about to catch hell for banging up this plane." Paddy coughed again and winced at the pain.

Diggins glanced at Legget, then replied, "You're right on that one. You're not touching a plane of mine until you learn how to fly."

Legget turned to the gathering rescue crew. "We need to get him and ourselves out of here before this thing blows up."

"Not going to happen today," Paddy said slowly. "There isn't a drop of petrol left to burn."

"Even though, can you stand up?" Legget said. "Diggins, grab his arm and pull him over to your side."

With help, Paddy exited the cockpit and made it down to the ground, where two medics were waiting with a stretcher.

"Sorry, gents," he said to the medics. "I'm walkin' away from this plane. Every man and boy with a pilot's license are watching, and I'll never hear the end of it."

He put his hand around the shoulder of his group leader and started toward the truck. With his other hand, he pulled the leather flight cap off his head.

He was still a little slow in speech when he turned to Legget and said, "I need a favor. I would really like to see Edith soon, perhaps today or tomorrow. I don't know exactly when. Do you think you can issue me an evening pass?"

"Yes," he responded, "if you go directly to the infirmary, I'll make it a forty-eight-hour leave. But," he said, waving a finger, "you must promise to sleep part of it."

"Not a minute," Paddy said, laughing. "I have a chance to see Edith, and suddenly I appreciate some others won't be so lucky."

Legget looked down at the ground as they walked; it had been the second narrow escape for Paddy in thirty-six hours. There was a quiet understanding between the men; not another word needed to be said.

Chapter Seventeen

Margaret's House
Amersham

Margaret's eyes were still red as she moved from the divan into the kitchen. She was folding a towel when Thomas followed her in and said, "Margaret, look, I'm sorry. I'm sorry that the news story upset you. If you're up for it, I think we need to have a very serious discussion."

"And what would you call that out in the garden?"

"I mean a discussion that's not about me or us. In fact, it's even bigger than England. It's about … humanity … mankind."

"If you ask me," Margaret said, "and you haven't, they should change the term to 'womankind.' It's obvious to me the men have had their shot and failed miserably. Thomas, you don't have to tell me this is an important time. I don't live with my head in the sand, although it looks pretty inviting right now."

"I'm not saying that. I don't think anyone realizes, to the extent that I do right now, what's coming is a turning point in a global struggle. The only country capable of turning back the Germans is the United States. It doesn't take a Sandhurst education to know it's impossible to invade Europe from New York City. The invasion must occur from the shores of England."

"The Americans won't even consider helping us," she said.

"Perhaps you're right, but regardless of what any American thinks, if England falls, it seals Europe's fate for the next fifty years. I might remind you; it's the same planet that the Americans call home."

Margaret said, "Americans. Surely there must be other ways. Someone will take up the fight. I believe that deeply."

"Despite your attitude toward the Yanks, it *will* be the United States." Thomas paused for a moment before saying, "When they declare war on Japan."

"*Japan?*"

"Yes. That's another story. Japan attacks the U.S., and two days later, for no apparent reason, Hitler, in an act of crushing stupidity, declares war on the United States."

"That doesn't make sense. Are you sure? Even a girl knows you kick the hell out of the first bully before calling out the next one. Especially if the next guy you're calling out is bigger than you."

Thomas held his arms out wide, laughing. "I knew it. Underneath that little-girl charm and mild manner lies a true military strategist."

"Don't make fun of me." She said. "I had it right, didn't I? Besides, you're not the only genius in the room."

"Well, my dear, I must disagree. There's only one genius, and it's not me. You're right; someone will take up the fight, but an enormous problem must be addressed before that occurs." Thomas closed his eyes as if doing so would somehow rearrange the forthcoming sentence, making it flow willingly into Margaret's head.

"Margaret, we're the only ones who can address that problem. It must be us." He waited for the explosion.

"*Us!*" she shouted. "*Us?* We're not even sure of who you or we are, let alone that we can come to the rescue of a continent. And don't call me dear unless you enjoy pain." She wasn't laughing.

"Margaret, please, if I can show you how, will you help me?"

"No!"

"Good then."

"No," she said again.

Thomas pulled back a chair and sat down. "I'm not sure how, but we need to make sure that England's leaders don't decide to surrender in what'll appear to be a hopeless situation."

Margaret threw her arms halfway into the air. "Oh, that's all, but you said that the Germans won't or didn't win the war. Do you see how silly this is? How can they 'didn't' win the war?"

"They won't and didn't; that part is straightforward. The problem is, without knowing why I'm here in your life, and with some things still a mystery, I'm not sure about anything."

"Thomas, I would strongly suggest you start making sense very quickly, or you'll have this serious discussion by yourself. Which wouldn't look any more odd than some of the things you've been saying."

"Okay, I'm trying to make it simple, but I don't have all the answers either," Thomas said.

"Simple? Nothing that has come out of your mouth has been logical, let alone simple, and by the way, did you hear me say no?"

"Margaret, take a deep breath." He put up his hands as though holding her off.

"This is scaring me. Tell me again about England winning the war."

"Eventually, England does, but it all would appear to come down to one meeting of the War Cabinet. At that moment, history, balanced on the head of a pin, is in the hands of one man. Churchill."

Thomas pushed himself away from the table and stood up. They were getting to the crux, and it wasn't going to get by the brightest in the room.

"Look," Margaret said, "it's a wonderful story, but am I missing something here? According to your version of history, they make the correct decision, right? As I said, why do we have to come to the rescue? Leave it alone."

Thomas was still standing with his hands in his pockets, knowing what was coming next wouldn't go over well. He took a deep breath and said, "Because that history hasn't yet been written."

Without her knowledge, Margaret's entire body went limp in the chair. The fact there was silence meant it was serious. Thomas decided to keep talking.

"Margaret, the events leading to that meeting are based on an incredibly small margin of error. If not repeated exactly, my version of history, the one where England wins, might not unfold. Churchill barely won the argument. In fact, with the information at hand, most say he shouldn't have won the argument. Honest men might come to different assessments and an equally valid but different conclusion." His voice had risen along with his hands.

He slowed down. "You're right. If history repeats itself precisely, there's little to warrant concern. The big question is, does it? If it does, then what am I doing here? Was I here the last time? Does anyone else have this knowledge? If I was here, did I use my knowledge to ensure the known result, or did it come about on its own?

"As I said, my perspective seems to be from the future. I have or had an intense interest in these critical turning points that affect the future of mankind. Ah, I mean …"

"Thomas Watson, you don't know what you mean. First you tell me one thing, and then—what do you mean in the future?"

"When we look back from the future, history is set in stone. However, in the past, history is being made every day," he said.

"Oh, no," Margaret said. "Don't you have anything in that head that makes sense? Thomas Watson, I'm seriously getting worried about *you*—not England.

"Thomas, I'm sorry, but it's all too much." She brought her palms together and touched her lips as though she were praying. "What happens now?"

There was a long pause as Thomas looked at Margaret and said, "Actually, I'm not sure. Although I know what should occur, I wasn't exactly given a plan of action."

Thomas could sense she'd had enough. He sat back down and reached for her hands.

"Look, we need to change the mood from dire to something approaching just dread."

"On that, we agree," she said.

Like flipping a switch, she sauntered around the table, sat on his lap, and threw the now familiar arm around his neck. She was grinning the 'Margaret grin.' Thomas looked at her for a second, captivated; he would never get used to how she could just stop him in his tracks with her pure magnetism.

"Thomas, why would you know *what* and not know why you know *what*?" she asked.

"I thought we stopped talking about that. Besides, that sentence sounds right out of my book, not yours."

"I don't remember anyone saying I couldn't talk that way. Why should you be the only one to act completely crazy?" she said.

"There should be a law," he said, "that says you can't have a mischievous grin pasted on your face without explaining the reason to the person most likely to be affected."

"What a bunch of rubbish. It would take all the life out of conversations, let alone barge in on every woman's right to have secrets."

Thomas looked around at the items she'd mindlessly rearranged while they were talking. He waved his hand toward the pots hanging from the rack, saying, "Do you know how to use any of these toys? Not that I'm trying to change the subject or anything. The fact is, I'm getting hungry."

"There, you see? You're not changing the subject in the slightest. I believe you should buy me a pleasant lunch. I would say we were on the same path in thought, wouldn't you?" she said, as the arm around his shoulder moved inward, putting his head in a vice lock. "I'll give you just enough air to say yes," she said through clinched teeth and a slight giggle.

Thomas started making low guttural noises and reached for his throat. With both hands covering her mouth, she jumped up and almost hysterically said, "Oh, Thomas, are you alright?"

He stood up, fixed his collar, like some peacock, and said, "Of course, we men also have our methods and secretive societies."

He bolted for the kitchen door as she yelled, "Mutant sod!" Just as a potholder hit the casing as he left the room.

Later, as they prepared to leave for lunch, Margaret suggested a place that sounded a little starched. Thomas asked if there wasn't something that wasn't as formal.

"Mr. Watson, when a man takes this girl, I mean *lady*, no, I mean *woman* out, it's not to a café or you're going by yourself."

Thomas felt he'd used up any good will he might have had earlier in the day, so he tactically let her win the battle, having dwelled enough on the war.

Chapter Eighteen

Kenley Airfield
11 Group Kenley Sector

Kenley wasn't so much an airfield as a straight bit of paved road surrounded by large areas of flat grassy fields. Across from the still-standing maintenance depot was the machinists' shop, destroyed in a raid a fortnight ago. As luck would have it, the red telephone box with its shiny crown on the top was still standing, although it lacked window glass in every opening. Paddy waited for the chap in the box to finish. Uniformed personnel could use the phone for non-military use and a very impatient Paddy was third in line, standing about, marking time. He'd gone through the debriefing, the medical check, and managed to catch some sleep. He wanted to contact Edith to see if she could manage some leave tonight. He never knew from one minute to the next if they could see each other; in fact, he didn't even know what her bit was in the war. She'd let him know it was definitely off-limits in their conversations and never brought it up.

He paced back and forth with his hands in his pockets, trying to think exactly what he was going to say, when from behind, he heard, "Well, Paddy Hemmingway, what're you doing here?"

Paddy turned to find Lonnie Garrah walking up to him. Lonnie was the WAAF (Women's Auxiliary Air Force) warrant officer at Croydon airfield. Lonnie and Paddy had a history, although it took place some time ago, and they'd parted as better friends than lovers. She simply didn't feel he would ever take their relationship to the next level. She still loved Paddy, and sometimes life was just plain maddening. Lonnie knew ending the relationship was the right thing for her. Paddy wasn't as sure. Later she realized she'd made a mistake, but it was too late.

The gold braiding on her cap gleamed in the sun as she approached. Her light complexion contrasted against her simply styled, sandy-brown hair and her crisp, dark blue uniform. Lonnie wasn't the pinup type who attracted that racy whistle from across the street. Lonnie wasn't served well if you were prone to book-and cover judgments, as her unique sparkle and deep humanity were found written on the pages inside.

Paddy's eyes widened a bit. It had been a few months since he'd seen her last, at an officers party in Brighton. They'd been having a great time when, curiously, she said she had to leave.

He smiled at the sight of his friend; he straightened and saluted, even though Paddy, an officer pilot, outranked her.

She gave a perfunctory wave of her hand toward her cap and said, "Oh, put your eyes back in your head and give me a hug." A young mechanic waiting for the phone pretended to ignore the scene as he pulled out a cigarette. Paddy walked away from the phone area and stepped back, holding Lonnie by the shoulders, looking her up and down. She had lost a lot of weight and went from a very attractive chubby to a set of three G-curves.

"Will you stop it?" Lonnie said as she could feel a blush rising and took a deep breath.

"Stop what?" Paddy said, sounding falsely accused of stealing the last cookie.

"Stop looking at me like it's 0200 in a pub. It's not going to get you anywhere."

"Lonnie, you look fabulous and, honest, I wasn't thinking that at all," he said, flashing a charming almost roguish smile.

"Yeah, and planes don't fly, or they do and some pilots can't keep them in the air," she laughed. "I just heard about your landing. Are you okay? That looks nasty," she said, pointing to a bandage on his head.

He reached up and touched the bandage. "Well, the canopy sort of up and swatted me, but Doc checked me out and I'm fine except for desperately needing some sleep. Thirty minutes will do wonders. Too bad I got it during the debriefing."

Lonnie shook her head, knowing the story was probably true. "How can a perfectly competent pilot get himself in such a position? Isn't there a limit to how many hours you can fly?"

"Well, normally, but things are getting a little frantic as we simply don't have enough pilots and planes to fly escort. A few of the bomber boys I know ended up on an impossible mission, and I felt I needed to support them. Unfortunately, it was after two scrambles earlier in the day. I had to ditch on the first but got a hot dinner as the Navy boys brought me back. That's the good news; the bad news is we lost Dickey Lee."

"Paddy, I'm so sorry. I know you two were really close." Lonnie could see the strain in his face and the tightness around his lips as he held back his feelings. "Why do men do that?" she thought. She opened her arms and hugged him. He grabbed her hard and just held on, and Lonnie could feel her old emotions rising in the moment.

Paddy continued to hold her and remained silent. Lonnie let him take whatever time he needed. He'd always been there for her, and she was grateful for this chance to be there for him. She felt his arms fall, and Paddy paused briefly, drifting off in thought. She chose not to interrupt whatever thoughts he was arranging.

In a few seconds, he finally said, "Actually, I'm not totally okay. Honestly, it was a bit of a scare, but it cleared my mind and straightened out my priorities?"

They were no longer in an embrace, but they still stood very close to one another. "Paddy, my boy, this doesn't sound like you," she said. "What do you mean priorities? What's changed?"

He put his hand on the inside of her arm at her elbow and led her away from the wreckage of the building.

He said, "Right in the middle of fighting the plane and sleep when I knew I was going off the runway, I had this crystal-clear thought. You can't wait until tomorrow to live your life, because there are no guarantees of a tomorrow, especially in the middle of a bloody war. I lost a dear friend yesterday. One minute he was there and the next he'd disappeared from my view. This morning, when I found myself alive and being helped out of the plane, I made a commitment."

Something moved inside Lonnie. "What kind of commitment?"

"I'm asking Edith to marry me, hopefully tonight. Denis said I could have a few days' leave. The big problem is her getting time away from that mysterious job. In any event, I need to do it now; I'm not going to wait. I don't have any plans, so it will probably be in a pub and not the Savoy as it should be. God, I don't even have a ring, so I'll probably wrap a bit of string around her finger and kiss it. I really don't know, but that stuff is just not important right now. Lonnie, I really love her, and I want to let her know, to show her now—not later."

A surge of emotion flowed through Lonnie's body. It surprised her, as completely different feelings had been surging through her body and mind only a second ago. Now she found herself having traveled a sort of emotional circle. She had never met Edith but was familiar with their relationship. She and Paddy had spent many a night talking about Edith over drinks. It was a peculiar position, as she found herself helping him work out the same frustrations with commitment they'd experienced when they were together. She knew he was serious by the look on his face and his speech had a particular intensity and deliberation.

Lonnie didn't know what to say. She faced what every schoolgirl faces when moving to a new boyfriend and someone dating her old one. What was it that made you look back when you had decided to go forward? Was it pride, selfishness, or just ego? She didn't know, but she had it right now. Knowing they'd decided not to take the same path, it would now be permanent. She could feel the emotion surface; her face was getting hot, and a tear started down her cheek before she could catch it.

Paddy was yanked back to where he was and what he had said. "Lonnie, that wasn't fair. I shouldn't have…"

"Oh, shut up. I'm happy for you, Paddy," she said, as she cleared another drop off her cheek. She emitted a single chuckle and said, "Can't you see that I'm happy for you?"

Paddy was silent. He realized life was a complicated emotional place, where things weren't always what they appeared. He'd hurt her, and it was the last thing he wanted to do. "God, I'm so stupid," he thought.

"Lonnie?"

"Paddy Hemmingway, you sod. You can't propose to a woman without a ring."

"Isn't proposing more important than some piece of metal?"

"No, there are certain things that are important to a woman, war or no war. They want a good man they can depend on, they want security, but most of all, they want romance."

"Romance? Come on, Lonnie, twenty minutes after I ask her. The Germans could be on the beaches. Certain things can't be obtained. Wedding dresses aren't exactly popping out of Paris right now. I'm not even sure I can see her tonight, let alone have enough time to get into London and arrange a dinner at a decent hotel."

"Some things are more important than others." Lonnie brought her hands together and with ease pulled a ring off her right hand. It was a simple band with a row of three small sapphires at the top. It was the first thing she'd purchased after leaving home—something she just wanted and didn't actually need. Lonnie grabbed Paddy's hand, placed it in his palm, and closed his fingers around the ring.

"Lonnie, you can't do this. …" He said.

She put a finger to his lips, and he stopped.

"You're not a woman. I wouldn't expect you to understand. I'm sure it will be too big, but it will get you past the moment. You must never

78

tell her and never try to give it back. You can get her a decent wedding ring later."

He started to talk again, and she interrupted. "Do I have your promise?"

"Yeah, but ..."

"Paddy, I mean it. Never tell her."

He looked at the ring in his hand and back at Lonnie.

"And there's something else you must promise me. If there are any more like you, Paddy Hemmingway, you must send them my way." She looked over. "The phone is clear; you better make your call."

She returned his hand to him and turned away. "I'm off to Birmingham, but I'll be back on Thursday. Let me know how it goes. You can get me here at the base."

She turned and walked away smartly as the emotions she was holding within let loose, and she started to cry.

"Lonnie, I didn't know." He called after her. "I really didn't."

"I know, Paddy," she said, facing straight ahead. "I know." And she was gone.

Chapter Nineteen

London
Embassy's Flat—Silvertown, East End

Night fell on the East End of London. Yuri was sitting at the table, writing his rent payment for the small flat he also kept on Leyton High Road in the West End and listening to Italian opera on the radio. They were so emotional, these Italians. It was great, but the trait made terrible soldiers. They'd design these incredible helmets with plumed feathers but couldn't shoot a gun. What good was that? He found it amusing that Hitler had made a pact with Mussolini. It was like the machinist going into business with Gucci. The Italian's only task was to hold a part of Africa, their colonial backyard. It was only a short time before they were routed. Soon, the Germans would have to secure the continent with their resources. Now they were doing the work of the Italians and still bound by the pact. The agreement wasn't good business; he wondered if this Hitler was as bright as everyone thought.

There were two loud bangs on the door, and Yuri thought it was about time. He'd been waiting since the meeting that morning with the ambassador. Wondering what the next hour held in store, he walked over to the radio, moved the station, and turned it off. On his way to the door, he opened his long coat hanging on the entry hall tree, pulled back the center lining in the back, and slipped the payment envelope inside the hidden pocket. He straightened the coat, looked one last time around the room, then walked over and opened the door. In front of him stood a stout young man with a round face in a brown business suit that looked two sizes too big.

"Welcome, Comrade Stakova!" the man said loudly in English.

Yuri leaned forward, looking up and down the hall, then walked past the man, leaned over the stairway railing, and peered down the open stairwell to the first floor and the front door. He'd chosen this flat because the entry foyer was visible by looking down from just outside his door. There appeared to be no one. Without returning the greeting, he pushed the man into the room and closed the door.

"And you would be…?" Yuri said in English to test the man.

"Comrade Joseph Surkovich Alexikov," the man also said in English. "It's a pleasure to meet such a famous comrade who has provided such exemplary service to the Motherland. All in the Moscow bureau admire you. I would only hope I can achieve this status someday."

"Comrade Joseph, if I may call you that?" The man nodded his head. "How long do you expect to be station chief of the London bureau?"

"Well," the man hesitated just a beat too long, "as long as I'm asked, of course. It's a very interesting question," he said, reaching up and removing his hat.

"If you wish to be here for an extended period, I would suggest that you not announce to the world that you're a spy and make me a rather obvious accomplice," Yuri said.

The man stammered, "I, of course, knew there was no one in the area. I looked, and there was no one there." He folded his arms. "Of course," he said.

"Of course," Yuri said, offering to put the man's gas mask on the small entry rack beside the umbrella, and put the man's hat on a hook. Yuri moved toward the center of the room. He turned to face his visitor, placing his hands into the pants of the suit provided by Mr. Stevens, the purveyor and exacting tailor at a small shop on Seville Row. He knew that Mr. Stevens's real name was Isaac Sharfberg, and his guest would have to make his shop one of his first stops.

Yuri said, "Comrade Alexikov?"

"Yes?" Joseph said.

"The regulations," Yuri said in Russian, "which I'm very sure you've memorized, state that we must speak English even when we're alone, so there's not the slightest chance we're mistaken for what we are. How is your English?"

In English, Joseph said, "It's very worthy. I studied and accepted top passing in my section."

"Grade," Yuri said.

"Grade?" the newcomer said defensively.

"Yes, you received a top *grade*," Yuri said in English.

"Of course, *grade*," Joseph said, folding his arms again.

"What're your plans, Joseph?"

In English, he said, "I'm requesting we," he paused and found the word, "proceeding the last case that must conclude before your leaving. I've information on entire local assets and," he paused, "ongoing operations. I've exact directives carrying out in short time but can't... proceed until this final issue is come to a... halt."

Joseph reached into the breast pocket of his coat, handed Yuri a sealed envelope, and said, "I've carried this perso... myself from Moscow. The director Mission Central pressures you complete very quickly this instructions and be home back with these directives, ah...directions."

Yuri realized that helping the man with his English was a lost cause. Besides, he sensed something far more important was developing between the two men. Yuri opened the envelope and read the letter inside.

> People's Commissariat for Internal Affairs (NKVD)
> Comrade: Yuri Ivanovich Stakova,
> 15 August 1940
>
> You're directed to retire the agent, Thomas Watson, for failure to provide the promised information for which we paid handsomely. With recent developments, this agent is considered outside our charge and can't be allowed actions beyond our control. Such activity would almost certainly compromise other assets in the region. Endangering existing operations isn't acceptable in the strongest terms with the invasion, but days or weeks away.
>
> This issue is your responsibility. Completion is mandatory, with updates to Moscow Centre as to your success.
>
> Upon completion, you're to proceed to the Hartford Street location in the port city of Glasgow and await further instruction regarding your transportation back to Moscow.
>
> Comrade Andri Ganova Schikova
> Director Foreign Operations
> Western Sector

He looked up at Alexikov and said, "Recent developments?"

"Yes, he…" Joseph started in Russian.

"English, please," Yuri said stoutly.

Joseph glared at the interruption. "Yes, it's the point you reported about more money."

Yuri stiffened. Watson did ask for more and Yuri was unhappy, but not unhappy enough to eliminate him. "Why was I not informed if the Centre took this so seriously?"

"You've been substituted on another, more meaningful directive. Watson matter is considered … abolished … ah … over. This case file is a single one I not receive … did not receive. Moscow wishes you completed this case file. How into this … mess did you arrive?"

Yuri resented the young man insinuating that he'd somehow failed. "It's not a mess," Yuri said. "I'm not sure what it is, as I don't have all the information."

"Well, Comrade, it is so, as the Bureau … deathly avoids with anybody, as in English say it, 'put out to farm.'"

Yuri walked over to the radio, turned it on, set it to an English station, and upped the volume a bit. He mentally drifted for a second, listening to the music, trying to gather his thoughts. Unfortunately, it was playing "A Tisket A Tasket." It was a good tune, but not one of Ella Fitzgerald's best. Anyway, he should have turned it on when his guest entered the room and started this conversation. "Please," Yuri said to Joseph, motioning to take a seat.

"It's 'out to pasture," Yuri said slowly.

"Pasture?"

"Yes, the English phrase is 'out to pasture.' I suggest you stick with the basics until your language skills improve." Doubts continued to grow in Yuri's mind. Walking over to a low cabinet, he opened the door, took out a bottle of vodka, and grabbed two glasses with one hand. He placed the glasses on the table before the divan, where Joseph had taken a seat.

With a broad smile, Joseph said, "Comrade Stakova, a most generous host indeed. Is vodka accessible here?"

"Yes, but I never drink it in a public place."

"Why is this?"

"Just being cautious, but I would think that would be obvious. I always drink the local beer," Yuri said.

"Oh, yes, the famous English beer. What is taste like?"

"Warm."

"No, not true. You're making fun with me in English. What is warm?"

"Теплый," Yuri said.

"No, this is not being true. I don't find it true."

Yuri looked at the man in front of him. "Joseph, have you ever traveled in any country outside the Soviet Union?"

"No. This is also interesting question."

The war didn't allow for the customary extensive language and customs training deployed in the past, which accounted for the decline in tradecraft. Back in the day, it was an honor for a spy to participate in brief excursions into their target country to work on accents, adapt mannerisms, and work to blend into the culture.

"How could the 'bright ones' not know they were exposing our operation and this young man's life, sending him out too soon?" Yuri thought. The answer was obvious; they hadn't been out of the country either.

"It's not important," Yuri said. "Back to our problem. We've known for some time the Germans have a message-encoding machine that's an excellent piece of equipment. They consider the daily random combinations of some encoding wheels to make the code unbreakable. There's a high level of suspicion that the British have made considerable headway at Bletchley Park in creating a machine that can decipher the transmissions. If this is true, it gives them at least partial access to top-level German commands. The Bureau wanted any information they could get on this project.

"One day, this Thomas Watson wandered into the embassy, wanting to know how he could make a lot of money. As head of security, I interrogated him and immediately suspected a double agent. It was just too easy, and he was too naive. Despite a good education, extensive checks proved he was a drifter and a con artist. He was made-to-order without any overt loyalties to his country."

"Overt?"

"Откровенный," Yuri said in Russian. Joseph nodded his head.

"Eventually, I put Watson on this project. We knew that a company called Hatcher Plc., a manufacturer of materials for uniforms, was secretly working on a project similar to one underway at Bletchley Park. Perhaps they were the same thing; we didn't know. Watson was to return with a plan on how he would put himself in a position to access the information."

"What occurred to the Mr. Watson?" Joseph asked, holding up his glass. "К Родине (To the Motherland)," he whispered, and they touched glasses, tipped them up, and felt the quick sting in their throats.

"Well, Joseph, it's hard to tell with this one. He came back, said he'd done some checking on his own, and proposed that he get close to the owner's daughter. I thought it was bold, as we'd already been watching the daughter. I was never very comfortable with him. He was quiet but could turn into a real charmer. It was apparent he didn't understand what he was getting into, but the possibility of getting some information on the project was too good to pass up. We put him on the high payroll, with a very large up-front payment, and waited.

"One day, unexpectedly, the daughter broke with the family, wanting to start a new life. She needed money and a place to stay, so, without her knowledge, one of our contacts arranged to have her accepted in a house even though she was unemployed. Watson continued reporting and making progress on his plan. Then without warning, he informed me that he'd married the daughter. I was very suspicious but somehow he pulled it off. As I said, he could be very effective regarding people. Other times, you wanted to watch your wallet. Watson and I met at a pub near him called The Stag House, near the Amersham Station, and we established ourselves as friends among the patrons to lower suspicions.

"Then he urgently wanted a meeting in which he demanded more money without convictions, almost like a child. I told him he was getting well above what we normally paid. He wasn't happy. In fact, he was a little threatening. Besides, other than managing to marry the daughter, he hadn't produced anything of value. Given what I know now, I think he has sold us out for a better deal and didn't know how it might affect his life expectancy."

"Comrade, how will this be done by you?"

Yuri looked directly at Joseph. "I have no plan yet, but a directive is an order that's acted upon promptly. An operation such as this, in a foreign country, must be executed carefully and without a trace."

There was strength in Yuri's voice to impress his guest.

"I'm interested," Joseph said. "Who was used to make the rental flat for Margaret? These informations weren't added to asset reports. This would be good to know also." Joseph found it interesting that Watson wasn't being completely truthful. Joseph was briefed on the incomplete reports before leaving. Joseph knew not reporting in full to superiors was a grievous error and could easily result in rather sparse accommodations in Siberia or worse. It was Joseph's first indication of the true meaning of Yuri's new 'desk job.'

"It doesn't matter," Yuri said, sidestepping the question. "The important matter is executing the directive before he's allowed to cut his deal with the other side and thereby compromise our operation. We can't let that happen."

"It's your case, Yuri. Joseph has many worries of my own."

Yuri looked at him intently. Joseph wasn't as slow as his English made him sound, but his job would require fluency in the local language. His lack of in-country training was just too obvious. Joseph wasn't of the caliber to be 'rising fast' in the Bureau and cutthroat in the process, as the ambassador indicated. He wasn't the new station chief. That meant someone else was out there—someone who met those qualifications.

Yuri hadn't told Joseph everything and perhaps had told him too much. Several things weren't adding up. There are too many holes. This wasn't being handled according to the rules, and field operations were always executed by the book. Yuri had Watson under surveillance, and there had been no change to his situation since the last report: he was at home with his wife. Watson wouldn't do something as stupid as cutting a separate deal unless he really was stupid. If he was about to go turncoat, a low profile was a very healthy thing, and the last few days, Watson had done exactly that. So far, the only unusual thing was the Moscow directive. Tomorrow, he needed to get more information.

Chapter Twenty

London
No. 10 Downing Street

It was early, but Churchill was already in his nightclothes. He often worked from bed, either in the morning or at night. He placed the papers down on his lap table and removed his spectacles. The manufacturing reports weren't encouraging. If the truth where told, very little of late had been encouraging.

He stared blankly at the wall while waiting for the secretary to bring the most current raw materials inventory, up to the last convoy. His impatience grew, knowing it took so long to create a winning strategy. They'd suffered setback after defeat, but they were still in the running. He'd barely stepped in the door, and history laid the fiasco of Dunkirk at his feet. Brave men, at significant peril, had turned the blood-soaked shores into a victory. This occurred only after he'd insisted that the nation's future depended on occupying that thin stretch of land, and soon the opportunity would be gone.

Any failure on his watch would result in the inevitable references in the newspapers to the Empire's resounding defeat at the Dardanelles. It occurred while he was First Sea Lord and would be his cross to bear. This was despite a commission citing the military's failure depended on occupying in executing his orders in the field as the reason for the failed operation. Still, the defeat stuck to him like gum to the bottom of his shoe and followed him everywhere. Whenever he stepped into the Office of the Prime Minister, he could hear the old whispers rise again. However, it wouldn't deter him from making decisions based on honesty and righteous ideals.

In trying to save the island, there was only so much he could do. Inside, he believed he was right to continue with his 'senseless stubbornness,' but he also sensed a rising tide in the country against resisting an invasion. He drifted back to the years when he was a soldier correspondent in South Africa, barely escaping from the Boers with his life and, upon his return, hailed a national hero. Things had been less complicated back then, right, wrong, black and white, with morals held in high esteem. Today, anything was acceptable without reference to the old standards, including bombing civilians.

Chapter Twenty-One

Margaret's Home
Amersham

Thomas awoke early and while lying there, wondered why his thinking existed in this gray area. "We're given control of only certain things," he thought. Which currently appeared not to include his life.

He decided that events were only to get better. After all, there was Margaret; she was definitely the silver lining in any clouds on his horizon. After their talk about his knowledge, the rest of the day was terrific, much like the day before. He would sit there completely fixated as she talked in high-speed animation, covering subjects that ranged from politics, history, art, family, and the contents of her kitchen. At day's end, they were exhausted and collapsed into bed, avoiding any outlying issues.

Margaret had awakened very energized. She indicated she wanted to punch that Hitler bloke directly in the nose every once in a while. Right in the middle of this hellish war, with all the talk of the coming German invasion, Margaret thought one of the best weapons against the Third Reich was to act as if it simply wasn't going to affect her life. She maintained she had a special secret weapon, a covert diversionary action, which she finally admitted was a picnic in the country.

Margaret went next door to lobby her landlady, Mrs. Somerville, into loaning them her old Austin for the trip. As Mrs. Somerville fussed about the counter, Margaret observed a very mischievous smile emerging on the face of someone who had become her dear friend.

"Well, I'll let you borrow the Austin on two conditions. One condition is that it still runs, likely killing the entire plan, and the second is you must grant me a promise."

"And can I ask what this promise of yours might be?" Margaret said, taking up a large blue enameled boiling pot and toweling it dry.

"Well, Kitten, of course, you can. It's just a trifle. It would bring me great pleasure to know how enjoyable your day was, so I can vicariously enjoy it with you. It's much better than reviewing one of my old memories. Simple enough, don't you think?" Mrs. Somerville said as she placed a dry dish in the cupboard. "I'm an old lady with simple needs."

"You're not," Margaret said, drying the last dish. "What I see is a very clever woman with a bit too much twinkle in her eye. That, madam, is what I think."

"Yes, of course, we all have our opinions now, don't we, young lady?" she said, laughing deeply.

Mrs. Somerville wandered into the adjacent dining room and opened two louvered doors that covered an ample storage space under a set of stairs.

The space housed the few bottles of wine Mrs. Somerville felt the need to keep on hand. She reached in, selecting one bottle and then another from a rack, inspecting them both until satisfied with one. Dusting the bottle off with the towel on her shoulder, she handed it to Margaret.

Surprised, Margaret said, "Do you know how hard it is to get a good bottle of wine these days?"

"Of course, young lady, that's why I'm giving it to you. At a picnic, there's nothing better than the aroma of a good Bordeaux, except its effect." She finished the sentence by pointing directly at Margaret with an unmistakable look. "If you're going to be in the picnic business, you must do it properly."

Margaret smiled, cradling the bottle in her hands, and said, "There's that grin again. This wouldn't have anything to do with the resulting story, would it?"

"Honestly, you're so young. You're more like a daughter." Mrs. Somerville moved to her credenza. She pulled out the top drawer, moved some items, and handed two petrol ration cards to Margaret.

"I'll never use these, and even if it starts without them, you're not going anywhere. If you ever need them in the future, I store them here."

"No, I think you should hold onto them," Margaret said.

"My God, woman, I can't drive," Mrs. Somerville said. "What on living earth would I do with petrol ration cards except trade them for butter, which you don't have to look closely to notice I don't need."

In the drawer, a large book covered in ornately stitched velvet caught Margaret's eye. "Mrs. Somerville, what's that? It's beautiful."

Slowly, Mrs. Somerville said, "That's where I keep Charles. Photos of the life we shared. I'll sit down someday, and we can go through them if you like, but not today."

"Oh, yes," Margaret said. "I'm very interested in stories, and I also know you've a few to share."

"Daughters," Mrs. Somerville said, shaking her head, "Off with you now, and don't forget wine glasses."

It took a bit of tinkering, but the Austin eventually fired up, though it was unhappy at the intrusion. Margaret and Thomas stowed everything in the boot and drove off.

Actually, Margaret drove. Initially, Thomas got behind the wheel but didn't feel very comfortable for some reason. They were just underway when, upon changing down for a slight upcoming hill, a most painful noise emanated from somewhere inside the beast. It sounded like he'd reversed the shifting pattern of the gearbox, and the Austin let him know in no uncertain terms. After Thomas's gallant, albeit uncoordinated effort, they pulled over to the side of the road, and Margaret graciously, after a hard laugh at his expense, took over driving.

With his newfound ability to concentrate on other things besides the road, he noticed there were not references to streets or village names. "How do they deliver the post without street names?" he asked.

"Oh, the postman knows them well enough. They removed all the signposts to confuse the invading hoards, or should I say Huns."

They drove to a favorite spot Margaret had all picked out. She recounted how her father had taken her to this old farm many times as a child and young woman. She had wonderful memories of long discussions and walks through the rolling hills. Her father would share his frustrations about business, friends, politics, and even his relationship with her mother.

Over time, she realized that no one lived at the farm, and no one was interested in fixing it up. It had a main house, very old and made of stone. Typically, it was almost impossible to destroy one of these houses; often, they rebuilt the interior, with repairs made to the stone shell and thatched roof. Here, however, a remodeling effort wasn't the plan. The grounds also contained a couple of outbuildings, including a huge barn. It was actually in good shape, with its large loading doors bolted shut. Margaret said that the small, regular-sized door directly to the left was the only other way in, but it too, was always locked.

After her father died, she stopped going to their 'special place.' It wasn't the same after her life changed and her relationship with her mother became strained. While she became independent and went off to school, Mother turned to shopping at Harrods, followed by great teas with the ladies, where they nibbled on delights while discussing the latest events in society.

Thomas unloaded the various items from the Austin's boot. They then walked through a thick stand of tall brush a short distance from the buildings and entered a wonderful little green meadow dominated by a massive solitary maple tree. Directly ahead, he could see formerly active farmland now covered with wild grasses as high as the tops of the fence posts. To the right was a line of fifty-foot-high cottonwood trees, planted double thick, that blocked off the view on that side of the meadow. Thomas thought he heard some activity, likely from a farm on the other side of the cottonwoods. They were the only sounds other than those of a natural setting. It was a perfect place to forget about the day and night of bombing and the strained lives outside this piece of rural world. Margaret busied herself, taking out the sandwiches and salad she had prepared, and lamented the lack of fresh fruit.

Then, with great fanfare, she pulled the bottle of wine out of the basket, holding it in the air, saying, "This is from your friend, Mrs. Somerville."

"My friend?" he said, surprise in his voice.

"Yes. To my surprise, Beth has recently taken a liking to you. Before, she didn't know you existed, and now she gets this twinkle whenever you're around."

"Well, I do have this intrinsic charm; it must be genetic," Thomas said, lifting his chin and showing his best side.

"What's *genetic*?" she said, laying out the food.

"It's... a type of... No, I think... The real answer is, I don't know. But I thought I did."

"There you go again," she said, followed quickly by a napkin holder sailing past his ear. "We won't be given over to that spooky stuff here. This meadow is sacred ground."

"As is anywhere you walk, I'm finding out," he said, blowing her an animated kiss.

"Eat your sandwich, Mr. Watson. It might be the last food you see from me for quite a while—unless you change your ways."

"The food was delicious, but the genuine attraction of the afternoon was conversing with someone so consistently quick off the mark, bright, and inwardly beautiful," he thought. They wandered to any subject, and he found the energy exchange refreshing and intoxicating. Thomas quickly found a sensitive liberal with an eye toward saving the world but equipped with the pragmatism required to accomplish the task.

At the end of the day, she convinced herself Hitler wouldn't win the war. Not because of any tactical knowledge but because evil, while it may leave destruction in its wake for a time, never really wins in the end. She believed in the over-powering limitless might of good and God, although she never used that word; instead, she related to an 'Everywhere Spirit.'

She said, "Mankind's existence is a balancing act or battle between positive and negative, yin-yang, salvation, and hell. The story of this battle is called history. You know, the stuff we teach to make a living."

She explained that if one could strip away all the dogma added to the original works, the same story would emerge in all the great religious books of the world.

Surprise after surprise spilled out of her, and Thomas was utterly fascinated.

"Whom have you shared this with?"

"Only you," she replied.

"The me now or me before?"

"You now."

"Why now and not earlier?" he said.

"Because you now appear to be the only one interested."

He pressed her further on her relationship with the old Thomas, and she was reluctant to provide any more details and wanted to change the subject.

She became reticent after that and busied herself gathering things and putting them into the basket. Thomas watched as she gently placed the plates at the bottom and folded the napkins.

She brought up the sides of the basket and inserted the small wooden pin between the wicker loops that held it closed, took a deep breath, and said, "Thomas?" She waited for a second before continuing, "were you married?"

"What kind of question is that?" he said.

"Well, if you must know, it's a damn important one. Now answer it or …"

He put his hand up again, in what was becoming a familiar gesture, "Hold it, okay. Let me think for a minute."

He sat there, trying to get a feel for his personal life, but like everything else, it was vague, and instead of memories, he had only feelings. He could feel the presence of a great love at one time, but he couldn't understand why it was gone.

"Time's up," she said.

"Actually, I'm married to you. Isn't that enough?"

"No, Mr. Watson, that's not enough. We've been over this territory before."

"Margaret, I think there was someone I cared for deeply, but for some reason, she's gone, and there has been this emptiness since. That's as clear as I can get."

"You don't feel you were married?"

"No, I don't feel I was married."

"Thomas?"

"Margaret, that's the best I can do. It's as close to the truth as we're going to get."

Satisfied she relaxed after that.

They continued to talk and regretted the end of Mrs. Somerville's wine. Then they nodded off in each other's arms in the warm August sun. At least Margaret napped; Thomas was too wrapped up in the wonderful feeling of having her that close and pretended to sleep so she wouldn't find an excuse to move away. "It was the most enjoyable part of the day," Thomas thought.

Slowly, the splendid clear day disappeared behind gathering clouds, and the temperature dropped. Undeterred, and leaning against a tree, they kept talking like a non-stop radio program.

He'd hoped to avoid thinking about his problem and, instead, spent the day trying to establish his relationship with Margaret. In the back of his mind was trying to keep her from any of the fallout his memories would bring. Then, during their conversation, he got an idea of how to get his knowledge into the right hands without exposing themselves. He would take the direct approach and provide the information to someone in the intelligence community, letting them present it as information from their usual 'mysterious' sources. Still, why would someone in the intelligence community believe him? Then he had the answer.

He knew the British had a super-secret intelligence organization at Bletchley Park. The government asked women to submit a unique crossword puzzle from the newspaper. Those chosen for the task took each piece of intelligence from spies and military observations and dutifully entered it by hand onto three-by-five-inch cards. They filed these cards in vast rows of dark wooden file cabinets. Within this organization, an extraordinary team of mathematicians, chess masters, and cryptographers worked on breaking the German military code used to issue orders to the field army from Berlin. A machine called Enigma generated the code. Ultra was also the name the British gave to the information intercepted and decoded. Unlike the other murky images, Thomas knew they'd ultimately credit this team with developing the first real computer, starting a technical revolution they couldn't have imagined. He also knew they were having trouble with some existing methods and equipment. Expertly arranged file cards could only take you so far.

The person heading up the work was a man by the name of Alan Turing. He was quirky but brilliant mathematician many recognize as a hero of the war. However, his work would remain hidden for the next thirty years under the security veil of the secrets act. If Thomas could gain access to him and reveal some information not generally known about his work, he hoped he might engender Turing's trust. This might give Turing reason to believe him and perhaps help in his plan.

Failing that, his second option was significantly more desperate. It required scheduling a meeting with the prime minister, and his chances of succeeding with that were close to zero. You needed a good reason to see the prime minister during wartime, and Thomas didn't have one he could discuss openly.

He presented his ideas to Margaret, and they agreed he should try his hand at Bletchley in the morning. It had taken some time, but she was now backing his effort, although she still didn't clearly understand why.

Eventually, they had to address the evening that would soon be upon them; a drive back in the dark meant taped lights and closed filling stations. In the first months of the blackout, more civilians died because of traffic accidents at night than bombings, so it was a situation neither of them felt was safe. They quickly packed up the evidence of a most enjoyable time and headed back to the car.

Chapter Twenty-Two

Outside Amersham

Pavel, an agent at the Russian Embassy who reported to Yuri, was neither comfortable nor happy. His legs were stinging from standing and leaning up against a tree. It had been an eternity since the Watsons had arrived and settled under the maple tree. Recently, he moved closer, attempting to hear what they were saying. Staying behind the tree was the only place close enough to listen to their conversation and stay out of sight. He really needed a cigarette and was hungry and didn't appreciate traipsing through the wet shrubs and grass in his dress shoes. He didn't think they'd ever stop talking and he dozed off for at least a few minutes upright against the tree. That wouldn't be in his report to Yuri, as it was horrible tradecraft and could get him fired. He hadn't known where they'd spend the day, so he'd hardly prepared for this marathon. "It's a good thing they didn't go mountain climbing," he thought.

When he moved closer to hear their conversation, he still couldn't make out everything they said. Did Watson say he was going to Bletchley? Pavel knew of this place, and everyone thought it was the hidden location of the machine. However, if he was going to Bletchley, it was most likely an attempt to find out more about the device than because he was going to tell the British that he was a Russian spy. This man was clever enough to escape execution and turn it into money.

Pavel had heard bits and pieces today, not the whole story, but he knew this was a significant piece of information, and Yuri would be very pleased. It was the kind of lucky break that would get him out of the field and into the political side of embassy operations.

He saw the couple packing up and loading everything into the car. They were farther from him now, and he couldn't hear any of their conversations. Moving closer was too risky as there wasn't enough cover, and he certainly wasn't going to lie on the ground. He'd given enough for Mother Russia today.

Pavel watched with amusement as the woman got into the driver's seat. He'd been on this case long enough to know that this wasn't any normal woman. On the drive out, Pavel, following from behind, almost overcame them when they stopped and changed drivers. First, he heard her laugh loudly, and then the car pulled away.

Still hiding, he picked up the sound of the engine and the rapid shifting of the gearbox as they drove away. He reached into his pocket and quickly lit up a cigarette. He decided he wouldn't follow them back and would make his way to the embassy instead. He needed to write this up, but most of all, he needed to call Yuri from a private place.

After a few lingering, deep inhales, his urge for a smoke was waning. He walked over to the tree to see if they had, by chance, left anything interesting behind. It was standard surveillance and an old habit; also, it was nice to walk a bit before getting back into the car. He bent over and picked up a small polished wooden ring that was definitely out of place. Perhaps it's a tiny bomb, he laughed. How did he get into this business? He took another long drag from his cigarette and held it a second before exhaling. In a way, he hated cigarettes. They were messy, and they were also inconvenient in his line of work. It was hard to remain hidden and observe with billowing clouds of smoke emanating from someplace where no one was supposed to be. He followed the path they'd taken to the car and took another look around, finding nothing.

"It's getting dark," Pavel thought. He didn't enjoy driving in the dark. Why did they come all the way out here? "Love," Pavel thought, throwing his cigarette down on the ground and crushing it into the damp earth. It left many unexplained actions in its wake.

Chapter Twenty-Three

After the Picnic

Again, Margaret managed the shifting and driving, winding through the green pastures and low hills in a semi-trance. The low sun flickered brightly behind the various obstacles as they meandered back and forth on the small, rural road.

Being at the farm felt like old times, allowing her to be in another world where she could avoid all the things that needed avoiding. However, on the trip back, each bright flash bursting from behind each passing tree and barn slowly drew her back into today.

She had been in control of her life two days ago, or at least she thought so, but the last two days had shaken her security. She'd also felt in control of her emotions, but that also was shaken to the core. What was this deep, overpowering emotion she was feeling for the man who had filled her day? This person who wholly and quickly obliterated any attraction she might have had for the same man two days ago? Marrying the old Thomas had been a mistake. Although a curious sort, she didn't hate him; it had been a fling gone wrong without the fling. She'd found the constant attention he'd bestowed upon her irresistible, his exciting, spontaneous lifestyle threaded through a time of war. He'd provided a little joy to balance the constant pressure from her mother, who had decided she was to follow the rules of the last century.

She'd entered the marriage with eyes wide open and on her terms, but she quickly became aware that something was unsettling about the man. Somehow she wasn't getting the entire story. Before their marriage, his intense interest in her family exceeded his futile but constant interest in gaining access to her knickers. She kept that situation at bay with the old reliable 'I'm not that kind of girl.' It wasn't true;

every girl was that kind of girl if she was with the right man. In this case, he wasn't the one. She knew it would become a serious issue after the marriage. To solve the situation, she informed the surprised groom minutes before the wedding that she wished to work on important parts of their relationship before they had a 'full' marriage. He could take it or leave it. If he accepted the premise, it convinced her she could work things out with his questionable side. As far as the full marriage, although backward to convention, she would eventually also work that out.

During their courtship, it hadn't been long before the misplaced attention directed toward her family had become uncomfortable. Her mother wouldn't hide her disdain for him. Nevertheless, he kept insisting on opportunities to win her over. Consequently, after a visit where he pushed the issue too far, resulting in a huge row, her mother took Margaret into the library and ordered her to stop seeing Thomas. The intense energy, exchanged equally between the two women, was the release of years of suppressed feelings, of tensions that had built up over everything from Margaret's independent ways to her capturing more than her share of her father's attention. Eventually, her mother realized the actual depth of her daughter, at which point a stone silence completed the block wall between them. Without another word, Margaret stormed out of the house, only belatedly realizing she'd left Thomas inside.

Margaret mulled the word 'ordered.' Upon hearing it, all other logic went by the wayside and doomed any form of compromise from Margaret. Had her mother understood the actual consequences of her dictatorial approach, Margaret was positive she wouldn't be married today. It was true she'd gotten herself into a strange situation. Even more peculiar was the old Thomas accepting the ridiculous rules she'd imposed. Why would he do that? There was no turning back if she was to make her point that her life was her own. She'd let her need to be contrary and defiant control her decision without considering the long-term consequences. More frustrating was the warning from the wonderful woman in the gallery. With the wisdom of a life's experience, the woman knew that Margaret was in danger of eventually doing precisely what she'd done.

The part that defied reason and shook her world was her feelings toward this new Thomas. They were on a runaway train, completely out of control, which didn't make her any more secure. She was experiencing unfamiliar, overwhelming feelings unlike anything she'd ever felt. Of course, there had been romances throughout her life, but they were always of her choosing. None of them had moved her. She'd always treated them indifferently, as though the real beau would appear and sweep her off her feet. Was this it? Was he it? Unlike the one before him, the new Thomas was utterly transparent but came with the unfortunate memory and fortune-telling baggage. She gripped the wheel tighter.

What in the bloody hell had happened in that bathroom? Could her life's true love mysteriously appear in the same person whom she regretted marrying? She didn't know how to handle it. She violently downshifted, increased speed, and charged the next bend. No more thinking; her heart was making it plain. This man was the love of her life, and she'd known it that first morning.

At a bend in the road she wouldn't remember, she traded the unanswered reasoning for complete surrender. In that instant, a tangible calm surrounded her mind and body.

Thomas put his hand on the dashboard to steady himself. "We could get you flying lessons in a Spitfire," he said. "On second thought, perhaps that's not fast enough?"

"Are you trying to get me to laugh?" Margaret said, staring intently at the road ahead.

Thomas observed a scene of perpetual motion with the determined gearing and hair flying in her face. "Me trying to get you to laugh, no, I wouldn't think of it presently. In a fit of selfishness, I would settle for you coming back to Earth before we both needlessly become casualties without taking a few Germans with us."

She didn't reply.

Thomas had also done a lot of thinking in the car while Margaret, utterly alone in her thoughts, frantically careened through the countryside. He knew that somewhere out there was a remarkable woman meant just for him. What he didn't know were the strange circumstances under which she would appear. Strange or not, it didn't change the fact that she was the one.

Surely breaking a speed record she'd set in the morning, Margaret had them back at the house with the added benefit of them being in one piece. They unloaded the things from the Austin and left it parked in front of the house. Inside, placing the basket on the kitchen counter, Margaret busied herself putting away the items. She had the empty wine bottle in one hand while bustling things around in the basket with the other.

"Hey," she said, "we're missing one of Mrs. Somerville's napkin holders."

Thomas looked at the quizzical look on her face while she held the bottle in the air. With arms folded and leaning against the kitchen doorway, he said, "Margaret, do you believe in love at first sight?"

"What?" Margaret said, her head snapping around to face him.

He repeated, "Do you believe in love at first sight? It's the same question."

"Sure, I do. Preferably, the man is absolutely gorgeous, on a white horse and pulling a wagon with sections of white picket fence. Oh, did I mention gobs of money?"

"Margaret, I'm being serious."

"So am I," she said. "Can you ride?"

"No, I can only horse around," he said with a huge grin.

"Thomas Watson, do I have to point out that we're currently married and, you think, but not sure, only to me? You know, bridesmaids, bills, dishes. A minor point that makes it a little late to entertain the particular concept of love at first sight," she laughed.

Thomas was heading to the bedroom, intending to put the picnic blanket back on the chair where it had been that morning.

"Where are you going? You just asked me a question."

She appeared at the bedroom doorway. She placed one hand against the door to steady herself while removing one shoe and then the other.

"As I said, I'm your wife, which should put that question to rest."

With a mischievous look, Thomas said, "Margaret, you didn't marry me. You married that other guy."

She glanced up, and the smile on her face turned into a curious look. "Thomas, I get the feeling that you're actually trying to be serious here. Could this be true?"

"Yes, I'm trying to reach a point here," he blurted.

"About us?"

"Yes," he said, "about us, about you and me. Although I might wander off to the occasional errant concept, there's something I know for certain."

"That's refreshing." She said.

"Margaret, I truly believe I fell in love with you at first sight. I want to spend the rest of my life with you and …"

"Well—it's—about—time," she said, emphasizing every word. Filled with the emotions of her own recent realization, she thought, "This was the man, the right man, and he just proved it."

"Oh, brother," she whispered, almost to herself, "Mrs. Somerville is really going to love this part."

"What does that mean?" Thomas said as he stood next to the bed.

Still standing in the doorway, Margaret had placed one hand on her hip while the other held an invisible cigarette with a limp wrist. She said, "Hey, sailor, got a light?"

Nothing hid the confused look on Thomas's face.

Standing right before him, she sauntered over and looked up with a very impish and determined smile. Holding his gaze, she tucked her hair behind her right ear and proceeded to undo the top button of her blouse.

"Oh!" he said, realizing her intent. "Where did that phrase come from?"

"I heard it in a Hollywood movie once. I've always had a soft spot in my heart for a guy in a uniform. It was Daddy's business, you know. Anyway, it's a lot more ladylike than shouting, 'I'm available!' across a crowded pub. So, Mr. Thomas Watson," she said, now on her fourth button, "If you're so damn good at predicting the future, try predicting what's going to happen now."

"That's easy. You're going to change blouses," he said.

"You *sod*!" she said, taking a playful swing at him, missing and spinning in the process. He ducked and grabbed her around the waist, pulling her toward the bed. He put his hand out to break their fall, landing on her. She immediately started to push him off and get up.

"Oh, no, you don't," he said as his weight held her down, thinking she was going to get up. "You, my lovely, aren't going anywhere, as I'm pretty convinced this was your idea."

"I'm not that kind of girl, Mr. Watson," she said as she stopped resisting. Her head fell back onto the bedspread as she said, "Okay, maybe I am, but who said I wanted to get up?"

"What is it then?"

"I want to be on top."

"What!"

"You heard me. This was *my* idea; now move over!" Margaret said with a shove.

He felt the pressure on his shoulder but didn't move. They remained face to face; a full twenty seconds passed. Before him was the complement to an inner part of his heart that had been missing for a very long time. Thomas was immersed in a sensation transcending all that had come before and any that would succeed. His senses were aware of everything. He knew this was right with a certainty that he couldn't fathom, let alone explain. He didn't want to explain. If there was sand in the hourglass of time, he would will it to stop. Each grain would stay in place at this exact moment, proving that raptured adoration defies the universe's physical laws. Then, with glistening eyes and emotion in his voice, he managed to whisper, "Margaret, I love you."

They looked at each other, and she placed her hand gently on the side of his face. She pulled his head down and slowly and deliberately kissed him, touching every part of his mind and body. He felt a soft, powerful energy mixed with a feeling of invincibility that only the love of your life could give you. They were one in soul, with Margaret first among equals.

"I know," she said after the kiss. "I'm a little overwhelmed with where my feelings have gone. I know I do love you, the you here today. Just promise me you won't go away as mysteriously as you arrived."

"I promise," he said.

Then, still face to face, she took her index finger and gently, but directly, placed it right on the end of his nose and said, "Now move over."

Chapter Twenty-Four

Russian Embassy

Viktor Grigoryevich Krivitsky confidently walked the darkened halls of the Russian Embassy as one of the elites in his country. His uncle was a member of the Communist Central Committee, placing him worlds apart from the working class. Viktor arrived on a diplomatic charter with three other embassy personnel earlier in the afternoon. He didn't know any of them and kept to himself while contemplating what might lie ahead. Viktor was a rising star in the NKVD, also known as the Company, but to excel against such meek and meager competition tainted the honor. Viktor knew exactly what he wanted in a sea of people supremely satisfied just to have a job.

Night had fallen as he surveyed the embassy, his credentials having gotten him the files he wanted to review on Mr. Stakova, the embassy's chief of security. Now having a master key to the entire Security Department, he borrowed any office he wanted. He reviewed the brief's information until his eyes started to burn.

He started his journey yesterday, and the grueling plane flight in a Soviet transport made him think of the bed in the flat he'd let earlier. It was time to consider calling it a day.

Down the hall, on his way out, Viktor saw a man quickly exit from the stairs and head back into the room he'd just left. The man's hurried step made Viktor think something wasn't normal. His trained suspicions came to the fore. Obviously, this man wasn't a diplomat, as they were, by nature, never in a hurry. To them, diplomacy was a many-tiered journey toward an unfocused point or unachievable agreement, rendering the entire process useless. Viktor saw the man turn the key and knob and open the door.

Pavel moved over to his desk in the middle of the large room. The space, empty of people, contained identical desks, each featuring its specific clutter design, reflecting each owner's concern for organization. Pavel's desk looked like a file drawer had fallen from the floor above and landed upside down right next to his phone, leaving its contents strewn about the entire surface. He pulled the chain under the lamp, illuminating an organized disorder exceeding any cryptographic system. He picked up the receiver near a stack of restaurant menus and knew Yuri would be very interested in his news.

Viktor, who had followed Pavel through the door, walked up to his desk as Pavel looked at his small phone book from his breast pocket. Yuri's home number was next to the name "Stags Pit," a local tavern that kept a portion of the embassy's vodka behind the bar.

The motion of a man offering him a cigarette from a newly opened pack startled Pavel.

"Papirossa?" Viktor said in Russian, offering him a cigarette.

Pavel looked at the unfamiliar face with its professional smile. He recognized the pack; they were a Russian brand of cigarettes known for their distinctive taste and aroma. Pavel hadn't seen one in over a year. Moreover, these particular cigarettes weren't the everyday smoke of the average Russian. Tsar Pushkas were hand-rolled from Turkish tobacco only at the Sokolov factory outside Moscow. The name referred to a forty-ton cannon commissioned by Tsar Feodor in the late 1600s. The tobacco factory, owned by the state, provided its products only to party favorites, which made his visitor a matter of interest. Pavel nodded and pulled one out of the orange pack, and it slipped between his fingers.

The man reached into his outside coat pocket and pulled out a pack of matches and a lighter.

"Zippo," the man said, tossing the lighter a few times in his hand. "Built like a Russian tank but by Americans." Yet, he struck a match and held it out, requiring Pavel to lean over to catch its light. The stranger then tossed him the book, suggesting they were beneath him.

Pavel reflexively caught the book of matches against his chest with one hand and slowly nodded his thanks. It was best to be cautious when faced with an overconfident jerk. Pavel silently drew in the biting smoke. Distant memories of long nights in basement taverns with his friends filled his mind. He could almost taste the ever-present vodka and the biting in his throat. Pavel continued standing, evaluating the man as he drew the cigarette close to his face.

The flash of the Zippo lighter brought him back as it shadowed the lines of the angular face and flared in the eyes that were looking directly at him.

"Class games," Pavel thought. "Always cause for caution."

"My name is Viktor," the man said in Russian. I just arrived today, and you are?"

"Pavel Nikitin," Pavel said casually, inhaling again. "Well, Viktor, welcome to London, the favorite target of the Luftwaffe." Pavel exhaled and shuffled some pages on his desk in an unmistakable gesture, but the man didn't move.

"How often do they bomb?"

"Nightly," Pavel said. "They bomb mostly factories, at least until two nights ago. Moscow has given them our location, hoping Germany's aim is good enough to miss our little piece of heaven."

"Pavel, what do you do at the embassy that would have you here at this hour when you should be at home enjoying a boring Moscow report and a glass of something traditional?" Viktor said, smiling. Meanwhile, he pulled open the left side of his coat and reached for the inside pocket.

Pavel knew the man was fishing for information, so he cautiously provided the standard line. "Comrade Viktor, I'm sure you can understand the need for security and the fact that they've instructed each department to not ..."

The man abruptly thrust his credentials at Pavel in a solemn, silent presentation. The visitor held them up for effect as he blew cigarette smoke right over the top of the wallet directly at his target. Pavel could see the NKVD's bright red and gold logo with the three stars below.

"Three stars," Pavel thought. Just below the stars, Pavel only had to see the word Colonel preceding Viktor Grigoryevich Krivitsky, and he quickly moved off the edge of the desk he was leaning on and stood erect.

"Please—please," Viktor said, obviously enjoying the deferential reaction. He pointed to Pavel's desk chair and, reaching over, grabbed a visitor's chair for himself. "It's late, and I've always believed that formality should go down with the sun. As I said, I just got here, and I'm trying to familiarize myself with the operation. What're your duties at the London bureau?"

"I'm a security agent."

"Who do you report to here?"

"Comrade Yuri Ivanovich Stakova. He's military liaison to the British, but undercover, he's station chief here at the embassy. All espionage and security affairs are his responsibility. He's a very good man."

"Were you on a project today?" Viktor said.

"The man was pushing a little too hard," Pavel thought.

"Yes, it was routine. My assignment is to monitor one of our resident agents. I'm sure you wouldn't be bothering with something of this nature."

"No, please tell me, is this the Thomas Watson problem?"

Viktor saw he'd surprised Pavel.

He said, "I understand Watson is working on obtaining information on the cipher machine that the British may use to decode German messages. This program is a big issue in Moscow Centre, so it's not a bother. Is there such a machine?" Viktor asked.

Pavel again became very cautious. "Enough information exists from several sources to believe the Hatcher family might be assisting somehow. However, we've never obtained any solid evidence. In fact, Watson has produced nothing of value other than stories of his female conquests while being paid to sleep with a beautiful woman. Thomas Watson is completely unreliable and a pain to everyone. He lives his life like a circus in which he substitutes sleight of hand and illusion for reality."

Viktor exhaled, looking past Pavel in thought, "Why has Yuri not been able to run the operation with better results? He's supposed to be a pro, but it makes me ask: Does he know what he's doing?"

"Comrade Stakova is excellent at his job. Obtaining results has been difficult because Watson is only interested in games and mostly money. There's also the real possibility that this machine doesn't exist."

"Well, my friend, unfortunately for Comrade Stakova, he should have answered at least that question by now. Anyway, priorities have changed with the invasion eminent, and with that comes reorganization."

"What kind of reorganization?"

"You'll know soon enough and in good order. You were in a hurry to make a call. May I know what it was about?"

Pavel, now sitting, tapped the end of his cigarette on the ashtray, taking measure of his following words. "Yes, I was reporting some observations to Comrade Stakova that I felt couldn't wait until morning."

"Then it must be of interest and…," Viktor paused for an uncomfortable length of time.

Pavel felt the pressure of silence and shifted nervously in his chair. The man clearly outranked him, and rank was everything in the Russian republic. Yuri wouldn't be happy at the intrusion, and Pavel knew, either way, he held a losing hand.

Viktor, schooled in the game of intimidation, knew it was working. He said, "I'll meet with Comrade Stakova shortly and could carry your message in person. I would prefer it that way. I would be your personal envoy," he added, smiling.

Again, Pavel felt the noose tighten. "Well, the current arrangement has me reporting..."

"*Pavel*," Viktor spat out.

It startled Pavel.

Viktor said, "The current arrangement is exactly why I'm here. It is part of the problem and not the solution."

The man's credentials, coupled with the curt manner and energy in this statement, left no doubt Pavel was in over his head. The Byzantine methods of Soviet security services were, by design, beyond understanding, and his best response was precisely the one he gave.

"Yes, Comrade Colonel."

Calm returned to Viktor's voice, "So, now that we're of one mind, what was this news that couldn't wait?"

"Last week, Watson asked Comrade Stakova for more money. Yuri refused to consider it and pushed Watson for results. Since then, we've increased surveillance on both Watson and his wife. The original agreement was extremely generous, so we viewed additional requests skeptically. Watson wasn't happy, very unhappy, you might say. Today I followed them from their house in Amersham into the countryside, where they had a picnic somewhere off the road. I tried to get as close as possible, but it wasn't easy. I managed to hear Watson say he was going to Bletchley Park tomorrow, but I didn't get the entire conversation."

Pavel continued, "Watson is very independent and clever and could be contacting the British. Perhaps to tell them what he knows, if anything, about the decoder. He's just unstable enough to blackmail the British and resourceful enough to make it sound like he's a patriot. However, a catastrophic alternative would be that he tells the British he's spying for us, thus putting the entire Soviet presence in the country at risk just before the invasion. The British could very well throw us out or severely restrict our operations. Even if I'm wrong, this is something Yuri should know."

Viktor's political senses came to the forefront in a rush, and he could feel his eyes grow large. This agent had just presented a once-in-a-career opportunity to provide heroic service to his country and, more importantly, reap the rewards. This was exactly the type of situation Moscow Centre had feared when they ordered Yuri to eliminate Watson and return home. Viktor knew the instructions in the directive presented by Joseph. Moscow thought Stakova had spent too much time in the field and could no longer count on his complete allegiance to the State. They were calling him back, or worse.

Viktor knew his uncle's position within the Central Committee guaranteed that he would stay alive. Nevertheless, before him was a potentially grave situation. Watson was obviously dangerous and needed to be stopped and quickly. There was no doubt. Knowing Watson had definite plans, Viktor had reason to act independently, and only one other person knew anything. If he acted quickly, he could eliminate Watson before his predecessor had the chance, making Yuri appear slow in reacting and Viktor taking the initiative in a dangerous situation. Moscow would view this decisive action as having averted a very public foreign policy embarrassment that couldn't damaged its espionage capability for years.

These weren't exactly his orders, so there was an element of risk and failure, which could end his career, but it was worth the risk. A lesser bureaucrat would leave well enough alone, but Viktor was an experienced field operative. He could feel the rush.

"Surely," Viktor thought, "Watson wouldn't be stupid enough to return to his house." He decided that it had to occur at Bletchley if he were to eliminate Thomas. It was the only place he could count on Watson being at a specific place and time. Viktor considered contacting the Centre but knew a decision would never arrive in time. Everything from the Centre came after the nightly shots of vodka and 'entertainment' provided by the State, so real decisions never emerged until late morning. Bletchley wouldn't be easy, but reports were that security was intentionally light to avoid scrutiny. Anyway, he'd completed field tasks of greater difficulty before. "No risk, no gain," he thought. Besides, three of his agents he'd previously sent into the country were without identification and were expendable. The other two were to fill out his new staff. It was a decision a man in his position must make for the greater good.

He emerged from thought and turned to the agent sitting across from him. "Pavel, for a field agent, your instincts are very good. I believe your thoughts about Watson are correct. However, there are issues in motion that prevent any obvious solution. For this admittedly vague reason, I want this information kept secret and only acted upon by Yuri and myself.

"Now listen carefully. Before formal notification, I'm informing you I'm the new station chief replacing Yuri, and you now report to me. I must repeat: Your observations today remain confidential and I'll present them to Yuri for our evaluation. Do you understand, Comrade Pavel?"

Saying nothing, Pavel picked up some papers from the pile on his desk while looking at the Colonel.

Viktor said, "Now, as your new superior, I'm reassigning you. You're no longer to be involved in the Watson case."

It surprised Pavel, and he said, "But shouldn't we tell Comrade Stakova of the change now, tonight?"

"I said Yuri and I would take care of it. Agent Pavel, your service to your country has been invaluable, and that will certainly make it into my report, but the reassignment is an order. Do nothing to change my mind as to your continued usefulness. You're to take a few days off until I contact you. Leave me your private number, and I'll call you directly with details on your new duties." Viktor added, "Being the excellent agent you are, I'm sure you have surveillance pictures of Watson. I want them and the file."

Pavel quickly saw through the charade but wasn't in a position to control anything. He could disappear into the frozen oblivion if he disobeyed the order and contacted Yuri. A few hundred top generals and State officials had disappeared whenever a paranoid Stalin had judged them a threat. He knew there was no one to witness the direct order, and if Viktor disappeared tomorrow, Pavel had no evidence to prove his side of the story. It was hopeless.

He jotted down his number on a sheet of paper, reached into his desk's middle drawer, shoved the packet of photos into the case file, and handed them all to the man.

Viktor smiled, and light-heartedly said, "Pavel, you must look at this as an opportunity. Take the time to catch up on some personal things because events will soon become frantic, and you'll be happy to have gotten this break in the routine. Now, off to your flat and a good book. We will take care of this, and Watson will no longer be a threat to our operation."

Viktor watched the agent leave the room and wondered if he would follow orders. He had to keep him out of the way but alive to provide the reason for his actions. It was a thin thread from which Pavel hung. Viktor thought, "The agent knows I have him in a box and better be smart enough to follow orders." He would assign an agent to watch Pavel's house in the morning.

Viktor pushed his foot against the desk before him and rocked back in his chair. Things were falling into place as if emanating from a grand design. Viktor was glad that at the last minute, he'd sent his assistant Joseph to the meeting with Yuri, as Viktor wasn't yet ready for Yuri to know who he was. Viktor knew that sending Joseph would make Yuri think he was dealing with a lower-level bureaucrat, not a gifted professional. Things would need to come together quickly for this to work, but he had the assets and was in charge.

Viktor smiled and reached down to the desk for the Tsar Pushkas and pondered his next move.

Chapter Twenty-Five

Uxbridge Operations Building

Two workmen quickly drew taut the last two supporting wires to one of the many antennae atop the Uxbridge Operations building. Yesterday a nearby bomb blast damaged a lot of the equipment and gear, causing all manner of havoc with the almighty RAF blokes inside. Thankful for a full moon, the men had worked into the night to repair the damage without lights. Nevertheless, whatever their assignment, it never was completed fast enough or in the proper order.

Standing up and stretching, one of the men said, "That ought to do it then."

"Yeah, and only a week late," said the other sarcastically.

"Those boys down below are a bit edgy, don't cha think?" the first said.

"Spot on that, mate, but that can't be good news, Martin," the other man offered. "Given what I think they do down there, it can't be good for us if they're feeling too much pressure."

"What the bloody hell do you know about what they do?"

"I've got me sources, you wazzack. Let's have a drag and a break before goin' down. No one will be the wiser."

The operations building on which the men stood was an old structure that no longer looked like it had before the war. Bulldozers plowed the surrounding ground against the walls until the earthworks angled from the ground to the roof. In addition, they installed two feet of reinforced concrete onto the top and another two layers of sandbags. The operations bunker was sixty feet below ground and accessed by two flights of stairs. The stairs descended into another world, knowing little of sunsets and days of the week. Inside this structure, ordinary people intensely labored twenty-four hours a day, protecting people they'd never know or see and people they loved and cherished.

Inside, Edith Bristo walked up to the watch guard and waited for him to place a new sheet on the clipboard before she signed off her shift. George was well into his sixties, but it didn't mean he'd lost touch with what brought a little skip to his step. While he was doing his bit for the war, it was a tad boring, and he found the shift change, when the ladies signed off, the most rewarding time of his day. Some were chattier than others, and some didn't even know he was there, but he especially liked Miss Bristo as she always had something to say and treated him with special respect.

He handed the clipboard to her with a smile and said, "How was today for ya', Miss Bristo?"

"George, you know how I love it here," she said with a pretend smile. "I'm sorry, George, that was rude and badly done. Actually, it got a bit tense as poor communication caused more problems than usual. Some German bombers got through without any resistance. We normally would have had our lads on them, but it will be okay for the next shift. Well, there it is, and I've already told you too much, and I should know better. After all, you could be one of those dashing undercover spies who looks harmless but can kill in six ways. Besides George, Mr. Undercover Spy, didn't we discuss you calling me Edith?"

"Well, yes, we did, as I remember. Edith, it is then."

"Any fish left in that river of yours, George?"

His eyes went wide, then narrowed, as a huge grin appeared. "If there be even one that's left, I'll have it for me own. I've had me a secret fishin' hole for forty years. I could bring ya' one; it'll be a beauty," he said, holding his hands five feet wide and beaming.

"Ah, I think both the fish and I would be much happier if it got to stay with its family. However, thanks just the same. See you tomorrow."

"And a good evenin' ta ya', Miss B... Edith," he said, touching his blue security hat and sitting back down. "She looked a little tired today," he thought. As she turned and walked away, he took in the rhythmic manner of her walk as she transformed something very ordinary into something exceptional.

Edith pushed up the sleeves of her light blue sweater as she continued down the hall. She looked at the numerous electrical cables, tubes, and wires strung along every wall in the building and hoped that they actually went somewhere useful. She was only sure about those that were part of the pneumatic Lamson tubes. She depended on that messaging system day in and day out.

She walked across the ring corridor and through a door into the women's cloakroom. Before the war, the girls were convinced that the room had been a museum for pipes. It contained at least one of every variety, running along the ceiling, the walls, and around the baseboards. Sitting in the center of the room was a double set of old gray school lockers. Based on each locker's size, the design originated before they required students to store books. However, it was a secure place to keep things like a handbag, a purse, or a pack of cigarettes but only one at a time. She removed her bag and placed the small lock in her purse to use tomorrow on whatever locker was available. There weren't enough for all the girls on all four shifts.

Edith had seen her life change in ways she couldn't have foreseen in the last few years, particularly the last six months. Edith had gone from having a shy personality, unsure of her adequacy, to realizing people quickly liked her. She had a way of finding something to share with those she met. Also, she had a natural knack for making people feel comfortable by connecting with them on this or that in a manner she found surprisingly easy. She had many friends, including men, who usually found it hard to start a conversation with someone who was popular and appeared to know everybody.

For Edith, it was a new aspect of her life. She grew up with two brothers who did all the talking as she and her parents did all the listening. Her brothers had her convinced she was below average when the truth was they were probably just being brothers. Despite their influence, she'd acquired new confidence at twenty-three and physically blossomed into a statuesque frame that didn't go unnoticed. Both traits served to disguise her East End heritage. She wore her hair in a way that masked the slightly full face she'd inherited from her father, and she wore any dress as if it was designed and tailored just for her. In her family, she was the youngest, and until recently, she needed to stay home. Now with her new job, she was finally out on her own, handling the responsibility and loving the freedom the pay increase had made possible.

Being hired in her current position as a WAAF at Uxbridge had come about almost by chance. Her duties included compiling a line readiness report on each squadron for all bases in the sector. The information established an order of battle for the day, used by Air Marshal Harris, who issued commands based on available assets. The problem was that the report was due before all of the maintenance crews were ready to commit to the serviceability of their planes. Their hesitance was especially true if their plane had suffered damage and required repair beyond general servicing.

Consequently, she had to rely on incomplete information from overworked ground crews who weren't the least interested in having women in the service area, let alone paperwork. Eventually, she won respect and cooperation of the crew chiefs. They wanted their plane in the air but were sometimes unsure of the job ahead. Edith proposed that if they committed based on their best guess, she promised they could remove their plane from the report at the last minute if needed. No one would know. It wasn't by the book, but it worked for everyone.

To Edith's surprise, Air Marshal Harris was very aware of the daily battle hidden between the pages of the brief that eventually arrived at his desk. One day, a major decided she could better serve her country by volunteering to work on a secret project. She would have to sign the Official Secrets Act, which carried rather severe penalties if breached. There was no description of the task offered other than the title of a plotter. He only said it was critical to the war effort and that they preferred women as they were prone to maintain their composure during intense situations, but they had to pass a math test.

She jumped at the opportunity. The additional money and an agreement with a new friend would allow her to share a flat. The distance to her new job would be too great to travel if she continued staying at home. The distance was the reason she gave when presenting the idea to her Mum and Dad. The new freedom had also made possible a social life, something that hadn't been as easy for her to create living at home as it had been for her brothers.

According to her family, her future was preordained; she was to become a clerk at a department store, making three pounds a week, which she'd done before the war. She was to continue doing this while waiting for someone to marry her so she could have kids. Somehow, society had decided that most women came up short in the workplace. The male clerks were the only employees allowed to ring up a customer's purchase at the department store because "women were not good at figures."

Her parents were stuck in the Middle Ages, and with her new life in full swing, being committed was definitely not her cup of tea. Or at least not until this cocky fighter pilot made a pass at her in Battley's Pub. Several times, in fact, over a few weeks, he plied her with clever lines without success. He wouldn't give up, and Edith wouldn't give in, as she had a small secret. She found men in uniforms not just handsome but quite dashing and knew it to be her weakness. Her protective caution had served her well, keeping her out of many a sticky situation. Eventually, Janet, her friend, and flatmate, said she was a fool and insisted she give it a go.

Janet had made it very clear: if Edith wouldn't give in, then *she* was going to ask him to the cinema.

Janet said, "Either way, we shouldn't lose him to some loose Piccadilly harlot."

She did give in, and things were never the same as Edith Bristo was in love. However, the guy was much less committed to discussing something as touchy as being "tied to the ground," as the pilots would say. Still, Paddy was kind and considerate, and she knew he had feelings for her, so she'd decided to ride it out and see what might lie ahead.

Chapter Twenty-Six

Uxbridge Operations Building

Edith approached the last security station on her way home with her coat over her arm. Duncan was at the desk, and George was out of sight. Duncan, a perimeter security guard, was in full uniform and armed with a pistol; he was very nice-looking and very married. Flirting with Duncan in his uniform was a lot of fun, and knowing she wasn't the only girl doing it, made it okay. Besides, he was too serious, the opposite of George downstairs, so he was an easy target. She silently placed her things on the table. He solemnly looked into her purse, pressed on her coat pockets, and returned them.

"Find anything interesting, Corporal, sir?" Edith said with a smirk.

In his best imitation of a deep official voice, he looked up and said, "Not this time, Edith, but I know you're smuggling something," They both laughed. She was pleased to have brought out his humor.

Edith said, "Of course I am, you silly bloke. I'm smuggling coats." Edith could barely get it out, holding her hand over her lips, laughing.

"Best be careful, Edith. This building isn't the place to be kidding around. People tend to lose their humor when they come in that door," he said, tilting his head toward the exit.

"Oh, come on, Duncan. What do we have left? Can't let the Jerry's take it all away. I know I asked yesterday, but…"

"Yes, I'm still married, and you're not serious anyway. Despite the collective effort, you're all jealous that I love my wife."

Edith handed the clipboard she'd signed back to him, saying, "Really now, it's that obvious, is it?"

They were still smiling when he opened the steel-reinforced blast door, and she walked out into the early evening air.

Edith worked the D shift, and today was supposed to be a special day. She'd worked six hours on and six hours off for four days and now got twenty-four hours off. That was the routine, over and over. Today was the fourth day, and she planned to sleep away most of it, but her supervisor asked her to return. Lucy, one of her co-workers, had not shown up, and with the increase in activity, he needed an entire crew.

Meanwhile, out of concern for Lucy, the supervisor had made some calls and found out the street where she lived was near a base and had been part of the bombing the previous night. He had the Home Guard involved in the search for Lucy, but they were still fighting fires, so he placed a defense priority on it, putting the reporting of information ahead of other civilians. Everyone loved Lucy, and his concern was personal and ran deep.

Sandbags lined either side of the section cut out of the earthworks for the entrance. Edith reached into her purse and pulled out the keys to her very used MG. Still walking toward the car, she heard someone call out her name. Turning, she heard the shout again and saw George's portly figure emerge from the dark, almost bouncing toward her.

"Miss Bristo, there's been a call, and me thinks it's tha' gentleman who rang up last week. He's in quite the rush sayin' it's very important that I bring ya to the phone."

A few steps short of Edith, George stopped and put his hands on his knees. He was red-faced and panting, looking like he'd run from the building and called out the sentence all in one breath.

"Oh, George, you didn't have to run," Edith said.

George took a breath. "He was very serious, and I thought it was important," George said as they walked side by side back to the building.

Edith knew Paddy would be the only man to call her, but why? Perhaps to apologize for leaving her short on a promised dinner on one of the few days, they both had off? He'd offered a perfectly believable excuse, but every woman knew she should leave some space around any claim made by any man and knew that women, more than they wanted to admit, broke the rule. Edith hoped they were creating something special, though inside, she was wondering. Is this the "I'm going to be busy for a while" call that every woman knew might be waiting just around the corner?

They approached the security desk, and George said, "You can take it on Duncan's phone; that ways you don't have ta sign back in."

"You're sweet, George, thank you."

"Hey, what about *me*? It's my phone," Duncan said.

Edith looked at Duncan and sarcastically said, "We can still share phones, Duncan, as we're just dating."

Duncan held his hand with his wedding ring right up to her face.

Edith waved him back and said, "It means nothing to homewreckers like me. Besides, I pledged my heart to George."

George said, "That's right, Duncan; let's give her some privacy now."

Paddy closed the phone booth door while waiting for Edith to come to the phone. The man who answered said to wait, so he figured she was still there. He leaned back against the booth as visions of the early morning flashed in his head. Something is wrong; it's taking too long. Perhaps this just wasn't meant to be. Other thoughts of that kind started drifting into his head when...

"Hello," Edith said.

"Edith, it's Paddy."

Edith felt an edge or perhaps a hurried note in his voice. She decided to try to lighten the moment and sound upbeat. "Well, flyboy, couldn't you get another date?"

Paddy said, "No, no, that's not it. How are you? I mean, can you have dinner tonight? I really mean, can I see you?"

Edith sensed something amiss because Paddy was never at a loss for words.

"Of course, you can; I mean, not tonight. I have to be a little hard to get. Any decent girl would make you jump through a few hoops to make it worthwhile." She waited through a few seconds of silence and then said, "Paddy, are you alright?"

"It's been a tough day."

"I'm sorry, Paddy, for joking around. I've to be back in two hours to pull Lucy's shift. No one else is available. Besides, it will take you over half that to get here."

Paddy grew angry, "My God, Edith, are you running the bloody war? What could be so important? I can't stand this war. What happened to personal lives?"

"Paddy, we've had this discussion. By tomorrow morning, I'll be desperate for sleep. Can we make it a late lunch? I'm scheduled for twenty-four hours off."

Paddy let out a very audible sigh. "I'm being ferried to the Castle Bromwich factory to pick up a new plane and won't be back until after seven in the evening."

"What happened to your plane? Why would you need another plane?"

"That's part of the story, I guess. Then are we on for tomorrow night? I promise you can sleep."

"Yes, Paddy, of course we are. I can meet you halfway at the restaurant. The MG is running fine, and Janet and I have coupons for enough petrol. It will give us more time together. Do you know a place?"

"How about the Fox? It's famous for surprises on the menu."

Edith said, "That will be wonderful. I can't wait."

"No, Edith, seeing *you* will be truly wonderful."

"I miss you, Paddy. I'm not trying to make this hard. Things are over the top at work, and if you knew …"

"Well, I don't, and it makes it hard. However, tomorrow night will erase it all. Edith?" he said. "I want to tell you something …"

Edith could hear Paddy's voice give way. She listened to a deep breath and, in another attempt, he barely got out, "I'll see you" and hung up.

Seeing Edith looking oddly at the phone in her hand, George returned to the desk.

"Everythin' 'right, Miss?"

Edith stared into unfocused space for a second and then responded, "Yes, thank you both. That was a very important phone call."

Duncan tried not to look concerned but said, "Your friend, is he okay?"

"Yes," she said with a smile far enough from natural that both guards let it go without further comment.

Edith stepped outside and said, "Good night, guys, and thanks again."

Chapter Twenty-Seven

Whitehall
War Rooms

Colville opened the door and said General Ismay had scheduled a time for a requested report.

"Yes, bring him in," Churchill said.

Ismay sat down in front of the PM's desk. He opened his briefcase and pulled out a single piece of paper.

Winston, watching his actions, said, "I once believed that a comprehensive report delivered on a single piece of paper couldn't hold anything extremely good or bad. On this, of course, I've repeatedly been wrong."

Ismay didn't smile as he supplanted a more significant gift in managing large organizations for a distinct lack of wit. In that venue, humor wasn't a useful tool.

"Mr. Prime Minister," he started in a very formal tone. "All the people have expressed their sincere gratitude at your minding the store in such difficult times."

"Thank you, General, it's most kind of you. It's most unfortunate they all don't work in this building. Nevertheless, it sounds similar to congratulating French Royalty for donating their estates to the people just before the guillotine drops upon its target."

Ismay scrunched his face at the image.

"As you requested, I've personally visited the locations in this Readiness Report. I've spoken with many managers, officers, and pilots, except the Czechs, whose lack of English is more than made up for by their zealous desire to stay in the air killing Germans.

"As you're well aware, the Germans have continued in their efforts to destroy our airfields and factories. Their concentration lately has been on Biggin Hill. As of this morning, it was almost out of action. The losses for yesterday and last night were 39 RAF aircraft lost in combat, with an unspecified number destroyed while still on the ground. The Luftwaffe lost 41. Of course, we cannot trade them plane for plane, as they'd win on attrition. The Southeastern airfields, starting with Biggin Hill, along with Manston, West Malling, Lympne, and Hawkinge, are undergoing repairs, with most available within twenty-four hours. In addition, only two RAF Sector Stations are in working order south of the Thames; the rest are under repair and will be running again shortly."

Winston interrupted. "That puts the Luftwaffe close to its goal. Nonetheless, it does not mean they're aware of the situation."

"Quite right, but it places us in a position where we can't take the fight to the enemy. At this time, our fortunes lie in the ability of the lads to bring back to serviceable order any plane not completely destroyed.

"All the radar stations are functioning except for the fifth. The estimate is seven to ten days to bring it back into service. Unfortunately, I couldn't hurry it along, but the A1 radar was hand-built, and spares aren't sitting on shelves.

"My conversations have revealed a stout concentration of their duties and the men's full awareness of the consequences of failing. I must say their enthusiasm was quite uniform, given such dire times. In summary, sir, your observation is correct. Göring is as close as ever to obtaining air superiority and being a hero in Hitler's eyes."

Before today's report, Churchill had moved some of the RAF's reserve fighters southward from other sectors, but the RAF found fewer and fewer fields to land on. It also left the north vulnerable to attack from Norway. The Royal Navy had moved reserve units from Scapa Flow, setting up a picket line off the Northern shores. Inland, Churchill had already moved regular Army divisions south as a ready force, positioned to react to the most likely landing beaches. Further inland, all was ready, including several established defense lines across the island, one following another. These pre-positioned lines aided in re-establishing control in the event of a retreat. All the lines were fully stocked with supplies and ammunition. The one noticeable exception was an absence of heavy artillery and tanks, most of which were still sitting rusting on a beach in Dunkirk. There wasn't enough time to compensate for losing an entire expeditionary force's equipment.

Ismay closed his briefcase and placed both hands on the top. "In all this, I must say, with the dogged determination of the lads on the ground, all they need is time. They've perfected rising ever faster after suffering a blow. God only knows, but this will be a big war won by ordinary people doing extraordinary things."

"General, as senior statesmen for this troubled island, I would like you to confine your eloquence to this room. Your thoughtful description of our lads on the ground will only serve to make me a *junior* statesman."

Ismay grinned without comment.

Churchill had finally gotten a lighthearted response from his friend.

He went on. "I want to thank you for your efforts on such short notice. Formal reports have an understandable tendency to polish even a sour apple. I wanted a straight description of the situation, and it's exactly what I received."

Chapter Twenty-Eight

Margaret's House
Amersham

In the early morning, Thomas and Margaret walked down the street arm and arm in relative silence. Margaret had decided they were going to a pastry shop for breakfast and was quite excited that Thomas was coming along. Ahead, a milkman's horse-drawn delivery carriage pulled away from the front of a small shop, just passing them by. He was making his early morning rounds and keeping a regular schedule like everyone else in the country. In the countryside, a carriage was a common sight, as all available lorries had been put to service in the war effort. As they approached the shop, Thomas saw a sign in the window: "More Open Than Usual." It was a sign common to customers and the world, referring to the tenacity a sorely tried population demonstrated.

Margaret and Thomas entered the front of the Saxby Bakery. Thomas recognized the shop as the one the older couple had been locking up when Margaret dragged him to the shelter. He felt that first night was much farther in the past than it was.

Stewart and Emma Saxby had purchased the shop many years ago to supplement their pension, which wasn't enough to cover their living expenses. They'd lived in the area for as long as anyone could remember. Kids called Emma "Mum," when they came in after classes to present pieces of anti-aircraft shrapnel that had fallen from the sky the night before. The child with the biggest piece won one of Emma's biscuits, leaving several sad faces hanging on the losers. Children created games out of whatever was available, from stacking bricks to holding secret club meetings in abandoned buildings. The shop was a nice neighborhood place in the morning and part of the fabric that made up the English experience.

As they walked inside, Thomas quickly encountered the glass presentation case and couldn't miss the extensive menu on the back wall just above a small work counter. The usual toasters and mixers covered the back counter. In the corner to the right was an icebox for cold drinks. Margaret had said she wanted to sit outside, but Thomas wondered what the other option was given the shop's small size. The temperature wasn't a factor; despite a morning chill, August seldomly got below 11 Centigrade at night and was generally the best month of the year.

"Emma, I don't think you've had a chance to meet my husband, Thomas. He never got a chance to get over here, which is why I always took my things bagged."

"Well, Mr. Watson," Mr. Saxby said, "it's nice to meet you finally. We know just about everybody in Amersham, and now it's nice to add you to the list."

Thomas nodded, and Mr. Saxby came around from behind the counter, showed Thomas a pair of wet hands, and said, "Just a second, be right there." He reached for a towel and extended his hand toward Thomas after a few quick wipes.

"Stewart Saxby, pleased to meet ya, Mr. Watson, after all this time and all. I've seen ya in the shelter, but most times ya didn't look to be talking none."

Mrs. Saxby shot him a look that couldn't warmed your choice of pastry.

"Well, what do ya want me to say?" he said to his wife. Turning back to Thomas, he added: "Wasn't that you that got knocked about at the top of the entrance when that explosion went off?"

"Yes, but the Service Guard looked like he took more of the brunt than I did."

"Oh, that's my friend Bernard Sheldon; Bernie's okay he's got enough of Mum's pastry in him," with a nod to his wife, "to blunt a tank shell he does."

Armed with a finger, Emma said, "That, Mr. Saxby, will be enough of you. Mind your manners if nothin' else. I'm sorry, dear," she said to Margaret.

Meanwhile, Stewart got a quizzical look and sported a "what did I do grin."

"Mrs. Somerville was in earlier and said you might be by," Emma said. "I think she gets up as early as we do. Now, what can we do to cheer up your mornin'."

Thomas was now hungry. He rubbed his hands together in anticipation.

"What a great place you have here," he said.

Looking up at the menu, he saw it contained a long list of treats, including a Traditional Welsh Cake from an "old Saxby family recipe." Queen Cakes, Crumpets, and Hot Crossed Buns. Then Thomas saw it: Scotch Shortbread biscuits. They sounded wonderful.

"I would like to try one of those," he said, pointing up. "The shortbread biscuits." He looked back at the case as he didn't know what they looked like. Mrs. Saxby reached in, pulled out a tray, and placed one on a small china plate.

Margaret was up on her toes, looking back into the bakery area.

Mrs. Saxby took notice. "Margaret, and what would you be lookin' for? As if I might not know."

"Oh, I just wondered if you had any strawberry turnovers, and they're just not out yet? They don't have to be fresh, mind you, but."

Mrs. Saxby glanced at her husband with the look of a mother taking breakfast orders for the kids. Seeing him proudly nodding, she said, "It just so happens that daddy made a couple for us this morning with berries right out of his Victory Garden."

"Made 'um me self," he said, standing closer to the counter.

"Yes, in a few more years, he'll be a full partner in the business," Mrs. Saxby said sarcastically.

"Oh, I wouldn't want to take yours. It wouldn't be right," Margaret said.

"Oh, I wouldn't fret none, we're done, and they won't last unless they go to the icebox. Then they're not fresh, are they?"

With a little bounce on her toes, Margaret clasped her hands together and said, "Splendid Mum, just splendid. It's going to be a good day."

Chapter Twenty-Nine

An Unexpected Visitor

Outside, Thomas and Margaret placed their teacups and the pot of hot water on a small round table. They sat, ate, and talked. They never had problems talking. A subject they could jump into deeply was never far away. He learned much more about this gorgeous creature with each conversation and he wanted more.

"What're you thinking about?" she said. "You went away."

He set down his teacup and said, "Have I told you I love you today?"

She leaned back, tucked her hair behind her ear, holding it while she thought, and then put her index finger on her chin. "Well, it was after midnight when we finally got to sleep last night. So I would say yes, Thomas, you've covered that for the day. However, if you truly loved me, you would forget that trip to Bletchley today.

In reply, he moved his head ever so slightly from side to side, and a pouting Margaret propped up her chin with one hand while leaning her elbow on the table. In silence, Thomas reached down, found the other hand, and squeezed it gently. He was about to say something when a large man approached from nowhere and stood right next to them. They both became silent.

The man, in his mid-fifties, had a strong face and was slightly overweight, dressed in a London Fog overcoat, impeccably polished shoes, and a fedora angled just enough to make a statement. In addition to the message his clothes conveyed, he displayed confidence as he purposely stood too close for casual conversation.

He startled Margaret, dashing the romantic moment, when he said a little too loudly, "Well, well, who do we have here?"

Thomas looked at Margaret and knew from the look on her face that she wasn't comfortable. Thomas picked up an accent from the man but couldn't place it. He wasn't British. As Thomas stood up to address the man, his metal chair fell back onto the paving-stone sidewalk. The loud bang only added to the drama.

"Hold on," Yuri said. "I don't think you want to go anywhere right now, and you're certainly not going to do anything to me."

Yuri's hands were in the side pockets of the overcoat. He took the left hand out and pointed to the right, still in his pocket, conveying it contained more than his hand.

Margaret looked into the pastry shop, but Mr. and Mrs. Saxby had wandered into the rear and out of sight.

"We need to talk," Yuri said in flat tones directed at Thomas.

The man was very sharply dressed, not common for a thief. Thomas said, "Look, we don't have a lot of cash, but you can have what we've got."

"I beg to differ, my man; you've a lot of money," the big man said.

"You must be mistaken," Thomas replied.

"That's enough for now. Wait until we get inside." Yuri turned and tilted his head toward the pub with the extra-large door on the corner across the street. He started toward the pub as Thomas and Margaret exchanged glances. Thomas looked at Margaret, motioned with his head toward the man, and they both got up and followed.

As they crossed the street, Thomas thought how confusing this was. If the man was a thief, why was he walking in front?

"Why are we going to a pub?" Thomas asked.

"Because of the back room. What would you think? Your memory must have taken a holiday. That explains a lot."

Thomas didn't want to explain that might be precisely the case.

A simple sign on the pub's massive door hung on a string that said "closed"; inside was a drawn shade. The man knocked loudly, saying, "Come on, Evan, I know you're in there. I need to use the card room for a bit."

Yuri grabbed for the doorknob, twisting it several times, more for the effect and noise than any chance he thought it would open. He knocked again, the shade moved aside, and a man looked out. The door opened.

Peering around the door, the man said, "Yuri, Thomas, what in bloody 'ell are yer two doin' here this time ah the mornin'?"

"A favor, Evan, it's just a favor. Can we use your back room to talk?"

Thomas concluded the big man must be someone out of Margaret's past, and it was apparent the visit wasn't social. Thomas looked at Margaret, trying to glean some message, and got nothing.

Evan wasn't too sure.

"We won't be long, and besides," Yuri said, "you do remember that shipment of Johnnie Walker that I was able to get through customs?"

Evan opened the door without another word and walked back behind the bar.

The man stepped back, letting Margaret and Thomas in first.

"Morning, Lem," Yuri said to an older man leaning on a mop. Lem nodded a response and looked at Evan.

"Mornin', Miss," Evan said, making circular wipes of the bar with a towel previously draped over his shoulder. "Well, it's early, but about time you gents brought someone to brighten up the place. I'd had me thoughts as to yer a spendin' all that time together in that small room." He laughed and looked at Margaret and quickly said, "Ah, oh, sorry, Miss."

Margaret didn't respond.

The big man pulled a chair out and offered Margaret a seat at a table.

"I think you should stay here for just a while until Thomas and I can talk," he said. "Oh, and Margaret, I trust you'll stay and not leave, as I wouldn't want to interrupt your morning with anything unpleasant." He looked at Thomas.

Margaret glared at the man; he knew she understood but wasn't too pleased.

"Somethin' ta drink?" Evan said.

"Yes," Yuri said. "A juice for us and something for the lady."

With an attitude, Margaret continued staring at him, then sat heavily in the chair and crossed her arms.

"Any kind of juice would be fine, right?" he said, looking to Thomas for a reply.

Thomas thought this was another strange experience and wondered how many more could lie ahead.

"Very well then," the man said with a look of indifference.

The big man led Thomas down a narrow hall with a door to the restroom to the right and another door facing it. Yuri opened the left door and motioned for Thomas to go in.

The room smelled of smoke and beer. In the center was a round card table surrounded by six chairs. A single light bulb with a dented tin shade hung overhead, barely illuminating the dark wood walls. The room was just large enough to accommodate the table, chairs, and bodies that would occupy them. The barkeep came in behind them, dropping off the glasses and making sure the door closed on his way out.

Margaret saw Evan walk back into the bar area. She stood up and said, "I think we're being robbed or something. Can't we call a constable?"

"Robbed? Don't think so, Miss, those two have been coming in here for the better part of...?" he looked up at Lem.

"Six months," Lem said.

That wasn't good enough for Margaret. She started toward the door, "If you won't, I can have someone here before they're out."

"Miss," Evan said quite loudly, "it's none of my business, and you can walk out that door, but the big Russian said to stay."

He put both hands in the air as if he was under arrest, "I just run my business and feed my family and try to make it through the war. But I highly recommend you stay, and that's for all of us."

Margaret stared a hole through the man as his hands stayed in the air. She looked at the other man, a timid shell; he nodded in agreement. Margaret kicked a chair. There wasn't much she could do. She decided to stay and not summon any help and just decided to wait it out.

Yuri took off his coat, "Well, aren't you going to sit down?"

Thomas figured silence was the best approach but was starting to resent always being on the defensive. In fact, his anger grew as he finally started to feel comfortable.

"You've gotten yourself into some real trouble," Yuri said. He looked right into Thomas's eyes. To Yuri, things were already not adding up. Why wasn't Watson talking a mile a minute with tons of thin excuses? There he sits like a cool block of ice. "Very strange," he thought.

"So, you owe me an explanation," Yuri continued. "Despite your rather animated promise to keep to the plan, you haven't contacted your handler for over two days. This behavior isn't good for you."

Thomas decided that whatever this was, he wouldn't be manipulated. Not knowing his history didn't mean he couldn't deal with the present.

"I'm sorry," Thomas said. "We must start earlier in the story, as I don't know who you are."

Yuri laughed loudly, shaking his head. He leaned back in his chair, his vest strained against his oversized waist. "You don't know what?" Swinging forward on the chair, he grabbed the glass before him. While looking at Thomas over the top of the glass, Yuri managed a chuckle and a sip of apple juice simultaneously. He made a face, "I thought you English had beer for breakfast?"

"I wouldn't know."

"That's good, very good. I never thought you had a sense of humor, but a guy in your position should get to the point."

"Okay, just what's my position? It's certainly my first time being robbed by a gentleman who frequents Seville Row."

"Сократите дерьмо or, as you say, cut the crap, Watson. I'm the only friend you have right now. You're persona non grata in the rest of the world. You know, that's not bad English for a dumb Russian on his third language. Did I tell you I also speak Italian? I spent eight years in Italy, a great country with beautiful women and magnificent food. It's a bad combination as the women get round like Russian women. The problem is that Russian women *keep* getting round. It's a curse."

"Well, you'll have to stick with English. I'm afraid I'm not as well-traveled as some in this room," Thomas said. "Look, I don't know you. I don't know what to say. I think I hit my head. I don't remember, and you'll have to take that for what it is."

The personality change sparked Yuri's curiosity. Thomas never addressed a question head-on. He always managed to wiggle out the side and change the subject if it didn't suit him.

"You remember where you live. You remember that very... how should I say it?... strong woman you charmed into marriage. By the way, this woman," Yuri said, motioning toward the other room, "is special and not a normal woman. Italian women throw things if they don't get their way. Russian women starve you to death. This woman convinces you she's right. I've heard these conversations."

Thomas didn't like Margaret pulled into whatever was going on. "Why would you care?" he said.

"You don't think we would pay handsomely for your services and not watch you?

Thomas looked directly at the man and said, "Look, I don't remember."

Yuri became very serious. "It's a lie, a stupid lie." He stared at Thomas and said, "You're mine, Mr. Thomas Watson, and I have to decide what to do with you, so you better give me a reason to be your friend."

"What's your name?" Thomas said.

"Are you serious?" Yuri bellowed.

"Look, are you going to tell me or not?" Thomas said, his voice a little higher than before.

"What a stupid question. Yuri, of course. Enough of the games."

"Yuri, I need you to tell me exactly what trouble Thomas is in before we can get anywhere."

"This is a joke with words. You're Thomas and why are you wasting time?"

"Will you tell me, or will we continue in these circles?"

"You speak of Thomas, yourself like you're not here."

"Look, answer the question, will you? What did Thomas do to make him persona non grata?"

"Okay, for your entertainment, I'll play this little game. Time is short, and there's a need for certain informations. Thomas is, I mean *you're*, an agent working for the NKGB."

"The Russian Intelligence, a resident spy?" Thomas said, his voice rising as he spoke.

"Yes, the same agency that paid all the money for informations about a secret project Hatcher Plc is working on for the government. You made the agreement, took the money, and broke the deal. Now, the way I have it figured, you're either tired of living, or you just got a better deal from MI-5 to uncover your case officer, which isn't good for Yuri. So now, you may have both of us in trouble. Things aren't in a good way, Mr. Watson. You've been absent from your work for over two days without informing us, which has raised some questions."

Thomas worked to comprehend what he was hearing.

"What's curious, Mr. Thomas Watson is that you're not acting like a man on the run. I watched the two of you before I interrupted your morning meal. To be honest, you act more like a man in love. The supposed hit you took must have been a mind-altering event, as you've never acted in such a way to your Margaret or been so direct with me. It's all for the best, as she was much too good for the old you."

Still trying to grasp the situation, Thomas said, "So I'm a spy? I don't remember that, and you'll have to believe me. I walked out of a bathroom, married to Margaret. Almost everything else is blank."

"Almost?"

"*All.*"

"Enough," Yuri said gruffly. "I don't believe you, but it doesn't matter. I can help you, but you don't see it. You need to give me all the informations you have, especially the site's location, or I'll leave, and you're on your own. I need it now before it doesn't matter and the invasion takes care of everything. Lists will be exchanged; people will disappear." Yuri slammed the table for emphasis.

Thomas shot back with equal energy. "There won't be an invasion. Herr Hitler won't conquer England. I'm certain of it."

It was the first pause in the conversation. There was an unusually long silence as the energy between the men dissipated, and Yuri tried to size up the man in front of him. Things were becoming confusing. He leaned back again, put his hands in his pockets, and, in a normal tone, said, "Oh, I see. You'll guarantee this, but you're only an army of one. The choice is yours."

Yuri stood up, took his coat, and carefully laid it on the table. Looking into the small wide mirror at the top of the coat rack, he became enamored with adjusting his hat. Satisfied with the fit, he stepped back casually as if they had been discussing the weather.

Thomas looked at the coat half hanging off the table's edge, creasing right through the pockets. "Where's the gun?" He asked.

Yuri was surprised at the question. "Thomas, I told you before. I'm trained in firearms but have seldomly ever had to use one. I wouldn't unless there was absolutely no other alternative. In fact, I'm surprised the trick worked. Other people use guns. For me, there are other ways, better ways. I'm a diplomat, not a thug."

Thomas wanted to establish some sort of defense and said, "Now, that's one thing I remember. I think I know my way around guns." For some reason, the thought felt true, so he went with the threat.

Yuri said, "That's a surprise. How could that be? When we struck our agreement, I asked you if you needed a gun, and you said you wouldn't know how to use it."

"Sorry, I don't know the answer to that."

"Watson, you've always been a strange man—very strange. Today, it appears, is no different. Life is strange, but I tell you, as this case progressed, it became undeniable that even if you had wanted Margaret

Hatcher, she deserved better than you. But now she won't have you, so it doesn't matter."

Yuri shook his head, pulled back the latch, and opened the door. "It's over; you've made your choice."

Chapter Thirty

Thomas is a Spy

Yuri left the small room where they'd been talking and returned to the pub area.

"Evan, I thank you, and we're even again."

As he walked toward Margaret, she stood up rather assertively.

"You see, Mrs. Watson, here he is, sound and safe," Yuri said, looking back as Thomas emerged from the hallway.

"Margaret, everything is fine," Thomas said.

She stared at Yuri angrily and said, "Don't lie to me, Thomas."

Yuri couldn't contain a laugh as he continued toward Margaret. With the humor still in his voice, he said gently, "You know Mrs. Watson, Margaret, if I may; I watch many American gangster movies. James Cagney is one of my favorites because he appreciates power and strength and knows how to get what he wants. To him, you would be known as a, 'tough cookie." Yuri laughed loudly. "Not a bad, how do you say it, style?"

"Quality," Margaret said.

"Oh, yes, quality. To have this isn't a bad quality, especially for the coming events in your country."

Yuri looked at her. He'd grown to like this woman, reached out to shake her hand, and Margaret moved back. Rebuffed, he resorted to a deferent nod, touched the brim of his hat with two fingers, and said, "A good day to you, Madam," and walked out the door.

Yuri looked up at the sky as he closed the door behind him. If this were a fair sky, it would tell him why things still didn't make sense after meeting with this man. Now many things were so confusing Yuri knew storm clouds were brewing in his world. He crossed the intersection and started up Chiltern Avenue toward Amersham Station.

Moscow had sent a man into his territory without his knowledge and offered him a nice retirement with a *dacha,* or second home, and a pension. Clearing up his last case wasn't going down as simply as it should. This Thomas Watson had gone from a clever and charming irritation to a curious person who knew more than Yuri did or knew nothing. That made him very dangerous to Yuri, who didn't like unknowns in his double world.

The stage had been set, and tomorrow it would be over—or would it?

Thomas and Margaret watched him walk out, almost in awe as much as confusion.

With her hands on her hips, Margaret turned to Thomas and firmly said, "Now is the time in the gangster movie when you tell me quickly what that was all about."

Thomas grabbed her arm and said in a low voice, "First, we need to get out of here."

He turned to the barkeep and reached into his pocket. Evan looked up from his conversation with Lem and waved a hand. "He's on account, Mr. Watson. Yeh, know that. Besides, now I'm even."

Margaret looked at Thomas without saying a word. They walked out of the pub and onto the street. Thomas said, "Let's wait until we return to the house."

Thomas needed the time to try to determine what had just happened. This morning, he was telling Margaret about things that would happen in the future. Then he meets a Russian who tells him he's a spy who has backed out of a deal and is in serious trouble. It didn't matter, old Thomas or new Thomas; it was now his problem. Regardless of what was to happen to him because of the old Thomas, he still needed to tell the government enough to keep Britain from surrendering. He still needed to get to Bletchley.

***

Margaret was sitting quietly on the couch, her legs crossed and one leg nervously swinging back and forth, waiting for an explanation. He determined she was about to explode, the Margaret version of patience.

"Margaret, the man said I was a spy."

She was astounded. "A *what*?"

"He said I was a spy, and you didn't know. They paid me money, and I was supposed to provide information about work your father's company is doing for the government."

At that, Margaret said nothing. She just stared at Thomas. The loudest noise in the room was the one you couldn't hear: Margaret was speechless.

In a serious tone, Thomas said, "Margaret, why exactly did you marry Thomas?"

"We discussed this at the picnic. It was after my mother, and I had the biggest row imaginable. I guess I wanted to get back at mother, and this was the best way I could think of."

With arms crossed and leg still swinging, she went on. "At first, he was overly attentive and concentrated on my every wish, which is exactly what I needed at that time. I have to say, I didn't tell him everything either. He didn't know I was a 'Hatcher,' whatever that meant. God knows it didn't stand for much at the time. I let him into that circle only after Mother and I made up."

Thomas said, "I'm sorry, Margaret; I think he knew exactly who you were."

"I don't think so. He never cared about my past, which was one of the attractive things about him. I'd renounced being a Hatcher and was prepared to leave it behind. However, he changed. We were working it out, and I thought we were making headway when, well," she said, flinging her arms in the air, "you walked out of the bathroom."

"Margaret, he married you to get information."

"No, he didn't. I … getting married was my idea."

Carefully, Thomas said, "Either way, he's taken a lot of money to provide the information to the Russians and not delivered, despite their constant pressure. Not knowing any of this, I didn't report to the handler, and they grew suspicious.

"That man said my time was short, and I had to come up with the information, but he didn't say exactly how much time. I think we're okay for now, but it has hindered my first goal, which is to get the information to Churchill. That's of the utmost importance. We can deal with the other later, or I hope we can."

"Are you still going to Bletchley?"

"If you've a better idea, I want to hear it right now."

"No, I don't, and you're not going to this Bletchley alone. I'm coming with you."

"Really, you can't be serious," Thomas said. "It's going to be hard enough for me to get in there, let alone bring along an entourage." Thomas winced.

"An entourage? I can assure you, I'm nobody's entourage, and I'm certainly not *your* entourage."

"Here we go again," Thomas thought. He tried to think of something that would make sense in her mind.

"Margaret, if you don't go along, it's safer for me because I'll have a lower profile."

"Watson, that's a trick, and you know it."

"Will it work?"

"Damn you, Thomas. You know I want to go, and your safety is the only argument that would keep me here."

"I know, but I don't want me hurt either. I'll ring up and see if I can get a cabby to take me there. I think it's safer than the train."

Ultimately, Thomas left for Bletchley alone, and Margaret wasn't happy. She'd been outfoxed and didn't feel good about it. She had a bad feeling about all this. She sat down and thought about the curious events of that morning and the Russian. Thinking about the other Thomas, she wondered why she hadn't caught on to his deception. Looking back at when she'd brought up getting married, she could now see he'd been following her lead. This new information helped explain why he went along with the strange bedroom rules she'd set and, due to the argument with her mother, the expeditious manner of the nuptials.

"What was Daddy doing that would generate so much interest?" she wondered. "And why would it involve the Russians?"

There was a dirty feeling she couldn't escape, knowing that the old Thomas had deceived her emotions. She felt violated and angry but knew it was her fault. Her only consolation was the feeling she had for the new Thomas. They didn't need to work on anything to make their relationship happy. From day one, it was like an exciting ride to happiness. The feelings for Thomas now were unexplainable, and their relationship was completely different, completely simple, and not driven by anything but love.

Chapter Thirty-One

Yuri Thinks He Knows

Yuri took the tube from the Amersham Station, intending to return to the embassy. Barely aware and deep in thought, he was trying to make sense of the meeting with Watson when he realized the doors had closed and they were leaving the Chalfont & Latimer Station.

Yuri looked around the car as he waited.

"Approaching Chorleywood," a voice announced over the speaker.

As the doors opened, the station agent yelled, "Mind the gap, people; move along."

Yuri waited as those getting off cleared the door and followed. After five or six steps, he casually turned around, putting his hand into his coat as if looking for something. He was giving the crowd time to clear and mentally making a note of anyone who didn't go up the only exit to street level. A rookie would make the mistake of waiting for Yuri while doing something casual; a pro would know the exposure of a tail was worse than losing it. Satisfied no one was following him, he headed for the stairs and out of the station with a small group of people with packages, bags, and places to go. It was a typical morning during the blitz in everyone's life, but it was the beginning of an unknown adventure for Yuri. Trained to avoid the unknown, as it was unhealthy, he figured this mystery would be the same.

Ideas started to form in his head, and the result was unsettling. He'd decided that Thomas was a type of double agent but doubted he worked directly for the British. This fact put the Hatcher woman in danger. Professing to spy for money would explain the lack of a political motive. However, Watson's true agenda was probably trying to find out what information Russia wanted, calculate how much the Russians knew, then sell the information to the British. The British would be very interested in anything regarding the supposed Hatcher machine. In the process, he would receive payment from both sides. That would explain why he wasn't very effective in gathering information. Yuri would expect this from the Thomas he brought onto the project, but the Thomas he'd talked to this morning was very different. Something was wrong, and he needed to find out what it was.

Either way, Moscow Centre wasn't taking any chances with the coming invasion and wanted Watson removed. They also wanted someone running the London station from the new school, steeped in Soviet doctrine and sworn allegiance to the tyrant who liked to call himself Uncle Joe. While cleaning house again, Joseph Stalin considered Yuri part of the trash. Just seven days ago, the NKVD, had assassinated Leon Trotsky. Since Stalin had taken power, almost everyone important in the government, and most of the military leaders were gone. Most of the Foreign Service people remained. Nonetheless, Yuri's file would tell the story of a man who was too independent and not in lockstep with the Kremlin. He knew there would be no dacha and desk job back at home.

For this reason, he needed to determine if Watson was playing both sides. If Watson told the British what the Russians knew, Yuri was positive the Russians would kill him before he could even get to Glasgow. He needed to keep up the front and notify the embassy of his intentions to follow the directive. That would keep the Russians from tailing him and possibly avoid his mysterious disappearance.

Yuri reached the street with the others and looked around. He found what he wanted barely twenty feet away and made his way over while reaching into his pocket. Opening the door to the red wooden booth and dropping some change into the phone, he dialed a number from his memory. He memorized the numbers of all his cases so nothing would be found if he was picked up or searched and his claims of diplomatic immunity were ignored. He'd done so religiously since it saved his life in Italy. He walked right out of the polizia station when the authorities were certain he was involved with a deported national. Yuri put the phone to his ear.

Still trying to justify her actions, Margaret decided that just sitting around and waiting for Thomas to return would drive her crazy. Walking over to the hall tree, she grabbed a scarf and coat and opened the door. Starting towards Mrs. Somerville's, the phone rang. She curiously looked at the phone and let the double ring go twice before picking up the black handset.

"Hello," Margaret said.

"Margaret, this is Yuri, the person that you…"

"I know who you are," she said.

"Well, then, is Thomas there? Can I talk to him? It's very important."

Margaret paused, "He's not available right now."

"Not available or not there?"

"Why should I tell you either way?"

"If my suspicions are correct, it's important to all of us, so please put him on the telephone."

Margaret didn't know where the Russian was and didn't know if she should be where he could get to her. "He stepped out and will be right back," she said.

Yuri would have believed most women but not this one. She was a clever fighter, and he knew Watson wasn't there. "Margaret, Thomas could be in danger. You must tell me where he went, as I'm one of the only people who can help him."

"You're lying."

"No, you're lying, but it doesn't matter because you don't have a choice. Either I can help him, or I'm the one harming him. Either way, you've nothing to lose, as I'll eventually find him. You'll tell me where he is because you've fallen in love and want to protect him. Either he went to a location that I don't know, or he went to Bletchley Park. I heard you say it when I walked up. Now, which is it?"

His using the word Bletchley startled her and broke the cadence of the conversation.

The phone went dead.

Yuri opened the phone box door and hurried back to the station. At the counter, he said, "Bletchley Park, please."

The older man behind the counter gave Yuri a sour look. "Well, that's going to be a very disorderly ride," he said. He turned in his chair and placed a large map mounted on a board against the bars so Yuri could see it.

"You'll need to start with the tube to Harrow-on-the-Hill Station and transfer to the Innercity, which will take you to Watford Junction. You'll need to get on the Silverlink rail service to Milton Keynes from there. Bletchley is the stop just before Milton Keynes. If you buy all the tickets here, then Bob's, you're uncle. All you'll need to do is find the proper train."

Yuri, feeling pressured for time, just wanted it done. "Yes," he said. "Quickly, please, I know the transfers." The man pressed the keys down three times on a machine, producing the tickets. He handed them to Yuri and pointed to the car just coming to a stop.

"That'll be yours, sir. Bit lucky, I would say. Hope you're this lucky the rest of your day."

Yuri walked quickly to the open doors and sat at the back of the car. As his weight settled into the seat, he thought he'd need more than luck to unravel what had once been a routine intelligence operation.

Chapter Thirty-Two

Bletchley Park
Milton Keynes

Between Oxford and Cambridge, sixty miles northwest of London, he came upon the town of Milton Keynes, Buckinghamshire. It's a minor stop on the way to Birmingham, an industrial city in the heart of the country. The Bletchley Station received its name from an estate Sir Herbert Leon started building in 1882 by the same name. In 1938, the government acquired the entire estate for the wartime headquarters of the Government Code and Cipher School.

Bletchley consisted of a beautiful Tudor main mansion and several outbuildings, including stables with a tack and feed house, a head groom's house, a dairy, and a large car park. They converted the buildings into offices. As the cipher task quickly grew, they built an increasing number of fabricated huts to house the overflow. Since the function had moved out of London, this eclectic collection of buildings was the center of British Intelligence.

Milton Keynes was a small old town, quite unremarkable except for some of the remarkable things occurring within the mansion's walls at Bletchley. In these most unlikely government buildings, some of the most advanced and creative forms of mathematical and technological knowledge came together to decode German communications. The resulting theoretical, technical, and electro-mechanical breakthroughs laid the foundation for what would become one of humanities' most significant creations in modern times. Thus, when the names of famous battles in the air, on land, and at sea were later declassified, this unassuming place would make the list of places where the war was won.

Here, Thomas had come and hoped to present his information to the right people. After several attempts and vigorous discussions, one cab driver finally relented and agreed to bring him all the way in from Amersham. The driver was suspicious: why didn't he take the train? Thomas had the driver drop him off at the train station, and, given everyone's wartime mentality, this increased the man's suspicions.

Thomas paid the driver and walked toward the train ticket counter to ask for directions. He noticed that off to his left, above a grove of trees, he could see the very top of the mansion and its chimneys. Directly across Sherwood Street was a worn dirt path through some woods that undoubtedly led to the Bletchley grounds. The trail looked not to be more than 200 yards long.

Thomas crossed the street and entered the footpath, quickly enclosed by greenery and tall trees. Halfway along the path, life disappeared to fade into the countryside, with the sight of trees and colour and the shining sun caring for it all. A peace came over him as he unconsciously slowed his pace to prolong his walk, taking it all in. Eventually, as did his wandering, the path ended at Wilton Avenue, which ran right onto the mansion grounds.

He headed to the mansion's main entrance, with its wide circular arch and formal entry. There was still a hint of the once-stately elegance the original master had instilled into its design, and under the care of its current owner, the whole complex looked in dire need of repair. He was stunned that there were no guards at the front and that fencing didn't surround the group of buildings.

Thomas entered the mansion. Just inside the front door and to the right was a small reception area that had been the Music Room during a more romantic time. The right side of the room consisted of three matching sets of ornately carved window frames. Each pane of glass faced the mansion's front and was carefully crossed with tape, keeping the glass from flying in an explosion. Bookshelves with diagonally grated cabinet doors covered the far wall almost to the ceiling. The original textured silk wallpaper flowed to crown molding surrounding a framed mahogany-coffered ceiling. In its day, the décor established an old-world grace and dignity since lost. Amidst this well-worn elegance, three military-issue grey padded office chairs looked decidedly out of place. Situated prominently in the room, and looking unmovable, sat a large metal desk. Behind it sat a very prim-looking woman with a neat perm and rimless spectacles. She was busy talking on the phone, using a very official voice and pretending he didn't exist while watching his every move.

She put the phone down and suspiciously placed a stack of papers into the top drawer of her desk as if to hide them from his view.

"Can I help you?" she said.

"Well, yes, I believe so. My name is, ah, Dunning. Yes, I'm looking for a Mr. Alan Turing."

"Alan Turing," she repeated. She looked away, and her forehead wrinkled as she searched her memory. She reached for a frayed manila file folder on her desk and started flipping through some pages stapled directly onto the inside of the folder. Significant effort was required for her to access the right page. After a second, she looked up and said, "I'm very sorry, Mr. Dunning. We don't happen to have an Alan Turing here at the academy. Do you know what department he's in?"

"No, I don't. You must understand, I wouldn't expect you just to let me see the man, as he's involved in some very classified work. I'm more than willing to submit to an interview about my intentions to talk with Mr. Turing. There are some things that I believe he's working on, and I could possibly be of help."

She wasn't parting from her assigned duties of keeping the public away and keeping suspicions to a minimum. The term Praetorian Guard came to mind as she rose to her feet to stand behind her desk. As she lightly rested her hands on her blotter, she said, "Well, in light of any other information, I can do a limited amount for you, Mr. Dunning. I have an item that requires my attention if there's nothing else. Can I ring you up a cab?"

Thomas thought, "Getting someone to talk to is going to take a while. How do you get to talk to someone in charge of one of the deepest secrets of the war?" The choice of starting in the morning was fortuitous. Seeing him could take weeks.

"No, but I sincerely appreciate the offer Miss…?"

She paused before finally relenting. Looking up she said, "It's Mrs., Mrs. Stimson."

"Well, Mrs. Stimson, at the risk of being a bother, I must insist that someone interview me. It's of the utmost importance that I pursue this matter."

Thomas had said it perhaps too vigorously as it elicited an icy response worthy of an old school teacher out of a worst nightmare.

She crossed her arms. "Mr. Dunning," she said rigidly, "I could ask that you leave, but of course, that won't be necessary, will it?" She spoke in measured staccato tones.

"Yes, you could, Mrs. Stimson, but I won't until I'm accorded at least a hearing with someone who can determine my motives and assess if I'm of any value."

Turning away, he promptly sat, solidly hitting the bottom of a stuffed chair and reaching for a magazine.

His motions were not, to say the least, received with a neutral frame of mind. Silent and motionless, she stood behind the desk for a full twenty seconds staring at Thomas. Mrs. Stimson was obviously used to getting her way in manners of "reception protocol." Eventually, a single finger started tapping as she reviewed the options, including shooting him dead, right then and there with her stare. She spun around and left the room through the only door other than the entry, closing it rather vigorously behind her. As she left the room, Thomas checked his watch and thought he'd nothing to lose in this effort, as the other options weren't much better.

Fifteen minutes later, she returned. Upon entering the room, she resumed her place behind her desk, firmly re-establishing her position of power. In a very dismissive tone, she started, "I said, without further information, there's little I can do for you. I have, however, found someone willing to talk to you. You'll follow me." She stood and headed for the door.

They walked through the door into an anti-room, down a short hall, and out a side entrance to the original old building. They crossed to one of the huts, a very long and narrow one-story building. Inside was a long hall that was a primary part of the building's design. It had many doors on each side facing the hall and abysmal lighting. Above each door was a single number. There wasn't a soul in sight. They passed about five doors, then she opened one on the right, leading him inside.

"Please have a seat, Mr. Dunning. I trust someone will be with you momentarily."

"Thank you, Mrs. Stimson, you've been most helpful," he said. She left without another word. She wasn't used to losing.

The interrogation room was a box not even ten feet square with a single bare table in the center with an old oak chair on either side. The whole scene was so cliché that it was almost amusing, as if torn from the pages of a detective novel. A mirror on one wall was obviously two-way glass, and a single light hung over the center of the table. Thomas waited ten minutes, pacing, folding, and unfolding his arms, knowing someone was watching him. Finally, a slightly built man entered, moving very slowly, not due to any injury or physical disorder, but Thomas got the impression that was how fast his world evolved. A pair of wireless spectacles with thick lenses adorned his boyish face. Thomas wasn't impressed.

"Mr. Dunning?" the man said. He extended his hand. "My name is Alan Turing. I'm very sorry about the confusion. You can't find anything on a list that's never updated. I see you got past our guard at the front desk." He was nervous and kept talking. "I must apologize. Mrs. Stimson is something of a legend here at the academy, and warmth isn't her best attribute. We think she has friends at the director level. Most of us think she'll be buried with the place," he said.

Managing a smile, Thomas released Alan Turing's hand with great suspicion. They both sat down. Thomas said, "I have to say that even after insisting on talking with you, I'm surprised you're sitting here."

As if bored, Turing pushed the wire frame higher on his nose with a long thin finger and said, "Yes, that might be. However, how can I help you?"

Thomas leaned back in the chair, one hand resting on the table. He took a long look at this, Mr. Turing. "I want to help," he said.

Turing nodded while turning back several used pages in a yellow notebook he'd brought in, stopping at a fresh one. Reaching into his shirt pocket, he appeared confused momentarily, then, after checking, found his pencil in his pants pocket. He examined its point.

Thomas briefly looked at the mirror and said, "The war is going badly, and there are things I can do to help the project you're working on."

Turing nodded again, acknowledging the statement, but didn't offer any comment. Instead, he leaned forward and put the date on the top of the new page.

Searching for somewhere to start, Thomas decided to try to get the man's attention. He looked at Turing and said, "The German high command uses a device called Enigma to encode messages sent to their commanders in the field. This facility is engaged in deciphering those messages, and I have information that might make the process more efficient."

Turing sat back in his chair with his legs crossed and wrote "Mr. Dunning" in precise letters under the date on his pad. He looked again at the end of the pencil, noting it needed sharpening, then placed it on the table, signaling he was done.

"Would you like me to continue?" Thomas said.

"Oh, yes, of course, Mr. Dunning."

This man didn't have the foggiest, but there was little choice but to go forward. "Each day, the Germans replace one of the five different cipher code wheels in their devices. To quickly decipher the day's intercepts, your machine must be modified to match the ever-changing wheel combinations."

Thomas stopped to observe, to no effect. "You're currently trying to do it with patch cables which, while effective, are laboriously slow. The United States is also secretly trying to build a calculating device to generate artillery-firing tables and has a similar problem. Your machine needs a stored program to follow. A program, changed in minutes, will make the machine practical, and I can help with this."

"Actually, I'm not sure you can help, Mr. Dunning, as I'm not working on such a project nor such a machine. I can assure you that..."

Mid-sentence, the door opened, and a large man stuck his head into the room. The man, dressed in baggy tweeds with a tie encircling a large neck, said, "Devin, that will be enough for now. Mr. Shane wants you to interview another visitor in Hut Twelve, Room Two. However, before that, the operator said she was waiting to put a call through to your office. Best be at it, man."

Thomas was very relieved that this man wasn't Alan Turing.

The frail man got up without looking at Thomas, gathered his notepad, and exited the room with defeated body language. "I wish you guys would decide," Devin said.

Devin wasn't happy and was still mumbling as he proceeded to his office a few doors down. He picked up the phone, and the operator said, "Mr. Fletcher, you have a call."

Devin said, "Yes, put it through."

Looking at the blinking light, the operator pulled out the plug and cable, inserting it into the connector next to Devin Fletcher's name. The action automatically disconnected her headset from the line; she saw both lights go on and went to the next call.

Devin's job wasn't the most prestigious at the Park, but at least he should be accorded the simplest respect. He could go elsewhere, but women, who accepted less pay and didn't complain, were filling many of the jobs that had been the domain of men. If he were military, it would be different, but he couldn't pass the physical because of his eyesight.

Chapter Thirty-Three

Bletchley Park Station

Yuri looked at the worn Bletchley Park sign hanging from the station's rafters. He could hear the phone ringing as he performed his usual scan of everyone nearby.

From the handset, a voice said, "Devin Fletcher here."

"Are you alone?" Yuri said.

Devin stood straight and looked around the empty room as if caught doing something embarrassing. "Wait," he said quietly into the phone and walked over to his office door. He casually looked outside into the hall and closed it behind him. Picking up the receiver, he whispered, "What're you doing calling me here?"

"Because I pay you money. It's important, so shut up and listen. There's a visitor there by the name of Thomas Watson. Have you seen or heard of him being there today?"

"No."

Irritated, Yuri said, "No? That's it?"

Fletcher took a deep breath and looked around the empty room again. Nervously, he grabbed the right lens of his glasses between his fingers, performing another unneeded adjustment. "That's it," he said.

"Well, Mr. Fletcher, that's not it," Yuri said threateningly. "You must find this Watson, convince him he needs to leave the Bletchley complex now, and I don't care how you do it."

"How am I supposed to do that?" Devin said.

Yuri said slowly and distinctly, "You're not listening. I said I didn't care."

"But I don't know who this guy is and even if I did …"

"He arrived within the last hour, probably wants to talk to someone important, and will need to be screened. That's what you do there, right? That's why I pay you money, to keep track of who's coming and going. Now, has anyone come in during the last hour or so?"

"Yes, two people. One was a WAAF, and she was in for training," Devin whispered, "and the other isn't your Mr. Watson."

"Why not?"

"Because it's not his name; what can I say?" Devin was genuinely uncomfortable.

"What was his name?"

Fletcher reached for his yellow pad and looked at the name written at the top. "Dunning," he said. "it's the only person I know who came in, so there's nothing I can do."

"Didn't it occur to you that he might not use his real name? What did he look like?"

"He was tall, with light brown hair, about 180 pounds."

"Did he have on a bluish shirt and khaki pants?"

"Ah ..."

Yuri waited. "*Fletcher*, get on with it."

Fletcher squeezed the handset, "Yes, that's probably him. Dunning wanted to see Turing, but they took him to another office," Fletcher lied. Even though he was alone, he tried to control his guilty body language. "I don't know where, but someone was very disturbed by what he had to say. He knows too much, so I can't help you, even if I wanted to."

"Devin, you've been on the take for two years. It's payback time. You need to find him, or he's a dead man, and if that happens, I'm not sure about *your* future. Am I clear?"

Fletcher moved the phone to his other hand as his sweaty palm made it hard to hold. He wiped the sweat from his hand onto his pants. "Yes, I'll go find him."

"Tell him he's in danger and to meet Yuri back at the station quickly."

"Yuri?" Devin said.

"Yes, that's the cover name he knows me by. He'll know who it is. You need to do this now."

"Okay, but what if I can't?"

Yuri heard him but paused dramatically and hung up. It was thin at best, but he couldn't think of anything else. He couldn't chance trying to get into the complex himself. Although it looked like one could walk right in, it wasn't as easy as it appeared. He looked around with a helpless feeling. He needed to discover Thomas's true allegiance but might have run out of time.

Fletcher sat down in his chair and stared at the wall. What was he going to do? He opened the desk drawer and pulled out his precious calendar notebook, deciding to leave everything else. He picked up the yellow pad for appearance's sake and walked out the office door. He quickly headed for the back of the building.

He didn't know what he would do but knew he couldn't stay here. Things were starting to unravel, and that Russian could start talking to the wrong people. He thought, "I can't believe this is happening to me." He thought supplying a list of names of new people screened at the complex would be harmless money. How important was it, for God's sake? You could see them walk in the front door. He had four kids and couldn't make ends meet with the government's salary. Now, the harmless effort had gone to places he hadn't dreamed of and placed the very family he wanted to help in danger. He opened the back door and escaped his hell at a rapid pace.

Chapter Thirty-Four

Bletchley
Meeting Dr. Turing

Thomas watched silently as the frail man left the interrogation room obviously flustered. A big bouncer-type man entered the room, followed by a gentleman who moved behind the now-empty seat at the table. They exchanged knowing glances, and the big man left the room, closing the door.

As the man pulled the chair to sit down, it was hard not to notice his significant shock of brown hair, which decided to do whatever it wanted without the consent of its owner. His dark, steady eyes fixed on Thomas as he settled into the chair. He had the look of a slightly erratic and sheltered professor with the most dreadful sweater, but, most importantly, Thomas recognized him.

"Mr. Dunning, I've been told of your discussion with my colleague," he said, pointing to the mirror. He placed his right hand on the table as if trying to bridge a psychological gap.

"Well, this is your lucky day. My name is Alan Turing," he said, extending the hand resting on the table for a firm, prolonged handshake. "I guess I should say, the real Alan Turing. Please excuse the cloak and dagger, but you haven't exactly dropped into the cinema, have you? I don't spend all of my time at this facility. I was here for a meeting in one of the other huts. They came and pulled me out."

He looked at Thomas and said, "Given your comments, you're quite well-informed, so I have to ask, have we met?"

"No, I can assure you we haven't, but I am greatly interested in your work."

Turing eagerly said, "Are you interested in mathematics?"

"No, not really. The sum of your work appeals to my sense of history. People will judge your work in the future, and those in the know will see it as some of the most important efforts in shortening the war."

"And how do you know this, Mr. Dunning?"

"Well, Mr. Turing, Alan, if I may, you're much more than a mathematician. You're one of the few people in the world with the capacity to devise an extraordinary algorithm new to your field. This is the basis for a formula used to sift through great stacks of information to find a relevant segment used in ciphering. Am I right?"

The attentive Turing revealed nothing, so Thomas continued, "What makes it extraordinary isn't the fact you did it but how you arrived at the solution. Your method speeds up the process by eliminating the information that can't be relevant, thus leaving a much smaller set that can be productive—instead of the other way around. It's like arriving at the right place by not going everywhere else. You call it exclusion."

"That's a little disturbing, Mr. Dunning," he said. He turned in his chair and looked at the mirror. Rising from his chair, he pointed toward the mirror and addressed Thomas, saying, "If you'll excuse me for a minute, I need to have a word."

At that exact moment, the door opened wide into the room, and the bouncer was in the doorway. The large man's head was turned, so he wasn't looking into the room but listening to someone outside. With the slightest nod to the mystery person outside, he looked at Turing and said, "Continue on for now."

Turing lifted his hands and said, "Sorry 'bout that, but like I said, it's disturbing information. You see, to my knowledge, there isn't anyone, including my staff, who understands the concept, let alone provide a lucid explanation. To eliminate that possibility, all information is compartmentalized. In addition, due to the secrecy, I haven't been able to publish any of my work. In fact, due to the pressure of war, I've been unable to transfer but the barest portion to paper for work at the lab, let alone document it formally."

Turing paused for a second.

Thomas was aware these were frustrating thoughts Turing had addressed many times before. "Alan, it must be hard. I can only imagine."

"Yes, it is, but that's not why you're here then, is it? So back to you, Mr. Dunning. Knowing you're aware of any detail makes this intriguing, mysterious, and possibly dangerous. Just what is it that you want?"

Thomas felt he was making progress. "Doctor, my primary goal is to convince our government that I've access to certain extraordinary information related to the imminent invasion. I wish to establish my credibility by providing important information that would benefit your work. Only after you're convinced my facts are authentic and my advice helpful would I ask you for a favor."

Turing said, "Again, what's this favor?"

"If you find me credible, I need your help presenting my invasion information to the proper people. To those individuals to whom I've no access. Please believe me when I say this intelligence is so important it could determine the war's outcome. However, we must act quickly, as time is critical and growing short."

Mr. Turing leaned back in his chair. "Mr. Dunning, I'm only an academic, a mathematician. Those prosecuting this war have the barest shred that I even exist. Besides, if I may be direct, given the secrecy of any projects we may or may not be working on, how could you provide anything specific?" Turing shook his head. "Actually, you may have answered that already with your previous comments."

His sentence trailed off. Thomas could see that Turing was tired, worn down by the constant political pressure, but more so knowing that every day the code remained unbroken, cost lives. Thomas's effort was starting to represent something Turing didn't need on his plate right now. Thomas needed to turn the conversation around quickly if he'd any chance to succeed.

"Alan, all I ask is that you try me," Thomas said. "I've already mentioned that your team has developed a calculating machine to decipher coded messages. Your team has hit roadblocks in getting your machine to decode and translate the intercepts quickly. Expediting the translation is where I can be of assistance."

"You continue with your inordinate surprises, Mr. Dunning. Okay, yes, we have a machine, and with that knowledge, you've crossed a threshold into a rather murky area where everyone is an enemy until they're proven innocent. Nevertheless, in an effort to move this conversation along, I must point out it's you who've created this state of affairs."

"You're right," Thomas said. "I'll accept what I've created. Nevertheless, am I within the mark?"

"Yes, it's a sophisticated information-processing machine we call the Bombe, after a favorite dessert. Not very clever, I'm afraid, but I had to come up with a name quickly. Anyway, it would appear I'm the only one who thinks it's fast or of any worth. As you said, it's because we can't decode information fast enough for it to be useful in the field. A special group of telephone engineers and I are pressed, quite strenuously to be truthful, into an effort to gain ever higher speeds. We've added more huts to house the increasing number of teleprinter machines needed, but we've hit a technical wall. That aside, it's truly inconceivable that you would know it exists. The enciphering machine and the deciphered information the Bombe produces, *when* it produces, are some of the most guarded secrets in the war."

Thomas knew it was sink or swim and had to play all his cards. "To deepen my state of affairs, I can tell you the machine is called Enigma, and Ultra is the information it produces and is known by the code name Ultra," Thomas said. "With the exception of a handful, no one in the British military has the foggiest notion it exists."

Thomas waited. Turing stared at Thomas for a long while and eventually shook his head in bewilderment.

"Alan?" Thomas said, looking for his approval. "There's so much to discuss and share. After the war, incredible advances in manipulating data will occur. Most of it will result from people building upon your work and I'll be considered the dawn of the computer age. Some will call you the father of the modern computer, which will give birth to something called the Internet, but that's a completely different story. You can't imagine how freely accessed information will impact innovation worldwide. But we need to discuss this later."

Turing was startled. "Well, I'll give you this, Mr. Dunning; you seem very confident and resolutely sure. Who are you? How do you know all this? You had to have known that revealing this information would place you in somewhat of a" he paused, "delicate situation."

Thomas knew Turing would end the war in seclusion, fighting the mental spirits let loose by the continual intense thinking. He would lock himself away for days, solving the problems made urgent by the times. He would run long distances like a fanatic to burn off the stress. Turing would also struggle with society's fixation on his sexuality in a time of few options. It was an undeserving legacy to one of the greatest minds of our age.

Thomas leaned forward as if he was sharing a classroom secret. "I know that your work's scope is so vast that I urge you to persist even in the darkest moments, even when you think it will surely drive you crazy."

"Actually, Mr. Dunning, some would say I've passed that mark," he said with a laugh. "But seriously, you have my attention. We need to establish where this is going?"

"Yes, I know revealing such information would certainly raise some eyebrows. After careful review, I decided there wasn't an acceptable alternative. For some reason, I'm very aware of your work, so it naturally led me here."

"For some reason, you're aware of the work?" He said with a questioning look.

"Well, anyway, I indicated I might be of some help. Of course, I can't help with your algorithms, but the key to increasing the speed is rather non-technical. The secret is accelerating the input rate. I know that the current method uses a huge patch cord panel that takes a team of women hours to set the machine for a new code. The patch panel settings trigger a relay that sets the many rows of drums." Thomas waited for Turing to acknowledge that he was right and to validate that he wasn't off on a lark.

Turing's face reflected his confused thoughts, "Yes, but how would you have come across …."

"As I said, I wanted you to know my information was accurate to gain your trust. Anyway, I think you already have all the elements to construct an input device using the half-inch roll of punched paper tape used in a stock ticker. Each tape program contains a specific set of instructions. We must punch the holes in a specific pattern representing the binary value associated with every switch. It's called a program. It's the same information that the women use to set the patch cords. Feed this tape between a light source and an optical sensor, and it trips the individual relays, completing the circuit. You'll have to rewire the patch cord panel to bypass the connector and feed directly into the relay. The machine set-up time is in minutes, not hours. It's all very similar to the needle cards in Jacquard's loom, where he easily changed the cards to alter the pattern woven into the cloth. Instead of a needle, it's light. Are you with me?"

Turing sat in a long, thoughtful silence followed by rapid unfinished thoughts. "A program, you say? This is very interesting. How would you keep the …?" He stopped and looked down at the table. Silent and still thinking, a very small, almost imperceptible smile appeared on his face.

Thomas could almost see his thoughts connecting into strings of new ideas. He absent-mindedly ran his right hand through his thick hair, then dropped his arm. Still staring at the tabletop, Turing turned to Thomas and said, "Of course, the optics could replace manually setting the patch panel and…." With both hands in his pockets, Turing jumped up and started pacing back and forth in the small room. Approaching the opposite wall, he began to lean against it, but after barely touching his shirt to the wall, he stood erect, pointed the finger at Thomas, and said, "Yes, a switch, a high-speed patch connection. My telephone engineers have developed a much faster electrical switch relay based on the old slower design. It's dreadfully expensive with delicate machining. In fact, we installed them, but currently, the patch cords still do the tripping. We didn't know how to combine the switches with the settings other than manually.

Thomas knew he'd achieved his primary goal, which was impressing Turing. It was a monumental first step, and he allowed himself a slight sense of optimism.

Chapter Thirty-Five

Bletchley
Dr. Turing

Turing was beside himself. "How absolutely fascinating."

He looked directly at Thomas with a full, wonderful smile. "There are a couple of problems, but that's a magnificent piece of thinking." He approached Thomas and asked, "How would you like to see what we're doing? I think I can arrange a…"

The door to the room opened with far more force than required and a civilian entered.

"Mr. Dunning," the big man said forcefully, "would you come with me? You're to be interviewed by someone else."

"Who could it be?" Thomas asked. "Why?" He looked at Turing, and they realized it was over, and neither wanted the exchange to stop.

Turing stood up and walked over to the man. "I don't think you understand what's occurring here." Turing gave Thomas a knowing look over the man's shoulder.

The big man told Turing, "He has said some things that are quite disturbing, and he'll need to come with me."

Alan Turing's voice rose. "No, no, I insist. What this man is saying is very important. You don't understand."

As the two talked, Thomas, with a quick, small motion, reached inside his coat and found his cab receipt. With the new man facing Turing, he placed it on his leg below the table level and reached for the pencil left behind by the first Mr. Turing.

"Please, Mr. Turing," the man said. "It's not your affair. I've my orders," he insisted.

Turing could still see Thomas writing something down over the man's shoulder and was now stalling. "Where's he going? Will I see him later? I *need* to see him later. You people can't control everything if we're to make real advancements here. I want to know where he's going!"

Turing turned to Thomas with a helpless look.

"Please follow me, Mr. Dunning," the large man said, walking out of the room, assuming Thomas would follow.

Thomas quickly mouthed to Turing, "Can we talk?"

Turing knew that the authorities saw this as a security breach and this man was in serious trouble. He'd warned him, but now, Turing knew he was powerless despite the importance.

When the big man realized Thomas wasn't behind him, he reached back inside, placed a large hand on Thomas's arm, and started leading him out of the room. Thomas grabbed and started to shake Turing's hand with both of his in what looked like a desperate attempt to keep himself in the room.

The man's pressure on his arm caused Thomas to let go and, walking backward, said, "I'll try to contact you, but keep up your work nonetheless."

Turing knew it wasn't going to happen. He might be able to see him in prison, but that was as close as it would get.

"Dunning!" barked the man.

Thomas almost shouted, "Perfect the tape input. It's the key to the output."

Turing watched Thomas briskly led toward a door at the back of the building. Casually he slowly opened his right hand and read the scribbled words 'Crown Inn' on the cab receipt.

"It was hopeless," Turing thought. "It wasn't going to happen."

Being manhandled, Thomas knew something had changed and suddenly started to feel his original plan of releasing the information was a desperate unworkable plan. Thoughts of escaping went through his mind.

Stepping outside, Thomas saw two very young-looking Royal Marines smartly dressed down to polished buckles and carrying side arms. In a random thought, Thomas wondered how someone living in a barracks managed a double-creased dress shirt in wartime. One marine walked in front of him while the other followed. The comfort that they were British was belied by the fact that they didn't exactly know who he was or his intentions. Again, war exaggerates everything, and knew it is wise to assume the worst.

"Where are we going?" Thomas said to the stone silence of the men around him.

Given the sudden uncertainty of his situation, Thomas felt a heightened awareness that made him acutely mindful of every detail, should it prove useful later. After a short walk, they passed what appeared to be the original horse barn on the estate, set off by itself as if its once-pungent odor might still be keeping the surrounding huts at bay. Its weathered wood gave it the character of a black-and-white photo. He assumed it was unused as there was no worn path to the barn. He noticed most of the huts were windowless boxes containing the mysteries of the war and the people who knew them. The paths between the huts formed a maze confusing even to the employees. Thomas saw a car park between two huts and a common across the street.

The first guard opened a door at the back of a hut and stood back, motioning him forward. The second guard closed the door and remained just outside. The civilian continued walking down the hall, talking on a large handheld radio. Again, Thomas entered a small room with the same small table. Unlike the other, this one contained two windows. One window looked out into the inside hall covered with drawn blinds. Thomas noticed the new room lacked the two-way mirror prominent in the last compartment. Natural light filled the room from a single multi-paned window about four feet square on the outside wall looking out at the shabby huts and the stables about 300 feet away. He couldn't get over how unimportant everything looked, but he knew better.

When they had entered, no other workers were visible, but Thomas could feel the energy in the building, the low, uneven noise of human activity. However, there wasn't anything specific he could discern.

Events rapidly diverged from the script Thomas had outlined initially in his mind. He wasn't quite sure of anything and was concerned about Margaret if he were to disappear. The marine who had entered with him said, "Place your palms against this wall and move your feet away so you're leaning against it. Anything I should know about?"

"No," Thomas said, noticing that the term "Mr. Dunning" had disappeared. He thought both marines reported directly to and received training from Mrs. Stimpson as they exuded her caring warmth.

The marine reached into Thomas's pocket and placed the return cab fare into a large, worn envelope with a clasp. When Thomas had left Margaret's, he'd purposely left anything behind that could identify him as anyone besides Mr. Dunning. He didn't want anyone tracing him back to Margaret. It meant traveling without an identification card, not recommended in wartime, but it was a chance he'd decided to take.

The marine stepped directly behind Thomas with his side to the outside window and patted him down. Instantly, two window panes shattered into the room, and the young marine grabbed his thigh and fell to the ground. Thomas, too, immediately hit the floor, flat on his chest, though he didn't know why. He could feel broken glass under his palms. Thomas hadn't heard gunshots, but the result was unmistakable. Blood flowed over the marine's hand as he gripped his leg. Thomas could hear strained breathing as the young man dealt with the pain. Thomas unbuttoned the soldier's collar and ripped open his shirt to ease his breathing.

"Hold on," Thomas said, moving closer and pulling the man's tie completely free of his collar. He then worked it around the marine's leg above the wound and pulled it tight. The young man grunted at the pain.

"How bad is it, son?" Thomas said.

In short grunts, he said, "Just the outside—of my thigh—I think."

Thomas could see the tourniquet was already slowing the bleeding. He reached for the leg of the table and pulled it over them as they sat on the floor. He grabbed several sheets of paper that had fallen to the floor and folded them over twice. He then grabbed a large piece of glass and, holding one edge with the paper, cut the pants open just below the bullet wound, exposing the wound.

"It went straight through, son. You'll be fine, but it won't feel good anytime soon. I'm sure we'll have help in a minute."

At that instant, the other marine flew in the door, his pistol drawn, shouting, "*Eddy?*"

He positioned himself against the wall next to the broken panes.

Slowly, the injured soldier on the floor said, "I'm okay; I think I'm okay."

The big civilian, radio still in hand, flew through the door, taking a position on the other side of the window. With his gun in one hand and the radio in the other, he began yelling into the device. "Hut 14—gunfire—marine down!"

The second wave of glass exploded into the room, most landing on the table above Thomas and the wounded marine.

The second marine fired three rapid, deafening shots through the open window.

"It's from the barn, sir, the Dutch door on the right. I saw the flash on the second shot."

"Cease firing, corporal!" the civilian screamed.

"Sir?"

"We might hit our people in the building behind it."

He started yelling commands into his radio to secure the grounds and get medical assistance to their location.

Thomas's mind was racing, trying to make sense of the contradictory events of the last hour. It didn't take a brilliant mind to realize that if someone chose to shoot at the exact moment he'd entered the room, they were trying to kill him. But who? Why didn't they try when he was between the buildings? The British thought he was a spy. They were about to take him into custody because of the secrets he'd disclosed to Turing during their meeting. It was a sure sign they didn't exactly see him as an ally, but they certainly didn't need to kill him. He was of more use alive.

No, this had to do with Margaret's Thomas and his involvement in spying on the Hatchers. He concluded Margaret's Thomas had indeed been working for the Russians and reneged on a deal.

Thomas thought, "Yuri's group thinks I came here to divulge what I know about their operation, which would make me very unpopular in their eyes."

The Russian had offered to help but couldn't unless Thomas turned over some information he didn't have. Thomas struggled to perceive any positive outcome.

Chapter Thirty-Six

Bletchley Train Station

At the station, Yuri was pacing back and forth between the phone he'd just used to talk to Devin and the ticket counter at the other end of the platform. Chances were slim that Watson would appear. Standing near the ticket counter, Yuri could see an older man walking toward him, hunched over as he dragged a large bag, his disheveled look the result of clothes he'd been living in for months. His face wore a life story much different from Yuri's own. Yuri managed a half-turn but couldn't walk away.

Behind him, a failing voice said, "Kin ye spar' a gift, sir?"

In a second, Yuri could see the beauty in the illogical picture of it all. Many overlapping human stories took place in the same space and at the same time. Some were in contact permanently; some came together but for a second, and some not at all. He was in the middle of a spy chase, war secrets were at stake, a man could be in serious danger, and here was this poor sod looking for a few quid. Out of nowhere, they were at the same place at the same time. As farfetched as it is, perhaps Thomas's tale consisted of two stories fitted end to end, and both were true. Yuri reached into his pocket, pulled out a pound note, folded it in half, and handed it to the older man without a word.

Yuri took the same path as Thomas, leaving the station but avoided entering the Bletchley property. Instead, he turned onto Roche Gardens Road, taking him alongside the complex and allowing him to peer into various places. The odds were long, but it was his only lead. He didn't know what he could do or what he was looking for. Making his way along the road, he walked and observed, then heard the security sirens on the grounds.

Chapter Thirty-Seven

Bletchley
The Common

The interrogation room was in chaos. Thomas crawled over and looked into the hall. The first doors were opening, confirming his guess that soon there would be total confusion. People were pouring into the hall, curious at the yelling and noise. Thomas looked at the injured soldier; he'd helped him to a half-sitting position against the wall but still under the table. He was conscious and alert. The man on the radio was looking around the window, casing toward the barn. The other marine moved to his comrade.

With the soldier in good hands, Thomas slowly stood up and moved into the hall unnoticed. Armed security guards were running at him. Thomas felt his whole body freeze. It only relaxed when they ran right past him, unaware he had anything to do with the situation. Thomas took several quick steps toward an exit door on the side of the building opposite the stables. He closed the door behind him and decided that in the uncertainty, he would get safe first and rationalize it later. A few hours ago, his grand plan looked like a tough assignment. Now it looked impossible.

The rhythmic sounds of heavy boots hitting the pathways and shouted orders seemed to come from everywhere. Yet Thomas couldn't see anyone but office workers all rushing to different destinations. This opportune situation wouldn't last long; he needed to use the current chaos to have the slightest chance of escape. His calm confidence surprised him, given his options were reduced by the second. The sensation inexplicably came from the same place that was the origin of all his mysterious ideas.

He hurried past several people running on the paths between the huts and took a left, which would lead him away from the stable area. Hearing a commotion from behind after passing the corner of the building, he looked back. Soldiers appeared in numbers from the other direction concerned primarily with surrounding the stables. An obvious reaction, but any shooter good enough to get so close was good enough to be far away. Thomas turned and ran, figuring he wouldn't draw attention because everyone else was doing the same thing. He passed several people and headed for the end of the last hut and the car park he'd seen behind the building. Walking bent over between the cars, he stopped at the rear of the last row and knelt.

Across the street was a neighborhood common, nearly a block square dotted with large trees and shrubs. A five-foot-high stone wall and cobbled walk ran diagonally across the square area, stopping about sixty feet short of each corner. In the middle of the stone wall, at the center of the common, was a fifteen- or twenty-foot opening spanned by a large wrought iron arch. On either side of the wall was a ten-foot planted area containing a thick growth of trees and large hedges. It looked like a good first place to hide. To get to it, Thomas would have to cross the road from the car park, in full view of the world, until he reached the hedges and the wall. After that, if he could quickly cross the common to the street on the other side without drawing attention, Thomas felt he could disappear into the neighborhood. However, he would have to do it now.

Backing up, he looked into the car's window to his right and the one on his left, without luck. Then trying another, he saw what he wanted. A grip of the handle and push of the button produced the glorious pop of an opening door, and he reached in and grabbed a newspaper. He didn't have time to look for a chance set of keys left behind; that would mean crossing the line to petty theft. He wasn't sure what he'd become but knew he hadn't fallen to that level. Taking a deep breath, he stood up while unfurling the newspaper, doing everything he could to appear taken entirely by the buxom lass traditionally on page three.

Slowly crossing the street, he watched for anything that looked like a threat. He still didn't know the location of the shooter. Until he did, he was far from safe. Reaching the other side of the street, he stopped and refolded the paper. Startled from behind, he jumped when a young boy rang his bicycle bell, rudely reminding him of his right of way on the bike path. The lad passed, saying something as Thomas tried to regain control of his racing heart and some semblance of calm.

As he approached the closest group of thick hedges, he looked around, ducked into them, and worked himself between the hedge and the wall. He then knelt and waited. He peered through the branches. His heart was still pounding, and his eyes were wide open as he tried to control his heavy, noisy breathing. Still acutely aware of an enormous amount of detail, he saw an elderly couple walking out of the park, but they didn't appear to have noticed his dash into the shrubs.

The only way to remain out of sight and cross the common was to make his way between the dense row of shrubs and the wall. One very troublesome problem was the archway opening in the center. Thomas wasn't happy about traversing that section in the open.

Weaving his way along the wall behind the foliage was tough, but he finally arrived at the archway. He could hear the increasing turmoil over the shooting in Bletchley Park. Right now, he had his own problems. He looked left but failed to look entirely around the wall to the right. He stood up quickly to sprint across the opening and ran straight into another man. Thomas felt the blow on his right shoulder and heard the man say something he couldn't understand.

Thomas barely remained standing, as colliding with the other person felt like hitting a big wall. Each surprised, they separated and, for an instant, just stared at each other. Looking at the man, Thomas could see his dark eyes widen and his face grow tense. There was no mistake: Thomas must have matched a briefing photograph, and the man was just as surprised as Thomas was at the unscheduled meeting.

The man was tall and large with a full face, wearing a simple hat and a civilian overcoat. Thomas rightly sensed he wasn't part of Bletchley's security. The man's hand quickly moved to the inside of his coat, prompting another one of Thomas's subconscious reactions. In one continuous motion, Thomas grabbed the barrel of the gun that emerged to control the direction of any fire while thrusting an elbow into the man's midsection, causing him to double over and swear in a foreign language. Thomas applied a second elbow to his temple when his head came down. What followed was the heavy thud of the man hitting the paving stones.

Thomas saw the muscles of the man's hand go free. Still holding the barrel, Thomas pulled the gun away. The man wasn't British, that was for sure; the swearing had sounded Russian. It was more evidence Yuri's men were coming for him after the warning this morning. He remembered Yuri saying he was a diplomat, not a thug. Thomas had thought he would have more time.

He dropped down, making sure no one saw them. Thomas lifted one of the man's eyelids and determined he was out cold. He moved into a defensive position with his back against the cold stone and examined the pistol. It was a Luger 9mm with a Krupp 801 silencer and a nine-shot clip. It wasn't your average sidearm. If he was the shooter, the silencer explained the absence of the sound when the marine went down, but it had to be someone else with a rifle at that distance.

Thomas ejected the clip. Holding it up revealed the empty spaces at the bottom, previously occupied by two rounds. He brought the barrel to his nose, screwing up his face at the odor. He thought it definitely wasn't a rifle, confirming the man was the shooter. Thomas realized that his plan of escaping toward the common must have been an obvious and anticipated move.

Crawling back over to the man, Thomas looked for some identification, holding little hope of finding any. Pulling back the overcoat exposed the empty holster but no more clips. He ran his hands along the inside of the coat's lining and thought he felt something. Ripping at the closest seam, it parted easily and produced a small slip of paper. Thomas looked up and around before unfolding the note to find a single telephone number. Placing it into his shirt pocket, he then, with considerable effort, pulled the man off the path toward the hedges and rolled him over, face down. Reaching under the man's coat at his back, he could feel the magazine pack attached to his belt. Upon snapping it open, three clips fell out—all full.

A distant thought prompted him to have a full clip when in a defensive situation. Thomas turned the gun to the side and again ejected the existing clip into his hand. Grabbing a full one, he slammed the new clip in. Pulling the top action back created the spring motion that loaded a shell and cocked the mechanism. All of it produced entirely too much noise. He quickly crouched down to the lowest possible profile and surveyed the area. There didn't appear to be any other activity.

Thomas resumed crossing the green between the foliage and the wall and started thinking about what he was doing. A short time ago, he was talking to Turing about computers. Now he was behaving and feeling like a spy on the run. Thomas looked at the gun in his hand. He wasn't sure how he knew how to handle the situation, but the fact that he could was a comfort. Perhaps Margaret's Thomas was more than just an opportunist. "Or," Thomas wondered, "maybe we just acquire the needed skills when needed." In any event, he needed to get out of here and fast.

Before standing up from his crouch, he detected movement behind one of the trees across the lawn to his left. He froze and focused intently on a man's feet in the space below a bush. Did the man Thomas had taken down have a partner?

"Does he know where I am?" Thomas wondered.

He saw the movement again, but it was moving away. Thomas thought the casual cadence in the steps wasn't normal for a person charged with adrenaline or fear. "The second man obviously didn't know there was a problem, but the man's care in staying out of sight behind the trees," Thomas thought, "belied his true intentions."

Staying low and moving from bush to bush next to the wall, Thomas made it to the end closest to the street. Before standing up, he set the safety on the Luger, pushed his overcoat aside, and stuffed the gun down his waistband at the back. It wasn't comfortable.

With a hand on the stonework, he pulled himself up and looked to the other side of the clearing. There was nothing. He looked back toward the feet beneath the tree. They were gone. Thomas wasn't sure it was safe, but he had to vacate the green, cross the street and blend into the people milling about the neighborhood houses and shops. Between the end of the wall and the street, there was another tall tree next to the sidewalk. Its sizable trunk would be his next cover. He started toward the tree, and the bark exploded next to his face when he arrived. Hitting the wet ground, he rolled to the side of the trunk, opposite the impact on the tree.

The position almost placed his feet into the road. "This is bad cover," he thought, reaching back for the gun. Thomas knew he was too exposed and needed to get back behind the wall. He surveyed everything in sight and listened with complete concentration. However, the only noise was the strained sounds of a car pushed to its limits, combined with the sound of terribly abused tires. Still lying on the ground, he turned half over to look toward the nearing commotion. His body stiffened in stark terror as, over the tops of his shoes, he could see a smoking vehicle headed at full speed in his direction. He thought about rolling out of the way, but there was too little time to react. The Austin hit the curb, and the door flew open.

"*Get in,*" the driver yelled. "Thomas, get in!"

It was—Margaret?

He got up and stepped toward the car. Just as he got a leg in, a shot careened off the car roof, just above the window molding.

"*Go!*" he yelled.

"Where?" she said, slamming the pedal with him half in the car.

"Anywhere," Thomas shouted, pointing a finger away from the direction of the shots, fully expecting another to come right through the window. Trying to get low, he slid down in the seat as his knees slammed into the dash. "Argh…. God, that hurt," he said, yanking the door closed.

"Hurt? You could be dead right now," Margaret said, fighting the wheel and jamming the shift lever into the next gear. "Fine bit of pitch you found, Mr. Watson."

From a distance, a figure in the shadows watched Thomas enter the vehicle. Then the figure looked over to the man lying in the park out cold. Angrily, he pulled out the orange pack and lit a cigarette. Sirens were blaring; Bletchley security was making their way to the park. It all meant he wasn't happy. They'd arrest the man still on the ground, but he didn't care. He pulled away, knowing next time would be a more significant challenge. Watson was now in the wind.

"What in bloody hell are you doing here?" Thomas said. "How did you find me?"

"Actually, I thought I was hopelessly lost following some impossible directions. Then I see you run across a park, fall on the ground and pull a gun out. What was I supposed to do?"

"I would say my directions were spot on, wouldn't you, dearie?" a voice said from the back seat.

Thomas turned. "Mrs. Somerville, what … what're *you* doing here?"

"What do you mean, what am I doing here? After all, it's my car."

"I mean, what're both of you doing here—never mind," he said, grabbing the door pull as Margaret managed a twenty mph corner at forty-five.

Immersed in driving and without looking at Thomas, Margaret said, "The Russian called after you left. He wanted to know where you'd gone and urgently needed to talk to you. I said you weren't available, and he asked if you went to Bletchley. It startled me that he would know. He must have heard us talking. I think he picked it up in my voice because the next second, he was gone. He might have been the one trying to shoot at you, although he said he wanted to help. He said it a couple of times. I didn't believe him."

Thomas thought about Yuri's jacket on the table this morning, his comment about guns, and his being a diplomat. "I really don't think it was him."

"It's strange," he thought, as the man also told him he wanted to help, but Thomas couldn't meet his terms.

"Thomas, why would someone be shooting at you? It shows that I shouldn't have let you go alone. That's it; I'm never letting you out of my sight as I'm responsible for at least part of this mess."

"Margaret, we can talk about that later. Right now, we need to get out of here. We definitely can't go back home. We must assume they have ministry contacts to trace the number plate."

"Not possible," said the voice in the back seat.

"Why not?"

"Because, when Margaret called this morning, I had my friend Vernon Bartlett take them off and replace them with an old set Charles had nailed up on the garage wall. Poor Mr. Bartlett, he'll do absolutely anything for a female."

"Anything?" Margaret asked.

"My heavens, woman, he also does what I ask him *not* to do. Besides, isn't this exciting?" Mrs. Somerville said, clutching her purse and bouncing it on her lap. "I haven't had this much excitement since Charles and I were at that little inn by the coast and... ah... well. Oh, Charles," she said, addressing someone with that certain twinkle. "May God bless your lovely soul."

"I'm going to take us to Mother's. Her house has a security detail, and she's on the Home Guards watch list," Margaret said, turning the car onto the main road. Thomas's racing mind was returning to normal. As Margaret increased speed, the air whistled through the bullet hole in the roof. With it, Thomas realized that he still held the Luger. He held it up and looked at it.

"Thomas, where on earth did you get that?" Margaret said, looking at the gun. "Please put it away; it's scaring me."

Still looking at the gun, Thomas said, "Actually, merely knowing what it *is* surprises me, and the fact that I know how to use it is beyond my comprehension right now. Besides, again, what're you two doing here?"

"Thomas, I'm a schoolteacher, not a criminal, and didn't have a clue what I was going to do when I got here. Nevertheless, I thought there would be trouble after the Russian rang off. That will teach you to leave me behind."

"Well, now, Margaret, you sound a lot like me trying to figure out why I know what I know."

"It must be contagious," she said. After a short silence, she looked over. "Thomas, you couldn't gotten hurt. If you loved me, you wouldn't be taking such chances, people shooting, and bullets flying."

"Loving you would be wonderful if you could just figure out why you had to be here. Then perhaps I would know why I know what I know."

"Blast you, Thomas Watson. You're not doing yourself any favors, if you know what I mean," Margaret said, trying to suppress a smile.

"I know what she means," said the voice in the back.

Thomas said, "The favor I need right now is for you to take me to the Crown Inn, but I think we should drop off Mrs. Somerville at the station."

" 'Fraid not, Professor. It's my car, and there ..."

Interrupting her, Thomas said, "Mrs. Somerville, I must insist. By now, you must have figured out that some people wish me harm, and there should be some concern for those around me. Also, I have to meet someone at the Crown Inn, and I'm unsure how long it will take."

Mrs. Somerville was buttoning the top button of her coat as if completely ignoring Thomas and said, "Do you happen to know where the Crown Inn might be located?"

Thomas gave Margaret a questioning look, and she shrugged and shook her head. He turned to the back seat, where Mrs. Somerville continued to button her coat.

In her own time, she said, "Well, that's it. I suggest we turn around, as I can assure you it's quite fruitless to venture further in this direction."

"Mrs. Somerville?" Thomas said in the raised tone of a parent.

"Mr. Watson?" she quickly replied, in a tone slightly higher.

Thomas knew he wasn't going to win this battle. "Okay, but the both of you can't be with me at the inn. You'll need to go and come back after my talk with a man. I'm not sure when he can get there. Actually, I don't know if he's coming, so we may have to wait a while."

Mrs. Somerville smiled the satisfied smile of the victor as she said, "Margaret, turn left at Addison Road. It's not the direct route that someone might expect."

Thomas looked in the back seat with a question on his face. Mrs. Somerville, cool as a cucumber, frail as a lark, looked at him and raised her eyebrows, saying, "Couldn't hurt."

Chapter Thirty-Eight
Bletchley
Common

Yuri's mind was racing as he'd placed very little hope in Devin and his ability or inclination to get his message to Thomas. He was nevertheless astounded to hear the alarm. Having made his way to a corner across from the common, he stepped into a bus stop shelter. He wanted to assess what form the alert would take. As he did, he saw Watson drop to the ground behind a tree, then jump into a car. A man was lying on the walkway near the archway, and he saw another man's back running down a street. Seconds later, the park started filling with Bletchley security personnel, and he didn't want to explain his presence.

He rushed back to the station, hoping to get there before Bletchley security could shut the stop down. He needed to avoid scrutiny before boarding. Slowing as he approached the station's shelter building, Yuri casually crossed the platform and grabbed the handle on the coach, pulling himself into the entrance. He walked down the car aisle, looking through the glass before sliding back a door to an empty compartment and entering it. Yuri was grateful he'd purchased roundtrip tickets.

Almost immediately, the platform started to slip slowly past the window just as two uniformed men came into view looking for Watson. One was running and waving an arm; the other grabbed the stationmaster. The stationmaster reacted by grabbing the wrist of the security person and throwing it off. It was obvious; the guard wanted the man to stop the train. The master's cap was shaking no as he pointed at one of the two large station clocks atop ornate iron poles.

He wouldn't stop a well-underway train on a continent that evaluated societies based on their efficiency of meeting train schedules.

A train held before being underway was an entirely different matter. Additional security arrived, and as the scene moved from Yuri's view, he could see they were still arguing. They'd call ahead to the next station, but whoever was there would have to rely on a verbal description of Thomas, now a wanted man.

Yuri was staring at the empty seat across from him. What a mess, he said to himself. Was the shooting a British operation? No, that didn't add up. They already had Watson in custody, and he was worth more alive than dead. No, it was not the British. The directive to kill Watson could only have come down from Russian security. Shooting Thomas was a job originally given to him by Moscow, and now, it would appear attempted by someone else. Was it a rogue Russian agent? Could it be a backup effort, making sure he got the job done?

This was a demonstration of brute force. Back home in Russia, where one grows up enduring the lethal power of the weather, woven into the psyche of every Russian is the concept of brute force. This attack was brute force, delivered as unprofessionally as Yuri had ever witnessed. A cobbled operation with expendable underlings directed from the shadows. Who was it? Did it matter? Except they might assassinate the wrong man, and Yuri had no reasonable explanation for why that could be true.

One thing he knew for sure, things were out of control, and Yuri's instincts were on edge. If he couldn't detect an observable pattern of today's events, he needed to disappear, for his own safety. However, the other thing he knew for sure was if Thomas was in danger, so was his wife, Margaret. If there was still time to act on it, Yuri had come to a decision. He needed some critical information and knew exactly where to get it.

Chapter Thirty-Nine

Crown Inn
Milton Keynes

"That's it there," Thomas said, pointing to the upcoming two-story brick building directly across from another village common. The Crown Inn was straight down Shendly Brook, originating as Bletchley Lane inside the government compound. Built in 1850, it initially had an addition on the left side that served as the village butcher shop. The shop had long been gone, and the structure now housed several flats, one of which Turing rented. The first floor gave residence to the Burnt Oak pub, which featured a large pour and the largest snooker table in the village.

Thomas stared out of the car as he visualized the chaotic scene at Bletchley. He winced in hindsight at how ridiculous and pathetic it must have looked to Turing, watching Thomas being dragged down the hall by armed guards. Thomas knew his detailed knowledge of the project had genuinely intrigued the scientist, but it also made him a wanted man. He should have expected the situation after being warned of crossing the line. Given any other options, Thomas certainly wouldn't have tried it, but, as they say, that was then, and this is now.

Margaret casually pulled around to the rear as if they were going to book in for the night. It also put the car out of direct sight of the street.

"What now?" Margaret asked as she pulled into an empty parking space alongside a huge red Lagonda, the required transportation of every successful country solicitor. Thomas looked down at the bright wire wheels that were simply too shiny. He thought, "It must be nice to have enough money that such details are completed by others and disappear in a wealthy person's life."

In the silence not filled by his reply, Mrs. Somerville leaned forward, looked directly at Thomas, and said, "I could use a cup—anyone?"

"Mrs. Somerville, this is no time for tea! I've made us all enemies of the state, and such normal pleasures have gone the bye."

"Mr. Watson, I would guess that you would be far less obvious if two ladies for tea accompanied you, especially if one looked like your mother. Besides, I'm dreadfully dry," she said, tapping the top of his seat. "Door, please."

"Thomas, I think she's right. We can move to another table or go for a walk when the man arrives."

With the day's stress evident in his voice, Thomas said, "Even though I'm putting both of you in danger, you're completely ignoring any of my attempts to keep you safe."

Mrs. Somerville turned to Margaret and said, "He's quite quick off the mark, isn't he?"

Margaret put her hand on his arm, "Thomas, it doesn't have to be all on your shoulders. We're not looking to be in danger, but if we can help in the least, we want to try."

From the backseat came, "You can add me to the list. More to the point, besides keeping you alive, what's this little adventure anyway?"

Resigned, Thomas gave in to the women and, upon entering the pub, surveyed the room, although he wasn't sure why. Given the time of day, it was close to empty, except for a pair of sharply dressed gentlemen pouring over stacks of paper higher than a pint. Choosing a table on the far side of the room, they all sat down. The waitress came over and said, "I know it's a bit chilly, but we've got a distributor special on Pimm's No 1."

Thomas felt like ordering one to help settle him down after the events of the last few hours but decided his wits were more important than indulging his need for a drink. Then the waitress looked to the barkeep and said, "Arthur, couldn't this be the gent Alan was talking about?"

A man with three clean mugs in each hand looked over and said, "Are you a Mr. Dunning?"

"Yes ... yes, I am."

Margaret looked quizzically at Thomas but didn't say anything.

Arthur walked around the bar and over to the table. Leaning over, in a low voice, he said, "Alan Turing is a close friend of my family. He phoned and asked me to ring him up if you chanced to arrive."

With evident relief, Thomas looked up and said, "Please, yes, if you could, I would be in your debt."

The man's friendly smile broadened, revealing a pronounced gap. "Come with me," the man said, waving over his shoulder to the bar. "You can have a word for yourself," he said, weaving between the tables and arriving at a small shelf protruding from the wall. "It's the only phone for all the rooms an' me business, so ya can't be long."

Arthur grabbed a note in his pocket, looked at it, and picked up the phone. After waiting a bit, he said, "Ellen, yes, Wellington 4397, please, an' there's a drink in it for ya to not put it on your log."

Thomas could hear the other person speak but couldn't make out anything specific except laughter.

Arthur said, "Ellen Bromley, I have me reasons an' I better not 'ear it comin' 'round or there be 'ell to pay."

The owner looked up at Thomas, rolling his eyes with impatience. Then breaking the look and staring intensely at the base of the phone, he said, "No, you're not going to get a short room let, neither. No, get me the number before I call your Mum about this nonsense."

After a few seconds, he handed the phone to Thomas and shook his head. "In me job, there's a lot to be known in a small village."

Thomas heard a ring, followed by a pickup and a voice. "Hello, Alan Turing here."

"Alan, this is," Thomas thought for a moment and decided to handle that issue later, "Mr. Dunning. Are you alone?"

"Great God," Alan said loudly, surprising himself. Then, in a much quieter voice, he asked, "Are you alright? Were you hurt?"

"No, by the narrowest of margins, I managed to avoid someone's attempt on my life. The last one today, I hope."

Turing said, "I can assure you, it wasn't the British, but I'm dumbfounded about who it could've been. You couldn't be mixed up in something, could you? Actually, from what you said, you could be of interest to any number of unidentified factions. None of them good chaps, I suppose, and not very visible. Anyway, our ... our conversation was rather odd but fascinating." Alan looked around his small, rarely used Bletchley office and, stretching the phone cord, walked over and closed the door.

"Well, they're certainly visible today," Thomas said. "They shot a hole in the car that got me out of there."

"At least you're all right. Where are you? Security is very unhappy at the compound, with talk of heads rolling and careers dropping off the map. They've poured all over the huts and surrounding neighborhood like ants looking for food."

"Believe me; it's not how I wanted to start my day. I'm at the Crown Inn," Thomas said.

"Well, splendid, that takes care of a lot we don't have to go into now. Are you parked 'round back?"

"Yes," Thomas said. "We've been here just a bit."

"Well, stay inside. I have a car and can be there in just a few, but we won't have much time. Are we all set then?"

"Yes, I would like to finish some of the things we discussed, including asking for your help," Thomas said.

"Don't know about that, as I said, but I would love to chat about the other items if we could. I'm on my way."

Chapter Forty

Crown Inn
Milton Keyes

Alan Turing emerged from the back near the kitchen and walked directly over to the table where Thomas was sitting alone. Margaret and Mrs. Somerville had taken a seat a few tables over, but that's as far as Mrs. Somerville would go.

Thomas stood up, offered his hand to Turing, then nodded to the women, saying, "My protective contingent. I think it's best they not be introduced."

"Of course, of course." Turing smiled directly at Margaret and, nodding, said, "Ladies."

Turing was nervous and a bit on edge as he removed his gloves. "I live here, you see, and came in a back way."

"I know," Thomas said. "That's why I chose this place."

Alan looked at him with almost deep concern, a look Thomas was starting to recognize. Actually, he had his own concerns about how comfortable it felt. Turing unconsciously moved his hat on the table as if wondering if this was worth the risk.

"I gave it some thought," Turing said, "about the danger of coming over here, but determined, with the invasion and increased bombing, well, the whole lot is on the line, is it not? However, I can't for the life of me figure out how you could possibly have all this information. Not knowing where I live, but the other, the technical pieces."

"As you said, we don't have much time," Thomas said, looking over at the other table, "and I don't want to put anyone else in harm's way if I can help it, so let me get right to it. I provided the information to win your trust, but now I realize it was more than clumsy. As you said, some of it only you would know. As to the source, that's a little more complicated, but if it can help win the war …"

"That's why I'm taking this chance," Turing said. "People's lives are on the line. One promptly deciphered message could save a ship and its crew."

Thomas was anxious to get beyond the issue of Turing's trust and how the man could help. "As to the other, I need help in delivering equally important information that will be of benefit to the prime minister and the country—our country." Thomas felt the last two words hover on his tongue. "All I need is ten minutes."

"As I said, Whitehall doesn't know I exist, and so it hinders any influence. Well, let's be honest. I've no influence. I've only met Churchill twice, and each time in a crowded room with others. That doesn't mean I won't try, but I want to be deadly honest."

"An interesting choice of words," Thomas said. Alan Turing smiled; he took his first full breath since they sat down. Thomas took measure of the man in front of him. "I think you might be surprised by the visibility and admiration you engender now and later. Unfortunately, your work is so advanced and important that public recognition won't be forthcoming soon. It will remain classified and unknown until well after the war."

"Recognition isn't at all what I'm about. My heaven is to return to university and bury myself in some pure research." Turing looked off to the side into mental space. "Oh, yes, I have a question. What did you mean by 'keep on it even if I think it will drive me crazy?'"

"Nothing, actually. Perhaps a reference to the fact that not a purely new thought has emerged that the church didn't call the thinker a heretic at the very least and mad at the worst. It might account for the fact that Newton didn't reveal his discovery of calculus for ten years and then only just before someone else was going to make the claim."

Both men laughed.

"Perhaps it's you that has run afoul of the church," Turing said. "What you've been saying is hard to understand. I mean, you talk as though we're in the past and providing information from the future. This would be most distressing to men of the cloth. However, I've chosen to put that aside for now, as what you're saying is so intriguing. I've already spoken with my staff, and they immediately realized the importance of the idea. My most gifted engineer started talking faster than I could listen and said he had to get off the phone to try something. I have some marvelous people on this project, but I think they're tired of the constant pressure resulting from the speed issue."

Thomas put both hands in front of him flat on the table. "So we arrive at the Bombe, your wonderful machine. As I indicated at Bletchley, it all comes down to an ability to modify the machine quickly to match the day's encoding wheels. After the patch settings are entered into the machine, your basic setup to handle data is functioning. At least that's how I remember it." Thomas realized what he'd said.

True to his word, Turing ignored the comment, saying, "We've known that's the problem, but several modifications, including the faster electrical switches, were only marginally effective."

Thomas then realized there was something he didn't know. "Can you resolve the wheel combination as soon as the Germans make the change?"

"Yes," Turing said. "I designed a mechanical logic engine that manually plows through combinations using brute force and the exclusionary scheme you referred to at Bletchley to arrive at the day's disk settings. It's rather slow because it looks at the combination for each disk, but it's effective. Again, we're back to, what did you call it, programming?"

Thomas could feel the escalating pace of their conversation. "I mentioned an optical reader. It's actually an array of optical or light-sensitive switches. Have those been invented yet?" Thomas knew he'd done it again.

Turing also knew but stayed the course. "Yes, they're vacuum photo electrics. Professor Reginald Jones delivered a classified paper to the war scientific group that suggested they might be working with them over at the Clarendon Laboratory at Oxford. They're trying to use them in ..." and he stopped.

"RDF or radar, as the Americans call it," Thomas finished Turing's sentence.

Turing sat back, startled. "You can't say that, let alone know about it. Other than what I'm working on, it has the highest security clearance requirement in all of England. It's bloody easier to steal the crown jewels from the Tower than getting information on that project."

Thomas's voice turned strong, "Ignore why and concentrate on how. You must obtain these optical sensors and set them in an array four across, sitting perpendicular to the punched tape running along underneath. I can't remember how big the optical switches are, but I'm sure you can adjust the tape's width to fit, stagger them, or use lenses. I think you can get them in under an inch, but it won't matter. What's the output of the logic engine?"

Turing said, "The switch settings for the day's wheel combination."

Patiently, Thomas said, "Yes, is it paper, physical settings, lights?"

"Oh, paper from a teletype machine, listing each switch and its setting."

"Great," Thomas said. "Then dismantle the teletype and, using just the mechanism driving the keys, create a mechanical way to punch the tape in the same switch sequence using a binary code. It will take a bit of rigging, but I'm sure it can be done."

Thomas stopped for a second as he wondered where this conversation was going. He started to feel strange—it was nothing he could describe to another person other than saying it was like the lightness you feel with a pint on an empty stomach.

"I just got it," Turing said quite loudly as if hit by a surprise thought. "All too often, things are simple once they're known. Did you know we double-wired the manual front patch panel to be fully accessible from the back? No, it was the other way around?"

Thomas shook his head, "No."

"It's due to a failure. Eventually, we decided that the time required to install a full switch panel would have to be paid. As a result of what was an expensive disappointment, we might have the answer, and it's much simpler than some of the things we've tried."

Turing tried to stand up but then sat down in a mindless need to express what was going faster through his brain than he could convey. It appeared he expressed deep thought or excitement with constant movement.

"Mr. Dunning, we can take the signal generated by the tape running over the light switches and run it through a conversion board where each signal is amplified with enough current to trip the relays that set the drums. It will be ugly and messy, but it can be done quickly. We can then bypass the front patch panel," he said, waving his arm in the air simulating the wires going from the front to the back, "by feeding it directly into the front patch circuit, but from the rear. Each front panel switch will be set to a neutral state and, being passive, will recognize only the signal fed from the amplifier board into the existing connection terminals, resulting from our previously failed experiment."

Thomas's face went blank. "I'm not sure I quite have what you're saying."

"It's okay, as the rework is relatively minor, so it shouldn't take long. With your tape idea, we go from teams of our girls manually setting the patch positions by looking at each line on a hundred sheets of paper to a direct electrical setting, which is almost instantaneous. Eventually, we could build and connect several logic engines together to decrease the time to resolve the day's wheel setup, each resolving for a specific disk."

Thomas realized why he didn't know where the rest of the conversation was going. Turing was providing it. Thomas held both hands up to get his attention and said, "Mr. Turing, Alan."

Turing absentmindedly turned to look at Thomas as if he'd just discovered him sitting right across the table. "Yes, yes, I'm sorry, did you want to …?" He quickly grabbed his hat, missing it the first time, and stood up, ready to leave.

"I really must get back to Bletchley." Today has certainly been interesting. Historic perhaps." It was time for my semiweekly beating over the head by the committee managers for failing to meet all but the most important milestone. The committee actually wants the machine to work. I'm afraid it has become a regular ritual." Then, with a beaming face and both hands in the air, one holding his hat, he said, "At least until today."

"You're there then?" Thomas said.

"I sure think so, and we can have it in full operation well before the next beating, which would be more than welcome." Turing paused before continuing. "You said some mighty interesting stuff today before being whisked off."

"Do I remember correctly, your first Bombe went online this month?"

"Well, yes, but in a few days. You said 'remembered.' It's quite a trick to remember something that hasn't yet made it into the world."

Thomas didn't want the subject to change. He needed to get Turing back on his agenda. "Ah, it appears to be a peculiar knack I have, but I must admit it can cause some concerns."

"I'm sorry to press, my good man, but how do you do it?"

"Not sure, really. The information is just there. As you pointed out, the one factor is the feeling I'm recounting the past, not foretelling the future." Thomas sat back.

Turing said, "Throwing everything we know about the world aside, it would mean you came from the future to pay us a visit."

"Perhaps," Thomas said, "but how or why?"

"That's easy," Turing said, "to tell me I need to use an optical reader just when they were losing interest in my being able to speed up the machine. Some want to use great rooms filled with hoards of women crunching away on mechanical calculators. Most aren't comfortable with a little electrical, or mechanical assistance to thinking, although it's perfectly all right to use a block and tackle when loading a ship. Perhaps you were chosen to spread the word?"

Thomas was pensive. "I do know one thing, the war is going badly right now, and it's going to get worse. Some on the war cabinet might try to force surrender."

Turing became somber. "Will they? Surrender, I mean?"

"No. I mean, I don't think so. I can't be sure, and that's why I need your help."

"Oh, yes," Turing said. "There's that Whitehall thing. See here, I promise to do everything I can to get you an audience with someone high up, but I can't hold out any hope for the prime minister. As I said, I'm afraid I'm just a scientist and not highly regarded right now."

Thomas also stood up, "You'll make the calls?"

"Yes, you have my word. Right after I set my staff."

"Please remember, I don't have much time. How will I contact you?" Thomas said.

"That could be a problem as there are no outside phones where I'm headed. All calls must be routed through a special exchange. Besides, Bletchley denies I exist, let alone forwards my messages."

Turing dropped his head in thought, then brought it up, saying, "I'll manage to find a phone somewhere and leave a message with Arthur. You can call the inn. Yes, that's it. The message might be a little cryptic, but I call in frequently, so it shouldn't arouse special attention."

Thomas offered his hand and said, "Then good luck to you, Alan, as I know you'll be successful, although you left me a bit pale at the last part."

Turing grabbed Thomas's hand; in his other hand, he held his hat with his thumb slightly folding the brim. "I know why you told me these things, but the larger canvas is how. For whatever the reason, you've ventured into a part of thinking beyond the comprehension of reasonable men."

Thomas studied the man and said, "Well, Mr. Turing, are you calling me crazy or a heretic?"

Both men laughed. Thomas continued, "Alan, I don't like being shot at or my family being put in danger. The easier road was to stay silent. But, as you said, the whole lot, England and Empire, is on the line."

Turing offered a pained smile, snuggled the fedora over the top of his unruly hair, and turned toward the rear of the room, stopping to say, "Get to somewhere safe, preferably not around here."

Thomas nodded. Turing had one glove on as he opened the kitchen door and disappeared.

"Thomas?" Margaret said from behind him. "We heard most of it. Do you think it will work?"

Mrs. Somerville put a hand on Margaret's elbow and said, "Kitten, we don't have a lot of cards, and there's no use holding them to your chest. Mr. Watson, I thought you did a marvelous job."

With the word Watson, Thomas stiffened. "Damn it all. Turing still knows me as Dunning."

"Who's Dunning?" Margaret said.

Thomas dashed to the door at the back of the room where Turing had disappeared. He opened it to the car park, observing in frustration, what must have been Turing's car turning onto the street from behind the inn. Thomas shouted and waved his arms to no avail.

"He's going to try to make an appointment for Dunning, a wanted man," Thomas thought and said to himself, "It's all for naught."

Standing alone in the car park behind the Crown Inn, Thomas thought of the young marine shot on his account. They'd be looking very hard for him right now, and Turing was right; he, Margaret, and Mrs. Somerville had to leave the inn.

Outside, the women appeared from behind. Thomas turned to them and said, "I think we have no choice but to hide out and play that last card at Margaret's mother's house. Most assuredly, there's watching Margaret's house, so it's not safe to go back there."

"That's our house," Margaret said.

"I knew that," Thomas said.

"Right, just making sure," she said, giving a strong tug on his coat sleeve.

Thomas looked at Mrs. Somerville, "As to your safety, I think you're fine. However, if you hadn't insisted on coming along, there wouldn't even be the chance of someone knowing you're involved."

"Thomas, dear," Mrs. Somerville shot back, "we've been over this before, and I think my contribution has exceeded any detriment I might have created."

"I can't argue that," Thomas said, "but you still put yourself in danger, and that's my concern and responsibility."

"Perhaps," she replied, "it was the danger that was equally *my* concern."

Thomas gave her a curious look.

"Thomas, she meant me being in danger," Margaret said. "She was concerned for me."

Very satisfied, Mrs. Somerville said, "Well, why does it always appear the same person has a head on their shoulders?"

Thomas's tone changed at the comment. "I'm concerned for you, that's all. I don't see why that's so bad."

Mrs. Somerville looked at Thomas and sensed the note of frustration in his voice. It had been a long day for all of them, especially him.

She said, "If I might say so, Mr. Watson, up until a few nights ago, I wouldn't have given a tuppence for your neck, but events have taken a course that's, to put it mildly, rather strange. It's a bit like you were switched at birth, but it happened to you as an adult. However, despite the odd situation, I'm very grateful that you've included me in your concern," she said, "very grateful."

Thomas also sensed the new direction the conversation had suddenly gone. "Look, Mrs. Somerville, that was a bit over the top on my part."

"Don't apologize to me, young man; I can take you out in a second." The line would have worked if she hadn't been laughing at the end of it. "In any event, may I suggest we drop me off at a cab stand?"

Both Margaret and Thomas looked at her.

"It's rather simple," Mrs. Somerville explained. "You two need the car, and many a night, I've arrived by cab as I don't drive, and I don't like taking the tube when it's late. This won't raise any suspicion, but I'm afraid all hell will break loose if you two come flying up trying to dump me off at my house. I'm afraid your days in my little flat are over."

"She has a point," Margaret said. "They'll be watching, whoever they are."

"I know it isn't the British that tried to kill me," Thomas said, "but they're uncomfortable with what I told them. There's no doubt that they'd like to continue our little conversation. The good thing about all of this is that they're looking for a person named Dunning. Only the people at Bletchley could identify me. The problem is, whoever tried to kill me knows what I look like, and I presume they're Russian, based on what that man Yuri had to say this morning."

Margaret moved close to Thomas and slipped her arm inside his, looked up at him, and gently said, "Thomas, Mr. Turing was right. We need to leave."

Thomas looked at her, recalling the chaos of the day. He reached out and pulled her close in a long deep embrace. "I'm sorry, Margaret; I never meant to create this mess." Then with hands on both of her shoulders, he squeezed gently and said, "I love you." She went right up on her toes, flung her arms around his neck, and kissed him, lifting her feet from the ground.

Mrs. Somerville looked at the two of them with pangs of envy.

"Are you busy later?" Thomas said.

Mrs. Somerville clapped her hands together, saying, "For God's sake, you two, set a mind to it and stop playing like you're teenagers in heat."

"Jealous, Mrs. Somerville?" Thomas raised his eyebrows.

Mrs. Somerville shot Thomas a look, "Absolutely not, Mr. Watson," she said. "It's just that it's time we get out of here, and there's a time and place for everything. With that, she glanced at Thomas and, with her mischievous smile, said to Margaret, "You never told me about your day on the picnic, and, yes, I could be jealous."

Chapter Forty-One

Turing's Lab
Bletchley Park

Leaving the Crown Inn, Alan Turing turned left off the street and drove towards Hut 8. Huts 3 and 6 also played a large role in the decoding but Hut 8 was where his office was located.

Gathering his things off the front seat, he proceeded quickly toward a side door labeled "Administration Offices Employees Only." Turing opened the door. To his left sat an attractive young girl, smartly dressed, with impeccable manners and perfectly combed dark brown hair. On one side of her desk was a large pile of papers she was trying to keep stacked and not sliding off down to the floor.

She looked up and smiled, saying, "Hello, sir," avoiding using names as instructed. Turing nodded while taking off his hat.

As Turing walked into his office he was met by Gordon Welchman, another Cambridge mathematician recruited for the task.

Turing said, "Gordon, look, I'm dreadfully sorry about my phone call. Looking back, I see it was mostly devoid of any value."

Gordon laughed, "Oh, I wouldn't say that. I haven't heard you so excited in a long time, and all it did was rub off on us. Your conversation sparked a few ideas we've been working on, and I had the lads clear their desks and minds because, I told them, whatever was coming would require our full attention.

"Gordon," Turing started, "I'm not sure it required quite that much drama."

"No, Alan," Gordon said, still chuckling, "you wouldn't."

"Fair enough. We've a lot of work to do, but I must make a phone call to keep my part of a bargain. After that, I'll be right out to terrorize the troops. It's an amazing story. I can't wait for you to hear it."

Reaching for his notebook, he unearthed the number to Churchill's office. Churchill once gave it to him, saying he wanted any pertinent information forwarded directly. Turing was under no illusions that this call might be a meaningless exercise. Nonetheless, he'd committed.

The double ring emanated from the handset for a long time. Finally, a shiny young voice answered, promising to relay the request if he would hold. Not one to tolerate idle time, Turing noted on a pad the instructions he would give his team.

One of the file clerks who had just started and whose turn it was to work the phones walked up to Colville's desk and, without knowing anything about who called, said a man wanted to talk to Mr. Churchill. Colville was annoyed and irritated. Completely ignoring the clerk, he stood up and shouted, "Mrs. Nell, I've a situation that needs your attention immediately."

Mrs. Nell was halfway to Colville's desk when Colville, vigorously pointed toward the clerk. He said, "Would you be so kind as to tell this young lady that a large majority of the people on the planet would like to talk to the prime minister, and her job is to stave off—well, all of them."

Mrs. Nell reached for the slip of paper in the trembling hand of the clerk and addressed Colville in her usual calm manner. "As usual, you're so right, Mr. Colville. I'll certainly proceed to have someone give Miss Denton the orientation we didn't have time to give her this morning, as she started on one of your assignments straight away."

The clerk froze in her tracks at the equivalent of attention. Even though it was her first day, and she was utterly ignorant of the office dynamics, she instinctively knew she'd landed right between the two political powers of the department. She was equally unaware that each executed their course of work with radically different demeanors.

Colville's resembled a bird that had mistakenly flown into the office, dive-bombing everyone and creating panic and bewildering moments of fear. This turbulent period was followed by calm, when it would perch on a rafter, only to start again. In contrast, Mrs. Nell was as composed as a mountain. Known as an unmovable force, she would proficiently implement her duties. And she would do so, disregarding any distracting hysterics.

Addressing the somewhat shaken person to her left, she softly said, "Ms. Denton, if I may have a word at your desk, please put the call through. I'll be over there shortly."

Ms. Denton jumped at the opportunity to remove herself from the crossfire. Mrs. Nell watched the clerk half run to her desk and waited the exact amount of time. Then, with a smile, she quietly said to Colville, "How right you are at the interruption, a situation we can address. Nonetheless, some of the people on the planet *do* get through."

At that moment, the forwarded call rang beneath Colville's hand resting on the receiver. It caused him to flinch slightly. Ms. Nell lifted her eyebrows and held up the clerk's note saying, "And Dr. Turing is one of them."

Colville stared at the woman whose crossed arms emphasized the effect of being deftly handled and knowing it was far from the first time. He exhaled deeply as his chair tilted back and, presenting a face of reconciliation, offered, "You're so right, Ms. Nell, and I thank you for your assistance."

Knowing she'd won the day but not wanting to demonstrate the slightest sign of improper decorum, she said, "You're most welcome, Mr. Colville."

Chapter Forty-Two

Turing's Office
Bletchley Park

Turing sitting at this desk had his left elbow holding the pad steady. Turing was on the fourth item, forgetting he was waiting on hold to Churchill's office.

"Dr. Turing, how are you today?" Colville said. "We don't get to speak often."

"True enough," Turing said, returning the phone call he'd placed. "As you know, we're trying to keep a low profile over here until we have redeeming news." Turing thought he would take a shot that had little possibility of success. "Is it possible that I could speak with the prime minister? I've, not redeeming, but very intriguing information."

"Unfortunately, he's in a meeting with Lord Beaverbrook, and they're planning on lunching in. Can I help with a return call?"

Turing thought momentarily about his promise and his deep desire to get started on his list. "I think that a message might do if you would. This morning at Bletchley, I chanced to have a most unusual conversation with a Mr. Dunning. The short of it is he demonstrated knowledge of my project and perhaps provided breakthrough information in the most detailed form. Curiously, it wasn't just that he knew our secrets, but he imparted new information that would instantly become new secrets. Sorry, a bit confusing, I'm afraid."

Jock Colville, writing everything down, stopped.

Turing resumed. "I know it's unusual, at the very least, and actually very disturbing if it weren't for the fact he was spot on in his recommendations." Bending the truth slightly, he continued, "In that conversation, he made it plain that the information he provided was only a way to enlist my help in providing even more important information directly to the prime minister. This new data doesn't concern my work, but he insisted it was timely and of the utmost importance in the war effort. He made me swear to do what I could to get him an audience with Mr. Churchill so that he could tell his story. I wouldn't be making this call, but given the caliber of the material we discussed, I'm given to try my best."

Colville looked down at where he'd stopped writing, "Just what do you want me to put down as a subject of the call or meeting? That an unknown private citizen wishes to convey to the highest authority secrets that don't yet exist? Doctor, in all due respect, how do I handle this?"

"Mr. Colville, I know my stock isn't high within the administration. Knowing that, I'm still willing to risk whatever influence I can bring to bear so that this man is taken seriously, or at the least given a chance to make a fool of us both."

After a brief silence from both men, Turing said, "Alright then. I acknowledge the uncomfortable nature of any message. Given that, I'll handle it myself in a meeting if you will. I also have means at my disposal and will take full responsibility."

Colville was unsure what to make of this strange conversation or how Turing would handle it himself, so he said, "Very well, doctor, I'll be back and hopefully we will see you tomorrow."

"Thanks," Turing said quietly and hung up.

Turing thought for a moment. It wasn't as if he was comfortable with any of this. He employed the best minds in an uncertain and emerging field on an almost unlimited budget. The team's extensive efforts had produced truly ground-breaking science, but not good enough. They faced the age-old problem of transforming it into a practical product.

They'd been digging and digging in the same hole to find the prize, and then, out of nowhere, a stranger appeared, dug a completely new hole, and found the magic box. The stranger did it by putting together solutions with information known only to Turing and his team, some known only to himself, and some not known at all. His group had the pieces, but Dunning came in and rearranged them into something more significant than the sum of those parts. Why would he do that, knowing the British wouldn't look on it favorably? They'd need to find out the origin of the knowledge, so harming him wasn't in the cards, but certainly, he was to be detained. Even stranger, Turing received this revelation in a chance meeting during one of the rare occasions he was actually at Bletchley, dutifully getting dressed down on those very problems.

Chapter Forty-Three

Milton Keynes

Looking to return Mrs. Somerville home, the group arrived at the taxi stand at the top of High Street in Milton Keynes. There a fare was certain from all the restaurants and shops. Thomas helped Mrs. Somerville out of the Austin and said, "Just not sure what's going to come about and not sure when we can get back to you."

"Then let me stay, so I don't miss any of the action," she replied.

Margaret gave Mrs. Somerville a tender smile.

"Oh," said the older woman, as she giggled. "I wasn't born yesterday. Besides don't you worry," she said, pointing to the purse tucked high under her arm. "I can take care of myself. This purse looks harmless enough, but it's a lethal weapon, and there are moves I haven't even shown you yet."

Thomas laughed. "Then it's a good thing I eventually started to grow on you."

"Good, my dear sir, Isn't the half of it. Now off with you two." She waved an arm toward the car.

"It's a bit of a ride," Thomas said. "Can I help with the fare?"

"You want to give me money? I've plenty of money; the problem is there isn't anything to buy because of the bloody war. Whoops," she said, her hand covering her smile. "Sorry, I've *never* done that before— well, maybe once. Now be off and call me when you can, but mind anyone listening."

"Don't you think that's a bit dramatic?"

"No, Mr. Watson, being shot at is dramatic. Or have you forgotten about that already? Now off," she said, looking down the street. As she started walking, Mrs. Somerville spotted a lone cab at the stand, put her fingers to her lips, let loose a shrill piercing whistle, and then yelled, "Cabbie, wake up, you're working."

Margaret and Thomas returned to the car and watched her walk down the street as only Mrs. Somerville could. One arm clamped tightly to her purse, the other swinging high like she was in a royal marching band.

Thomas sat back in the seat with his eyes still on Mrs. Somerville. The lights through the windscreen reflected the slight motion of his head and his soft smile as he thought, "Women—what amazing, wonderful creatures."

Margaret was sitting next to him, watching his head go back and forth in some silent opinion. She closed the door and sat still and silent, making her impossible to ignore.

"What?" Thomas said.

"You know what, just like you know cricket."

"It was a harmless thought about the most dangerous of subjects: women."

"Thomas Watson, you don't know about danger until you've seen me mad. Now take me to a hotel, buy me dinner, and wipe that smile off your face." With that, she moved over, kissed him quickly on the cheek, and quickly moved back to the driver's side.

"What was that?" Thomas asked.

Her only response was starting the Austin, putting it into gear, and shooting off past the taxi stand where Mrs. Somerville was banging on the roof of a cab waking up the driver.

Chapter Forty-Four

Whitehall
War Rooms

After hanging up from a call, the prime minister contemplated the news. The report had informed him that two U-Boats attacked Convoy SC 2 and sunk three ships, resulting in all hands lost. The other loss was the main cargo ship consisting of military provisions and a substantial amount of tinned meat. Churchill had wanted that specifically to help lift morale. The subs attacked while surfaced, avoiding detection by the British ASDIC (sonar). Hitler's Kriegsmarine was slowly dominating the lifeline England had established with North America.

A knock on the door disrupted his thoughts. Colville looked around the door as soon as the light had gone off on Churchill's phone.

"Mr. Prime Minister, may I interrupt with a curious update?"

"Only, Mr. Colville," he said too loudly without even looking up, "if it's bloody good news and not another weight to be borne by these shoulders. Answers are what I need, answers to the…" Churchill stopped, and the stillness created an uneasy moment by any standards.

After the pause and in a moderate tone and manner, he continued, "I would be most happy to entertain the details of your curious update, Mr. Colville. You may proceed."

In an unusual move, the chief of staff entered and closed the door behind him. He said, "I've been asked by Mr. Maston, security head at Bletchley, sir, to report a disturbance at the compound."

Colville looked at his notes, "It concerns a Mr. Dunning who appeared at the complex wanting to talk to Dr. Turing. Dunning escaped both an attempt on his life by an unknown assailant and the best efforts of our security to arrest him. They have another unidentified man in custody. This Mr. Dunning, probably an alias, had extensive knowledge concerning the Ultra project, which caused a great deal of alarm. Dr. Turing who was quite beside himself, indicated that this Dunning was of great value and that we needed to locate him. He felt strongly that Dunning is in a position to help with the project."

Colville looked up from his notes. "I find it hard to believe that this Mr. Dunning or anyone else could possibly have the rarified credentials to be of service on that project."

Colville knew he had to mention the phone call but didn't want any part of Dunning's oblique information. "I talked to Alan this morning about this Dunning, but nothing came of it."

"Perhaps the gentleman is an angel," Churchill replied. "God knows Turing needs one. At any rate, nothing could be more important, Mr. Colville, than this Turing business. Whatever we can do to increase the effectiveness of the Ultra project must be pursued.

"Jock, see to it that Dr. Turing can access this Dunning, assuming we can find him. I want no excuses for not getting this blasted effort on track. It can save lives, let alone the bloody country.

"Also, tell Mr. Maston to proceed with securing the entire compound. I never believed his tactic of maintaining a low profile in the community was better than just locking the place up."

"Yes, sir, I'll see to it at once," Colville said.

Chapter Forty-Five

Yuri Visits Pavel

Yuri's legs were starting to talk, the bane of every person who ever stood watch. He'd been in front of Pavel's second-story flat for almost two hours. If he was to unravel this maze, he had to talk to Pavel. He was the type who always knew everything. Most of the time, it was more than he should know, yet Yuri had always trusted the man. Pavel was usually home at this time, but Yuri was smart enough to know that loyalties can change quickly. He knew using the phone was out of the question, as he didn't know if Pavel was alone. He had to get inside.

A sliver of light was sneaking out between Pavel's blackout curtains. Yuri had hoped his extended stakeout would determine if someone had Pavel's place under surveillance. He saw an agent was assigned, unknown to Pavel, which made him feel better about Pavel's loyalty. After a cigarette, the agent made a round every fifteen or twenty minutes. The agent was trying to hide inside an abandoned building between rounds. The hiding place was good, but he couldn't see all approaches unless he was on rounds. It meant Yuri had access to the back of the building between trips. Yuri had watched the agent, recognizing him by his height and distinctive walk. It could only be Sergei; an agent everyone called Аист человек (stork man); he was one of Yuri's men. Sergei wouldn't have customarily monitored a house using such poor vantage points, so someone had given him specific orders he was following.

Yuri decided not to subject his man to making the same loyalty decision he would press upon Pavel. At the right moment, Yuri made his way around to the rear of the building he'd entered a hundred times. Up the stairs and down the hall had him looking through the rough translucent glass in Pavel's door for shadows or anything amiss. After a few seconds, he couldn't see or hear anything. Could Viktor and Pavel be waiting for him? Was Pavel a hostage or worse?

Yuri knocked on the door and heard movement on the other side, so he stepped to the side of the door and waited. He reached over and knocked again.

"Who is it?" It was Pavel's voice.

Yuri lowered his voice and, using his acquired English accent, said through the door, "Sorry 'bout the hour, mate, an' no offense, but I was expecting a lady ya know. Am I early?"

Yuri waited as the doorknob turned and the door opened. It was Pavel, but was he alone?

Pavel stuck out his head, looked at Yuri, and then down the hall behind him. As Pavel turned to check the other direction, Yuri noticed Pavel had his arm behind his back. He motioned Yuri inside as he brought the revolver to the front and reset the safety.

"Did Аист see you?" Pavel said.

"No. I taught him, remember?"

"Then why is he the only one here?"

"My guess is he's following bad orders."

Pavel motioned to the small kitchen table. "I have hot tea."

"No, my friend, I shall keep my stay to a minimum."

Pavel screwed up his face. "By the way, that was a horrible accent."

Yuri smiled, "It fools the English, well, sometimes. Anyway, I didn't want anyone to know I was seeing you and had to be sure you were alone."

The men gave each other a bear hug. "How are you?" said Pavel.

Yuri let out a sigh. "To be honest, my friend, I don't know."

Pavel looked at his friend with concern. "Yuri, the knives are out. I don't know much more. I was told, more like threatened, to stay here and not talk to anyone, which meant you."

"Who would give such an order?"

"A very dangerous man from Moscow Centre."

Yuri described Joseph.

"No, no," Pavel said. "This guy's mind and body are like one of Stalin's tanks. He has the authority and mental capacity to take 'devious' to another level."

"Tell me what you can."

"I was coming back last night after tailing Watson and his wife out in the countryside. I heard that he was going to Bletchley in the morning. That didn't sound right, as he didn't have any business being there except to talk to the British authorities. If he did, what would he have to say except things that would compromise Russian security? Therefore, I returned to the embassy to phone you, and this colonel in the NKVD walked in behind me."

"NKVD? What's his name?"

"Viktor Grigoryevich Krivitsky. I've never seen him in the hall or anywhere else. He was very casual and friendly, like a subtle assassin. He insisted on knowing what I was doing. I tried to tell him I reported to you and that he should know the standard procedures. That's when he pulled out his identification with great satisfaction and arrogance. He then tells me he wants to know everything. He knew I had no choice. There was no way he knew I was tailing Watson, but he knew his name.

"This Viktor is an egotistical ass and tells me he's now in charge of security and that I report to him. He becomes very interested when I tell him about Watson going to Bletchley. Actually, he was too interested. When I say we should contact you, the conversation stops. He tells me I'm off the assignment, that he'll bring you up to speed, and the two of you'll handle it. The man purposely maneuvered me into a box. He knew I would be in trouble if I didn't follow directions exactly. He then told me to return here, keep quiet, and take some time off. In other words, disappear."

Pavel looked at his watch, walked over to the window, parted the drapes, and looked across the street.

"He's still there. I'm sure he chose that place because I can see him. Sergei is a good man. Anyway, since I'm on vacation, you must assume my field duties, as I can't. Especially the 'Actor' drop off."

Yuri nodded. "Yes, yes," he said, distracted. "I'll check everything."

"What's going on, Yuri? Where do I stand? Where do all of us stand?"

"You do what he tells you, and you'll be fine. If you get the chance, tell everyone else the same thing. My guess is he's in over his head, and his ego sees some opportunities he can capitalize on."

"I don't think so, Yuri. This guy may be a Moscow Centre badass, but he's clever and devious. Be careful."

Yuri thought about what the Ambassador had said about them sending an agent and things becoming unpredictable.

The phone rang loudly, an unsolicited interruption. Pavel looked at Yuri, who conveyed no expression, so Pavel picked it up after the second set of rings.

Without waiting, the caller said, "Pavel, this is Comrade Viktor. I want Watson's address."

"It should be in the file at the office."

"I said I want the address. I'm not at the office, but it shouldn't make any difference; get me what I want."

Pavel could feel the tenseness and urgency in Viktor's voice. Something had gone wrong. "Of course, comrade. I'll get it right away. I'll need to get my pocket notes."

"Well, do it then!" Viktor pushed his hand against the back wall of the booth in frustration. "Is *everyone* an idiot?" He thought.

Pavel's coat was hanging next to the phone in the entry hall. He recovered his notes and found the page. He silently showed it to Yuri with a question on his face. Yuri thought for a moment. Pavel didn't have any other options, so he nodded his approval toward the phone. Whoever this Watson was, he wasn't dumb enough to go back there. They'd probably end up at her mother's estate.

Picking up the receiver, Pavel read off the address, after which Viktor immediately rang off.

"Someone tried to kill Watson at Bletchley today," Yuri said. "Two gunmen, but Watson got away."

Pavel looked shocked. "What? At Bletchley in daylight? It was him, Yuri; it had to be. I know it."

"Has he filed with the embassy? Do we know where he's staying?"

"Sorry, Yuri, I don't think the embassy even knows he's here."

"Too bad," Yuri went into thought. "Since I know he's going to Watson's, I could search his place or confront him when he returns. I'll find him; I have to."

Yuri moved toward the door. "Look, Pavel, my friend. You're caught in the middle. If you have to get involved, follow his orders and play his side of the game. If you must shoot, miss. Do you know what I mean?"

Pavel smiled. "Of course. I learned from the master." He slapped Yuri on the shoulder. "I'm almost the best."

Yuri slapped him back, saying, "Almost? It's as if you *almost* missed the bullet. Do you have a torch?"

Pavel was still laughing. "Yes," he said, reaching into a cabinet above the sink. He handed it to Yuri. Pavel then walked over to the fuse panel on the wall and pulled on it, bringing it out from the wall a few inches. Pavel reached inside the wall and extracted a cloth bag. He removed a pistol from inside the bag and placed it on the table. Then he pulled out several other items. Yuri reached down, picking up three passports beside a bundle of British pound notes and Russian rubles. He opened the Spanish one and looked up with a smile.

Proudly, Pavel offered, "As I said, I learned from the master."

"Yes, almost," Yuri said with a smile.

Pavel looked at Yuri. "I know how you feel about guns, but you can't go see a guy like this armed with an order of fish and chips and expect to defend yourself."

Pavel pushed the pistol forward. "Come on, Yuri, you know I'm right. It's clean and not registered with the British."

Yuri could see the machined edges down the square outer barrel and the deep criss-cross design making up the grip. He thought about the contents of his locker and relented and stuffed it into his outer pocket.

"There are two clips in there. Be careful."

Yuri said, "It won't matter if I can't find him."

"Just remember, he's ruthless and arrogant, a dangerous combination." Pavel chopped off the last word, having thought of something. Pavel remembered Viktor throwing him the matches because he wasn't good enough for his Zippo lighter.

Yuri stepped back as Pavel dashed past him to his jacket by the door. Yuri could see Pavel searching every pocket. He looked up with a beaming face, the kind of smile that warrants finding the number of the only girl that said call me in the last ten years.

"I think he's here. Without thinking of the consequences, his ego carelessly threw it at me."

Pavel held up the matches. Printed on the front were the logo and the words "Plough Inn."

Yuri smiled, took the book of matches, and read the address: 52 Parson's Mead. "I think I should go."

Pavel walked over to the window and looked out again. "Sergei is just now walking over the bricks and into the building, or what's left. You should go now.

"Then it is," Yuri said. "I'll contact you when I have some answers, and if I don't, play the game."

Chapter Forty-Six

Viktor Sets Up Watch

Viktor knew he'd planned the operation well. The embassy's knowledge of the layout and uses of the different huts at Bletchley was essential. There were guards everywhere, but every hut had a specific purpose, and only one held the security team that would interrogate Watson. He also had a roving team in a car covering possible escape routes, which ended in the park shooting. Nevertheless, at the end of it all, they missed the critical shot. Only an incompetent idiot would miss at such a distance.

He'd taken a chance. Success would have meant being honored for his bravery and assertive action, but it failed. Viktor needed to change what could become a messy failure into a success. Keeping a resident spy from going to the British, thereby compromising the entire in-country effort, would make everything right. He still intended to stop Watson but needed to do it quickly.

Viktor shouted at the embassy agent who was driving. "Stop at the next phone box." He got out, made a short call, and returned to the car with a slip of paper.

Viktor gave the driver the address and said he needed to be there in a hurry. Viktor's mind raced as the driver pulled up two houses short of Margaret's. He didn't expect Watson to be there but hoped the man might be that dumb, so he had to cover the possibility.

The driver and Viktor slowly walked up to a side window. The lights were off, and the blackout shades were open. It appeared no one had been here during the evening and it was empty. Viktor quickly approached the front door and told the agent to pick the lock. He did so quickly, and they both rushed into the house with guns drawn, checking all the rooms.

Viktor angrily shouted, "Check the backyard and alley."

Flipping the lights on, Viktor could barely control his anger. He needed to get Watson now, and he couldn't go shooting all over London. His next attempt had to be successful. He would report the initial unsuccessful attempt, blaming the inept shooters, and when he'd straightened it all out, he would bask in the glory of Moscow's admiration. The first step was finding the couple. In addition, he needed to return to his room at the inn because the other idiots in his group would be calling for instructions. The last thing he wanted was some half-wit wandering around, getting caught doing something stupid.

"No one out back," Dmitry said. "Comrade Krivitsky, we must turn out the lights or draw the shades as we will have the local warden asking questions. He'll know we don't live here."

Viktor ignored him and ordered, "Stay here and set up observation from across the street or somewhere, but don't let anyone see you. If they show up, break in and hold them. If Watson tries to escape, kill him and leave. If not, I want to question him about Bletchley."

The agent did not reply. Dmitry, one of Yuri's men, was caught up in something, but he didn't know what. The colonel's credentials were enough to make him obey any order, but this wasn't going smoothly. Being very careful with every step, he asked, "Do you want me to call you if they show up?"

"Of course, you idiot."

"Comrade Krivitsky?" The agent said hesitantly.

"What could you possibly not understand?" Victor almost shouted.

"I'll need a number to call if you won't be at the embassy."

Irritated, Viktor wrote a number on a slip of paper he found on the dining table. Looking over at the telephone shelf in the wall, he also noted that number, just in case. He handed his number to the man and said gruffly, "You can get me here. Keep trying. I'll send a man to relieve you in a few hours."

"Yes, comrade."

Viktor opened the door and said, "If Comrade Stakova shows up, put him on the phone to me immediately. At gunpoint, if you have to."

"But..."

"You've your orders. Follow them!" Viktor barked.

The door slammed shut. Dmitry had been in the country for over two years and knew how the embassy worked. It avoided, at all costs, this kind of visibility in the community. If Yuri knew the orders Viktor was following, he would have his badge. Unfortunately, this comrade jerk outranked Yuri. The agent heard Viktor start the car and loudly speed away, certainly drawing the attention of anyone in the area. Dmitry thought, "This man might have the credentials, but it doesn't mean he knows his way around in the field."

Quickly turning off the lights, the agent walked outside to see if they'd raised any suspicion. The deserted street and the houses on either side appeared to be deserted. With that, he started looking for a good place to set up his post. He needed a cigarette, but decided to wait until he could get himself hidden. He had a photo of Watson and a description of his wife. In a blackout, knowing what they looked like would be useless unless they entered the house.

Viktor grabbed the wheel tightly and retraced his route back to the embassy. From there, he was sure he would recall his path back to the inn where he was staying. He struggled with driving; it was black, and every vehicle was upon him quickly. He knew he had to get back in a hurry, to be there when his fieldmen called his room. He had Joseph look over Yuri's place in case he showed up, which was unlikely.

Chapter Forty-Seven

High Street—Milton Keynes

Mrs. Somerville saw the driver in the cab. He sat motionless, waiting for his next fare. His thoughts weren't in the car as he calculated how much money he could send to his family in Bangalore. After doing the addition for the third time, it still didn't add up to the amount he'd promised. People weren't going out at night while the bombing continued. It hurt his ability to provide for his family, the solitary reward that made his sorrow over the separation bearable. His options were limited to working longer hours and making do with less.

Sitting there in frustration, he heard someone whistle. He threw his arm over the back seat, looking through the rear windscreen toward the sound. He saw an older woman confidently approaching his cab from behind. Then he heard the thunder as she hit the roof with her hand. He swung the driver's door open and stood up. On his way around to open the door, he said, "Madam, it's late. It's not good for you to be here. Please let me get the …"

"No need, young man," she said, motioning him away with her hand. "I can get in a cab by myself, but it's an awfully nice gesture."

Mrs. Somerville closed the rear door and said, "How nice and warm it is here."

It was his first fare in an hour, and he was grateful. His heritage and tradition generated his concern for his new fare. He said over the front seat, "I don't mean to suggest you're unwanted, but Madam, you shouldn't be walking around alone after the blackout."

"You're Indian?" she said.

"Yes, but."

"How delightful, I think it's so far away and hardly ever think of it."

"It depends, of course, on the point of view," the cab driver said. "It's here that feels like the other side of the world."

"You're absolutely right. How horribly narrow of me. Can you take me to 128 Chesham Road in Amersham?"

"Yes, mum." He pulled down on the shifter, getting underway.

She leaned forward and said, "It sounds as though your heart, as it should, is still back in your country."

"It's because my family is there, and I'm stuck here, unable to leave the country due to the war. Any entry or exit is prohibited. I must stay to make money, but someone I don't know says I can't see my family." He touched the brake and rounded a corner.

Mrs. Somerville thought about the separation. There was a certain gentleness about the man; there was also the fact she couldn't remember when a cabby had made a genuine attempt to open her door. "You've chosen a dangerous profession, driving about on the streets, where all the cars are without headlamps, whizzing about crashing into one another."

"It's not a matter of choosing, as much as what's not desirable to others. Only what's left is available to a foreigner like me."

Mrs. Somerville looked out of the cab at all the blacked-out windows going by. She saw a home guard on his rounds, shining his torch into a parked car. She thought of Margaret and Thomas and hoped they were safe and well. Events weren't going as she would have planned if she was the planner. The world was going off on its own and doing a terrible job.

She remembered the day the man standing at the door had introduced himself, flashed a badge, and asked if he could come in. Over tea, he told a story of England needing everyone's help. Then, very much to her surprise, he produced a letter from Churchill himself. It clearly outlined that a young woman from one of Britain's finest families might have access to sensitive information. This information could interest the wrong people, creating concern for her safety. In reality, she was just a teacher, but even the possibility made her a hostage threat. In the letter, the prime minister clarified his concern for the woman's safety, but confining her against her will, or even having her protected or followed, would be counter-productive.

The man had indicated the authorities knew that she owned the house next door, and would she consider letting it out to the person in the letter?

The man noted that, with the government offer of a small subsidy, the current tenants had agreed to move to a different location. The young couple had received no explanation and had made no inquiries. The motions of war created interesting, unexplained situations in the lives of everyday people, and their situation was no different from similar stories they'd heard.

She was to place an advert and wait for a Margaret Hatcher to apply. She was to turn all others down. Her single task was monitoring the woman's security and reporting anything unusual or anything that put her in danger. The man indicated security was very tight, resulting in specific instructions for communication.

Initially, she felt supremely useful doing her bit, helping protect someone important to the war effort, regardless of who it was. Somewhere along the line, Margaret had moved into her heart and stayed there. She sincerely hoped the little security charade wouldn't change their friendship. Mrs. Somerville wondered if Margaret would believe that what started as a patriotic effort ended up a personal mission. That sense of duty requiring secrecy engendered compassion and love.

"It was easy to love Margaret," Mrs. Somerville thought. In many ways, she represented the qualities we wanted to see in ourselves, like a bright spontaneity, enlightened outlook, and declared independence. It masked her need to be loved for what she was and not for her last name.

Drifting to her youth long ago, the former Miss Leeds wished she couldn't been like Margaret; but she was to live in a different era. Women of her time were the lost generation. She'd nothing to show for it but the loss of Charles, the one thing she'd come into this world to find.

The car came to a halt and brought her back to the present. She looked at her house as she pulled money from her pocket purse.

"Up just a bit, to the next walkway, if you could." She looked at the meter and handed him some money, and the driver readied the change.

Dmitry had to move across the street and down to an empty house that was being renovated before finding the proper position. Fortunately, this one allowed him to observe unseen the houses and street before him. As soon as he settled in, a car approached. Without streetlights, he didn't know it was a cab until it passed directly in front of his position. He saw the brake lights go on as it stopped right in front of the target house.

First, there was excitement at his good fortune, followed by disappointment as the cab moved forward, eventually stopping at the house next door. Dmitry moved slightly to get a clearer look as the car door opened, and a woman emerged. Even in the dark, she definitely did not match any description he'd received. The woman and driver exchanged a few words.

Mrs. Somerville leaned into the cab's window and said, "Sanjay, that covers the meter and a little bit. It's not much, but you send that little bit home. I'm not rich like the queen, but you, on the other hand, are certainly a gentleman, which is rare in these parts. If I need you, can I call the company?"

Sanjay gave her a big smile, "Of course, mum," he said. "They'll direct me to you if I don't have a fare. The chances are good."

Sanjay started to get out of the car, and she said, "I'm fine to get up the steps but would be most grateful if you could look me to the door."

"Of course, mum," he said.

Dmitry watched as the cab driver stood by his door and waited while the woman walked towards the house.

Mrs. Somerville heard the repeated distant booming and flashes of light in the sky as the nightly attacks commenced. She unlocked the front door, waved at the cabbie, and walked in. She made the rounds on the windows, pulling the last two curtains together.

She quickly dressed for bed, feeling the day's excitement like a weight on her eyelids. She hoped she'd not upset Thomas. She could see his frustration. What was he dealing with anyway, and why had he changed? She straightened out the blanket on either side of her, pulled the covers to her chin, and let out a deep, troubled sigh. The fact she'd grown to consider Margaret a daughter was simply a direct result of who the young woman was. There was no doubt; she must leave the message, as she had no choice. Things wouldn't be the same tomorrow and the day after tomorrow.

Chapter Forty-Eight

Yuri Goes To Viktor's Room

The Olde Plough Inn wasn't far from the embassy nor Pavel's flat. Yuri knew Viktor was at Margaret's and had some time. Still, he was walking as fast as he could, and nothing would hurry up the process except a lucky cab that had not appeared.

Yuri reached the inn's front entrance and pressed the door, letting himself inside. The noise hit him full-on as customers were shouting and laughing. The bottom of the inn was a pub, the rooms to let upstairs. He looked through the smoke collecting toward the ceiling. Across the room, over a chest-high counter, was a simple sign saying "Rooms." Yuri approached it and looked around. To his left was a man behind the bar pulling two pints. He held both glasses in one hand, the other high on the elaborate handle that said, Mackeson Stout. With a nod, the man indicated he would be over.

When the man finally came over, Yuri pulled out his embassy identification and had it on the counter. The keeper looked down at the flash of the gold medallion and said, "Yes, sir, how can I help ya? Mighty pretty credentials. Are you with the police or somethin'?"

"No," Yuri said. "I'm actually with the Russian Embassy; I'm working with the British to search for one of my countrymen who might be in the country illegally. It doesn't necessarily mean he is, but the British are pressing for an answer. I think the invasion has everyone, including myself, a little jumpy. Is that how you say it?"

"Jumpy, it is for you, my man. As for me, just plain scared. How can I help?"

"I believe the man has checked in here, but I don't know the room. Have you had a man with a discernible accent book a room during the last 24 hours, and did he leave his passport when he checked in?"

"Why, 'course, governor; it's the law. I know exactly who it might be. Thought it was kinda strange the way he talked, with a British passport and all." The keeper pulled a set of keys out of his pocket and opened the lock on a cabinet door directly behind him. "This looks like a wood cupboard, but inside is metal per the regulations for pubs with rooms. Someone sitting at the end of the bar closest to Yuri pointed to the man beside him and shouted, "Lyle, this is what's paying the rent. My mate here is in desperate need of a Scotch."

"Hold on to 'um, if ya got any. Can't you see I'm busy with a gentleman? Certainly comes before the likes of you."

"Well," the-down-in-the-trousers patron said, "if that don't …" Lifting his glass toward the ceiling, he addressed everyone in the pub. His voice an octave higher for every pint consumed since nightfall as he had to shout for the rest of the house to hear him. "Did ya hear that, lads? I'm takin' me business somewhere else, I am."

The end of his proclamation was met with heavy laughter and someone yelling, "But Scotty, yer such a stingy laggard, it's the only pub that'll let ya in." That brought down the house.

The innkeeper placed a British passport on the counter, and Yuri saw a picture of Viktor for the first time. "Well, the passport certainly looks good, although it's probably not real. We've someone tailing him, so I know he's not in his room. I'm afraid I'll have to look around up there."

"Well, I'm not sure I can do that. It's not me business to be breakin' the law, ya know."

Yuri tapped the British passport and said, "Yes, I know. The boys at MI5 aren't keen on having missed this one and are looking to keep it quiet, so there will certainly be no questions. Sounds like politics to me, but I just do what I'm told."

"Okay, but don't come back 'cause I'll not be admittin' ya got this from me." He handed Yuri a key and said, "Number Six, through those doors at the top of the stairs, straight to the end of the hall before the escape."

With his senses on high alert, Yuri walked up the steps between the counter and the bar and between two swinging doors. Yuri felt apprehensive as he made his way down the hall. He stopped just before the door to Room Six. Standing with his back to the wall, Yuri listened for any sounds. Satisfied, he inserted the key and opened the door, letting it swing open. Cautiously, he listened again before looking around the corner and stepping through the doorway into the room.

There was a subtle odor, but he couldn't place it. He flashed his torch, navigating around the bed and over to the window. There he stepped on something—a suitcase. He closed the curtains and directed his light downward, retracing his steps back to the open door; he closed it and turned on the ceiling light. The bed was along one wall next to the window and the entrance to the loo.

He returned to the canvas suitcase he'd stumbled on in the small space between the bed and the window. Knowing it wasn't a serious hiding place, he checked the bag anyway. The case was normal, except for the double-lining, standard Russian issue. It contained only clothes and personal items. He put everything back exactly as he found it.

Yuri wasn't sure what he was looking for but continued the search. Viktor was an agent and wouldn't carry anything incriminating on him, so if he possessed anything of that nature, it would be hidden here or buried near a tree somewhere.

Yuri dispensed with looking under the bed, a place where Viktor would only hide something he wanted to be found. Yuri was surprised at the private loo, given the age of the inn. Viktor would have had to request the amenity. "It was small," Yuri thought, clambering up onto the seat of the toilet and shining the torch into the top of the tank. He then looked under the dank, tiny sink, which appeared to be from the era of Henry VIII. He checked the walls for loose tiles and ensured the baseboard hadn't been removed.

His image in the mirror above the sink caught his eye. The streaks from the corroded silver crossed his face. It was a snapshot of where he was today, and the picture wasn't pretty. Viktor was a problem; only a few times in Yuri's career did he have to get his hands 'dirty,' as they said, in the field. It wasn't his preference, but he was more than capable, if not usually willing.

The hinge resisted as he swung the mirrored door open. Behind it were three empty glass shelves, held up by slots on each side. They looked dusty, as though never used, thus never cleaned. Even though the single ceiling light was on, he pointed the torch inside to get a better look. With the increased light, he could see each shelf covered with an even coat of dust—except the center one. There he could see a very small clean area, on the edge of the glass, with the curve of a fingertip. The back edge of the center shelf obstructed the two screws that held the cabinet in place, and they were missing. He could see where the cabinet met the wall with the mirrored door open. He looked around the outside edge and found two places where the wall was slightly marred, a sign someone couldn't tried removing it but giving him no hint of when. It couldn't been fifty years ago. The center shelf had been pulled, and the screws were missing. "Very poor tradecraft," he thought, "for a rising member of the party and the golden boy of someone."

Yuri put the torch down and closed the mirror door. He grabbed each side of the cabinet and gently rocked it back and forth, pulling it toward him. It came out straight away, revealing a brand new envelope tacked right in the center of the back wall. Due to the small space, he placed the cabinet on the floor outside the bathroom. With the torch's light, he looked carefully at every aspect of the envelope, then carefully pulled the tack and took it off the wall. He opened it.

Yuri's eyes opened wide with surprise. In his hand was none other than Viktor's orders from Moscow Centre.

Unaware he was holding his breath, Yuri carefully read the words to the bottom. He held the letter for a moment and felt his mind and body relax despite what was bad news. He had the complete picture and enough information for the first time since meeting with the Ambassador. Planning is much easier if you know what you're planning for.

Moscow Centre felt the invasion was imminent and German soldiers would soon be on the ground. If a decrypting machine were somewhere, it wouldn't take long to discover. The Germans would then modify their codes, rendering the machine worthless. Despite the non-aggression pact between the two countries, Stalin deeply distrusted the German leader. This made obtaining information on Hitler's intentions towards Russia the highest priority. If England were soon to be occupied, the Germans would take a different attitude toward the Russians. Moscow needed a high-profile operative in London, not a diplomat. The Watson operation, now considered useless, was to be terminated. Viktor was to have Yuri kill Watson, and Viktor was to kill Yuri. It was business as usual, Moscow-style.

Knowing any extra time in the room was dangerous and unnecessary, he refolded the letter, and put it back into the envelope as he found it. He put the tack into the same tack hole and gently tilted it with his finger to exactly where it had been. Viktor would know the exact angle. He picked up the cabinet on the outside floor and carefully put it back into place. He surveyed the mirror, looking for any of his finger marks. Outside the loo, on the floor, were several pieces of wall material from the mirror cabinet; he picked them up, and put them in his pocket.

After turning off the lights and opening the blackout curtains, he headed for the door. He opened it an inch, listening for anything unusual. Only the muffled sounds of the pub came up the hall. Yuri stepped out and looked up and down the hall, finding it empty. He locked the door behind him and was heading for the pub area to return the key when he heard the sounds of breaking glass.

Chapter Forty-Nine

Olde Plough Inn

Before Yuri heard the breaking glass, Viktor had walked into the inn's front door like a man with a purpose. He looked at the crowd, despising that he had to choose some dive for cover and not accommodations equal to his rank. Viktor saw the barkeep look at him as he walked through the door, and given the look on his face, Viktor thought he must recognize him from when he checked in.

The barkeep finished serving a customer and went to the inn counter.

"Evenin', sir, can I help?"

"My key," was all Viktor said. The man placed his counter towel down but did so very curiously. Viktor couldn't define it, but his experience noted it anyway. With a turn, the owner unlocked the key cabinet, moving his head back as it swung past his face. He reached for room six's key and pulled it off the hook. Viktor could see the room keys, and his body tensed.

"Where's the other key?" Viktor said loudly.

"Sir?"

"Where's the other key to my room I said. Where is it?"

"The maid may have it," the keeper said, knowing that the other man might still be upstairs and didn't want any trouble. "Can I pour ya a tall one on the house?" He started walking over to the bar, but Viktor didn't move.

Scotty wobbled into the room from the loo, walking by Viktor and Lyle to his usual end stool. Still buttoning his pants, he was just in time to hear Lyle offer Viktor a free beer and noticed the man did not respond.

Viktor was incensed; service maids don't carry a bundle of keys to every room; that's why they invented master keys. He knew something was wrong. He scanned the room.

Scotty looked askance at any man who would refuse a free drink. He rested his head on his hand, but his elbow slid too far when he misjudged the distance to the countertop. Scotty slipped off his stool and came too close to Viktor.

"I'd be takin' it, mister," Scotty said. "It's not likely you'll see another offer like..."

Viktor, shoving Scotty aside, stepped toward the short stairs leading to the rooms. Scotty fell back onto a table fully laden with mugs. He landed sideways as he slid off, and the table tipped onto its side. Eight or nine mugs hit the stone floor, shattering and covering the floor with glass. With that, the noise level rose, chairs scraped across the floor, and everyone stood up.

Yuri stopped in his tracks as he heard the commotion coming from the other side of the stained glass doors at the end of the hall. He looked at the key in his hand and decided not to chance it. To his left was the noise, and to his right was a door leading outside that was likely unlocked. He moved quickly, running to the door at the back of the hall and turning the knob.

Viktor pushed past the innkeeper, the key in his hand, and ran up the six steps to the doors. People yelled at him as he pushed both ornate doors open as hard as he could and scrutinized the hall before him and the hall to his right.

Yuri had just closed the door behind him and rushed downstairs into the night. He knew he couldn't clear the back alley quick enough if someone had a mind to immediately survey the area from the stairs. Reaching the ground, he wedged himself between a wall and a lorry. Moving his head, he could see the top of the stairs through the side and front windows of the vehicle. Yuri hoped Viktor would determine the lorry was too close to hide behind, and Yuri's size and difficulty breathing proved the theory was very close to the truth. The door at the top of the stairs burst open. At the top appeared the silhouette of a man very much in a hurry. The man leaned over the railing, searching for movement in the constricted passageway, but just as quickly retreated inside.

Next, Viktor headed to his room. In front of his door, he didn't want to warn anyone inside by using the key. Without hesitation, he kicked the door in, instantly throwing his arm and gun into the space. Using the light from the hallway, he looked for something to shoot. Taking in the whole room at once, he replaced the gun and made the bathroom in two steps. With the light on, he stood in front of the mirror, looking at the edges. "Clean," he thought. Opening the mirrored door, he cursed as he saw the fingerprints on the glass shelf and the empty screw holes. He yanked the cabinet out of the wall, with the glass shelves jostling inside, and saw the envelope but wasn't satisfied. Moving closer, he examined the lower corner of the envelope tacked to the wall and saw it aligned perfectly with one of the plaster laths running horizontally across the wall. Still, he wasn't sure. He'd been sloppy, but the missing key was still the only evidence that someone might have been there. Just then, the phone rang, startling his already tense nerves.

The door to the room was still open, and patrons in various stages of inebriation shouted at Viktor as he went to the doorway. The innkeeper tried pushing the men back down the hall and into the pub area. Viktor's eyes met the owner's. Viktor's intense stare let the barkeep know he was best left alone. The keeper understood and headed his clan, protesting Scotty's treatment, back down the hall toward the bar.

Yuri wasn't going to waste any time. He made himself as small as possible to remove himself from the uncomfortable position. Keeping low, looking at the stairs, he quietly exited the passage and onto an adjoining street. He knew exactly where he was going.

Chapter Fifty

Room at the Inn

After dropping off Mrs. Somerville, Margaret and Thomas knew they badly needed to find a place to hide and get some needed rest before engaging with Margaret's mother the following day.

Margaret drove for a bit in the general direction of Mother's. Twice they stopped to see if anyone was following them and found nothing but dark roads with dark houses. It was a precaution that would now be part of their lives until Thomas could get the mess straightened out and their lives back to normal.

Thomas looked over at Margaret concentrating on the road, shifting gears. Today wasn't the result of something he did; he was sure of that, but the responsibility was his, which put Margaret in danger. With his growing feelings towards her, he sensed anger, thinking someone out there could hurt her. He wasn't going to let that happen.

"Thomas," she said, "something has been bothering me."

"Could it be my propensity for silent unshared thoughts?" he said, trying to get a witty response to relieve the tensions of the last hour, which had been rather cloak and dagger.

She ignored his attempt, saying, "After you left for Bletchley, remember I said the Russian called."

"Yes?"

"He's the only person besides me who knew you were going to Bletchley. Since the British didn't shoot at you this morning, it could only be that Yuri guy. All we need to do is turn him in, and we're safe."

Thomas looked at Margaret as she looked at the road. "First, there was the one who tried to shoot me, and another two men in the park, so this is bigger than just him. Second, do we know who Yuri is? Who do we turn in? Do you have an address? I would love to surprise him at his place while he was sleeping."

"Right, Thomas, and what would you do?"

Thomas caught her eye and said seriously, "Whisper in his ear."

"Thomas, you couldn't hurt a fly." She looked at the road and back at Thomas, who hadn't moved, and, in a curious tone, added, "I think."

There was a prolonged silence, then looking out the rear, Thomas said, "I'm pretty sure no one is following us. Whatever you can find for an inn."

Thomas flew forward as Margaret hit the brakes. With his hands braced on the dash, he asked, "Are you alright?"

"Of course I'm alright. You said to find a place, and we were right next to one." She shifted the car into reverse, then headed back to a stately house converted into an inn for the duration of the war.

At the desk, the matronly innkeeper gave Thomas a suspicious look after signing in as Mr. and Mrs. Thomas Watson for one night. She glanced at Thomas's hand, where there was no ring. Thomas looked around at Margaret, who said, "He would never wear one."

"I'll need to see your identity cards," the innkeeper said.

Thomas knew this was a problem. It was against the law to be without an identity card, and he'd purposely left his at home.

"I was robbed today," Thomas said. "My wife has an identity card that matches the address I wrote down. I know it's not ordinary, but we need a favor."

Margaret showed the innkeeper her card and said, "This is a stop on our way to my parents' house in Fernhurst, Surrey. Hatcher is my maiden name."

The woman looked up with interest. "Sir Ian Everett Hatcher?"

"Yes," Margaret said. "He's my father."

"Mr. Hatcher helped out a close family friend who couldn't fend for himself nor his kids. It wasn't his fault; he almost died in an accident at the mill. Probably 'fore you was born, young lady. Anyway, I don't forget those kind of people, nobody does. They seem to be all gone now."

She fiddled with the bowl of matches on the counter, then said, "Well, I guess I can look 'round it this time. Not for you, mind ya but your father, so it ain't none of me business. That'll be three shillings all-inclusive—paid in advance."

As if his lack of an identity card weren't enough, noting on the hotel register that they were from nearby Amersham, the lady was unconvinced by Margaret's assertions that they were married.

Margaret's attempts at restoring her pride took another severe blow when she had to borrow a nightgown.

"You can leave the key in the box in the mornin' or," she gave them a look over the top of her glasses and added, "tonight, whichever."

As soon as they entered the room, Margaret collapsed backward onto the bed, the nightgown in her hand. Thomas could now recognize the symptoms of Margaret on overload.

He lay down next to her on his side and said, "I think we need something to eat, and today's events should be off-limits during dinner. Directly across the street, I saw a stuffy-looking restaurant with a full car park. It could only be a good sign. What do you say we try it out?"

Margaret threw her arms around him and said, "You said you loved me today in front of Mrs. Somerville."

"Could mean it's true then," Thomas said. "What do *you* think?"

"It better be true. My reputation won't be worth a glass of water in the entire town by tomorrow morning. You must do right by this unfortunate girl," Margaret pouted.

"Oh, I don't think you're so unfortunate," he replied. "The whole 'Lady Hatcher' thing sounded pretty convincing."

"What do you mean? It's true. Besides, you weren't doing anything, and we would have been on the street in another minute. I saved the evening, and now you have to buy dinner. Kiss me, sir."

"As you wish, my Lady Hatcher," he said mockingly, quickly holding her free arm to the bed. Just as she started to protest, he rather vigorously put his mouth to hers. She changed her mind for now but having observed the unfolding saga of Margaret, Thomas knew it was no guarantee of anything in the future.

Chapter Fifty-One

Yuri to Safe House—Leyton High Road

It had taken Yuri over an hour to get near the Euston Station near Regents Park. The air raid sirens had gone off earlier, and the station had emptied, making it hard to get lost in a crowd. Yuri decided to wait up the street until the clear signal sounded and things got back to normal before making a decision.

Eventually, the all-clear signal filled the air. Finally, a shopkeeper raised the small rolling security panels on his newsstand across from the station.

Yuri walked up to him and said, "You're open late."

"Got ta be open when ya can, I say. Lucky for me, people still read."

Yuri stood at the stand and scanned the magazines. Occasionally he dropped his head to look closely at a specific cover but only to bring it up again, looking in another direction. Finally, he handed over a shilling for the weekly in his hand and stepped into the street, taking advantage of a final glance both ways for traffic and anyone of interest. He proceeded across the uneven road, looking down at the publication, realizing he'd purchased *The War Illustrated*, with a picture of two helmeted civil defense wardens looking through a large hole in a wall. Across the top, the banner read, "Nazi's target church." "It's only going to get worse," he thought, stepping onto the curb.

Amidst the comfort of a bustling humanity, a busy station, and the noise of an engine building up steam, he ventured toward a shop offering travelers biscuits and tea. It was next to his destination: six long rows of metal station lockers. He made a circular pass around the entire lot. The first two rows featured small boxes, big enough to hold children's books and the like; the lockers in the third row and onward were large enough for luggage. Toward the end of his pass, he reached into his pocket for the key. Yuri turned the key in one of the larger lockers and opened the door. To his relief, nothing had changed since he'd packed it nearly three years ago.

He pulled at the two leather bags, dust floating up as they landed on the floor. On one knee, he unzipped the smaller of the two. In the bag, he stored a supply of clothes, money in several currencies, a rail pass, and passports to key escape destinations. It was Yuri's other identity. He took the handgun from his pocket, placed it out of sight in the bag, and zipped it closed.

The other bag was longer but more slender. In it were personal items, more clothes, and more money, in case he became separated from either bag. It looked the lighter of the two but weighed more. Inside was a Lee-Enfield MK I rifle, standard issue to the British Army.

Yuri was as experienced in the ebb and flow of life as he was in the tradecraft of his profession. He knew nothing ever remained the same because there was always a human factor that demanded change. If change was inevitable, he believed, then you had to be ready. He'd arranged for these items within days of his arrival from Italy. He'd also rented the flat on Leyton High Road as a safe house, which he occasionally used when he wanted to be alone and away from the embassy residence at the docks. Its primary purpose was to act as a secret, safe place for him to go in case of trouble from any faction.

After declining help loading his items into the boot, Yuri got into the cab. His arm rested on one of the bags sitting close beside him as he said, "23 Fredrick Place, do you know it?"

"Indeed, sir, be about 20 minutes if the German bastards are done for the night. Traveling late, you are. Hard to hear the sirens on the train."

"Started after we pulled in," Yuri said, his mind already drifting into possible events ahead. "Been a long day; think I'll close my eyes a bit," he added, knowing it would stop the chit-chat.

They arrived before he knew it though he was almost sure he hadn't nodded off. "A mistake," he thought. He must be more careful.

"Here we are, sir, but are you sure about the address?"

"Yes, there it is. How do you drivers remember all these streets?"

"Born here, sir. Still live in me mum's house. Streets stay the same; it's the world that changes."

"Yes, indeed," Yuri said as the driver opened his door.

Dropping the bags on the street, Yuri paid the fare and bid the driver a good night. He fiddled with the bags while watching the cab disappear into the night. Yuri then walked to the corner and turned left onto Leyton High Road. The expansive common to his right was pitch black, giving the impression the world's edge was just 30 feet away. In the day, out his flat's window, he could observe the common maintain its steady position while confusion and fear gripped all of London. "Commons also don't move," Yuri thought with a smile.

Yuri turned left into an alley behind all the buildings along Leyton High, which took him to the rear entrance of his flat. Two trips up the stairs carrying his packed bags had them in the sparsely furnished flat. Inside he slowly lowered himself into an oversized old leather chair and finally allowed himself to feel relaxed. He was sure not a soul knew about the place except Pavel. Until now, he'd never kept anything in the place that could be connected back to him. Anything of that nature had been stored in the locker.

Yuri thought about his increasing lack of control and the shifting information. The rules of espionage required him to tie up loose ends and protect his people. Every year, another story would emerge pointing to the serious consequences of not extracting cleanly. Leaving behind a messy operation caused unwanted investigations that increased visibility. Never a good thing in the spy business.

Chapter Fifty-Two

The Fox Restaurant

Margaret and Thomas quickly crossed the unlit dark road. Thomas pointed out a building at the far end of the street. It had just been hit and suffered serious damage, but no fire was evident. Official beams of light from dozens of torches crisscrossed as crews arrived and police knocked on doors, evacuating people. It was cordoned off with bright rope to keep bystanders at a safe distance. Inside the secured area, some very impressive uniforms stood, discussing the situation. It was an unexploded bombsite, and they were waiting for the UXB crew, also called Sappers. These men dealt with defusing unexploded ordnance. Thomas thought, "No one could possibly receive enough pay to hover over an unexploded bomb and render it harmless."

Considering the chaos that was his life, Thomas found it normal, that they were having dinner just outside of the evacuation zone of a potential disaster. Thomas held the door to the restaurant open for Margaret. They entered a room with an inviting ambiance and that was warmed by a fire in a large fireplace. Once inside the doors, except for one uniformed patron having dinner with a woman, there was little evidence of a war going on.

The Fox was an old, established restaurant known for providing items on its menu that were missing at other places. Rumor had it that the owner had connections at the officer's commissary, but there wasn't a soul interested in discovering the origins of scarce good food. Subdued light filled the interior of the Fox. At the same time, hushed conversation hovered over white china and fine crystal as patrons enjoyed their meals with a respectable decorum exercised by the upper level of society who dined there.

"No fish and chips here," Thomas said.

"Oh, hush, it's so romantic, don't you think?" Margaret said. "Mother loves this place."

"Why didn't you say you knew about this place?"

"I didn't, but Mother has described it, and there's no mistaking the walls."

Thomas looked around at the walls, a veritable gallery of painting after painting of various scenes, all with a common theme: A hunting master with his assistants herding packs of hounds chasing after clever and resourceful foxes. Genteel riders, in brightly coloured formal hunting livery on a chase, their backs ram straight as they jumped over obstacles. All the while, the hunt servants and staff trailed, prepared to serve an extensive country lunch and afternoon tea, regardless of the hunting master's results. Thomas found it all a very traditional, although a delightful waste of time.

Thomas took their coats to the cloakroom. He placed their mask containers alongside the others. Some enterprising people had decided that if it was mandatory to carry the masks, one could make money converting them into a fashion accessory. As a result, the containers came in various sizes and colours, some occupying the bottom of large handbags or attached to umbrellas, and some just covered with gay cloth covers.

Thomas returned to find Margaret talking to a man dressed in a tailored Italian suit, with slicked back hair and that wide smile reserved for well-paying regular customers.

She must have introduced herself as the maître d' clasped his hands and said, "I'm so sorry, but your mother's table is taken, as we weren't expecting you. I do, however, have a quiet place for two by the fireplace that I feel would be more than sufficient."

Without waiting for a reply, his extended hand presented a path to the empty table somewhat separated from the general clientele. Holding Margaret's chair, he slid it under her at just the right moment. Then, his smile gone, he stared at one of his waiters and nodded down at the table with a look that could kill an armored battalion. Then, his face instantly transformed back to its glowing persona; with a slight bow, he said, "Andre will be at his best tonight, just for your pleasure."

Once he left, Thomas looked at Margaret, laughing, and said, "I think I can understand why your mother would want to come here—but why would you? The maître d' is as phony as a wooden nickel."

"What's a nickel?" She said.

Thomas paused.

Margaret had learned to move on when he would get that off-into-nowhere stare. "She likes it because the mood and the menu are magnificent, and she just happens to have an account here."

"I thought you refused any help from the family."

"I did," she said, dedicating an unusual amount of attention to arranging her napkin in her lap.

Thomas sensed that the relationship with her mother was much more complicated than it appeared. There were apparent feelings, but why did she deny them so? They ordered, and Andre was, indeed, at this best and a lot warmer than his boss.

Over dinner, they both wandered off, discussing subject after subject, again at lightning speed. Thomas thought life was much nicer when they concentrated on each other instead of the damned 'problem.' He looked at her face while talking and wondered what the future held for them both. Whatever it was, he was becoming acutely determined that it included this bundle of energy which, at this exact moment, was waving her arms, telling a story about her mother and Churchill.

Churchill had unexpectedly accepted one of Mother's dinner invitations, which sent the guest list in a flurry. Usually, inviting the man elevated the event to its own level on the social circuit. Despite the many less-than-favorable memories, Churchill had not only accepted this invitation but, the jesture completely outflanked her mother. He presented her with a basket of flowers and captivated her guests with wide-ranging dinner conversation and a warm toast to the hostess, proving charm is a potent instrument, especially when rendered with a subtle hand.

At another table, Edith looked around at the restaurant's décor. She'd never been to the Fox because it was way beyond her budget.

Paddy looked up at the waiter and said, "Yes, you can take them away. Do you have any Champagne?"

"I'm very sorry, sir, but not this evening. The supply, sir," he smiled a knowing smile, "is quite irregular."

Paddy laughed. "Yes," he said, looking down at his flight wings, "I can understand. I understand the officers club can't keep a consistent supply either."

Feigning surprise, the waiter said, "Now, isn't that an incredible coincidence." He reached for the last plate and said, "Will there be anything else?"

"No, but could you give us a minute?" Paddy said.

"Yes, indeed," he said, looking around the now half-full restaurant. "The table is yours. Take as long as you like."

Paddy looked over at Edith, and for a long moment, they just stared at each other. Edith was unsure where the evening was going and didn't care. She'd decided to take whatever time she could get and hope it was the beginning of forever. His almost breathless phone call from the airfield, had surprised her. He didn't know that she was aware of his crash before he'd described it to her. During the retelling, he was very emotional, and she knew that it affected him in a way that had changed his usual confident fighter-pilot demeanor.

"So, how did *your* day go?" he said.

Edith leaned over the table on her folded arms and looked up at Paddy silently.

He stammered, "It's a simple question, asked by people all over the country. You spend most of your time there, and I just want to know about your friends and if you enjoy what you do."

She thought for a second; this was painful as he was so right. "I'm sorry, Paddy. You, of all people, should know the outsized rules that come with war. It affects all of us in ways that aren't pleasant. Some don't even make it, so can we discuss something else?"

"I hate this damn war," he said rather firmly. "It changes everything. People want to move on with their lives, and some kraut decides he's better than everybody else. At such a human level, it's not fair."

Edith had sensed he was different when they spoke on the phone and this was more proof. She wanted to hug him or just do something other than sit across the table. He was agitated about something and wasn't letting on.

"It's about time you got some time off," she said. "You've been flying non-stop for days. Nevertheless, how on Earth did you manage leave? Not that you didn't deserve it. And on my night off, no less. You must be very clever."

"My squadron leader said I couldn't forty-eight hours, but I had to promise to spend most of it sleeping, directly because of my flying."

Holding her cup of tea in two hands, she took a sip, smiled, and said, "Well then, perhaps we should get you back to base since your squadron commander certainly knows best."

With a boyish grin, he looked into her eyes and said, "I told him not a wink if I can help it."

With a chuckle, she said, "I guess it's not such a crime to steal a little of a man's sleep, but you have to promise to get at least a few winks."

Paddy closed one eye and said, "Does that count?"

She playfully tried to kick him under the table. "No, but it's a start, you brut. Is that all men think about?"

"Mostly," he said with a smirk, "…'cept me, of course."

"I don't believe you for a second, and it's obvious, Captain Hemingway, my morals fly much higher than yours."

Edith waited for a laugh at her poor analogy or his usual quick retort. There was only a long silence; then, he shifted in his chair. He hadn't heard her or had chosen to ignore the comment. She decided to leave him alone.

"Edith," he finally said, mindlessly turning over a salad fork left on the table.

She felt a cold reality slowly drift down her spine. She'd never encountered Paddy talking in this tone. She put her cup down. She sensed something was about to happen but didn't know what it would be. Did he have to quit flying because of the accident? Was he seriously injured in a way that didn't show? She felt the first touches of panic. A distinct pang of uneasiness occupied the pit of her stomach, the same space shared by fear. "It's okay," she said to herself. "Whatever it is, I'll help him through it—we can do it together," she thought.

"I told my commander the time off meant more to me than anything in the world, and if he didn't give it to me, I was going anyway."

Edith heard this but wasn't quite ready to believe it. She had waited a long time for any hint that said she was something special in Paddy's life, for any small demonstration that confirmed they shared the same feelings for each other. After all, she loved this man and wanted him to know it, but the 'don't ground a flyboy' philosophy always kept her at bay. She'd just been enjoying him—but now this.

Paddy shifted to the side in his chair and brought his left hand up to the table.

Edith looked at him; his eyes were glassy, humble, and afraid. He nervously looked to the side, then back at her again. She held her breath.

Paddy pushed through the emotion in his voice. "There's only so much time in this world before we're just a note in history," he said. "We search and search, and you know something is right at some point. You shouldn't hesitate when it happens because life is a funny, wandering road." He reached across the table, touched her hand, and held it tight.

After a moment, he took a deep breath and said, "If we were reading this in a book or watching a play, the words would be perfect, but it's just me. So here it goes… Edith, I love you more than life itself."

He opened his left hand, and in his palm was a gold ring with three small sapphires in a row. She stared at it in amazement, then looked up and followed a tear running down Paddy's face and onto his pressed uniform shirt.

With all her might, Edith fought back not tears, as they were flowing, but for her composure. She lost the battle, resulting in cascading emotions, and she couldn't speak.

"Will you marry me?" he said.

Across the room, Margaret stopped mid-sentence in describing her father's love of his country house and looked over Thomas's shoulder. Margaret saw a woman quietly crying and a man holding her hand, placing a ring on her finger. He looked dashing in his blue flight uniform. She thought, "He's probably one of those Spitfire pilots that go headlong into a pile of German planes while we watch in horror from the ground."

"How absolutely adorable they are," Margaret said, discreetly motioning toward their table.

Thomas turned to look.

Margaret silently continued observing the couple for a few seconds, absorbing the ritual, enfolding and caught up in the emotion. Then sitting straight upright in her chair, she said, "Thomas, that man is proposing marriage over at that table." She sighed, and after a few tears came to rest on the white linen cloth, Margaret said, "God, how she must feel."

Thomas also had them in view. "Are you sure he's proposing?"

"Yes, I think so. There are *not* a lot of times when a woman cries and smiles at the same time."

They stayed long enough to see the couple holding each other as they walked out the door. Thomas and Margaret left a short time later.

Back in their room at the inn, Thomas noticed that they got into bed and, for the first time, seemed to be comfortable with each other. Thomas thought how perfectly wonderful this woman was and how, deep inside, he knew a Margaret would never come his way again. Lying side by side, Thomas placed his arm around her. Given what had occurred in the day and the amount of time they had for each other over dinner, this was a special moment in their relationship. He was about to remind Margaret of her loose moral character and then suggest how he had to make a decent woman of her when he heard the now-familiar deep breathing. She'd fallen sound asleep in his arms.

Chapter Fifty-Three

The Hatcher Estate

Thomas opened his eyes to the morning light. At the same time, he heard movement and purposeful noises not usually present if both occupants of the room were still in bed. He looked over, and sure enough, the person he fell asleep holding last night was missing. Without moving, he said, "Margaret?"

"Thomas?" she said without missing a beat.

"What're you doing?"

"What most people do when they rent a room for the night? I'm getting ready to leave. Care to have a go at anything a bit more complicated?"

"Ah-oh," he said, rolling his eyes before putting the pillow over his head.

Margaret crossed the room and grabbed the pillow between his hand and ear. Then she pulled back the covers and said in a very high voice, "Good morn-*ning,* Mr. Watson, known international criminal and rogue spy, or have you forgotten? We have a serious problem we need to work on, and it ain't gonna' happen with you sleeping the day away."

"What happened to last night?" Thomas said. "Does all that romance and love automatically disappear in the morning? I've survived gunfire; tomorrow, I ship out to some foreign land, and you could make this soldier a very happy man. Please come back to bed?"

"What romance and love?"

"Last night, before we went to sleep, it was wonderful. Don't you remember? It was heaven," Thomas said with a beaming face, and his arms stretched wide.

"There *was* no last night, and you're going straight to hell with this nonsense. We have only one other option, as I see it, and we might as well find out if it works. You asked me to help, and I can't think of a greater sacrifice than going to my mother, hat in hand. Now up and at it." She hit the man rising from the bed with the pillow to emphasize her final word, "…soldier."

It was under an hour's drive from the inn to her mother's. The morning was beautiful. Having playfully jousted earlier, their banter gave way to contemplative silence as they drove along. Margaret was concerned for their safety as the Russian obviously meant them harm. Thomas was sorting out the layers of information, deciding that contacting Churchill was still his only course of action. As he stared out the window, the suburban landscape gave way to the countryside.

Margaret was driving, and he put a hand on her knee, which wasn't far away in the small car. She looked over and, with a bright shining face, gave him a wonderful smile, saying over the motor noise, "*Was* there a last night?"

Thomas just smiled. After a while, he said, "Do you mind driving?"

"No, not at all," she laughed, "especially when considering the alternative. Do you mind being a passenger?"

"No, I don't mind at all, especially when I'm in the hands of one so capable."

Margaret looked at him twice between glances at the road, wondering at the differences between the two men she called a husband. She said, "We're getting close."

They traversed a series of small rolling hills. Upon cresting the last rise, the Hatcher Mansion unexpectedly appeared, taking up most of the horizon. Thomas was stunned to see the monumental building standing alone at the end of the long driveway, looking like it was part of Whitehall. The giant front gates were open during the day, flanked by home guards within a quick walk of the entry. Margaret slowed down and waved at one, George Alton, in uniform. He was also the estate's livery smith and did his bit on the odd days of the month.

Thomas simply couldn't believe what was looming before him. It prompted a thought from a part of his mind that gave birth to all the other orphaned thoughts that filled his life. As the house drew closer, he said, "Over the meads of our pleasant land of England, there lie spread the stately seats of her nobles."

"What?" Margaret said.

Since the 1700s, the community of Fernhurst had been considered the countryside. However, the constant expansion of the largest city in the world had continually crept ever closer to this enclave of serenity. Fernhurst was now and had always been home to those with abundant wealth, heritage, and attitude. It hosted the most prominent estates and mansions within a social distance from the heart of the Empire while maintaining the proper isolation from the endeavors of the working class.

The Hatcher Estate was initially part of a large land grant presented to Frederick Hanover, the Duke of York, in 1815 as a hunting reserve. Frederick was the second son of King George III, whose commitment to taxing the New World for the military protection of the crown led to the loss of the American colonies in 1776. In the 1820s, Frederick built a large country estate with extensive French gardens and outbuildings that was, for a time, the signature country residence of the greater Hempstead area. Frederick died in 1827, and Sir Lawton Everett Hatcher, a successful businessman, purchased part of the reserve and the mansion complex. He also served his country, without portfolio, in many projects for the royal family. After making it his home for several years, Hatcher and his wife retired to their small cottage in Scotland. His only son Ian Everett Hatcher I, Margaret's grandfather, inherited the estate. Margaret represented the fourth generation to occupy the home once built for royalty.

The surrounding subtle rolling hills, covered with dense and fertile woodlands, gave the land a natural texture absent in the smooth, even planes to the Northeast. Although the Hatcher Estate was a small portion of Frederick's original grant, it still encompassed almost 700 acres of land and the surrounding moors. Outside of the grounds and gardens, the land remained in a natural state, with a caretaker to manage the wildlife.

The crushed rock entry drive quickly separated into a divided driveway, about 400 feet long. In the center were the straight lines of perfectly cone-shaped shrubs, each surrounded by carefully tended underplantings. The decorative shrubs were each exactly five feet high, limiting any disruption of the visitor's view of the mansion.

The Hatcher Mansion itself was a neo-classical three-story structure. Local limestone covered all of the outside surfaces and, given the years, displayed a certain amount of weathering. A Greek cornice dominated the prominently centered entrance that, with the crown's permission, had been refaced and carved with the Hatcher family motto: *Famulus Regis Et Patria* (Latin for Serving King and Country). Four substantial Doric columns, set in a straight line, supported the cornice, and between the two inner columns, wide stone steps rose to the portico. This led to a single oversized and imposing black door.

Chapter Fifty-Four

Hatcher Estate—Margaret's Memories

When the Austin came to a stop in front of the mansion, it let out a sigh as if coming to the end of a long race. Thomas looked at Margaret, pointed his finger out the car's window, and said, "This is *your* house?"

"No," Margaret said. "This is my *mother's* house. Mine is in Amersham."

She went on. "Now remember, we saw her last week. We took the intercity train over."

"You said your mother doesn't like me."

"That's a good place to start. As I said earlier, you came into her life without her consent. You're the cause of her not hosting my wedding, the major social event in her life, depriving her of Society's center stage. She blames you for us going off and secretly getting married, although it was my idea. Actually, now that I think about it, you should be ashamed of yourself."

"Why did you want to go it alone?"

"Because 'the event' and who I married became more important than my happiness. But that's neither here nor there. You're the outsider and you're being held responsible. If she stays true to form, she'll order a drink shortly after you arrive to alleviate whatever she thinks she has to deal with and start talking nervously."

"You're kidding, of course," he said, thinking of the hour. Margaret just shrugged her shoulders.

They walked up the steps, and Thomas looked up at the enormous door as Margaret rang the bell. "You gave all this up for me?" he said.

"Don't start with me, Thomas; this will be hard enough. What are we going to tell her?"

"I suggest we play it by ear to see where the pieces fall."

She was now noticeably nervous. "Thomas, you're not taking this seriously. We need her help, and you, the absolute wrong person in the world, is asking for it. We'll need some sort of plan to ease her into the idea of providing any help at all."

The door opened. "Too late," Thomas said.

"Pardon, sir?" said the young girl holding the open door. She looked directly at Thomas. She was dressed in a uniform, starting with a gray ruffled cap that covered her forehead and tied in the back. Her dress was black, and over it, she wore a white lace pinafore that looked like the fanciest apron on the planet.

Upon noticing Margaret, the girl said, "Oh, ma' Lady, how good to see you. I'm so sorry, but Alistair asked me to get the door. Come in, come in. Let me take your wrap and things. Lady Hatcher is in the library. Is she expecting you, as she has a guest—Mr. Portman, the solicitor." She leaned forward to Margaret and whispered, "He usually never stays long, but he's been in your mother's private office a good bit today."

"No, Marion," Margaret said. "We didn't phone ahead. But it will be okay. We can wait in the drawing room."

Thomas handed over his coat, their masks, and hats as they moved into the entry foyer. He noted that daughters don't usually need to arrange for a time to stop by their parent's home, let alone ring the bell. He looked at Margaret and wisely chose not to say anything.

They heard voices from the back as a man rounded the corner and, in a deep voice, said, "Marion, my hat if you would be so kind."

There was no sign of 'Mother.'

Marion half-curtsied and said, "Excuse me, Miss; I must fetch Mr. Portman's things."

"That's fine, Marion. We can let ourselves in." She turned and looked toward Thomas, wanting him to follow.

The perfectly appointed interior of the Hatcher Mansion befitted the neat exterior. There were ornate marble work, woodwork, and paintings everywhere. The entry foyer rose two stories above a rectangular floor of ivory-coloured travertine tiles set on the angle.

On the right, a gently curving, grand, rosewood staircase rose to the open second-story balcony. Directly ahead on the back wall, above an arched opening, hung a sizeable intricate verdure tapestry depicting another fox hunt, this one reflecting the manor and its original use as a hunting lodge.

To the left was the largely ceremonial main stateroom where Frederick entertained in the evenings. The room featured a collection of

Louis XVI floral marquetry cabinets and a bronze reproduction of Donatello's almost feminine interpretation of David. An imposing fireplace dominated the center of the stateroom's far wall. Deeply carved into the mantel's center was the name "Hatcher" in script, also added after the royal residency had ended. Besides the carving, the mantel was free of appointments and looked bare.

Parchment-coloured paper covered all the paintings in the room, except for one of Sir Lawton Everett that hung above the fireplace. On either side of the fireplace was the essential embodiment of heraldic insignia: the ancestral coat of arms. These were actual shields decorated with the family design and were the sole right of knights to display with honor. The shields were a purely British tradition that started with the advent of full-body armor. The head-to-toe protection made identifying a knight as a friend or foe impossible. So the design on their shields provided clarity on the battlefield. The shield on the right was the house of Hanover, and on the left was the house of Hatcher. White linen dust covers hid the room's furniture.

Thomas thought he was aware of the vast gulf between the classes. He was most certainly wrong.

Margaret noticed he'd stopped while staring into the room. She offered, "Almost the entire staff is off on the war effort, making ammunition or constructing planes. The house is too large for what staff she has left, so they've shut off some rooms."

They walked into the drawing room. Everything was normal except that the lampstands probably cost more than a car. It was apparent to Thomas they used this room daily. The fireplace was lit, warming two facing divans separated by a low glass table. The right side of the room was predominantly glass, facing toward the rear of the house and overlooking a perfectly groomed immense green landscape. Outside, a kitchen garden and a small glass hot house sat to the left of a small outbuilding.

Thomas walked over to the window, taking in the acres of rolling green lawns, trees, and shrubbery. A short distance away, near a stand of full trees, an older man carried a woven basket. An undergardener in training accompanied him. The older man stopped and, reaching down, picked up a single solitary broad leaf off the recently cut grass. He looked closely at its underside for a brief moment, showing it to the young man, before placing it in the basket. Then he reached up into a nearby tree, lifting a branch, half turning it over. Satisfied with something, he moved on.

Margaret came up from behind Thomas, took his arm, and leaned against him.

233

"That's Ned Pomeroy, the head gardener. He has been with the family since before I was born. He's one of the few who long ago became, as my father would put it, a working family member.' Ned and Father had a unique relationship. They had the habit of disappearing for hours. They'd locate a new bottle of Scotch from the gardener's tool cabinet and an old folding table and find a hiding place in the hedge garden. There they'd solve the problems of the world, playing cards, until the last light was gone."

Margaret looked up at Thomas with a grin. "Father always bragged that he lost enough to put Ned's daughter through school. So, when she graduated from Wembury Medical Academy as a full surgeon's nurse, nobody thought twice about it."

She paused, "Father took care of us all."

She raised her other arm, pointing toward a small building with an unusual oriental flavor in its design. "Over there's a garden whimsy. In the old days, the landed royals would compete, building these elaborate little cottages that performed absolutely no function. Father had that one shipped from some manor in the North, reassembling it on the top of that knoll. It took months and was one of his all-time favorite projects.

"It was also very special to me," she said, yanking Thomas's arm and displaying an oversized smile.

Thomas gave in. "Okay, I get it, and why was it so special?" he said.

"Well, since you asked, I had my first kiss under that roof. Poor Nigel," she said, lost in an image in her mind. "He and I were walking in the garden, anxiously being chaperoned from this very window by Mother. She was uncomfortable with the prospect of me walking alone with a boy, especially after I told her I would cause a fit in front of him if she didn't relent."

In mock surprise, Thomas said, "You? A fit? I don't believe it."

"Yes, and it would have been a good one too. Of course, I knew that just the slightest prospect of boorish behavior traveling back to mother's friends, with their perfectly mannered daughters, would have been unbearable. My lone concession was agreeing to stay in sight.

"Just as the motion of Mother, moving to improve her line of view, caught my eye, a downpour drove Nigel and me to the whimsy for cover. Oh, Thomas, it was too funny for words. In seconds, there was an all-out alert, with Mother in a tizzy directing Mr. Pomeroy, now holding an umbrella, to bring us in forthwith. He did this dutifully but only after feigning to have understood we were in the potting shed. According to Mother, he was wasting precious minutes." Margaret laughed aloud at the memory.

"There we were, for a priceless few moments, conveniently out of sight. Nigel started to mumble and look at his shoes. There was just enough time for him to ask politely, but I would have none of it. I went to the top of my toes and just kissed him mid-sentence. I was a starry-eyed fifteen and madly in love. He was about to try again, and I wouldn't let him."

Thomas said, "Why not? You see, that's the problem with women; just because they're in control, they don't have to act like it."

Before Thomas could properly make his point, a male voice said, "Lady Hatcher, may I?"

Thomas turned to see a butler standing in the doorway. Hearing a conversation in progress, he asked permission to enter the room. He appeared to be somewhat over sixty and stood ramrod straight. He was dressed in what looked like a comfortable tuxedo covering a very trim and healthy frame. His posture, the cadence of his voice, or just his tone created a palpable presence.

"Alistair," Margaret almost shouted as she rushed across the room. "Where have you been?" she said, bussing his cheeks. "You weren't here last time. The evening spun off with me forgetting to ask where you were."

Alistair turned to Thomas, offering his hand and saying, "Welcome, Mr. Watson." They firmly shook hands. When Thomas released, Alistair kept his grip, looked down at their clasped hands briefly, then glanced up with a gentle smile.

"Oh, Alistair," Margaret said sharply, "when Mother isn't around, would you please call him Thomas? Now, tell me, where on earth did you disappear to?"

"I had to ask Lady Hatcher for some personal time as I finally located David. Thankfully, he was one of the rescued survivors at Dunkirk."

"Oh, Alistair, that's such great news. What happened? Where was he found?"

"At a recovery hospital where the boys were sent, but in the chaos, the records followed sometime later. He was a frightful mess. The doctors called it 'shell-shocked.' I think he was just a scared boy who became a soldier and hadn't anticipated the horrors of war. Those lads were lucky to be alive, let alone back home."

Margaret, with deep concern, asked, "How was it possible all those soldiers were able to get off of one beach?"

"He said he was able to catch a ride with three others in a small pleasure craft. Just one of the hundreds of private boats Churchill called to service to bring our boys home. David said he saw an older man and his son just off the French shore. The man was waving his hat, trying to get someone's attention. David and his mates left everything on the beach without hesitating and swam out. The owner turned out to be a master seaman. Together they battled a rough Channel sea, with the boys constantly bailing. A little worse for wear, but safe they are."

Alistair looked down, "It's starting to come out that over 35,000 soldiers were left behind. They were fighting inland, protecting those on the beach, and didn't get picked up by any of the rescue boats. They're heroes as far as I'm concerned, as they helped save my boy and over half a million others. His mother would literally strike me from heaven if I ever let anything happen to him. God rest her soul."

Margaret interrupted, "What a sad, sullen story. Those boys are the ones who'll keep us safe, and, yes, thank God, all is well with David. We shall all be grateful."

Then, without thinking, Margaret said, "Alistair, I want you to meet Thomas." Perfectly appropriate, as in Margaret's mind, he'd never been there before. Putting her fingers over her mouth, she realized what she'd said. The butler was, to put it mildly, a bit confused.

Thomas said, smiling, "Alistair, some things need to be explained. However, now isn't the time."

"Of course," he said with a perceptible nod. "If I may be excused now, as Lady Hatcher should be along any minute."

"Why do you stay here and put up with Mother? With your qualifications, you could work at Buckingham as the King's valet, with a good raise in rate at that."

"Ah, your Father … well," Alistair stumbled for words. He finally smiled at Thomas, "I think now isn't the time."

He gave the slightest bow from the waist, smoothly took a half step back, turned, and left the room. Margaret said, "He was father's valet and head of the household but so much more. When I was younger, he looked after me with a level of devotion I just didn't appreciate at the time."

"He's very dedicated," Thomas said, sensing the depth of her emotion.

"One time, when Father was off at one of the factories, after a good rumpus with Mum, I stormed off to my bedroom. In the middle of the night, I managed to make my way out of the service entrance and tried to run away.

"I realized it was very dark, scary, and cold after a while. I was hiding in the doorway of some building, hoping the sun would come up soon, when I heard Alistair gently calling out from a distance, trying not to startle me. He slowly approached out of the darkness and quietly explained it wasn't safe for a twelve-year-old to wander the roads at night. This gentle man had followed me for what had to be a mile, somehow staying out of my sight. He was the only person, other than Mr. Pomeroy and Father, who could have gotten me to go back to the house. Mother never knew. When things would get tense around the house, Alistair and I would share a wink every now and then, with him waving a finger side to side, knowing what I was thinking."

Thomas shrugged his shoulders. "I'll remember that the next time you wink at me, then turn up gone."

"That, my good man, will never happen."

Moving over to a tall, beautiful cabinet with curved glass doors, he looked at the myriad pieces displayed inside. Most were made of wood, some with metal fittings; all were well-used or old. Staring at a piece but addressing Margaret's last comment, Thomas said, "You said, 'my good man.' Isn't that something normally exchanged between two men?"

"Normally, ought to answer your question, Mr. Watson—normally."

He looked at her, saying, "Indeed it does, Mrs. Watson." His attention shifted back to the cabinet. "This looks interesting," he said, his nose almost on the glass. "It's a collection of something, but what?"

"It's my father's collection of items used in weaving textiles. Some are very old. Despite my lack of interest, I had to know the history of every spindle, shuttle, and bobbin. Every time he added another piece to the collection, I got the whole story. Go ahead, pick out something."

"Oh, yes, I can't resist," he said. He pointed to three thin flat wooden boards, each about five inches wide and twelve inches long. Threads along each edge attached the two together but allowed them to move independently. Each board contained holes punched in a six-by-twenty-six pattern. With a smirk, he said, "You can tell me about this one."

"That's the easy one. In 1801, a person named Jacquard used the holes to control the pattern being woven on his loom. You might say," she paused for additional emphasis, "he was to weaving what Gutenberg was to printing."

Thomas crossed his arms, making it obvious he was very pleased with himself.

"You're looking awfully impressed with yourself without cause," Margaret said.

"That story is good," he said, "but only partly right. You only get a B+."

"Rubbish, I don't get anything but A's, which is far from what you can claim. Anyway, how would you know? In fact, you're the one who asked—remember?"

"Don't ask me how I know because I thought we wouldn't go into that anymore. You said Jacquard was the first to use punched holes on a weaving machine. He wasn't."

"Was, too," she said.

"Was not."

Margaret glared at him. Thomas adjusted his coat and removed an invisible piece of lint. "Jacquard was, in fact, the first to use wooden punched cards strung together, making him very famous and successful. However," Thomas said, pausing, "a guy named Basil something used punched holes in stiff paper seventy years before that."

"Did not."

"Sorry," Thomas said, "you lost the contest."

Margaret moved between him and the cabinet, poking him in the chest with her finger. "I didn't lose anything because you had the wrong answer, making it the end of this conversation."

Chapter Fifty-Five

Mrs. Somerville's Home
Amersham

Shortly after rising that morning, Beth Somerville brought the kitchen cabinet doors together, pressing them firmly against the latches. She kept pressing them for a moment, pausing in distant thought, finally admitting that she had to choose. She picked up the pen and paper from the small telephone shelf on the wall and placed them on the dining room table. Pulling up a chair, she touched pen to paper. Its movements would write the words that could lead her life down a path she'd never expected and wasn't sure she wanted to travel. The reason she'd agreed to help no longer directed her actions. Her impulse had transformed from a desire to be useful to her country into a need to protect someone she cared for as if she were her daughter.

The government had made it clear: if she thought Margaret was in danger, her only responsibility was to make contact, keeping it brief. The man had indicated they'd take care of everything else. However, was she in danger? Today she was sure Thomas loved Margaret, while just a week ago, she'd thought him the kind of opportunist who could cloak the darkest of intentions with innocence and charm. Still, she hadn't thought he posed a threat to Margaret. Margaret was trying to build something of a life with someone she believed cared for her.

It was an important decision. Beth wondered if notifying the authorities would jeopardize her relationship with the new Thomas. In their shared times alone, Margaret had confided that she suspected Thomas possessed a shady side. Nevertheless, Margaret persisted out of a desire for love and comfort. To Margaret, nothing could withstand her persistence if she was to decide it so. After all, she'd withstood the towering will of her mother and won. At least she thought she had.

Beth looked at the paper. She finally decided that Margaret, having been anywhere near the shooting, changed everything. The man had told her that if Margaret was in danger, so was England. She shook her head in frustration and started writing.

To: Dacha
Believe Princess in danger, awaiting instructions.
Actor

She placed the small paper in a plain envelope, wrapped it in wax paper and put it in her purse with a piece of chalk. She went into her bedroom, and to the right side of the headboard reached between the mattress and the box springs. After several unproductive stabs, she caught her breath, coming upon the object. Back in the front room, she grabbed a warm muffler and stopped. Where was her mask? "It's always here," she thought. She closed her eyes at her stupidity. Her memory for the little things wasn't what it had been. She'd left it in the cab.

Beth sat on her divan, looking out the front window sheers. She smiled as she recognixed the car pulling up in front of her house. She put aside the things on her lap and she made her way to the hall and front door.

Sanjay watched her as she covered the twenty feet to his car.

"Good morning, Sanjay. I'm thrilled you could make it. I must say your dispatch man wasn't at all encouraging. I need to go to Camden Town Station."

"You mean the stop after Euston?"

"That'll be the one. Never been there, but it should be across the street from a park."

"You want me to take you to the Amersham stop or directly to the Camden Town Station?"

"Young man, I'm perfectly capable of walking to the underground at Amersham myself. You must get me to this address or close to it."

"Camden Town, mum, you must know this part of town isn't the best."

"I know. Given my wishes, we both wouldn't be going there, but urgent business leads where it leads."

They continued the conversation they'd started the night before. Touching on the war, his family, and what he did with his friends during his short time off. Eventually, they arrived in the area. Sanjay slowly drove past the station to the street named on the piece of paper.

"Is this it?" he asked.

"I think so," she said, re-examining her instructions. "Sanjay, it's over there in the park square."

"I'm sorry, mum. I know it's out of line, but what possible business could you have here? The green is known to harbor less-than-desirable people. I know this to be true."

"Sanjay, you're a gentleman. I appreciate your concern, but believe me when I say you don't want to know any more. Besides, it's obviously someone's idea of a joke."

Beth knew this was one of many drop-off points and was intentionally out of the way. The big wigs making the decisions usually dealt with men and didn't expect to ever direct a woman of her age to such an unsuitable location. She peered out the window with a displeased look.

"Sanjay, I think you must come with me briefly, as I'll need some help. Would you do that for me?"

"Of course, mum," he said, stepping out, making sure not to open her door.

She felt uncomfortable and clutched her purse close. She realized how thankful she was Sanjay was with her.

"We're just going over to that bridge," Beth said.

The cab driver and the woman walked into the common, delighted it was empty of people. A small decorative walking bridge barely ten feet long rose over a rock-filled riverbed that only saw water in a storm. There were square posts at either end of the bridge. They had originally supported gas lights but had fallen into disrepair long ago. Standing at the foot of the bridge, she moved to the lefthand side, holding onto the lamppost. Looking down made her afain grateful Sanjay was with her. The edge of the dry river fell steeply and down well over a foot. With no proper handholds, it would be a challenge to get back up, let alone not land on her backside going down.

"Sanjay, could you help me put this letter under that dark rock?"

"I would be happy to, mum." Effortlessly, he climbed down and completed the task.

"Youth," she said to Sanjay. "As soon as you know how life works, you lose the ability to work it. Thank you very much."

"Now, if you don't mind, can we take our leave?" Sanjay said as he looked around for no one in particular.

"Gladly, Sanjay, if I can ask just one more favor. Can you go over to the letterbox at the corner of the green and, using this chalk, place an X six inches high on the side toward the station?"

The cab driver's eyes became curious, but he held out his hand.

"I know. Crazy, isn't it? But upon that, our chores are complete, and we can retire to the warm confines of the cab."

Mrs. Beth Somerville, a dear friend of Margaret, had put the future in motion. She knew the next step was to return to the house and await a reply. Waiting would be difficult as she didn't know how or when they'd contact her.

Chapter Fifty-Six

Turing's Laboratory

After yesterday's phone call to Colville, Turing stayed at the lab with his group, working through the night. The hours flew as they incorporated the new ideas the very mysterious Mr. Dunning supplied. Skepticism prevailed but gradually gave way to the practical realization that his suggestions could be the answer.

There were still problems, to be sure. Particularly troublesome was Foster's task of converting the teleprinter into something that punched the proper holes in the tape, matching the original written command. The other issue was the instruction sent to the electrical switch controlling the position of the drum. In a flash of brilliance, Gordon came up with the idea of a conversion board, but as a pure one-off prototype, it was a trial-and-error effort. Nevertheless, the time had come to test the principal concept, even without a sample from the teleprinter crew.

Turing said, "Are we ready?" Everyone nodded.

For the test, they had a single set of wires from the electrical switch mounted into the hardware cabinet that ran to the output side of the conversion board. Another single set went from the input positions on the board to the new photocell assembly.

Gordon walked to the other side of the cabinet where he could monitor the switch. Duncan hovered over the conversion board. Turing slipped a piece of paper, manually punched with a single instruction, between the cells. Three distinct clicks followed as the relay adjusted the drum to the new position.

"Whoa," Gordon yelled.

"Are you alright?" Foster asked.

"Bloody hell," was Turings reply. "It kicked the switch."

Turing looked at the switch settings written on the punched piece of paper. "Gordon, read off the setting."

Out of sight behind the cabinet, Gordon read off: "Set one is twelve, set two is nine, and three is fifteen."

"Exactly!" Turing yelled, throwing his arms in the air. "Just like we designed it. Right, boys?"

"Damn right, Doctor," Gordon said. "Now it's a matter of creating the wire harness to connect the switches to the conversion board."

"That's a valley full of wires," Turing said, "and we must test each."

Duncan was looking at the bottom of the board and said, "We'll need some help with the mechanics. Can we pull in some people with clearances?"

"I'll work on that," Turing said, but first, another test. "Gordon, get your hands out of there for a second."

"Why?" Gordon replied from behind the machine. "I'm going to marry this thing; I'm in love."

Turing slipped the paper between the cells again and waited. There was no sound. "Nothing happened," he said.

"Of course not. You fed it the same instruction," Gordon said.

"Bravo, Gordon. That's why I hired you. If it switched the first time correctly, we could send each instruction twice as a parity check at no cost in cycle time. One error resets the switch back to zero. We can probably dispense with the parity at some point, but not now."

They'd eventually need a real coded message with the wheel settings, Turing knew, but they weren't there yet. Another group worked on converting the settings into the punched tape equivalent that would be used when Foster's teleprinter was ready. There was a sense in the group they were getting close, at least finally making progress.

Chapter Fifty-Seven

Meeting Mother
Hatcher Estate

Margaret wasn't happy with Thomas telling her she'd lost when it wasn't the truth. They didn't have the opportunity to resolve the issue, though. Thomas could hear the rapid click click click of footsteps across the marble tile as Lady Hatcher approached. It was as though an energy force was moving in. Soon, he would finally meet this legend. How was he going to ask her for help? Right now, it appeared to be a stupid idea. Somehow, Thomas needed to win her over, but his method would have to be different, something that Margaret's old Thomas had never tried. Without a list of previous efforts, it would be pure guesswork.

Still, out of sight, Lady Hatcher said, "Margaret dear, is that you?"

At last, she emerged from the main entry hall into the drawing room. With an awkward hesitation, she walked up to Margaret and placed her hands on the side of her daughter's shoulders. Margaret's mother was obviously glad to see her daughter but held her there at arm's length. Thomas was surprised at the somewhat subdued reception given that Margaret was her only child and guessed that overt displays of emotion weren't proper for England's elite.

"What marvelous timing," she said. "Marion was just laying out breakfast. You simply must stay for some food. After all, it's your mother talking."

Margaret said, "I know it's early, but we have something to discuss with you."

"Come, come over, and sit down," she said, ignoring Margaret's comment. Lady Hatcher placed a hand on Margaret's back and directed her toward the facing divans in front of the fireplace. Lady Hatcher moved the stitched pillows and sat, crossing her arms and legs. "Yes, then," she said.

This was followed by an awkward few seconds of silence when she, in an almost obliged manner, looked up and said, "Oh, ah, Thomas... And how are you today?"

Thomas joined them on the divans, trying to decipher any obscure clues in her tone of voice and body language that could help him. Unfortunately, the clues were so obscure he determined it was like studying the backside of an unknown painting. Lady Hatcher was a totally opaque and superficial personality, giving away nary a smudge common on the back of every artistic effort.

With that, he offered, "Actually, Lady Hatcher, I'm doing quite well, thank you, and you?"

She looked directly at him and then briefly looked at Margaret. Thomas felt Margaret's hand on his knee, noting the somewhat pained smile fastened to her face.

Lady Hatcher replied, "Well, other than how war can clip your wings in ways one never thought possible, I guess I'll survive. The new 'day girl' I was excited about bringing on lasted a fortnight. She accepted a job changing linen at the Navy hospital. I offered her more money, but she said I had missed the point. Simply can't understand young people nowadays."

"Mother, there will be others."

"Perhaps, but meanwhile, things are getting behind. We closed down all but one of the guestrooms, thinking you might need it and without help, more rooms are sure to follow. Before long, I'll be forced to stay in my bedroom all day."

Trying for sincerity, Thomas said, "Things appear to be bad all over." The line landed flat.

Thomas winced and, trying to recover, said, "How is the business going? I think the war would generate a nice increase in the order rate for your textiles." He shifted on the couch and removed a pillow that looked nice enough but made it impossible to sit comfortably. That's when Thomas noticed Margaret's mother hadn't responded and was just staring at him.

She said slowly and more thoughtfully, "Now, Thomas, that's very odd. You've never had the slightest interest in the actual state of the business, let alone discussing the order rate. However, your relentless delving into the content and location of the company's projects was more than irritating. What, may I ask, has generated this change? Also, when did you decide to start calling me Lady Hatcher?"

In a motion, she summoned Marion. "Marion, dear, would you have Alistair prepare me a gin and orange?" She quickly returned to her commanding cadence as he and Margaret exchanged glances.

"In here, Madam?" Marion said.

"No, I shall have it with breakfast."

"Mother, it's not important; he was just trying to be polite," Margaret said, trying to save Thomas from what could become a tense moment. "You didn't like it when he called you Mum. You said he didn't have the right, despite the marriage."

"He didn't, young lady; I barely knew him."

Margaret tried to turn the conversation away from going off the cliff. "Why was Mr. Portman calling so early in the morning? I don't ever remember him up before mid-day."

Mother's thoughts returned to the conversation. "He came for a proxy signature on a board vote this morning. I never go anymore. Those meetings are just too dull and smoky. Men and their cigars, it's a dreadful habit. I tried to pass an amendment that they couldn't foul the air when the owner was in attendance. Mr. Campbell called a break, taking me aside, and tried to explain, as if imparting a secret known only to men, that it was a necessary part of the thinking process. What a heap of rubbish. I acquiesced because he's succeeded in keeping everything on an even keel through some spotty times.

"Anyway, one of the factories sustained serious damage from this constant bombing. Mr. Campbell called a meeting to approve a short-term repair loan, as all working capital is in inventory. Your father always knew when someone was ready to take on added responsibilities. Giving Mr. Campbell an opportunity to prove himself was a masterstroke. I just don't know what I would do without him."

Thomas said, "Perhaps Mr. Campbell should contact the War Office. After the first bombing, I know that they decided to make long-term funds available to damaged factories critical to the war effort. I believe it's Sir Walter Mildmay, Chancellor of the Exchequer, who stated that it was the highest priority and all efforts would be made to cut the bureaucratic process."

Thomas thought this was an informative addition to the flow of the conversation, but it turned out he was wrong.

All he got was a blank look that contained no ill will but he was anxious nonetheless. Lady Hatcher remained hard to read. She turned her head away from looking at Thomas for a moment. Deep in thought, she absent-mindedly reached for the fabric of her dress, precisely rearranging the folds into other folds.

"Ready, Ma'am," Marion said, entering the room during the silence.

With breakfast called, Margaret's mother promptly rose from the divan and stepped around the glass table. She put her arm around

Margaret and started toward the dining room. Thomas, left on his own, followed.

"It's just lovely that you're here. Will you be staying in your room? I left it made."

At that point, Thomas smiled as he brought up the rear. He'd set upon a plan. It was apparent the other Thomas hadn't tried to win her respect or even get her attention. Every time he said a word, he felt it was out of turn. Thomas needed to gain her attention. If he could gain her respect, that would be even better.

They walked down a vast hall and turned left into a wonderful surprise—a bright, warm day room, serving as a private informal eating area. A rectangular table, surrounded by large, heavy chairs, dominated the center of the room. To the left, aligned with the table, stood a tall glass wall separating the room from a solarium on the other side. Hanging plants from the iron roof supports hung down, all overflowing their containers with colour, highlighted by sunlight shining through the glass ceiling. Some of the plants, having just been watered, were still dripping. The solarium floor was wet, leaving the impression that Mr. Pomeroy had made a timely disappearance. The whole effect was just short of a splendid Monet painting.

Marion had already added two table settings and moved the flower arrangement from the center to avoid obstructing their conversation. Marion pulled the chair back with considerable effort, and Mrs. Hatcher sat down, saying, "We lost both of our footmen to the war effort. This resulted in our breaking some centuries-old rule stating that only men can serve in the dining areas. The war has also attacked social stability and tradition."

Margaret sighed. "I'm sure the only people that care are in the same situation."

Ignoring the comment, Mother started directing. "Margaret, you sit here, and Thomas, you there."

Thomas saw it as the perfect opportunity and said, "Actually, I prefer Margaret sit over here by me, so she can enjoy looking out the window at those lovely flowers. What a splendid area and right where it can be enjoyed."

Mrs. Hatcher sat for a moment, either unable to understand or think she hadn't heard what was actually said. Thomas felt he was starting to get her attention.

Alistair came in with her drink on a tray, placing it directly to the right of the butter dish in front of her plate. Silently, she reached out and took a less-than-demure sip before putting it back down. Then, as if nothing had happened, she said, "Marion darling, would you tell the kitchen maid to go back to Fortnum & Mason to get more of that black tea and those delicious tiny jars of caviar? I would like them for the ladies this afternoon."

"Yes, Ma'am," She replied.

Mrs. Hatcher returned her attention to the table, addressing Margaret. "It will be quite the surprise from the standard fare of cake and cookies. I know they'd rather lunch at the Strand or the Berkley to ogle the dashing wing commanders or young Guards officers. However, it's my turn to prepare for the afternoon. So they'll act their age and settle for a nice lunch in and cards."

"I think they'll be delighted," Thomas said. "How many will there be?"

Ignoring his question, she raised her arm, turning her finger in a circle, motioning toward the vase of flowers. "Marion, could you turn that vase a bit so that wonderful orchid from Mr. Pomeroy's hot house is facing us?"

Marion did so while looking at Mrs. Hatcher, waiting for the exact position, and Lady Hatcher saying, "Marvelous."

"Thomas, there are six of us; there have always been six of us," Margaret's mother said, unconsciously reaching for her drink again.

Thomas was sure his former self wasn't usually this engaged.

"Now Margaret, you'll have those fluffy eggs you like, and Thomas, you'll have those dreadful bangers—a taste you share fully with Alistair, which, if the truth be known, is the only reason we always have them on hand."

Thomas looked up at Marion and said, "Actually, if it's possible, I would like an egg omelet with oregano, and Margaret would be thrilled if you could come up with a cream cheese turnover with strawberries."

With wide eyes, Marion cleared her throat and looked at Thomas, and then she looked at Mrs. Hatcher and then at Margaret, who had placed her hands in her lap and had a delightful smile on her face. Other than that, Marion didn't move or speak.

Thomas thought, "I've done it again."

"That sounds wonderful," Margaret said. "Do you have them? How, on God's earth, can you get strawberries with the war and all? I'll bet Uncle Ned has planted delicious secrets in his victory garden."

Chapter Fifty-Eight

Mother's Other Side
Hatcher Estate

Lady Hatcher's hand sent Marion out of the dining room, and she stopped just before touching her glass again. She put her hand back in her lap and, with her head looking down, raised her napkin to her lips. Then, for the first time since Thomas had entered the front door, she looked straight at him. She held the look long enough to draw attention.

Lady Hatcher's husband had always said that the head of a large business required clarity and the ability to address problems head-on. He admired his wife not for what she'd become but for what she'd been early in their marriage.

Then Lady Hatcher said, with the weight and intonation long the purview of England's ruling class, "I must apologize to you both as I've been deliberately vague about Mr. Portman's presence this morning."

Thomas and Margaret both noticed a change in tone and demeanor. Gone was the controlling social butterfly she chose to present to her daughter and the world.

Thomas thought, "I'm correct about there being two sides of Mother. One was the world of social relationships, the pastime of the invested class, shielding her from the realities of 'duty'." Thomas felt he was about to be presented, or confronted, with the other side of the painting. Perhaps just such comportment is what initially attracted Mr. Hatcher.

Margaret sat up and looked at Thomas with wide eyes. There was no mistaking she'd noticed the change, and it caught her by surprise.

"Marion?" Mother said rather loudly.

The maid hadn't gone far and re-entered the doorway. Before she'd gone two steps, her employer raised her arm with her hand bent at the wrist. Marion stopped dead in her tracks.

"Get the door, would you?"

"Yes, ma'am," she said, pulling the double sliding doors together.

Lady Hatcher continued, "He's not returning a paper to the board, as I said. Mr. Portman has an important meeting at the War Office where he's presenting secret company contracts for final signature. In those contracts, we agree to continue providing specific assistance at the request of the highest levels of government."

She turned and looked at Margaret. "This is just the sort of assistance your father and your grandfather repeatedly provided in their service to the crown."

She pushed her chair back a few more inches from the table and said, "Thomas, I'm troubled, or perhaps intrigued is a better way to put it. Actually, it's more in the area of things not adding up. For the brief time we've known each other, you've never called me Lady Hatcher. You didn't last week, nor the times before, but you did this morning. You'll remember early on, in our private meeting, I indicated Helen was more than proper. We discussed how the tone was more important than the word."

"The *tone*?" Margaret's voice went up. She looked at Thomas, about to go off. "I don't remember that conversation. Why wasn't I invited?" She was barely able to contain herself. Thomas did his best to give her a firm look, hoping it would convince her to let it pass.

Mrs. Hatcher continued, "Thomas, seldom do you participate in our conversations except when trying to obtain information regarding projects within the company. Until then, you pretend to be interested when you clearly are not. You never offer opinions because you have none. Further, under no circumstances do you ever present contrary ideas to those I present. You're always very careful to avoid any behavior that may place you out of favor. I've always felt such an exchange would lead to your revealing more of yourself than you're willing to share. The affluent have developed a keen eye concerning those whose sincerity is less than genuine. Thus, I've held you in contempt as a shameless interloper and opportunist, among other strong feelings."

Margaret bolted straight up out of her chair. "*What?*" she almost yelled.

Thomas grabbed the back of Margaret's dress, gently pulling her back into her chair. She was so distracted by her anger she stayed seated for a full second. Then, on her way back up again, Thomas put a hand on her shoulder, saying, "Margaret, I'm the one taking the beating, so let her have her say. I'm asking you to listen for two more minutes. Please let her continue."

Margaret's face was contorted and red as she looked at her mother. Thomas felt the pain of Margaret's death grip on his leg under the table.

"Thank you, dear," her mother said.

"I find this a bit awkward, but I heard you discussing something before I entered the drawing room. I heard you talking as if Thomas was a first-time guest here. Just before I made my entrance Margaret, you described things you'd covered previously with Thomas. If you remember, all three of us were standing at the glass cabinet when it occurred. In addition," she continued, "you've always eaten those dreadful sausages except once, when Alistair had the last of them. Add that to your business knowledge for specific projects I wasn't sure you knew existed. I guess all of that's innocent enough, except in this case. Then you combine it with information that won't be public for another two weeks. More than *that,* it's currently a state secret."

Margaret and Thomas just looked at each other in silence, both feeling as though they were caught in the act of something illegal or, worse, embarrassing. Nothing prepared them for the direct confrontation put forth by Mother.

She turned to Margaret and said, "Margaret, dear, Sir Walter Mildmay hasn't yet announced this particular program. In fact, due to the extreme secrecy, the honorable chancellor was only to be made aware of its existence upon the proposal's acceptance. Only a few people in the government have the power to restrict information elected officials require in the course of their duties. Yet Thomas approaches the issue as though it were general knowledge."

She slowly placed her napkin onto her empty plate and continued to look directly at Thomas—directly into his eyes. She then cast a contemplative glance toward the terrace and back to Margaret. The room had a palpable silence.

Then, without the slightest bit of anger, she said, "You're not Thomas, are you? I know it's not normal; in fact, I know it's not possible. Conceivably a twin, or perhaps an actor, I've no idea, except to know what I've seen."

Thomas looked at Margaret. She looked back while turning her hair behind a left ear.

Thomas thought for a second. Before him was no social dilettante; she was intelligent and perceptive, and she knew it. The subject concerned her daughter, the family business, and her country. Dutifully, wanting answers, she cut right to the core.

Margaret took a deep breath and blurted out, "Mother, that's why we're here. We desperately need your help with something that could save England and win the war."

"Well, there it was," Thomas thought. "Mother like daughter." They both had an intrinsic manner of getting right to the point. Every moment he spent with Margaret compelled him to admire a woman he barely knew. She had said we needed a 'plan' to *ease* Mother into helping them. Now that Margaret had hit her mother over the head with it, what would follow was anybody's guess.

"Mother, Thomas isn't Thomas in the way, well… he is but not the one we know."

"That's an intriguing sentence," her mother said. She reached for her gin and orange, raised her eyebrows, and said, "Care to try again?"

"Several days ago, the Thomas we know went away. I don't know how, and neither does, well, Thomas. One evening another person or personality walked out of the bathroom and into my life. We both know I married Thomas because he did not meet with your approval. If I'd married my new Thomas, neither of us would have had a problem. However, that's not what's going to be difficult to understand. Thomas, can you…?"

"Lady Ha, I mean, Helen, I don't exactly remember anything before that time. What I remember or, more precisely, what I sense, are current events. I know about events before they occur. However mysterious, that's the explanation for knowing about the program the chancellor has yet to announce."

Lady Hatcher took this in with an eerie calm, characteristically giving nothing away.

Thomas, knowing there was no reasonable explanation, continued.

"I don't know why I have this ability or knowledge, but it's especially true concerning the war. England is destined to stand tall and set an example for the continent. They, I mean, *we* will eventually defeat the Luftwaffe and Hitler with the aid of the Americans."

"The Americans?" Mother said. "They're isolationists and could give a tinker's damn about England. They wouldn't give 2p for our troubles."

"That's true today," Thomas said, "but not later. The Japanese will attack Pearl Harbor. The next day, Hitler declares war on the United States, giving Roosevelt a reason to get America involved in Europe. Right now, Hitler is determined to conquer England. Given the poor state of the RAF, the moment is closer than anyone will know until after the war."

Mother quickly said, "Preposterous. You can't possibly know what people will be thinking after the war. You can't know this!"

Having to defend an impossible situation, Thomas said, "I don't know how; I just know. I'm also certain that we will win the war. However, other than not surrendering, I'm unsure how."

"Mother," Margaret said, "he predicted the bombing of the civilians in Berlin the day before it was in the paper. He told me exactly what was going to occur. He doesn't know how it works, Mother, but I truly believe he's correct."

"Helen, very shortly, the war cabinet will try to force Churchill to consider some type of surrender."

"Nonsense!" she said.

"No, Helen, there will be a meeting on September seventh; they'll debate the risk of defending an invasion without air cover. The debate will be close, and all I know is that Churchill's persuasive performance convinces the cabinet to stay the course in the face of compelling evidence otherwise."

Lady Hatcher was confused. "But you said we will win the war."

"An excellent point, one Margaret and I have discussed. Yes, if everything goes according to my memories and those men make the same decision. However, because the issue isn't definitive, they could come to another decision. In history, there are examples where, for no obvious reason, events appear to take the path not obvious."

Thomas reached for his water glass and took a sip. "With this ambiguity, it can't be left to chance. I must get to Churchill and stress the importance of not giving up the fight. I know that coming from me, it's not a convincing argument, but I can tell him things that may get his attention. He might press harder in the meeting to accept nothing less than continuing the effort if there's just an iota of trust. It might just be the margin he needs. We need to prevail."

Chapter Fifty-Nine

Breakfast
Hatcher Estate

Sitting at the end of the table, Lady Hatcher was trying to grasp the extraordinary information presented to her. There were so many interacting parts. This wasn't the old, bad Thomas but the new, good Thomas. However, this Thomas could foretell the future. He's the Thomas Margaret loved, and she had to admit that despite his unbelievable story, there was a warm transparency about the man that had been absent in who or whatever existed before. In addition, a bond formed with her daughter that she'd longed for but was beyond her reach. She decided that if a close relationship might come out of such a strange situation, the change to Thomas was secondary.

She addressed Thomas: "What makes you think he'll believe you? What makes you think I believe you?"

"Because we can't take the chance, I'm wrong," he said in a definitive tone Thomas hadn't used in her presence before. "I tried to contact someone at Bletchely Park whose work I was aware of, but was kept from talking to him."

"Mother, yesterday we think someone tried to kill Thomas at Bletchley."

"What?" she said. "This tale is getting beyond believable."

"I was shot at several times and escaped when Margaret came 'round in a car in the nick of time."

"How did they know you would be there? Who are they?"

Thomas shook his head, "I don't know. Perhaps they work for the Germans. If they do, they've very good intelligence—extremely good intelligence. *Who* isn't as important as why. Some faction wants me out of the way. We suspect it's something involving the original Thomas."

Margaret's mother shook her head. "If all this is true, and it's a big if, what are your plans? Why did you both come to see me?'

"Mother, you're the only one we know who has contacts high enough in the government to get a meeting with Churchill."

"My dear Margaret, surely you don't think I'm going to just ring up and get you a meeting with Winston? We're in the middle of a war."

"That," Thomas said, "is precisely why you have to do it."

"Well, that's not a good enough reason, even if he would take my call."

"Lady Hatcher, have you seen this morning's paper?"

"No. Mr. Pomeroy interrupted my morning routine."

Thomas sat up straight in his chair. "Late yesterday and last night, British bombers struck a factory near Berlin. It wasn't successful from a military standpoint but was on a political and propaganda level. Churchill will declare, 'This Island Nation shall not cower, nor shall we in the slightest think in such regards.' Get your paper, and it should confirm and validate my information."

"What if you've already read the paper this morning? Forgive my bluntness, Thomas, but what if you're lying?" she said.

"I'm not lying. And what would I have to gain except your questioning my sanity?"

Lady Hatcher shot back, "I'm sure it comes as no surprise that I've already addressed that possibility."

"Do I look or sound like I'm struggling with clarity?"

"No, you don't," she said. "But things of the mind are seldom that simple."

With a detectable smile, Thomas said, "Then we're left with what do I have to lose?"

The Lady raised her voice, calling out through the door. "Marion."

The dining room door opened. "Yes, Ma'am."

"Can you get this morning's paper from the patio table or from Mr. Pomeroy in the kitchen?"

"Yes, Ma'am," Marion said as she did a small curtsy and left the room.

A silence filled with foreboding, hanging between them while they waited for Marion to return. Lady Hatcher rotated the glass in front of her as she waited, taking the time to contemplate the impossible information.

Eventually, they heard Marion run up the hall from the patio and then stop and slowly walk around the corner into the room and hand

Lady Hatcher a newspaper. Helen opened the half-folded paper, and the front page confirmed the bombing of German munitions factories in a raid personally directed by Churchill. It was in retaliation for a previous attack on London's civilian population. She perused the body of the article for an eternity.

"You won't find information about how bad the airfields are. I can assure you that," Thomas said.

"No, I wouldn't expect to find a status of our defenses given to the world. However, your quoting of Churchill was only close."

Thomas thought he heard just a hint of respect.

She looked up from the paper at Margaret. "Dear, what do you think of all of this?"

"What he has described is the possibility that we may have to surrender. On one hand, I can't think of anything so outrageous, but I can't think of anything that could be of more importance. I agree, Mother, it's impossible Thomas would know this, but he has proven to me he knows something about the future." She paused before continuing. "He has also proven to me he's not the same Thomas I married."

A silence followed this; neither of them interrupted. Margaret drifted, then blinked her eyes, snapped her head up, and said, "Anyway, the stakes are enormous, so why not let him try? What do we have to lose? If we can get him in front of Winnie, he'll have the information, even if he chooses to ignore it. If he does use it, he doesn't have to tell his cabinet where the information came from."

"Okay," Mrs. Hatcher said, "so assuming all this is true, what's next?"

"Mother, at some level, you have the ear of Churchill."

"You're wrong, my dear. No one has the ear of the Great Mr. Churchill, including, it would appear, even himself. He's bullheaded and not inclined to consider war policy from the wife of a former friend, or worse—a supplier."

"Mother, there has always been more to Daddy's business than weaving miles of khaki uniforms. You said it this morning: there was a secret project at one of the factories. That's got to count for something."

"Yes, the mysterious factory," she said. "It's under the barn on our property by Chartham Hatch, but you can't tell a soul. Did you know there's abundant working space under a barn's straw-covered floor? I didn't. It was a surprise to me. People go in and out through tunnels a half-mile away. Churchill and your father agreed to the arrangement long ago."

Margaret leaned over, gently placing her hand over her mother's. Her mother, for an instant, started to draw back and didn't. "Mother, I've always resisted your help, even when you meant well, and I should have accepted. Looking back, I'm not sure why I didn't. However, I'm sure there's something to this, and I can't explain it, but it's become a part of me. I know there isn't a shred of logic here, but I'm asking for your help. Please, will you help us?"

Thomas's eyes were wide open, and he was in wonder and disbelief. In a few short sentences, Margaret had summarized the unlikely situation, presented a logical plan to solve their problem, and, against every instinct in her body, just asked her mother for help.

Mrs. Hatcher felt the moment deep in her chest and looked at her daughter as if for the first time. Perhaps this side of Margaret is what her husband saw, and she'd missed, being too preoccupied with trying to present her daughter to Society. Margaret didn't need Society; she didn't even need a mother until now, and she said so.

Lady Hatcher, a tyrant, captain of industry, pillar of society, and parent, put her hand on top of Margaret's.

"Yes, of course, dear, but I'm not sure the question is, whether I *will* help as much as if I *can* help. What am I to say? My son-in-law reads tea leaves and has some targeting information for the next raid?"

"No, just get Thomas a meeting where he can present his information, and Mr. Churchill can decide from there. Surely he owes you something from those years with Father?"

"Oh, he owes me all right, but I'm not sure he remembers he owes me due to his particular condition on numerous occasions." She reached for her gin and orange and said, "Marion, please come in. I know you're right there."

Marion popped in too quickly. "Yes, Ma'am."

"Bring me the phone and Winston Churchill's number from my directory."

"Oh, Mother, I can't thank you enough."

Mrs. Hatcher turned to Thomas. "You know that if you're wrong, it could have repercussions all the way to the factory floor. I need to hear you're absolutely sure you know what you're talking about?"

"Yes," Thomas said, "I know I'm right. What I don't know is why I know."

"Given what's at stake, I wish you were more in the category of positive on both counts."

Marion returned with the number Lady Hatcher had requested and brought the phone to the table from the end of the room. Mrs. Hatcher put on her reading glasses and held the paper with the number as she dialed. Then she waited, her eyes drifting over to Thomas again as if re-emphasizing her point.

"Please connect me with Mr. Churchill. Yes, you may. It's Lady Hatcher. No, it's not important—it's critical." She looked up as though dealing with a thick servant. "Young man, I *know* he's busy. I know he's fighting a war. I'm not daft. Just connect me as I have some information that may be of use. *Now*, please." She glanced at Margaret with a very irritated look on her face.

Margaret silently said, "Thank you."

Her mother returned to the phone, saying, "Young man, he's always in a meeting. I didn't think he would be standing around discussing the latest run at the cinema. Get him now and tell him who I am. Then tell him he owes me this phone call for disrupting countless dinners. That's right, dinners. Tell him now. If not, get me Colville on the line."

There was a long period when the three of them just stared at one another as she waited with the phone at her ear. There wasn't a chance the young man would dare hang up on a "Lady Hatcher," but he might hope beyond reason that she would tire of holding. The young man felt the power of her insistence and knew there would be a price to pay. However, interrupting the PM was a sure way to place himself at the point of the man's anger.

The minutes wore on as they waited, almost like whoever spoke on the phone first would break a curse. Then...

"Lady Hatcher, it's Winston. May I ask why you favor me with a call on this busy day?"

"Winston, sorry, I know you're busy, but I've a request that I realize is out of the ordinary. Will you meet with my son-in-law for just fifteen minutes?"

After a slight pause, Churchill said, "That's it. No reason? Barnes said you had information that would be useful in the war effort. Not, mind you, that I wouldn't consider your most welcome request anyway."

"Winston, you haven't changed a bit."

"Indeed, 'tis not true. I no longer dip my cigars. The doctor said I had to cut down on my brandy consumption." He laughed loudly and continued more seriously, "Lady Hatcher, you've brightened my day with this call, but things are a little sticky right now. If you can be more specific about your pressing matter, I promise to have an aid give it priority attention."

"No, I can't go into it over the phone. It's not something I think I can explain anyway. Thomas Watson, my son-in-law, will have to do that, and it needs to be done in person and privately."

"Things are in quite a bind now. I think I have to ask if we could meet at another time. Just a couple of weeks would make it easier."

"We don't have a couple of weeks. England doesn't have a couple of weeks. That's why you're busy and exactly why he needs to see you. Winston, in all the years you've corrupted my husband, I didn't complain, nor have I ever asked you for a favor other than for you to try harder at making the ashtray, a request that I might add consistently went ignored. Give my son-in-law fifteen minutes, not because he's my son-in-law but because I think he can help in your efforts, and this is my bloody country too."

"Now, now, Lady Hatcher, there's no need to be at a loss for words. Being the cause of some subtle changes in a few dinner party agendas doesn't usually give one this much latitude. After all, it was *your* husband who was the source of many stories of dubious truth sure to be included in my legacy."

"Mr. Churchill?" She drew out the name in a long slow phrase.

"Helen, I shall concede to your strenuous and ill-timed demands." With gentle humor in his voice, he said, "However, I wish to add that through the delightful years of our friendship, I was never quite able to ascertain which of you was the most stubborn. It pleases me greatly to have finally found the answer. Have him call Colville straight away for an appointment. I'll try to see him but only as soon as it's possible. You have my word."

"Mr. Churchill," she said, realizing she'd actually been successful, "your gracious consideration is beyond reproach."

"As is my respect for the Lady," Churchill said, and, as was his habit, immediately rang off.

She looked at Margaret. "He said to call Mr. Colville for an appointment."

Margaret brought her hands together, touching her lips. "Mother, oh, thank you so much."

Impetuously, she was up from her chair and placed a kiss on her mother's cheek before either internalized the action. Margaret, realizing her impulsiveness, backed up to her chair.

"What would her mother do?" Thomas thought. "What would *they* do?"

For all the drama the moment presented, it fell flat. In a surprisingly short time, Lady Hatcher said, "Why, thank you, dear."

Chapter Sixty

Thomas and Viktor

After Lady Hatcher's phone call, Thomas called back, asking for Mr. Colville. Informed he was out, Thomas could make the appointment with Barnes, who already knew the story. "It's going to be an interesting meeting," Thomas thought.

The three of them finished breakfast on a much more pleasant note, with Thomas explaining his other thoughts about the war. Margaret's mother appeared genuinely interested, although she surely had trouble believing most of what she heard. Thomas tried to change the subject by asking questions about Margaret's childhood. The subject did not go over well, as Margaret and her mother had decidedly different memories of the same events. Overall, the remaining time wasn't as uncomfortable as the disaster he'd encountered immediately after walking in the big black door.

Lady Hatcher left to prepare for the ladies and her tea, explaining it would take much of the afternoon.

Margaret and Thomas wanted to spend time together, and Margaret's bedroom was the perfect place. Except for the staff's attention, the room remained as it had been when Margaret had decided to leave the family. Obviously, her mother did not believe it was permanent.

With the social areas occupying much of the bottom floor and the service staff living quarters up on the third floor, Margaret's room was in the family living area on the second floor. Several windows overlooked the grounds and, according to Margaret, let in far too much light in the morning. The room was large, almost half the size of the house she rented from Mrs. Somerville. The décor included pictures, stuffed animals, and brightly stitched, theme-based pillows. However, for the most part, there was nothing to indicate it was a little girl's bedroom, except for the four-poster bed whose canopy was a vivid flower pattern matching the bed cover. Instead, the room took on the same motif of neutral silk wall coverings and heavy furniture seen in the rest of the house. All very plush and, one would think, hard to leave. Later, the low flame in the fireplace and the onset of night cast a wonderful flickering radiance about the room.

Margaret was busy exploring a dresser drawer as if her past or clues to her future were in a hidden corner.

Standing at one of the windows, Thomas was locked in an unfocused gaze. Again, he was turning over events and trying to put the picture puzzle together. It would get close but was always beyond his ability to locate the final few pieces. From his back pocket, he removed and unfolded a piece of paper.

"What is that?" Margaret said, almost slamming one drawer shut, finding little of value, and moving on to another.

"It's a loose end that's been at the back of my mind all day."

He showed her the scribble, saying, "It's a phone number, but the real question is, whose phone number? I found it on one of the men at the park. Except for the gun, that's all he had on him."

Margaret just looked at Thomas without saying a word.

Holding the piece of paper up, Thomas looked at her. "If we're going to get to the bottom of this, we need to know who wants me dead."

"That ought to be simple. It's that Yuri character."

"If it was that simple, then why did he give me a chance to come clean when we were at the bar? Besides, there's a feeling that I get. I have a hard time thinking he was responsible for the shooting in the park. I don't think he would use a gun unless he didn't have a choice, and he had choices."

"Thomas, besides being scatterbrained, you're now being monstrously naïve. He wants the information he thinks you have about some bloody machine and is ready to kill for it."

"But I do know something about a machine."

"*What?* That was the old Thomas. Not you, Thomas. Or don't you remember again? Please tell me it's not you. I mean old…"

"No, I haven't left my senses. It's not the same information that the old Thomas had, or at least it's not the same kind or the source is different."

"Thomas Watson, I made a promise to help so we could get past this and to a life we can call normal. I can't do it if you don't start making sense. There's a point you start making sense—right?"

They exchanged looks.

"Thomas, answer me."

"Margaret, the Russians think I'm someone else, a spy they hired to get some information about a project your family's company is working on, something you or perhaps even your mother doesn't know anything about."

"I can assure you my mother knows *everything*. I grew up as her daughter, remember?"

"What about your sneaking out in the middle of the night and Alistair finding you on the doorstep?"

"Well, maybe almost everything."

"Anyway, they want the information, and giving it to them is the only way I can think of to get us out of this mess."

Margaret's eyes rolled back with her head in an unmistakable gesture. "You actually think they're all going to turn into harmless stray cats after you give them the information?"

"No, but I have a plan."

"You have a plan? I thought we were following my plan. The one that has us leading a simple life after we get this straightened out."

"Margaret," Thomas said. He grabbed her hand. "Think for a minute: It's the same plan. It just contains a twist."

"Twist," she said. "You won't know 'twist' when this is over. Kiss me."

Thomas emerged from his deep thoughts, saying, "Now that's a plan."

"But there's a twist," she said smiling, "only if you're not going to call that number."

"That's sexual blackmail."

Margaret said with arms stretched wide, "Welcome to the real world of women versus men. When it counts—we win."

Quickly leaning forward, he slipped the paper between two fingers, grabbed her face with both hands, and kissed her. He had intended it as a hit and run, but she pulled him down and straddled him, with both hands pushing on his chest.

"You sod. That's no way to treat a proper woman. You can't just say and do what you want and think I'll fall in love with you. Or stay in love with you." She stopped and thought a moment. "Either way, your brain is messed up, buster." She rolled off of him and fell onto the bed.

Sitting up, Thomas put the slip of paper on the bed stand where a phone sat. He looked at the number and then looked at her.

"Margaret, I have to call," he said. "How are we going to get this resolved if we don't take some action? Besides, for all we know, the person at the other end might be of help."

"Sure, and cows fly. For heaven's sake, what'll you tell him anyway?"

"Depends on who it is. I'll tell whoever it is what he wants to hear. Let's at least find out who it is." Thomas had the phone in his hand and dialed the number. "It's ringing; it's direct."

Thomas heard the click as the other end picked up the receiver. He heard a shout. "Where have you been, you idiot? I've been waiting. It was supposed to be a hit, not a gun battle in the middle of London. What the hell went wrong?"

There was a pause, and Viktor said, "Answer me. Who's this?"

"What do you want with Mr. Dunning?" Thomas said.

"Dunning, who the hell is Dunning? Who the hell is this?"

Thomas tried again, "What do you want with Watson?"

There was silence at the other end. Finally, the voice said, "You're in a great deal of trouble, Watson. How did you get this number?"

"It doesn't matter. What do you want with Watson?" Thomas placed his hand over the phone and whispered, "It's not Yuri, but he sounds very Russian."

"What do you think?" the voice continued. "We want what we paid for and handsomely. Your arrogance has made you many enemies, and Moscow isn't happy. We want the information about the machine."

"Where's Yuri?" Thomas asked.

"Comrade Stakova is finished. They're not happy with him either. I have been sent directly from Moscow to clean up his mess before the Germans limit our actions or worse."

"So, you're the one who tried to kill me?"

"You amateur players are so, how do you say it, childish. What were you doing talking to the British? What do you want me to think? You're the one who wanted to play the game, make money, and play with your girl. There can be only one reason you're talking to the British, which can't be good for Russia. We're not allies. Or have you been living in a shelter?"

With egotistical authority, the voice went for the close. "There are many things left unresolved. The only way for this to end favorably for you is to meet me and give me the information."

Thomas purposely waited for Viktor to finish his threat. "Wouldn't it be childish to walk into a trap? I'm afraid I must be overly cautious, given what has occurred. If we meet, I must choose the time and place."

"Fine, but this must happen quickly. Moscow isn't patient. I need an explanation for why you were at Bletchley and you need to give me the information you were paid for."

"I'm prepared to provide you with both but I want to guarantee my safety and my wife's."

The voice was forceful, "Because of your actions, you have few options. You must give me what I want and then leave the country."

Thomas paused again. "That will be very hard."

"It will be worse being dead. This I can assure you."

Thomas continued playing the game, asking the questions of an amateur player. "Can you and will you guarantee our safety? Can you get us out of the country?"

"Yes, I can, but only with protection from my people. You've made many enemies and I don't control the world. If we know about the project, then so do the Germans. After the invasion, they'll eventually find out you were playing both sides with information they think is critical. You don't have a connection to German intelligence. Consequently, the Germans will see you as an enemy of the state, and, of course, this isn't good for both of you. I'm the only one who can get you out of the country. But only after I'm satisfied with the information you must provide."

"Unfortunately, you make a lot of sense," Thomas said. "Once the Germans are in the country, they'll relentlessly search out anyone who could be trouble. It's only because of this that I'll agree to meet."

Viktor replied quickly. "How will you find a place that I know won't be a trap?"

Thomas returned with, "What do you mean 'so you'll know?' We're the ones who should be worried about security. I thought I just made that very clear."

Knowing he didn't hold the cards to force the location, Viktor agreed. "Okay, but it must also be secure from my side."

"It is. The location is in the Richmond district. Do you know where that is?

"Of course, I've studied the whole area as part of my assignment. I'm a professional, which you're not. This is obvious."

"Here's the deal. I'm only going to do this once and at a specific time. It has to be tomorrow morning. It's a place I stayed during some tough times when there was little money. Everyone knows everyone, so taking over a flat for any observation or deploying anyone on the side streets will be very difficult. The whole neighborhood will be watching. The people there are very suspicious of the authorities. Any actions of this nature will make them think it's directed at one of them and act accordingly. It's on Richmond Hill Road. Any cabbie can find it. A green in the middle of a housing terrace is visible as you crest the hill. The road ends there, and you can have a look about. It's right out in the open. You must meet me in the green at precisely 11:30 a.m. If you change it, the deal is off. Is that clear?"

"That's interesting," Viktor said as he fumbled through his jacket on the bed for his cigarettes. "Precision isn't something you've ever demonstrated. Why the change?"

"You might be surprised when you see the information. You must arrive before I do, and I must see you alone in the circle. If I see anything untoward, you'll find this information is wanted by more than the Russians. I might not be in the first car you see, so if you're thinking about shooting up the neighborhood, you may give up your scheme too soon. There won't be another chance. Bring two open tickets for the Pan Am Clipper to Lisbon and two entry visas in our names."

Viktor laughed, "And where will I get visas that quickly?"

"Don't play games. You know the embassy can create anything it wants and does. Do you agree to everything?"

"It appears I have no choice. You have it all worked out. I want the information, not you. I'll direct my people not to interfere with you getting to the airport, but only if I'm satisfied. Remember that's not the last of your problems as Lisbon is full of Nazi spies."

"The rest is my problem. Be there and be on time."

Thomas hung up the phone and looked at Margaret.

Margaret's face wasn't happy. "Are you really going to meet him with no information? And, by the way, I'm not going to Lisbon."

"Don't worry," Thomas said. "We're not going anywhere. We don't have to, remember? The Germans aren't going to invade."

"Thomas, you can't meet with this guy. He's an assassin. He doesn't play nice, and meeting him will accomplish nothing unless you kill him to get him out of our life."

"Precisely," Thomas said.

Chapter Sixty-One

Margaret's Bedroom

Hatcher Estate

After Thomas called to set up the Richmond appointment, there was nothing to do but wait. They both enjoyed the unexpected pause in their lives, which had become non-stop since that Yuri person appeared next to their table. They spent the afternoon mostly walking the grounds, where Margaret recounted more childhood stories as they happened upon this secluded bench or that beautiful grove of trees. Eventually, they came upon the now-famous pagoda, circling it as Margaret giggled.

"Enjoying the memory of your first opportunity at controlling men?" Thomas asked.

"First?" she said.

"Pardon me for the insane assumption that there were no previous opportunities to exercise a female's ethereal mastery over the weaker sex."

"Thomas, you're a lovely man, and I see no reason you should continue down a path that will provide you with nothing but bruised ribs." She jumped in front of him, her right hand clenched and the other pointing to his side. "Right there. Buised. Got it?"

Thomas spread out both arms, his body forming a cross, and said, "Strike me. Strike me now. Punishment gladly take I, for far greater the rewards from Lady fair, than ever the fate of less ... fortuned souls."

He barely got out the last two words before giving in to laughter and realizing his soul had better start running for its life.

They ended up back in the room. Margaret kicked off her shoes and flopped on the bed, as she'd undoubtedly done a thousand times before.

"You should feel privileged, you know. The other Thomas never got in here."

"In where? Oh, you mean not, like … in …"

"Watson? Your mind can't be that warped."

"Oh, yes, it can," he said with a huge smile.

She sat up to emphasize her precise meaning. "Not in this room. I wouldn't let him inside this room."

"Is this about pagodas?"

"I don't want to talk about it."

"Good," he said, "as I have to change the subject and cover a few things."

"Nooo," she said, flopping back down and clutching a small pillow embroidered with a saying. "I don't want to."

A few seconds later, she said, "Mother really changed, didn't she?"

Thomas didn't say anything, having drifted into his own thoughts. He was wondering how he was going to handle the inevitable.

Realizing her comment may not have made sense, she said, "Oh, I mean from what I'd described. She went from this hollow socialite that's just the personality match for the owner of this place to a military contractor baron." Margaret rolled onto her side, resting her chin in the palm of her hand. "It just doesn't make any sense. Why didn't she show me that side of her when I was young? It could have changed everything."

"Is it not obvious?"

She quickly focused on Thomas's face. "Obvious? Would I be asking if it were obvious?"

"It's entirely possible she wasn't that person when you were young. It's possible she rose to the situation that confronted her. She acquired that side to maintain the family reputation and the family business. However, there was no reason for her to give up the façade of the comfortable and familiar empty-headed hostess. She decided she could have both worlds."

"My mother isn't empty-headed, and I would look to your future sentences and review them carefully."

"Why are you getting upset at me?"

Margaret frowned. "I guess I was defending my mother." She sounded confused and surprised.

"There are worse things," Thomas said.

"It's you, Thomas. You're the one with these crazy stories that are turning my life upside down. You're the one who made me come here to ask for help."

"And look what happened? Or weren't you paying attention when your mother went with the emotion and let you hug her, then overtly let you know she enjoyed it by saying thank you. When was the last time that happened?"

"I honestly don't know." She rolled over on the bed and stared into space.

"Margaret?"

"Ah, oh," she said, again putting the pillow over her face.

"We need to discuss tomorrow, Thomas said. "You need to stay here. It's too dangerous to be with me. That much ought to be obvious. I'm going to the meeting with Churchill alone."

She tossed the pillow aside. "Yes, you are when I can fly. We're in this together, remember? We're at my mother's house, asking her to believe you're someone else. Then we asked her to set herself up for ridicule by exposing the notion to the outside world."

Thomas said, "That doesn't make it any less dangerous, and our agreement didn't mean putting you in harm's way. I don't want us to figure this out and not have each other. Frankly, I'm finding it hard to even consider living without you for any reason."

She looked at him, and he wasn't smiling. "Thomas, that's wonderful to say if you mean it, but you can talk away to your heart's content because I'm not listening." She rolled over, returning the pillow to her face.

Thomas looked at a hidden Margaret. "Things are getting clearer. No, I mean focused. No, the feelings are closer to actual things than before."

In muffled tones from under the pillow, he heard her say, "What the hell does that mean?"

Thomas looked at the little girl lying on the bed.

She tilted the pillow, saying, "I don't care what it means because I wasn't listening."

"Well, it's important, so you might want to try. Take the government's finance deal we discussed with your mother. The reasoning and purpose are clearer to me. What Turing is doing is clearer, and when I have these thoughts, they're starting to become connected."

He waited for some response, but she was still playing the ignoring game. Thomas changed tactics. "Do you know that radio will eventually come with a moving picture that will show the person talking?"

Her eyes went wide, and she said, "What? Thomas, you can't go around saying anything you want. Let's see. Yes, someday tea kettles will fly over the moon, replacing cows. And the king will find it in his interest to invite me to dinner. See, I can do it too."

"I'm trying to point out that some of what I can remember might help us. And that something is changing. The feelings and visions are much clearer. There definitely won't be an invasion, and England will maintain its independence after the war. Women help win the war by working beside men, instead of men, in many cases. Women's role in society changes forever."

Margaret's face was expressionless. "You don't have to tell me things are changing. By the way, where did that tough guy come from?"

"What guy?"

"The mister tough guy you became while talking on the phone. Combined with the gun you had in your hand at the park, there are obviously things I don't know about you. I guess that shouldn't come as a surprise. However, Richmond Hill Road? How in God's name can you remember that and not know we're married?"

"I read it somewhere, or I just knew it."

"Right, have you forgotten you'll see Churchill tomorrow morning? Remember the little phone call my mother made?"

"Of course, I remember, but it works out that there's enough time before my meeting."

"You're not going there, Thomas; there isn't time. What's this all about? You can't go anyway, as there's the issue of this confounded all important information—there isn't any."

Thomas said, "Well, I have some information, but I won't give it to him. It's just a hunch. I can find out if it works and not be anywhere close."

"What're you going to do, send the other Thomas? The creep I used to find so attractive."

"And you don't find me attractive?"

"Really, Thomas, get serious here."

"I am serious. I don't know if this will work, but what do we have to lose?"

Margaret grabbed the phone, put it in her lap, and started dialing. "I'm calling Mrs. Somerville to see if she's okay."

She finished dialing and then said to Thomas, "For your information, we have a lot to lose." She kept the receiver up to her ear. "No one is answering."

"For my money, she's smart enough not to be there."

"Do you think she's worried that's she's not safe?"

"I don't know," Thomas said, "but I can assure you there's a reason for everything that woman does, and nothing is by accident. Give her the benefit. If I promise to drive by tomorrow and check the place, can we go to bed and get some sleep?"

"Thomas, you said that like you were a little puppy. How cute. The answer is no. I mean, we can go to sleep but not to bed, and you can blame yourself. I warned you."

"How can we go to sleep if we're not in the …"

"Don't start the word games," she said. "It won't get you anywhere."

"Okay, you win; to sleep it is. I won't argue."

"Really?" she said.

"Yes."

"But what if I wanted to make love and was just playing hard to get?"

"Margaret," Thomas said laughing, "you *are* hard to get. You don't have to play at it."

Chapter Sixty-Two

Safe House

Like the first, Yuri started the second morning at the safe house sleeping late. Sleep had been elusive since the day of the shooting. He knew being gone from his apartment for one night wasn't unusual. However, missing two nights, with Joseph at the embassy, meant everyone would know something was different from the norm. Yuri had put the pieces together, at least the ones that concerned him, but he had a long list of obligations to his people that he had to take care of.

It was sad, but all things, good and bad, eventually end. What was the reward for spending his entire career serving his country? He'd received his country's undying gratitude in the form of a contract on his life. He blamed Stalin more than his country. Under the czar, although built in layers of classes, life was stable. Workers had their fair share of complaints, but the upheaval was mainly for the benefit of those in charge.

Yesterday, his first day on the run, consisted of several important tasks, including getting a new British passport and an exit visa. The British had changed the document laws and required more information, meaning everyone had to get new passports and visas. The ones he'd had in the locker were the old style. Both his Russian civilian and diplomatic passports, as well as those for other countries, were still valid. Being a diplomat had its advantages, but sometimes it attracted attention, and it became necessary to travel as a civilian.

Normally, he would have the new British papers made at the embassy, but that would have created a record someone could access. Consequently, he contacted the same underground resource everyone used for such work. The man went by the name of "The Printer." His ability to forge almost any document to near perfection, official or business, made him the stop of operatives from many foreign governments. Given the nature of his business, each customer had to follow a strict protocol. He required an appointment to avoid one government operative or agent from running into another, not so much to arrange a busy day. That wouldn't be good for business.

It had taken Yuri most of the day to work through the security requirements that identified him as a previous customer. First, a chalk mark on a lamp pole. Two hours later, a trip to the Hampstead Heath rail station and standing by the domestic ticket window. There, "The Printer" could identify a customer safely and anonymously from anywhere in the crowded station. If all was safe, The Printer usually paid a random young boy who knew nothing to walk an envelope over. Inside was an address for somewhere else in the city. Only after staking out the second location would he meet face-to-face. Customers paid in cash, upfront, and only in Swiss francs. He wasn't the kind of person you wanted to cross. The stories were out about those who were responsible for a security breach. You played by his rules, or you stopped playing—permanently.

The visa and passport were prepared quickly, but the procedures took up most of the day. In the afternoon, he stopped at a nearby newsstand, carefully aware of the people around him. Displayed were newspapers with busy headlines and important stories, but not a single letter about the huge story unfolding in his life.

"ИРОНИЧЕСКИЙ (ironic)," Yuri said to himself. He didn't know the English word.

Yuri left his flat, knowing he was on a mission that he couldn't explain to anyone. Viktor's fixation with bringing in Thomas changed everything. He looked at the common across the street from his flat as he walked toward the first step of his exit plan.

Chapter Sixty-Three

Mrs. Somerville's House

The double ring of the bell startled Mrs. Somerville. She placed the kitchen cloth on the counter and went to the phone. The voice on the other end asked if she was alone and safe. It was all charming but unnecessary, given the situation. Then the caller gave her the correct code word to verify his identity.

The voice said, "I have your note," and then gave brief detailed instructions for a meeting.

"That's odd," she thought. "It's so close."

Mrs. Somerville knew she'd been asked to follow the procedures exactly, but she was still mistrusting and hesitant. Margaret was in danger and hoped the note she'd written and dropped off would protect her, but there was no way of knowing for sure. She didn't know why the British government had asked her to keep an eye on Margaret. It was all very casual, with no pressure or compensation, and they'd said she could stop at any time. Ultimately, her continued participation was based on the friendship between the two women from different eras. As far as Thomas, she didn't know what side of his multiple personalities to believe. The new side, unlike the other, put Margaret first, even over his own gain. Indeed, both sides of that man were in one body, but their minds had grown up on different planets.

Mrs. Somerville balanced these thoughts like a performer spinning plates on the end of a pole. Which one would wobble with the weight of deception? Making her decision, she grabbed the notepad and pen to write a message to her young friend, just in case she came by and started to worry. She wanted to be extra cautious. How could she ensure getting it to Margaret and only Margaret? She couldn't just write it out for the world to see. Things were too strange and unpredictable.

Frozen for a moment with pen in hand, she looked at the sideboard. That'll do it. She smiled and quickly completed the steps that solved the thorny problem. She checked her purse for money and keys and headed for the door.

Chapter Sixty-Four

Hatcher Estate

The light that entered the room's windows was bright as Margaret awoke and realized her head was resting on Thomas's chest. She moved just a bit.

"Are you awake?" Thomas said.

"That I am," she said, kissing his chest and reaching up, tussling his hair.

"Good, I've a little boy problem, and I've been waiting way too long." He moved his legs over the side of the bed and went to the bathroom.

Margaret said, "You better come out of there, Thomas Watson." She was waving a finger imitating the dressing down of yesterday.

"What's the hurry; I've plenty of time before my appointment."

"Typical," she said, "I didn't mean that."

"You can come in and stand guard outside the bathroom to make sure I come back out," he said, quickly taking the last step inside, avoiding the pillow that hit the door.

With the door as protection, he looked around the edge, saying, "What's it with you and throwing things, along with the occasional thrust to my body? There must be other ways to deal with not getting your way."

"Marrying didn't give you the right to expect me to change in any way. It just gave you the right to observe whether I decide to."

He did come out, but not until after gingerly placing a finger on the mirror. He was glad she couldn't see him in the uncertain action. There was still a lot that was beyond his understanding.

After dressing, he wandered out into the hall. He asked a staff member where the kitchen was and was given directions to the kitchen on the lower floor. On a lark, he asked if anyone could make him a cup of coffee. After a concert of wrinkled noses, Mr. Henfield, chief cook and ruler of the area where they all stood, mentioned they did indeed have some as Alistair, the head butler, occasionally had it with an abundance of milk. A short time later, Thomas leaned over the cup in front of him. He drew in the aroma and was sent somewhere in his mind where memories should be stored. "Good memories," he thought. But none he could discern. Nevertheless, in the void, he thoroughly enjoyed the experience.

Thomas studied the empty bottom of his second cup and said to everyone, "Thank you. You really must try sometime."

Looking at each other for guidance, they all agreed with various gestures and mumbled replies.

Thomas looked at his cup again and the kettle in front of him. Knowing time was short, he asked, "I don't want to be a bother, but is there a way I can take some with me to warm a cold ride into London? I would be most grateful."

He encountered another round of anxious and worried looks from a staff trained to provide anything at a moment's notice. "We certainly aim to please, sir," Mr. Henfield measured out, "but there's not a single thermos flask in civilian hands."

Thomas was ready to pass on it until a tiny voice broke the silence from someone hidden in the back of the group facing Thomas.

"Pardon me, sir, will this make do?" The newly hired middle maid moved to the front, holding a canning jar with a tin-coloured screw-on lid. Mr. Henfield looked sternly at the young upstart, talking out of turn.

Before Mr. Henfield could administer a lecture on the limits of station, Thomas said, "Splendid idea, young lady! That's just the thing."

This caught the ranking authority with his mouth open and caused more than a few shuffling feet.

With a grin, Thomas said, "A perfect no-spill answer to portability, but it might be too hot to hold." The comment was followed by another few seconds of discomfort, after which the same young lady pulled a kitchen cloth from her apron, wrapped it around the jar, and held it out for all to see. This time, she dared not utter a word, so she looked straight ahead, lips tight.

Mr. Henfield looked at Thomas and, reading his grin, turned to the maid and said, "For heaven's sakes, child, get Mr. Watson a clean cloth."

"Yes, sir," she said, bolting for the kitchen linen cabinet.

Thomas held his hand to Mr. Henfield, shaking it strongly, saying, "Sir, a superbly trained staff. I'm very impressed and will convey my thoughts to her Ladyship."

Mr. Henfield smiled, saying, "We try hard to be of service, Mr. Watson," and with a glance toward the small figure holding the now freshly wrapped jar, added, "each and every one of us."

Margaret's mother wanted him to take the driver and the Mulsanne, but he felt uncertain of the day, not wanting the burden of a driver stuck smoking and polishing the Bentley's fenders for hours. He decided to stay with Mrs. Somerville's trusty motorcar. However, he had to admit it was a beautiful and tempting offer. Alastair had come out with him to the garage. He told him that the Bentley was the ninth off the line in '33, their first year in production. Margaret's father was a complete child when around the car. Alistair related one instance where Sir Everett Hatcher managed to coerce a friend of his wife's, leaving after tea, over to the car. She was one of the stuffiest, most insolent of his wife's social circle, and he proceeded to bore her to death with a tour of its sparkling motor.

"Really, Mr. Hatcher," she said, "couldn't you just pursue the hunt and play polo like the other gents? I can assure you. I've no interest as to a turbo-charger thing."

She'd taken the bait and, with a broad grin, Sir Hatcher reeled her in. "Why Lady Winthrop," he said while adjusting the front of his trousers, "it's what every decent gentleman should have under the bonnet—don't you think?"

With that, one of the last remaining pillars of Victorian society huffed out a very guttural sound. Aghast, she snapped her umbrella into full bloom, turned her full dress with the other hand, and directed herself back to the safe confines of decent company.

During this time, Churchill was sitting in the back seat testing the glassware. He said, "Well done, lad. Well done. Your heralded career in mixed company just got shot down."

Thomas and Alistair laughed, but the story ended when Margaret came into the garage, saying she and Thomas weren't quite finished with their conversation on whether she should stay at the house.

Thomas proceeded to present what he thought was a reasonable case. "Margaret, if nothing else, you're safer out here than in the bombing areas. On top of that, I don't want Viktor or someone finding me, which would put you in harm's way. I can't have that."

"You can't have that? When did you think it was yours to have?"

It was the first serious disagreement in a wonderful start to a relationship. In the end, driving off, he felt the gearstick vibrate as it searched for the proper site to eliminate the pain. Glancing at the wing mirror, he saw Margaret, grow smaller, standing with hands on her hips and with imaginary steam coming out of her ears, like in a cartoon. He was definitely in love.

Chapter Sixty-Five

Whitehall War Rooms

Churchill had just concluded a meeting with the home secretary and a few of his key people. Colville entered to continue orchestrating the leader's day and deliver an important message. Colville was holding his notorious clipboard in his left hand while trying to flip some pages with his right, two fingers doubling as a paper clip for yet more paper. Colville, realizing something, stepped back to close the office door for privacy. Churchill was certain that this man's unlimited but well-disguised patience, unique sense of order, and complete dedication to the job at hand made him one of the more important figures of the war.

"Yes," Colville started, "Director Petrie placed a rather high priority on this. There was gunfire at Bletchley involving Mr. Dunning, a visitor at the time. Security has arrested two men without identification, but only one was armed. Mr. Dunning, for unexplained reasons, managed to escape. Details are still coming in, so it's a bit sketchy. This Dunning knew enough about the Ultra program to raise serious concerns. They have full manhunt out."

"Why wasn't I informed yesterday?"

"I can't fully answer that. I'm sorry. I can check into it right away."

"Don't bother. The director has his own problems. Keep me up on it."

"Also," Colville paused, avoiding eye contact, "Mr. Prime Minister, we need to address a rather bothersome matter. It's the appointment you promised Mrs. Hatcher, who rather abusively got through to you directly during my off-duty hours. My sincerest apologies. Perhaps you have noticed Corporal Barnes is no longer on staff."

"Yes, yes…" Churchill said slowly. "I wouldn't be too hard on the corporal, as he went to battle completely unarmed with an unusually formidable opponent. There's a long list of brave and capable men who've battled and lost to our Lady Hatcher when she finds the need to emphasize her position. None of us has fared well, I'm afraid. Let's see him back for another try."

Churchill's tired mind willingly wandered at the name of Hatcher, providing visions of much simpler times, including the sport of teas and stuffy dinners and garden parties with even stuffier people. He longed in his heart for the return of an era seemingly lost. However, it wouldn't include his dear friend Everett if it were to re-appear.

"Your schedule, sir, is extremely tight, given your expressed desire that the visit to Uxbridge not be endangered. Actually," Colville said, as he flipped back to the last sheet and paused to read Barnes's note, "it's not specifically Mrs. Hatcher. The corporal's notes indicate it's with her son-in-law, a Mr. Watson, married to her daughter, Margaret."

"Really," Churchill muttered, his eyebrows lifting as he leaned back in his chair.

To Colville, this wasn't a good response. He carefully studied the man before him for signs that threatened his schedule. He observed him wandering in thought, not his typical manner of gnashing out information for a clear decision.

Churchill's memory served up another vision of his lost era. His memory smiled, remembering an evening when little Margaret stole his bowler, only for him to find it later that evening in the library, cocked atop a magnificent bust of the Duke of York. The footstool used to accomplish the act gave the perpetrator away. While drumming his fingers on the desktop, the great man took a moment to savor a growing outward smile.

At Churchill's request, some of the projects his friend Everett worked on were vital to the Empire. Thus, his company became an unofficial but very valuable and important part of the government. Late one evening, alone in the library, Everett had addressed his friend after a long pull on his cigar.

"Winston, I know this. Some won't appreciate our efforts for the king. My friend, I'm a husband and father, and don't want not to leave anything to chance."

That evening, Churchill had promised Margaret's father to protect Margaret and her mother, regardless of his position in government.

Many, inside and outside the country, would have liked to curtail Hatcher's influence, and it would appear they were successful. It was still a government secret, but the crash investigation revealed evidence of an internal explosion before the plane crashed. Churchill dearly missed his old friend and stridently wanted to keep his promise to look after his wife and daughter. He also shouldered a heavy burden, harboring the guilt that he might have contributed, even in the slightest, to the loss of a great man.

"Mr. Prime Minister?" Colville said, looking up over his papers, waiting.

Churchill returned to the moment, saying, "I'm afraid we will need a bit of your magic, as I must see this Mr. Watson, if only briefly. It's a long story that can be told only over a two-hour cigar.

"But he could arrive at any time, sir," Colville said as he turned to the door, trying his best not to show any irritation. Once again, he would need to rearrange the constant train of dignitaries who felt access was their right piled up at the door. Many of the upper class who entered the military found it hard to accept that their rank, or lack thereof, limited their station's usual civilian access and privileges. There were times, Colville felt, the PM didn't fully appreciate his efforts in dealing with the many inflated personalities that insisted on access to his schedule. In his most diplomatic manner, he constantly persuaded them that the war's outcome did not depend on their getting face time with the prime minister.

Mid-step, he heard Churchill say, "Jock…?" Colville stopped. "How is your little girl?"

Taken a bit off stride, Colville said, "Well, ah… she's doing fine, Mr. Prime Minister. Despite our best efforts, she continues to run the household at her leisure." Colville paused, begging the question of the great man's newfound interest.

Duly prompted, Churchill looked up and said, "It's just sometimes the level of work obscures what's truly important. I may forget to ask of such things; it's not that I've forgotten. Your efforts are exemplary, with a yoke that wouldn't be present with another man occupying the rather small confines of this chair."

"Thank you, Mr. Prime Minister," Colville said. "We'll make due, sir." He continued to the office door. "Once again," Colville thought, "the man's timing was impeccable."

Chapter Sixty-Six

Margaret Calls Mrs. Somerville

Margaret didn't think losing an argument meant defeat. Losing didn't really mean it was a bad idea; it just meant you lost the argument. With that in mind, as soon as she saw Thomas drive off, she went upstairs to ring Mrs. Somerville again. She stubbornly let it ring well beyond what was practical, indicating her concern. She decided to be driven into Amersham to check on Mrs. Somerville before taking the underground to join Thomas at the Ministry.

She rang the garage, where Brenan, the chauffeur, picked up the line.

"Brenan, I need to go into Amersham this morning. Don't bring the car around; I'll come down to the garage."

"Lady Margaret, I can't do such a thing as her Ladyship has instructed me against doing precisely what you're asking. There was no mistaking her meaning and the consequences of letting you leave the grounds," Brenan explained into the phone.

Margaret said, "Brenan, you dear man. I'll be down in a second."

Brenan's pensive look met Margaret as she approached the garage. He was placed in a sticky situation and wondered how he would handle two direct orders—the mother's order, carrying the weight of authority, and the daughter who was an insurmountable force.

Margaret saved him the trouble. Tapping his shoulder with a smile, she walked right past him and got into the driver's side of the service staff's lorry. "Brenan, where are the keys?"

"Lady Margaret, this is most disturbing, as I see no positive outcome for you or myself."

Margaret, showing impatience, said, "Brenan, if you don't say anything, who'll know? None of the house cars will be missing, and we go out via the service road."

The man stood silent.

"I can't drive into Amersham and just leave the lorry, as I'm going into London proper and coming back with Thomas. You need to drop me off."

"There are still the issues of directives, ma'am."

Margaret moved over into the passenger seat, looked at the chauffeur, and pointed at the seat next to her. "Quickly," she said, "I'll make do with Mother if there's a fuss."

Chapter Sixty-Seven

Amersham—Mrs. Somerville's Home

Less than a minute before Margaret's call, Mrs. Somerville had traveled well down the walkway after locking the door behind her. She was off on a mission she hoped would ensure Margaret's safety. Given the circumstances, she crossed the street and headed in a most unusual direction. Back in her dining room, the phone rang, filling the empty space with the sounds of concern from its caller. Now, well across the street, Mrs. Somerville wouldn't know Margaret was calling and thus would miss the opportunity to explain her actions and to tell her friend to stay at her mother's. As a result, there would be no contact, and events would take their course.

The man who had called Mrs. Somerville to give her directions looked at his watch, knowing time was short. Passing through the door of the shop, he entered another world dominated by the aroma of baked goods. "It's very curious," he thought, "that just a whiff can send my mind back to the farm where my father planted the grain and my mother used it to make every baked good imaginable." His mother was a master at getting all the children to eat the same thing every day by pretending it was something new. Now in England, the pleasant memory of his boyhood returned over forty years later. "In some ways," he thought, "time doesn't exist, or how can I feel like I'm next to my mother, in her kitchen, putting my hands on the hot bread, and still be in London?"

"Can I help you?" Emma Saxby called from the back of the shop as she reached into an oven wearing an oven mitt. "Bread rolls are coming out right now. The kids love them." With a jovial note, Emma looked at the man and added, "Big kids too."

"Just the thing," the man said.

Mrs. Somerville, busily making her way to the shop, was pleased to see only one person there, which would make things a bit easier. The man was sitting at a table outside, facing the other way, looking rather unkempt and a little seedy. Again, doubt drifted into the thoughts controlling her actions. Her pace slowed as she approached him, stopping behind, a few steps short. With her purse held tightly just above her waist, she spoke the password: "Princess?"

The man threw his chin over his shoulder, and his body followed. A scowling, questioning look distorted his face. Standing up, he quickly downed the rest of his tea and, with hardly even an attempt at pleasantries, said, "Missing your wits, lady? Do I look like a bloody princess?" The jerking of his body followed a mumble as he promptly stomped away.

"Well, that went well," she thought. "Now, what do I do?"

Inside the shop, the man paid and took the bag sitting on the glass display case. As he rolled the top of the bag over, he could feel the warmth from within escape, holding it closer to his face to catch the aroma. At the same time, he saw movement outside the window. A woman approached a rough-looking man sitting outside at one of the tables. After a few words, the man got up and walked away. Still holding the bag up, he looked back at Emma said, "Thank you. What a nice shop you have."

"Good day to you," Emma said, followed by a light-hearted, "Mind the bombs now."

The man politely acknowledged what he hadn't heard. He was now looking at a picture he'd pulled from his coat pocket. With a moment's glance, he moved to the shop door.

Mrs. Somerville, still surprised at her encounter, saw another man appear, closing the shop door behind him and walking over. The man closed the distance in just a few strides.

The man, bag in hand, laughed and motioned to the figure walking away, saying, "Did 'princess' confuse him?" He offered her the seat the man vacated. "Please," he said, positioning the empty chair to facilitate conversation.

Mrs. Somerville looked at the chair next to the table but remained standing.

"As you wish," he said, nodding to the other chair. "May I?"

She nodded and watched him sit down and unwrap the top of the bag.

With his nose firmly planted as far down into the bag as possible, he took two deep breaths and said, "Do you bake?"

Mrs. Somerville, still standing, answered, "Why are you offering me a job?"

The man laughed as he took a roll from the bag and tore a piece from it. "No, I understand you've done quite well on your own. However, there are some things more important than money."

Mrs. Somerville watched as the man stuffed the piece into his mouth. He reached up, handing her a note written in her handwriting.

"Mrs. Somerville, I'm Dacha," he said. "My real name is Yuri Stakova, the person who's very grateful that you are looking after Margaret Hatcher."

"I don't think so," Mrs. Somerville said. "I may be old, but I know enough to expect a British secret agent to sound like one. Your accent, it's Russian or something, not that your name wasn't my first clue."

"Who said I was a British agent?" Yuri said. "Besides, do all British agents have to sound like one?"

"No, but the man who interviewed me on the phone said he was from MI5. He told me that after any drop-off, I would get a phone call the next day to arrange a meeting. The person on the phone, who said he was Dacha, also sounded British," she said. "There's logic to this; I'm not just rambling on, you know."

"Something like this, perhaps? I want to thank you for the compliment," Yuri said in a British accent. With a charming look, he continued, "It's hard sometimes to get just the right rhythm, let alone the accent."

Mrs. Somerville stared down at him in shock and thought, "Good God, had she been working for the Russians all this time?"

Returning to his native accent, he continued, "It's tough to judge a foreign accent, listening through these ears," Yuri said, pointing to his head. "I know you have questions. It will all become clear, but at this moment, we must address important matters."

"You bet, like why would you, a Russian, be involved in protecting Margaret Hatcher, a British citizen? Besides that, why would I agree to assist a bloody foreign country, pardon my language? I don't even know if you're who you say you are."

"Mrs. Somerville, how many 'Dachas' do you have in your life that also know your contact identification, 'princess,' and happen to have a note, written by you, to me and whose instructions created this meeting."

Yuri's smile waited for a response.

Mrs. Somerville didn't say anything but sat down.

"I also handle her husband, Thomas Watson, another Englishman who happens to be a Russian spy. At least, I think so; today, I'm not so sure. He was supposed to be getting information from Margaret."

"What?" She leaned forward, putting one arm on the small table. "Let me get this straight. As a passionate British citizen, I'm watching over a child who couldn't possibly have a drop of information anyone could want. Moreover, *I'm doing it for the Russians?*"

Mrs. Somerville was beside herself. "But wait," she put her finger in the air like a schoolteacher, "as a ridiculous aside, you think her husband is one of *your* spies—but you're not sure? Hells bells, I'm confusing myself. You look bright enough to know that no sane person, and with you, I'm assuming a lot here, would be in such an upside-down position. So," she said, throwing her purse onto her lap, "although there's little you could say that would convince me, why would you do such a thing, and why would I continue to help you?"

"Why does anyone do anything? Usually, it's a devotion to your principles."

"That, my dear sir, is a dapper pile of horse crap. I'll give you one more chance."

Yuri leaned back and broke into a laugh. "Mrs. Somerville, there are no national boundaries when it comes to beliefs and principles that are branded into your life by the force of pain and agony."

Mrs. Somerville silently looked at the man, thinking of her and Charles. "Perhaps we have one thing in common," she said. "So what do you believe, Mr. Stakova? Whose side are you on? Because right now, I'm a traitor."

"With my belief in freedom, I think you should consider me on the British side," Yuri said. "In my country, they stole freedom from the hands of our children before they could feel the choices it provided. I've seen firsthand the horrors of those who wished to impose their will on others. No one can take back the terror already taking its toll there, but your country has this chance to stop the terror that lies before us. This man Hitler is no different from the tyrant that's killing my homeland, except Hitler is worse and German. If one is to be unjustly ruled, it's only slightly better from the hand of Stalin. The world must stop both Hitler and Stalin. I have no love, as you say, of England, but I know your government is against both monsters. That's why, as you say, I'm upside down."

He paused and looked at her.

"The man knew his heart," she thought. At the same time, Mrs. Somerville knew he hadn't answered her question about her being a Russian spy.

Yuri put the bag down. "Time is short, and we must come now to the urgent matter. You've done a great job, and your country is grateful, but there are never secrets forever, and this one is no different. You might be in danger and must leave to a safe place."

"In danger, from whom?" she said. "We've covered most nationalities, so, just for humor, why not throw in the useless Americans?"

"Danger is danger; it matters, not the source," Yuri said. "Is there someone watching the Watson's flat?"

"Yes," she said slowly.

"All the more reason you can't return to your house until I've taken care of some tasks that will set things right."

Mrs. Somerville looked at the man before her. "Since we're into questions, I have one. How do I know you're not the danger? My interest is in Margaret's safety, and what keeps me from going directly to the British authorities?"

"My interest is in everyone's safety, and we must do it my way as time is short. You're free to go to MI5, but some in MI5 don't know we exist due to how this is structured. It's a time of war, and how will you explain agreeing to look after a fellow citizen for the Russians? Not just any citizen, mind you, but someone whose family manufactures military equipment for the government?"

"What?" Mrs. Somerville wasn't happy.

"It's the truth, I must say."

Anger was in her voice. "I don't believe it. But it doesn't matter. I didn't ask for this."

"Beth, can I call you Beth?"

She didn't respond.

"Beth, I didn't ask for this either." Yuri was searching inside his coat, feeling for the lining pocket. He handed her an address and two keys to the Leyton High Road apartment. "You must go there and stay until I can get there. Don't open the door to anyone except me unless there's a phone call or you hear the code name princess. Yes? Do you feel comfortable doing this?" Yuri said.

"I don't know," she said.

Yuri thought for a moment and looked across the street to the pub where he and Thomas had talked.

"Mrs. Somerville, may I ask you a question?"

"I'm the one with questions."

"How is your relationship with Margaret and Thomas? Do you know them well?"

"Margaret is like my own daughter. You'll never find a purer heart. Thomas? Figuring that one out is a little more difficult."

"Please," Yuri said, "could it be he has put on another of his many coats?"

She smiled; it was the first real evidence this man had provided to prove that he was who he said he was. The curious question made her a lot more comfortable.

"Well, Mr. Dacha, it's apparent you're also confused about who's the real Thomas Watson. Margaret said it was amnesia, and there it must lie, as I don't have a better explanation. However, I can assure you that the heart of the Thomas she originally married doesn't beat inside the man she's with now. I'm not sure how this can be true, but it is," she said.

"I, too, am not sure, but I agree," he said. He'd picked up the bag again, and another piece of bread muffled the words. "That's why we must do something to save them both. However, you've done your part and must go to the rear door of this flat, not the front entrance. I don't think it's being watched, or I wouldn't send you there, but you can never be too careful. Inside, you'll find some of my things and some food. You must promise to go directly there, do you promise?"

"No," she said. "Not until I take a few passes at the stations, ensuring no one is following me. That would be obvious, even to the old lady next door. You're not very good at this, are you?"

Yuri crumpled the now-empty bag in his hands as he smiled. "Do you know where Margaret and Thomas are?"

"No, they dropped me off the day of the shooting. I think they were going to go to her mother's."

"I saw you pick up Thomas at Bletchley. Were any of you injured during the shooting?" He studied her face and said, "No, Beth, I wasn't responsible for that, but I know who was, and *he* is the danger, and I must say, a danger to us all."

Yuri rolled the watch on his wrist and started to stand. "I'm late and must go."

She looked up at him, "This is so strange and diffused."

Yuri looked at her quizzically.

"Unclear," she clarified.

Yuri nodded and looked again at the same sky that had betrayed him a few days before. "It's the nature of the business."

"What business?" she said.

With a pleasant but serious expression, he looked down at her and said, "Freedom, Beth, freedom. Now, I can't protect you unless you promise me that you'll go to the flat after your precautions and stay there. To do the things I must do, I need to know where you are and that you're safe. If it makes you go, you may tell your close friends inside," he nodded to the bakery, "but no one else, is that clear?"

She looked into his eyes briefly and said, "Okay, but if you don't help Margaret, I'll be the danger. Is that clear?"

With that, he smiled, touched his hat, and headed toward the train station.

Beth watched him walk away. After the phone call from Yuri, she knew the meeting would be at Emma's. After that, she wasn't sure what would happen. That's why she told Margaret in the note; Emma would know where she went. It was impossible anyone would know where Emma was located except Margaret, so that wouldn't put Emma and Stewart in danger.

She re-read what she'd just finished writing and returned to the shop. "Emma, dear, if Margaret shows up here looking for me, can you give her this note? I think she might be in some danger."

Emma was concerned. "From that man outside? He's the same man who talked to them the other morning."

"Talked to Margaret and Thomas, together?"

"Yes, just after you left," Emma said. "I went into the back, and when I came out, they were gone. Didn't think much of it. Did I miss the mark?"

Mrs. Somerville thought for a moment. This information didn't clarify anything and only made the issue harder to understand. He was supposed to be protecting Margaret. Why would he talk to both simultaneously if he was directing Thomas to work Margaret for information? She considered her options. Finally, something genuine in the manner of the Russian solidified her decision. She turned to Emma, "If Margaret shows up, can you make sure she gets to this address? She'll be safe there. It's where I'll be, but I would feel better if she had someone to go with her."

Emma took the note. "I'll take care of it. Just you take care of yourself."

Her husband was listening and said to his wife, "Ya should arm her with a bag of y'ur hard rolls. Blame potent as a rock if..."

"Mr. Saxby, that'll be enough out of you."

Emma was concerned. "How long will you be there?"

"I don't know until things clear up, I guess, whenever that might be. I guess I should tell you not to give that address to anyone else."

Emma had a worried look. "You let me know how you are, or I'll be in a fit of worry."

"No need to worry about me. You've got problems of your own," she said, looking at Stewart.

Emma looked at her husband walking into the back and said, "Beth, love is a mysterious force in this universe. I'm hoping someone figures it out someday."

Chapter Seventy

Mrs. Somerville's House

Sitting in the back of the car, Margaret was waving a finger, "Brenan, pull over here and drop me off. I don't want to be too close."

The driver, who had eventually agreed to take her into town, did as he was instructed but wasn't happy. He'd had an excellent job for over ten years, and he knew it. Some didn't have a job, and he wasn't interested in giving someone a reason to sack him.

"Miss Margaret, if Lady Hatcher finds out I brought you into town, she'll have me 'ead."

Sitting beside him in the front seat, Margaret put a hand on his shoulder. "Nobody is going to find out, I promise you. Just go back and don't say a word. Not even to Alistair."

"Too late, I'm afraid. I wasn't going to do this on me own, when everyone else was plain too afraid. Alistair was the one who said he 'ould have me back."

"It's okay; I'll handle Mother."

"Well, I jus' glad someone can." He realized his fear let that slip. "I mean…"

"Brenan, I know exactly what you mean, and it's okay. She isn't that bad inside, but how would anybody know? Now go." Two blocks from her street, she got out and shut the door.

Margaret stood at the corner bus stop with a view down the alley bypass behind her row of houses. She paused, pretending to rummage through her purse while stealing glances, looking for any clue that a guard was watching the house. She could safely take her time, as any man would see her diversion in her purse as the equivalent to a woman breathing.

Grigory Dorokhin, was a rookie agent who reported to Yuri. However, Viktor had flashed his credenctals and ordered him to watch

Watson's house and notifiy Viktor if they returned. Surveillance duty was an agent's lowest endeavor, and his replacement was thirty minutes late. He stood hidden between two large shrubs across the street from the front of Watson's house. He had a full view of the front door. He figured the families on either side of him had left town as it was too quiet. It was his good fortune not having to worry about them, and he could smoke without giving himself away. He finished the cigarette and dropped it atop an ever-growing mound of butts. "This assignment was stupid," he thought. There wasn't a chance in hell that anybody would return to a place that was surely being watched.

This Krivitsky, Viktor, or whoever, was an arse who could see nothing but his resume always in his face. Who was he, anyway, flashing his credentials and giving orders? Where was Yuri as thoughts of his boss's safety entered in a fleeting thought. It had been over forty-eight hours since anyone had heard from Yuri and at the worst possible time. This Victor had mobilized everyone, and Yuri, the girl, and the guy were nowhere to be found.

Margaret started walking up the bypass slowly, feeling the fear grow in her arms and legs. She was going to do this. Without an answer from her friend, she absolutely had to ensure she was okay regardless of what could happen. After all, her relationship with Beth and Thomas had gotten Beth involved anyway. It was her fault, and she had to know.

Along the back fences, the growth of hundred-year-old trees and shrubs had grown tall. These houses were among the first in the township before the sprawling edges of London engulfed all the surrounding countryside. Stopping behind Beth's house, she stepped into a row of tall bushes out of direct sight of anyone who would enter the bypass. It was almost certain they were watching her place next door and would spot her if she wasn't careful. That meant she had to get Beth's attention and get into her house and out of sight as quickly as possible.

Reaching up, she moved some branches and looked at the back of Beth's house for a few minutes. There weren't any movement or lights, but that didn't mean she wasn't inside. It wouldn't be as simple as seeing her in a window or coming into the backyard to empty trash. How could she find out without standing in plain sight and knocking on the door? Margaret heard a man and a woman talking as they turned into the alleyway. They entered the second house on the right through the rear gate. Having seen them before, Margaret felt relieved.

Dorokhin's anger grew, and he decided to leave before his replacement arrived. He looked at his watch, deciding to finish with a last every-thirty-minute walk around the block before leaving. He casually strode to the sidewalk from his hiding place and looked up and down as he crossed the street. He had his hands in his pockets, walking casually. There were a few people out, but not many. His instructions were clear: hold them if he could but don't let them leave the house. If necessary, kill them both and do it professionally and quietly. He knew it was part of his job as an agent, but it rarely happened. He wondered if he could do it if the situation arose.

Margaret looked at the ground around her feet and saw some planting stones. If she could make some noise at the back of the house, it would rouse whoever was inside, friend or foe, while she remained hidden. Margaret reached down and picked up a small rock but still heavier than she would have liked. It had taken years, but she'd conquered the stigma of throwing like a girl, and it had come in handy during her childhood, winning the challenges placed before her by stupid boys at garden parties. She even defended herself from a fox in the woods who had decided she was nothing to fear. Got the animal right in the flanks, then quickly climbed a tree when the mother fox appeared. Knowing the object was heavy, Margaret drew back and gave it an extra bit of effort. Her target was the bottom of Beth's back door, a good fifty feet away.

Unfortunately, the extra velocity kept it high, and it sailed right through the fixed pane of glass in the window at the top of the door, taking the side curtain with it. "God," she thought as she ducked down out of sight. That's exactly what she didn't want to have happen. Someone could have heard that from St. Paul's, let alone scare the hell out of her friend. Angry but out of sight, she waited. Nothing happened for several long minutes. If she's not there, where could she possibly be? Perhaps her sister's, but she should have thought of that back home when she had the number. She had to get inside to find out.

She moved to the gate, pulled at the latch, and rushed to the back porch. Using the neighbor key Beth gave her, she opened the door. Stepping on the broken glass, she cautiously entered the house, pausing to listen for any noises and then closing the door behind her. Moving slowly and quietly, Margaret made her way through the kitchen and headed for the dining room. Thinking of calling out, she spotted a note on the dining room table. She listened for anything before going into the room. After a moment, she looked around the corner, and the house appeared empty. Checking the bedrooms, she returned to the note and unfolded it.

At the top was the name Kitten. Once, her dear friend had used that name when they were joking around, and the name stuck. She said Margaret was a playful little kitten with claws that needed to be respected.

Kitten,
Had to leave and not sure when I'll be back.
I wanted you to know. Charles will tell you where I went.
Beth

Charles? Margaret thought a moment. She looked at the photograph of the handsome man in uniform neatly framed and hanging on the wall. Then remembered the conversation they'd been having when Beth opened the drawer, and Margaret noticed the ornate picture album.

Beth had said, "My Charles is exactly where he should be, in heaven waiting for me and in my picture book, always in the top drawer of my sideboard."

Dorokhin rounded the corner, turning into the dirt alleyway. As usual, he passed several houses before arriving at Watson's home. Giving a general look around, he entered through the now-familiar back gate of the Watson's property. Once on the porch, he checked that the back door remained locked. He stood on the porch for a minute, looking across the street to more gates and backyards. "What a lost part of the world," he thought. "Why would the Germans bomb it, needlessly angering the British and causing certain retaliation? The British papers used it as a rallying point. If the Germans were so precise, then they were precisely stupid."

Proceeding toward the gate, he looked at how each owner had changed the look of the originally identical houses. In the process, something caught his eye. The back door of the house next door to Watson's was ajar with a hole in the glass window. His training had taught him that anything appearing unusual usually was. He thought it was probably kids looking for cigarettes, but it didn't matter. His job was to be aware of anything, assuming any part could influence his present assignment. He decided to check it out.

Margaret pulled back on the knobs of the sideboard drawer and saw a velvet-covered photo album neatly tucked into the front right-hand corner. "That was easy," she thought. Picking it up, she was surprised at its weight. She placed it on the table and opened the hardbound cover to discover another note. Anxiously she grabbed and unfolded it.

Kitten dear,
If you read this, please be very careful. It's not just Thomas in
danger as some wish you both harm. I've done what I can to protect you,
and want desperately to explain how I know. Go to Emma's where I'll

leave a message telling you my location, so you won't worry. Please go back to your mother's; it's the safest place.
   Your friend,
   Beth

  As agent Dorokhin approached the rear wooden door, he stepped on a piece of glass that had landed outside on the porch. He looked into the kitchen through the window, and nothing looked disturbed. He couldn't see anyone or anything indicating recent activity, like food on the table. "It's just a simple burglary," he thought, and he was off duty and hungry. He pulled the door shut and started to leave. His shoulders dropped as he acknowledged the standards his boss and friend Yuri demanded. He returned to the door.

Chapter Seventy-One

Yuri's First Phone Call

Riding into London, Yuri thought it was fortunate he had checked the drop-off. It was a narrow miss created by Viktor, taking Pavel out of the picture. Yuri had a series of things he had to do before he could disappear. Time was short. He knew Viktor's men were hunting for Margaret and Thomas. In addition, Yuri was the only one who could reveal Viktor's stupidity at Bletchley, thus making himself an essential target for Viktor. The directive from Moscow he'd found in Viktor's room gave the man all the cover he needed to pull the trigger.

Yuri entered the phone box and slowly picked up the receiver. He knew the heavy Bakelite object wasn't all it appeared. It would carry the weight of a necessary disclosure, the key to opening the next door in his life. Yuri's size always made him uncomfortable in call boxes. He turned and looked out the small panes for anything or anyone out of place. There was a smartly dressed man across the street. He'd been standing there for several minutes. Yuri started to put the receiver back as a cab approached, taking the man away. He looked the other way to see if a backup existed, but the street was quiet. "Am I being too careful?" Yuri wondered.

"Never," he said aloud as he heard the familiar dings of the change falling. That's the reason he'd made it out of Italy alive. Through the handset, he listened to a young woman's voice saying, "Number, please."

"Wytell 2975," he said.

"Good day," she said, but Yuri didn't hear the usual connection being made.

She came back on the line, confused, saying, "I'm sorry, sir, I don't have that available on my switchboard. Please hold while I get my supervisor."

Upon hearing the number, her supervisor said, "Stella, patch it to my office, please." The supervisor turned the key at the end of a chain, opening the safe. The phone rang through to the small connection board in his office. He answered and said, "Could I verify that number, please?"

Yuri gave it to him again.

The man flipped through a small book. Locating the number, he discovered it was a military switchboard and restricted. He flipped again to the section where each phone number in the Wytell code had a password next to it.

"Sir, I'll need a password to complete the call."

Yuri said, "Ghost town."

The supervisor's attention drew more focused, as he never thought he would ever deal with this type of situation. He was happy he'd paid attention in training much more than a year ago.

"Thank you," he said, reaching up and inserting the proper cords into the super's board. He listened for a single ring, assuring the connection before an automatic cut-off. The call traveled outside any regular public system, as it was a direct connection and end-lined at a single device.

A large red phone rang twice in a virtually secret, heavily guarded room. The room was the field communications office of an unknown section within the British Intelligence Service. It was located deep inside Blenheim Palace, Oxfordshire. The palace, named after the Battle of Blenheim in 1704, was a key victory for the English over the French. In an act befitting the nation's gratitude, Queen Anne had ordered its construction for the esteemed leader of the victorious English Army. With the gardens still under construction, John Churchill, 1st Duke of Marlborough, moved in, and it was to be the family estate of the Churchills for the next 300 years. It had been the birthplace, but never the residence, of Winston Churchill, who decided, after a bombing and fire, to allow MI5 to occupy the estate.

Agent Erin Kirkway, the field watch commander, waited for the second ring before he answered, "Watch Desk."

Yuri hesitated a brief second before speaking.

"Hello?" the agent said.

"I need to speak to a nine-nine-two contact," Yuri responded.

"Are you in immediate danger?" Kirkway asked.

"No"

"Can you hold for two minutes?" he said. As per regulations, he wrote down the number.

"Yes," Yuri said.

Kirkway looked at the number he'd written down, making sure it was the number he'd heard. His job was to be the field agents' singular contact and write detailed reports. If matters dictated, he conveyed operational issues to the bigwigs, literally upstairs. In his three years of service, the last two as watch commander, he'd never made contact with someone in the 900 series.

Agent Flaherty stood, feeling the key hanging from his neck swing back to his chest. He locked the office door from the inside and then hurriedly passed a row of padlocked cabinets. He stopped and paused at the imposing twenty-inch-thick steel and concrete safe known as Blenheim's Box. Running his thumb across the top of the safe's dial, he removed a thin film of dust. He thought momentarily; he hadn't opened the safe in a while. Was the last number twenty-eight or thirty-eight? He cursed, as they wouldn't let him write it down. He spun the safe's dial back and forth, entering the combination, and the handle wouldn't move. He tried again, using thirty-eight. Holding his breath, he pushed down, hearing a loud clang as the resistance gave way. At the same time, the red light above the door went out, and the green one next to it lit up, indicating the disarming of the explosives meant to destroy the documents inside. Erin shook his head. A bloody light and a piece of wire were the only things between him and permanent retirement.

He continued pushing the handle down until it stopped and pulled back on the thick door. Before him was a series of internal drawers, each two inches high, running the twenty-four-inch width of the box's interior. He grabbed the thumb handle on the one labeled "Nine-Ninety" and, as it opened, looked at three red folders. He grabbed nine-nine-two, pushing the drawer closed with his other hand. On the front of the folder was a large label declaring the contents MI5 C Top Secret – Private and Confidential, followed by some small print threatening to quickly rearrange anyone's normal life if they didn't follow the rules. "As if the explosives weren't enough," he thought. MI5 was Military Intelligence Section 5A, in charge of domestic security, also known as just plain Five. Department B handled the section's field agents—C didn't exist.

He opened the folder and stared at the first page containing the contact information, instructions, and a brief assignment description. In a subconscious act, his eyes grew wide, and his forehead creased to his hairline. The contact list usually contained the agent's handler and a secondary emergency contact. His job was to make a quick connection between the contact and the field agent. Upon reading the file, Erin was astonished; the only authorized contacts were the director general of security and the prime minister. Normally, the men he handled in the field were double agents, working for an obscure entity called the XX (Double Cross) Committee. They were usually foreign agents caught spying and, under threat of death, convinced to work as double agents with the British. To no one's surprise, they usually cooperated, feeding false information back to their counterparts in Germany. However, this call was from a foreign agent turned to spy on his own government, and who was in charge of recruiting British nationals for that job. Having thought he'd seen every form of deception, even he had to think twice: "tatDo all nine ninety's play those twisted games?" He wasn't sure.

Agent Kirkway moved quickly back to his desk and picked up the phone. "Code name?" he asked.

"Treasure," was the reply.

Kirkway said, "Code confirmed. You wish to report?"

"No," Yuri replied, "I need to talk to someone in the file." Yuri wondered if the system was going to work. It had been years since he'd made direct contact, with all communication going through dead drops in the field.

"May I have your general location?"

"London proper," Yuri said.

Kirkway looked at his list of public phones in and around London and said, "Kentish Town Station at the corner of Caversham Road and Hammond Street in two hours. Can you make it?"

"Yes," Yuri said and hung up the phone.

Erin Kirkway was very grateful that upon hearing the nine ninety number, he instinctively gave himself the longest amount of time regulations allowed to return a requested contact. He needed the time, as the contact list did not contain handlers, but the names on the list were some of the highest and busiest people in government. They weren't easy people to contact quickly, if at all. Also, the file predated the XX Committee, so Erin wondered if he should contact its chairman, Oxford don, Sir John Masterman. He concluded he should start with Sir David Petrie, the PM's director general, unofficially inform Masterman and then place an optimistic call to the prime minister. He would then cross his fingers.

Chapter Seventy-Two

Thomas at Whitehall

Thomas put his hand on the sandbags stacked higher than his head. It was strangely familiar, matching a scene in his mind, except the picture was black and white. As he drove through the city, he only took a few wrong turns, surprising himself by finding it quickly. After all, Whitehall hadn't changed location and… what a strange feeling. Where does all that come from? Why would he know how to get to Whitehall? The source felt closer, for lack of a better way to put it, but not close enough. The sandbag was cold. Before him was a stairwell from which he might not emerge. Once he divulged his information, they may find him just as much of a risk as they did his Mr. Dunning. Nevertheless, he had no choice.

He'd descended the steps and come to the guard when it hit him. He didn't have any identification. What could he have been thinking? Dumbfounded, he stood before the guard as the man waited for Thomas to say something.

"My name is Thomas Watson, and I have an appointment with the prime minister scheduled through Mr. Colville."

"Yes, sir, your identification, sir," the guard said as he picked up the list of the day's authorized entries. "Well, let's see, Thomas Watson, you say?"

The guard ran his finger down the page and said, "Yes, Mr. Watson 'ere it is." The guard then looked up, waiting for the ID, and said, "Nice bit of a day today, in' it? With it I'm stuck between these walls with a draft up me shorts."

Thomas had defensively put his hand inside his coat as if reaching for something when he finally dropped the arm to his side and said, "Well, Officer, I'm afraid I don't have any ID."

"Well, now, Mr. Watson, surely you mus' know it's a crime no' to carry any form of identification and during war, quite dangerous to no' be able to identify oneself to authorities."

"I know, but if you could just call Mr. Colville, he can verify my appointment."

"That's all well and good, Mr. Watson, but how do I know you're the actual person 'ere for the appointment? You're not coming in to flirt with the ladies now, are yah? No, you're coming in tah see the prime minister whose safety and security the lot of us take somewhat seriously."

Thomas was stumped. Given the magnitude of his mission, it was pretty unbelievable that the everyday rules of life and war were restricting his presenting the information.

"Mr. Watson?" the guard said a little loudly.

Pulling out of thought, Thomas said, "I'm sure Mr. Colville can straighten this all out."

"Will Mr. Colville be able tah identify yah on sight?"

"No," Thomas said as he crossed his arms in frustration, "as we've never met, but I could describe him to you." Thomas knew exactly what Colville looked like. He was so close.

The guard's shoulders visibly dropped, and the situation grew less defensible by the minute. He leaned downward for something under the desk and continued, "Mr. Watson, as we are no' just on a need and authority basis, we also require every person be visually familiar tah the entry guard or someone else inside. If no', you're very heavily searched and must be accompanied by armed guard."

"I fully understand. I know this is very unusual and you must do your job, so do whatever you must. It's the meeting that's important."

"Of course it is, Mr. Watson, that's the whole of it, is it not? No one asks to see the prime minister and enters through here now. They always go through Ten Downing and the connecting shaft. Therefore, you see that you're in a very unusual position from the top. Given the rest of your story, I would say yah are no' very bright or just plain daft."

Behind him, Thomas could hear someone coming down the steps. He turned to see two more guards and started feeling a little desperate. The guard must have pushed a button or something that Thomas did not see.

"Could you please call Mr. Colville and find out what *he* wants to do?" Thomas now knew he should have brought Margaret as Churchill could at least identify her, but it looked like it wasn't going to get to that point.

The guard looked up to the men behind him and pointed toward Thomas. There was a loud snap as one of the new guards took three steps back, and the other new guard said, "Stand still, sir, like a good gentleman."

The new guard started patting him down, checking all his pockets but found nothing.

Thomas had never felt so stupid in his whole life. Why hadn't he thought this through? He was angry with himself for being so shallow and stupid. Daft, if you like. He could've gotten a letter or something from Margaret's mother. Why did he think he could just walk in, even with the phone call to Churchill?

This time the footsteps came from below, and a captain appeared. Thomas's hopes dimmed as he ran out of options. The last thing he needed was to sit in a cell for a day, missing the time he needed to get to the prime minister. Today was the day all hell would break loose, and tomorrow was too late.

The original guard had backed away from the guard desk and began explaining the situation to his superior. At the end of his explanation, they both turned and looked at Thomas.

The original guard stood beside the captain during the moment of silence. Thomas sensed this was his last chance. He started thinking through his situation. Someone was trying to kill him, and that put Margaret in danger. He was accused of being a spy in a baffling conversation with a Russian, who just might be the person out to get him. He had no facts to support anything in his story, and all he was trying to do was save the country. At that point, his hopelessness turned into anger.

"Captain?" Thomas said, and the man looked up. Taking a deep breath and with a firm, steady voice, Thomas said, "You need to pay attention as you're going to have to make a decision that might just affect your career. There's no way, at this moment, I can prove who I am. However, I've some time-sensitive information upon which the nation's security depends, and those facts will come out eventually. When it's discovered you didn't follow up fully to the extent within the framework of your responsibilities, your arse will swing from the highest point within sight. I suggest you do what you have to do, but do it. Mr. Colville would be a good place to start."

Slowly the guard crossed the few steps between Thomas and the captain, making eye contact with the other station guard.

The captain remained cool under the verbal assault and started to say, "You can fully under…"

Close to shouting, Thomas said, "Captain, given my understandably weak position, I've nothing to lose here. Arrest me and pay the price or get Mr. Colville."

Thomas now had a guard firmly attached to each arm and could feel their strength as his weight shifted from the soles of his shoes. It was all too symbolic of the diminishing hope he felt.

The captain looked at Thomas in a considered manner that had to be admired. His hands moved to the front of his belt as his mind weighed the situation.

Calmly he said, "Handcuff him."

Colville put the phone down, shaking his head as he realized the day was falling apart. Why did everyone think one could just call and see the most important man in the world as if ringing up for tea? He dedicated himself to maximizing every minute of the PM's time, thus, in his own way, shortening the war and saving lives. "It was just astounding," he thought. "The nerve!"

The captain stopped in front of Colville's desk and saluted. "Yes, captain, what could it be now?" Colville said.

"Sir, I've a situation at the George Street entrance. A Mr. Thomas Watson insists he has a meeting with the prime minister and is simply without any identification. On the verge of normal stability, sir, he insists I contact you to verify his story. Given his desperate situation, I hesitate to bother you, but it's just a gut feeling, sir. I have him bound and detained at the desk. Should I just arrest him, sir?"

"Watson?" Colville said, "At ease, Captain." Colville shuffled the papers on his clipboard.

The captain placed his arms behind his back. "Yes, sir, he says it's important, urgent in fact. If I may, sir, there's just enough wrong with this that something might be right. Sorry, sir, but can you identify him?"

"Yes, he's on my list, but I can't identify him, nor can I assure you that the PM can. I'll need to make a call. Bring him down but keep him bound. Put him over there with an escort."

Thomas looked around the area where he was sitting. The noise level in the room was high, with banging typewriters, people talking, and phones ringing. Thomas saw the name Colville on the desk from across the room. Since being escorted onto the floor, the man hadn't looked at him during the flurry of activity Thomas witnessed. After two phone calls, Colville had signed a communications folder and stood with his finger pointing somewhere while vigorously talking to a uniformed office worker.

The captain stood beside Colville's desk, his feet apart and arms relaxed behind his back. Directly across from Thomas, on the opposite wall, two guards stood at strict attention like bookends on either side of the very suspicious Mr. Watson.

Thomas shifted his weight forward, away from the back of the chair, easing the pain in his wrists. At the same time, he felt a relaxed hand placed on his shoulder. He looked up, and the guard gave him the 'stay seated' look, like one given a child whose time in the corner had yet to expire.

One of the telephones rang, filling the room. It must have been Coville's as he picked up the phone and, smiling into the receiver, looked at Thomas. Shaking his head, he spoke, and after a bit, Colville put the phone against his chest and said something to the captain, who motioned to bring Thomas across the room to Colville's desk.

Colville said. "What's Lady Hatcher's daughter's middle name?"

Thomas didn't know. He simply didn't know. Thinking quickly, he said, "Her first name is Margaret, and you can confirm Lady Hatcher's habit of ordering a gin and orange every time I'm a guest at her house." Thomas hoped Margaret's mother could confirm the unusual statement.

Dumbfounded, Colville looked at him. An unmistakable look of disgust quickly replaced his confusion. "I don't have time for this." Through a tight jaw and clipped noises, he said, "Need I point out … that wasn't the *question*? Nor point out the question *wasn't that difficult?*"

"I'm sorry, Mr. Colville, it's the only answer I can give you," Thomas said.

Still holding the phone to his chest, Colville looked to the side, trying to contain his anger. He pointed back to the chair, and Thomas returned to his seat. Colville returned to the phone and quickly performed a 'what's the use' gesture with his arm. After a polite, smiling salutation, he very gently placed the phone down on the hook as if the phone were a bomb that might explode. He'd just experienced all he wanted of Margaret's mother for the day.

Colville said something to the captain, accompanied by a stern gesture in Thomas's direction. The captain came over and said, "Un-cuff him." Looking at Thomas, he said, "Please stay seated, Mr. Watson, and I would mind your manners as you wait." He looked over his shoulder at Colville. "While I'm glad I made the right decision, and I'm relieved my arse will remain on the ground, you, on the other hand, are standing on thin ice."

He looked up and said to his guards, "Back to your posts, men."

Thomas's hands were around a warm cup of tea, offered to him by a woman who looked like she was in charge of most of the people. She must have spoken to Colville earlier about getting him some tea while he waited. She was utterly indifferent to Colville's manner.

Upon receiving the cup, he looked up and said, "Thank you, Mrs. Nel."

With apparent surprise, she said, "You're welcome, Mr...." and she waited.

"Thomas Watson," he said, standing.

"Mr. Watson," she said slowly. "Have we met? I'm sorry."

"No, we haven't, but I think I saw your picture once." He remembered seeing a much older, wonderfully soft woman and remembered the name, but again where escaped him.

"Well, you certainly have a fine memory," she said before walking away.

The image in his mind was surprisingly clear. Things, in general, were getting clearer, except there was no explanation of why the information was there in the first place.

Chapter Seventy-Three

Margaret Checks on Mrs. Somerville

Margaret heard glass break and pictured someone at the back door. A wave of fear flew through her body and mind. She froze. Her friend always entered the house from the front, which meant it had to be someone else. The note was specific about her being in danger. Margaret knew she should either get out or hide. The front door wasn't an option, as she would be in full view of anyone watching her house next door. Thoughts connected to memories, and she moved to the other side of the room. Dropping to her knees, she opened the louvered doors to the storage space under the stairs. She awkwardly worked herself into the small space and closed the doors behind her, grabbing the fixed slats from the inside.

Dorokhin checked around outside to see if anyone could see him. Satisfied, he slowly pushed the door open and called out in Russian, "Is anybody here?" He moved through the kitchen and, this time in English, called out, "Hello?" He entered the dining room of what appeared to be the house of a grandmother who loved to knit and used a bit too much perfume. Then, to his left, he saw an open drawer and an open photo album on the table.

Trying to hide, Margaret held her shoulder against the wall while bending her legs back in the tight space. Then terror gripped her heart; she'd left both notes on the table, in plain view—unbelievable.

Dorokhin saw the notes on the table but his English wasn't good enough to understand the message. He decided the back door just meant someone had broken into the house. Thinking he heard a sound in the back rooms, he reached for his firearm in the holster under his arm. He slowly moved to the bedroom area and checked out the rest of the house, finding nothing. Coming back out, Dorokhin walked by Margaret twice as she stayed silent, despite the cramp beginning in her right leg. She grabbed her calf and bit her lip as the pain and fear brought tears to her eyes.

Holstering the gun, Dorokhin walked over, unlocked the front door from the inside, and swung it open. His replacement, stationed behind the bush, was surprised as they locked eyes. The agent closed the door behind him and headed toward his replacement.

"Why were you late?" Dorokhin demanded.

"I'm not late," protested the new man. "Besides, you were missing when I arrived. What were you doing coming out of the house next door?"

"Someone broke into the back of the house and I wanted to make sure it wasn't the Watsons trying to hide. You can tell that Viktor guy it was boring."

"You tell him. I'm not even talking to that guy unless I have to."

Inside, Margaret heard the door close and assumed they were both outside since she could barely hear the exchange between the two men. Quietly she pushed open the door to her little space and straightened out her leg, trying to alleviate the pain. Standing up, she rocked back and forth on the leg while berating herself for being so careless. The agent had undoubtedly seen Thomas's name, and it would be evident that Beth was somehow involved. That's exactly what she didn't want. She didn't think he could link the names to the bakery, so Beth wasn't in immediate danger.

Margaret tried to get to a simple train of thought. Why did Beth know they were in danger, and why on earth was she involved? Margaret thought about dropping her off last night. They shouldn't have left her alone, but she'd learned that it was hard to change Beth's mind once she had it set. Margaret had come to see if she was safe, and she wasn't. Margaret knew her next step was to go to the bakery. She cautiously looked out the sheer curtains as the two men argued in the street. Occasionally, the original agent would vigorously wave an arm at one of the houses in his conversation. If she were to leave undetected, it would be while the agents were together.

Margaret thought about grabbing the notes that caused her so much anxiety. They were lying there just below her outstretched hand. However, if she took them and the man returned, he would know someone had been inside. She cursed and made for the backdoor of the house. Slowly she opened the door and went out, through the back fence, and into the alley. Which way to go was answered when she saw a cab drop off Mr. Bartlett at his rear gate. It was almost directly behind Mrs. Somerville's. As she approached the cab, Mr. Bartlett tipped his hat and said, "Mrs. Watson, good day, and aren't you just the thing to brighten up an already sunny morning."

"Hello, Mr. Bartlett," she said. "Thank you, but I'm in a bit of a fix."

"Well, you came to the right place. What can we do for you?"

She asked the cab driver, "Can you give me a lift to Saxby's Bakery? I know it's not far and not much of a fair, but I'll pay you extra."

Mr. Bartlett answered for his longtime friend in the cab. "Of course, he would for the likes of you, Mrs. Watson, wouldn't you, Emery?"

"I can speak for myself, judge; I don't need you to be mindin' my business." Emery looked out of the driver's window and, with the warmest of faces, said, "I would be delighted to take you anywhere you wish."

Emery then addressed his friend with a long, drawn-out "Well?" The judge was still enjoying the reason for his brightened morning. "*Judge*," the cab driver said like a schoolmaster, "even a schoolboy would know to get the door."

Judge Bartlett opened the door and said, "Now, Emery, you behave yourself." They both knew that Margaret's feminine attributes were the subject of many of their frequent discussions in Judge Bartlett's back garden.

With that in mind, the judge added, "You know what I mean, dust off the gentleman in you and make sure you treat her like a lady."

"She *is* a lady, and I don't need you to be telling me; I can see for myself."

The former judge, Vernon Bartlett, peered into the back seat and said, "You let me know if this rake is anything less than perfect." He laughed.

"Gentleman, I'm in kind of in a hurry. Can we go?" Margaret said.

"See, Emery, she's giving you the benefit of the doubt."

Emery put it in gear and said out the window, "You would be good to lose my phone number, you old dodger."

"I can't; been in my memory for fifteen years," the judge shouted over the sound of the engine taking off.

"Emery, is it?" Margaret said.

"Yes, ma'am."

Realizing he would take the shortest route, which would take them back in front of her house, Margaret said, "Can you take me to the bakery by going up Chesham Road and around? I don't want to be seen by someone."

"Well, that's sad for most of the world, now, isn't it?"

"Emery, this is very important."

"Yes, have you there in a jiffy."

Emery approached the intersection and turned away from the direct route to the bakery. As they drove away, Margaret looked back and saw the new agent running around the corner at the other end of the alley. Presumably, the other man was going in the front. Margaret slid down in the seat, thankful she'd considered the consequences of taking the notes.

She approached the bakery and asked the cabbie to drive past it and drop her off. She reached into the purse slung over her shoulder, and extended payment to the cab driver.

"No, Miss, no fare today. But on your next walk around the neighborhood, can I ask you to tell that friend of mine how I was the perfect example of a lady's gentleman?"

Seeing that it was faster than getting him to accept pay, she said, "Yes, of course, I will." He began to open his door. "No, Emery, don't get out; I'm fine." Margaret got out and closed the door behind her.

She walked down the sidewalk and took a cautious look at the shop window. Inside there were two of the many children who stopped by every day.

Emma noticed Margaret outside. Having taken care of the boys, she said, "Out with ya now, both of ya, till tomorrow."

Margaret entered as the boys left. Emma pointed to the rear of the store with a towel in her hand. Passing Margaret, Emma reached out, turning the Open sign on the front door.

She could hear Stewart and another man talking as she walked behind the counter and through the door into the working part of the business. Emma was right behind.

"Is Beth okay?" Margaret asked.

"Yes, dear, she's fine; she was by earlier today."

"Yes, I know; she left me a note saying to come here."

In a different and more serious tone, Emma said, "After a conversation with a stranger right outside, she came in and said you might come by. It was quite a serious conversation, but I didn't pay it any mind except I didn't know him, which was strange." Reaching into her apron pocket, Emma continued, "After he left, she came inside and asked me to give you a message, along with this key and address."

Margaret looked at the address. "I don't know where this is."

"Beth said things had changed, and both of you were in danger. If you showed up, I was to tell you to go to the rear of this flat, not the front, and you could find her there."

"Did she say anything about Thomas?"

"No, it was quick, but she made me promise I would get you there. She was concerned, anxious even. Very unlike the woman I've known for years. So, I called Bernie, the warden, and he said he would go with you to make sure you get there safely."

Bernie, who had been sitting at a table speaking with Mr. Saxby, stood up. "Yes, indeed, I'm not sure what's goin' on, but I want ta help."

Margaret smiled, acknowledging his concern and offer. "Bernie, everyone can always depend on you. You're such a dear."

Emma looked at her husband and said, "Can't you see Margaret needs something to drink? Where are your manners?"

Stewart looked up in surprise, saying, "Course, mum, I was jus' goin'," and bolted for the icebox a few steps away. Stewart soon handed Margaret a cold glass, and she suddenly realized what Emma had already determined. The last few hours were tense for Margaret. She took a long drink of the cold sweet tea and exhaled. She raised the glass and said, "Stewart, that's wonderful."

She paused in thought. Until the Russian read the note on the table, Margaret was sure Beth was safe and not connected to the troubles she and Thomas faced. However, Emma said she talked to her much earlier after meeting the stranger. After that encounter, Beth somehow concluded she needed to go somewhere safe and that Margaret should follow. Why? The answer lies with who the person was.

"Emma?"

"Yes, dear."

"You said you didn't know the man. Can you describe him?"

"Yes, he was big, but he had a gentle manner. He had a full face, slightly round, thick features, and was well-dressed. Not the likes of those around here." She glanced back at her husband and Bernie, who was still waiting to help. They exchanged confused glances as Bernie pulled his belt up, to no result, as it retreated to its previous angle.

"Did he sound Russian?"

"He came in and left with but a few words. But, no, he had no accent that I could hear."

Margaret was very concerned and had to understand why her friend thought she needed to go to a safe place provided by a stranger. The physical description fit that Yuri person, but he definitely had an accent. She didn't know about the one Thomas called Viktor. They'd dropped off Beth two nights ago at the taxi stand, and Margaret knew she'd gone home because she'd written and left the notes. Then why didn't she answer any of Margaret's calls? Beth's involvement was a serious concern and changed everything, and she had to let Thomas know.

Margaret had made her decision and stepped toward the man in uniform. "Thank you, Bernie, for being here, but now that I know Beth is safe, there's something I must do, and I'll be okay."

On her toes, she placed a kiss on the man's cheek. Again, Bernie self-consciously yanked at the front of his trousers.

"Thank you all," Margaret said, moving toward the front of the store. "You've been wonderful, and I'll be back to fill in the mysterious details."

Chapter Seventy-Four

Whitehall—Thomas Meets Churchill

Thomas had been waiting for over an hour, with Colville routinely coming and going out of the prime minister's office. With the latest emergence, he walked over, saying, "Mr. Watson, the prime minister, will see you now."

He raised his arm, whose first duty was directional management, pulling the sleeve back from his watch. "You've exactly fifteen minutes. I'll show you in."

Colville's hand was on the door as it swung open. Thomas stepped in, and before him sat perhaps the most outstanding natural leader the world had seen—or perhaps will ever see.

Sometimes the simplicity of appearances hides the true impact contained therein. That was the case with the office of the prime minister of England, on whose desk lay, undetectable to the naked eye, perhaps the most challenging task anywhere on the planet. He shouldered the responsibility from an office in keeping with the dowdy décor of the transatlantic telephone room. The low bookcase to his left contained various personal memorabilia items. Layers of maps covered the yellowed wall behind him, and on an ordinary desk were the typical articles of a manager: a two-piece pen set with an open bottle of ink, a blotter, and stacks of files. The only exceptions were a communications box with lighted buttons, red and black telephones, and an ornate wooden box, presumably for cigars.

With a gruff voice, Churchill put down the phone and said to no one directly, "Sometimes, in the course of difficult times, no news is good news."

"Fifteen minutes, Mr. Churchill," Colville said, staring at Thomas. He exited the room.

Thomas glanced back at the door, saying, "He's very dedicated. My name is Thomas Watson." He extended his hand.

The prime minister remained seated. "Sometimes dedication is just not enough. Fortunately, in Mr. Colville's case, it's mixed with a great deal of natural ability. The effort before us needs more people like him." He motioned to a chair.

Thomas withdrew his hand and sat down in one of the three chairs lined up in front of the desk. Details were starting to drop into place, but it always seemed within the structure of the current conversation.

Thomas offered, "Sir, I can assure you that Mr. Colville's place in history is secure."

"Are you a historian or a fortune teller, Mr. Watson?"

"To be truthful, it might be a bit of both, but it's not a good way to start."

"Agreed. It's an area I'll choose to avoid. So, Mr. Watson, how is Margaret?" the man said.

"She's very, very Margaret," Thomas said with a half laugh, hoping to ease into what could be a fateful few minutes.

The man smiled. "Amazing lady that one, hard not to give her a whole battalion of Royal Fusiliers, point her toward Germany and, with a lightened heart, take a holiday. I could especially use her today."

Thomas took the opening, choosing his words carefully. "It will get worse before it gets better."

"That's not an exceptionally bold bet, Mr. Watson," Churchill said. "I find it hard to think you're very good at cards. Time is limited before Mr. Colville fidgets in here, changing the subject and the present company."

He leaned back in his chair before continuing. "Despite your somewhat inept charge at the castle gates, you've managed to see, with a strategic assist, the nobleman that resides within. That assist is a dear relationship with Lady Hatcher through her husband. She's a wonderfully complicated woman who has, over the years, failed miserably at the part of a shy flower but has excelled at being the beautiful rose, which can only be handled by its uninviting stem."

Looking to his left, Churchill rotated his chair and said, "Mr. Watson, it's not often, in fact, never, that I receive a call such as the one I participated in last night. No, I should say I was subjected to. So young man, how do you propose to save England?"

Thomas began, "Mr. Prime Minister, this will be unlike any meeting you've ever had."

"Indeed, it already is," Churchill replied.

"First, I must ask for your patience as I try to establish some form of credibility, as, without that, we won't get anywhere. What I have to say involves information I'm not supposed to know and will appear, at first, to imply I'm a spy, which I can assure you I'm not."

"That's comforting. Very comforting," Churchill said, almost absent-mindedly.

Thomas drew a deep breath and said, "I know that at this time, Fighter Command is dangerously short of fighter planes. They're shorter yet of pilots and fields for takeoffs and landings."

"Well, you're a spy that reads the newspapers, I see, how clever."

Thomas ignored the comment. "Later today, you'll go to the Uxbridge facility to catch some of the action, as you like to say."

At first, half-listening or not listening, Churchill looked down, appearing to read a paper atop his desk as the sentence registered. At the mention of Uxbridge, the prime minister's head and eyebrows went up.

"Not many in the Kingdom save Mr. Colville, and my wife knows my schedule. You've moved out of the realm of just well-read to actual spy. I hope you have an explanation." Churchill pulled a cigar with a damp end from his outside breast pocket and rolled it in his fingers.

"I hope to do two things," Thomas said. "The first is to prove I've valuable information that's secret, in fact, not known at this time, and, second, to prove that I'm on your or our side, to keep from being shot."

"You better be expedient. Thomas, is it?"

"Yes, today …" Thomas started.

"Young man," Churchill interrupted, "you said 'not known at this time.' Do you mean not known to our intelligence services or not known to me?"

"Not known to anyone, and please give me my fifteen minutes, or you'll think I've taken flight to fancy. Information not known to anyone," Thomas paused and looked directly at the prime minister, then continued, "as it hasn't occurred yet."

Instead of the major reaction, Thomas expected, Churchill just moved the unlit cigar to his lips and smiled as he said, "You're not the type I would have thought Margaret would have taken a fancy to, flight or not."

Thomas continued in an urgent tone, "I must be quick. Later today, you'll witness the largest German air attack to date, totaling over a thousand aircraft. We will repel the attacks, but at the end of the day, if the Germans were to continue the battle, the RAF wouldn't be able to defend southern England."

Thomas took a breath. "Luckily, the Germans will also suffer extensive losses, and the second attack won't occur. At 18:30, England will essentially be defenseless."

"Please, Mr. Watson, why are you doing this?" Churchill reached over to the box on his desk and pressed a button. "It's heresy. I've honored the request of a very dear friend, and you've chosen to belittle the relationship with this nonsense."

The door opened, and Colville entered the room, excited that he could pick up even a few minutes on his schedule. "Your time has expired early, Mr. Watson," he said as his arm directed Thomas to the door.

"Sir," Colville said, I've Mr. Bixby waiting, and there have been reports of another civilian bombing with casualties, this time in Richmond Hill just across the …"

Thomas rose from his seat a bit too quickly, startling Colville and the prime minister. The adrenalin coursing through his system raised his voice. "Sir, I need you to believe me. Within your government, specifically at Bletchley Park, there's an effort to decode quickly…"

Without even turning to the door, Colville yelled, "*Captain!*"

Thomas spit out the words as quickly as he could: "To quickly decode intercepted Enigma messages. The resulting data is called Ultra, and only a few people know about it, and it will, I promise, stay that way."

At that moment, two men grabbed Thomas and pushed him to the ground, his arms pinned behind his back once again. Unable to brace himself for the fall, he hit his head hard on the floor but turned just in time to land on his cheek to avoid striking the full front of his face. Thomas grunted at the impact of a knee in the small of his back but managed to say, "… the codes of the German high command."

Thomas increased his cadence as the two men picked him up off the floor. "You can't decrypt the messages fast enough …" Before Thomas could stand on his own, the men pulled him forward, and his shoes dragged along the wooden floor behind him. He struggled against the two men as they cleared the door. "Lord Halifax will call you later today for a meeting of the war cabinet to be held tonight." Thomas was now almost shouting. "He's preparing the cabinet to adopt a proposal of surrender to forestall an invasion."

"Captain, this is unforgivable," Colville yelled, then added even more loudly, "Get him out of here," followed by "You're not to leave the building without seeing me, is that understood?" His eyes rolled, looking up at the ceiling.

Churchill watched the drama unfold, standing at the doorway of his office. He looked at the man lying on the floor beside Colville's desk.

The captain, down on one knee, locked eyes with Thomas. "This is a very interesting or very disturbed man," the captain thought. Thomas heard a snap in the background. With Thomas still in the firm grip of the two soldiers, the captain said, "Come now, Mr. Watson, before I'm forced, with no lack of pleasure, to bring you to harm."

Thomas felt the pain in his shoulders as the two men started to lift him. Again, he tried to get his feet in a position to stand.

"*Wait!*" Churchill yelled. Everyone stopped. "Put the gun away, captain."

Chapter Seventy-Five

Yuri's Second Call

Yuri had given himself plenty of time to reach the contact point, with a constant awareness heightened by the presence of Viktor.

Leaving the Kentish Town Station, he walked down Hammond to Caversham and turned the corner. He kept walking, as he did not notice any public call box right away. It appeared as soon as he passed a flower wagon with its large umbrella. As he approached, he saw a young man silhouetted inside the darkly lit enclosure. Yuri looked at his watch. "Five or six minutes," he thought. He nervously paced past the stand, looking at the colours of the flowers. How did anyone come up with flowers amid a damn national conflict? Vividly, the blooms sat grouped in rusted tins, representing one of the divine creations that did not wage war.

"A little pickup for the lady, sir?" the vendor said, pulling a bag out from below a counter.

Yuri drew back to the comment and looked at his watch again. He ignored the vendor and returned to stand right beside the telephone box, so the young man inside could see his impatience. The figure looked back at Yuri, continuing to talk, staking out his rightful territory, having been there first. "The old man will just have to queue it up," the kid thought.

Yuri could tell by the kid's posture and facial expressions that he wasn't talking to his science teacher but with someone of more personal interest. Yuri was out of time; he needed to do something. He could drag the kid out of the box, which would cause a scene opposite of what he wanted. The flower man would immediately run for the constable.

Moving closer and staring through to its occupant, he reached into his pocket, placed a one-pound note against the glass, and waited for the reaction. The lad said a few quick words, hung up, and opened the door.

Yuri extended the money. The kid took it and held it up, saying, "Pleasure doing business with ya."

Yuri said nothing and grabbed the door just as the phone started ringing.

Agent Kirkway had dialed the number and listened to the busy signal. The agent looked at the clock again, confirming it was the right time. He dialed the number a third time, relieved to hear the double ring.

"Is he there?" Petrie said, putting down the red file folder he'd just absorbed.

"I'm sure, sir. They don't generally ring up here to order tea." Kirkway bit his tongue as Petrie gave him a cold stare. "Sorry, sir," he said, as he thankfully heard the receiver at the other end pick up. He turned and motioned the director toward a second phone.

Director Petrie picked up the second phone and held it to his ear.

Kirkway said, "Watch desk, code name?"

"Treasure," Yuri said.

"Hold for Mr. Petrie, Director General of Security."

Petrie came on. "Petrie here; what's your situation?"

"Hello, director. It has been some time. Have you reviewed the file?"

"I didn't need to, but I did."

"Then you're aware of my unusual situation."

"Yes, very aware."

"Then first things first. Margaret Hatcher is secure at her mother's house. Recent developments have forced me to terminate this assignment, which I'll explain. Moscow told me to gather whatever we could on a suspected project underway at Hatcher Plc. I recruited a Mr. Watson for the job. It's all in a previous report."

"Yes, I'm familiar with it," Petrie said.

"Watson proved to be very unstable but somehow married Margaret Hatcher."

Petrie, taken by surprise, said, "Married? Are you sure?"

"Yes, and despite the marriage, he produced nothing of value on the assignment. All other efforts at uncovering the existence of such a project have also come up empty. Given his ineffectiveness and instability, Moscow issued a directive for me to eliminate him. The same directive ordered me back to Moscow. However, I've discovered Moscow secretly sent another agent into the country, and this agent has gone rogue."

Yuri continued, "As to Watson, except for possibly placing Miss Hatcher in danger, I had no interest in Watson's destiny until recently, when he changed."

"Where's Watson now?"

"At the Hatcher Estate as of yesterday," Yuri said. "They both are safe given the estate's private protection. However, there remain several issues that need to be addressed. I met with the local asset charged with observing Miss Hatcher. She's at a safe house on Leyton High Road 26B, a secure location known only to me."

Petrie looked over to Kirkway, who quickly wrote down the address.

Yuri continued, "Her name is Mrs. Beth Somerville. She's in the file. She'll need to be brought in. She'll only open the door to someone using the identification of 'princess.' The embassy is unaware of her involvement. She has taken a personal interest in Miss Hatcher's safety, going beyond the original monitoring assignment. She has done an excellent job."

An impatient Petrie said, "So Margaret and Watson are safe, and the asset is at the safe house. What about this agent?"

"His name is Viktor Grigoryevich, a colonel in the NKVD, and he's very dangerous. Moscow has ordered me back after eliminating Watson. The real truth is I'm on Viktor's list. He has orders to kill me, which he'll find is not so easy."

"We can help," Petrie said.

"No, if the trail comes back to British intelligence, it leads to Margaret, and someone in Moscow will open another investigation, putting her back in danger. I must eliminate Viktor, and they must know who was responsible. Only then will Margaret be safe from the embassy, which was my commitment. I believe I've then completed my end of our agreement."

"Mr. Stakova, we also committed. You must also come in, as we promised to provide for your safety."

"No, Mr. Petrie. Moscow Centre has decided. Even without Viktor, Moscow would have had a cot in Siberia with my name on it. I can't stay in England. I need to disappear. We both know the rules, Mr. Security Director; you can only be a double agent once and then can no longer be trusted. To lie once is to lie twice. As you say, I've done my bit, and it's time to move on. It's finished, I'll take your secrets and disappear unless you choose to insist on 'protecting' me. In that event, I'm back in a game and will certainly bargain for my life with what I have. To convey any information to anyone at this time isn't in my best interest, so our incentives are one and the same, are they not?"

"Yes, I guess that's true enough," Petrie replied. "Have you made arrangements? Can we help you there?"

Yuri's smile came through in his words. "I arranged to leave the country the day I arrived years ago. In addition, your government provided the necessary documents at the time of our agreement. Of course, I'll not be using them, as you would then know the name I'm using when I travel. Besides, if you help me, someone must know where I'm going, which is never good. Please, it's not a matter of trust; it's a matter of procedure."

"True, sir, very true," Petrie said. "Never try to be clever with someone who has mastered the ability to stay alive. Mr. Stakova, I know I speak for the prime minister in saying we can't thank you enough."

"Mr. Petrie, if I may, Margaret Hatcher started as an assignment. Separately, somewhere along the line, it became an affair of the heart for both Mrs. Somerville and myself. Miss Hatcher is truly unique, capturing your heart in a single beat. It's too bad she'll only know me as the enemy. To me, this matters."

Looking at Kirkway, Petrie said, "If it's of concern, then I'll be sure to address it."

"Thank you. I'll not be leaving right away. As I said, I must address a few issues before I'm free to travel."

"Such as…?" Petrie asked.

"Housekeeping," Yuri said. "I must clean up some things which affect both our houses, actions I'll take to contribute to Margaret's safety and, perhaps more importantly, to mine."

Yuri thought for a moment before exposing his friend. "There's a man at the embassy I trust who might be of service to your government in the future. His name is Pavel. You might convince him to cooperate for the right incentives, namely political asylum, and relocation. However, I can't guarantee this. As to the Russian Embassy, nothing was learned of the special project of any importance."

"One thing," Petrie said, "you indicated something about not trusting Watson until recently. What did that mean?"

There was a noticeable pause before Yuri's response, "This I'm not sure about. He has certainly changed. He was a complete liar with two faces, not very bright, and not someone you would trust with even worthless things. He was incapable of true feelings for Margaret. All he cared about was money. Recently, he changed into a serious man on a mission. He would say interesting things like there would be no invasion and Germany wouldn't defeat England. But we both know that at least the boats will be coming—perhaps any day."

"Well …"

Yuri allowed the man his biased opinion and continued, "That aside, more than one person, including Margaret, thinks the current man isn't the same Watson she married. He might as well be another person. One day, when I pressed him for information, he was completely unaware he was working for me. My ah…instincts told me he wasn't lying. However, he's not a threat to Margaret, so I see no reason for action. Indeed she's safer with this ah…new, different man in her life. There, you have it. Don't ask me to explain it as I can't, but I'm one of the believers."

Yuri knew this moment represented the end of a chapter in his life. "Then it's done, Director. Thank you and the prime minister for allowing me to oversee Miss Hatcher's safety and a second chance to survive the war. I hope he thinks his decision was the correct one."

"I'm sure he does," Petrie said, listening to the muffled thud as the swinging receiver at the end of the cord gently hit the back glass in the small space.

Petrie hung up the phone. So ended one of the most interesting cases he'd ever followed. He turned to his agent, asking for the file. "Is this all of it?" Petrie asked.

"Yes, sir. It's Section 900. Everything that exists is in that file, then placed in that safe."

"Fine," Petrie said, placing the file under his arm. "Restore security, and I'll write the debriefing report myself."

He reached down to the log and, confirming it was the current log sheet tore the almost empty page from the binder. He said, "You're to replace whatever notes you had for earlier in the day from memory, but do *not* refer to anything regarding this file or this phone call. This event never happened. I must be certain of your understanding. Am I clear, sergeant?" Petrie raised his eyebrows, expecting an answer.

The sergeant stood up, saluted the civilian, and said, "Understood, sir, fully, sir. It was just a normal morning."

"I hope so, son. Carry on."

The sergeant closed the door behind the director and locked it. Kirkway walked over to the safe, secured it, then turned to his log and started reconstructing his entries earlier in the morning. In doing so, he considered the consequences of error in his pre-war job as a department store manager. Any minor failures couldn't result in his being sacked, but here one slip of the tongue, and he could be shot.

Chapter Seventy-Six

Churchill's Office—Thomas On The Floor

The captain was surprised at the strength of Churchill's command to stop.

"Yes, sir," the captain said, freezing in mid-movement like a figure in Pompeii.

The prime minister walked over, stopping at Thomas's feet. Still rolling the cigar between his thumb and forefinger, he looked down at Thomas for a full ten seconds, then said, "Mr. Watson, a spy with unimagined abilities could, in the remotest sense, know the information you've provided. However, the most beloved Halifax won't call me for a meeting scheduled for today, as this very morning, he requested a meeting for tomorrow. While meetings of this sort are certainly not out of the ordinary, it's extremely suspicious that you would be aware of something no one else could know. You see, Mr. Halifax and I were alone in my quarters during our discussion. Indeed, I've yet to inform Mr. Colville, whose job it will be to gather the members due to the uneven nature of the morning."

Thomas turned his head as much as he could and said quietly, "I still believe the meeting will occur today."

Churchill turned to the captain, who had returned to normal form. "You and two men stay down here." He looked up at the room crowded with soldiers and at the anxious stares of every worker. "The rest of you fine people can go back to work. I wish to thank you all for your devoted service. Colville, in here with me, and that would include you, Mr. Watson."

Thomas felt relief saturate his body. He stood with the captain's aid and felt the handcuffs fall free from his wrists. Thomas put his hand up to his face, only to encounter a sting. He winced.

The captain noticed the action and said, "Sorry, sir, I think we couldn't avoid that."

Churchill said, "In a minute, I too will know whether to apologize."

Back in Churchill's office, with an almost uncertain motion Churchill waved Thomas to the same chair, ignoring Colville, who continued to stand. Churchill also remained standing behind his desk.

Thomas was still breathing heavily as he accepted the seat.

"How is it you can know about Ultra? My first fear is the secret's been let out," Churchill said.

"No, it's still a secret, and it will remain so throughout the war," Thomas said.

"You've found that the Hatcher firm is involved with this. Is that where you got your information?"

"No," Thomas offered. "Lady Hatcher knows of the project but not the details, and Margaret knows nothing." He knew it wasn't entirely the truth.

"Well, then?" the PM said impatiently.

"Sir, I wish to continue with my recount of events to occur this afternoon, but you might find it advisable that we continue the conversation alone."

"Bloody 'ell," Colville shouted.

Churchill silently looked at Colville as he searched for a way to move this unusual situation forward and get to the nut of it. "Mr. Watson, do you love this Margaret I hold so dearly? Can you tell me why you would place her in this position? By simple association, this path you've chosen could be doing her a grave injustice."

Waiting, Churchill looked directly at Thomas.

"Mr. Watson?" Churchill said, a clear edge to his voice.

"Why?" Thomas said.

"Why do you love her?" he repeated with irritation. "Tell me, and you should be quick about it," he said, reaching across his desk for his lighter.

Thomas was surprised at the query and wasn't quite sure of what to say. It was as if he knew he had only twenty words left, and they had to be exactly right. "Because she was born sixty years too early," he said. "She should have been born in an era when a woman could be prime minister."

"Good God, man," Colville said in disbelief. "Have you no respect?"

Thomas continued, "Margaret is a woman *before* her time, as much as her mother is a woman *of* her time. My association with her and the path I've chosen should tell you the importance I place on the events coming later today."

The great man stared at Thomas in thought. Still standing in front of his desk, he started toward his chair, saying, "Mr. Colville, could you give us a moment?"

Colville was speechless and stood frozen in his spot.

After sitting down, Churchill looked at his exacting gatekeeper as if a teacher was waking a student sleeping in class. He said, "*Mr. Colville?* Would you be so kind as to get the door?"

Colville, with an astonished expression, left the room without a word.

"Thank you," Thomas said, feeling the pressure ease. After a pause, Thomas said, "It's an odd question."

"If so, I believe it fits quite nicely with some of your odd statements. I thought it an excellent method of finding out if you had your wits about you. The test was to determine if you would continue to blabber about your fantasy world, which, even now, I'm beginning to doubt is pure fantasy. The mere thought, you must surely understand, leaves me in a somewhat uncomfortable position."

Somewhat frustrated, Thomas said, "Mr. Churchill, I don't have a source for the information. I wish I had something clever to say to give you confidence in my intentions. I don't. I woke up one day married to Margaret and don't remember anything before that except…" Thomas stopped.

The man waited.

"Except, if I may, I know some things that have yet to occur." Thomas winced as if in anticipation of being called a lunatic.

"You've already proven one with the statement about Halifax. He's very unhappy with my leadership, and given things are going badly, not completely without reason."

With notable caution, Thomas said, "He wouldn't be unhappy if he knew the whole story."

"And I presume you know the whole story?"

Thomas wasn't sure he wanted to reveal the whole story and decided to stay with the subject at hand. He said, "I know enough, sir. Halifax spent yesterday and most of today gathering support for a resolution, which he'll present at a time he feels will place you in the weakest position and that he hopes will force you to sue for peace at the earliest."

"This isn't hard to believe, given the state of our defenses," Churchill said.

"Mr. Prime Minister, that weakened time will be after a battle later today during your visit to Uxbridge. After today's attack, he'll have numbers that reflect the day's battle," Thomas said. "Sir, the numbers will reflect substantial losses. They'll be the smoking gun he'll use to support his position, to sway the War Cabinet to his vision of what's best for England. He'll go into the meeting feeling very confident."

"Well, Mr. Watson, I've the same numbers from yesterday, and I can assure you, it's all he needs. If the next battle places us in yet a deeper state of peril, continued resistance, on the face of it, becomes a position that's ever more difficult to defend. The leader of my ever-present opposition isn't without his grounds nor insincere in his efforts." He mindlessly fiddled with the lighter while looking at Thomas.

"Sir, I believe you understand that events don't always logically flow to the statistics or even the obvious. I know you, and perhaps only you, have a vision for the proper outcome of this war. Moreover, I'm positive you intrinsically possess the personal ability to transfer this vision into reality."

Churchill stopped flipping the lighter over and said, "If things are as bad as you say, a state I'm not altogether ready to deny could occur in *your* theory of the universe, Mr. Watson, just how does one play this hand?"

Thomas leaned forward to emphasize his answer. "Mr. Prime Minister, it's one of your greatest leadership performances. You convince the cabinet that in the face of logical evidence to the contrary, it's an obligation, bound by the blood of those who've given the highest sacrifice, to defend the Kingdom to the last standing stick. To know that these brave boys preserved the hope of presenting our children with the grandest of humanity's gifts, the opportunity to build upon the best of our civilization."

Churchill stared at Thomas with a look devoid of any sign of emotion. "That was an impressive bit of oratory for one who comfortably resides on the cutting edge of insanity."

Thomas smiled, changing the mood, "I must admit, sir, it's very possible some of those words are your own, pulled from my fragmented memory. If credit is due, I suspect it's yours."

Winston's forehead furrowed at the comment. "Again, a memory of the future?"

Thomas nodded.

"I know that this will not sit well with you, Mr. Watson, but a memory resides in yesterday; of that, I'm most confident."

Thomas continued cautiously, "Knowing the future gives me an unusual look at the present, which will become your yesterday. Moreover, what resides behind yesterday will determine what occurs in the future. My memories tell me you—we—win the war."

"As eloquent as you make it sound if your memories are correct, what's the problem, Mr. Watson? Let events proceed of their own accord."

"Though I've no logical explanation, I believe I'm here to ensure my memories and your upcoming decisions are the same."

Still, in a quandary, Churchill said, "It's been an intriguing rhetorical exchange, but it doesn't answer the question of why I should not accept the agenda of my foe if it benefits the people under my present stewardship. Mr. Watson, I love the story, but what's the problem?"

Thomas thought, "There it is again. If all turns out right, then what's the problem?" What he would say next would determine if presenting the information would be enough. The response carried the weight of Europe and a free people. He needed to say just the right thing, or it could be lost.

Thomas said, "I'll have to answer your question with a question. Mr. Prime Minister, have you decided to fight on, despite the condition of the RAF?"

Churchill took the time to light his oft-used cigar but not the time to deeply draw in the smoke and savor the taste he so dearly loved. "Honestly, Mr. Watson, I haven't come to that decision, but if I could stop time, I would, as the more that passes, the murkier this saga becomes."

Thomas waited. "For reasons unknown to me, I think I'm here to assist in your decision to fight on, that today matches tomorrow's history."

"Where's here?"

Thomas looked puzzled.

"If you can explain 'here,' you must define 'there,' and in that, we discover the source of your knowledge."

In a wistful tone, Thomas said, "I know not of a 'there.' As I said, it's more information than memories. Our dear Lady of History hasn't seen fit to give me a 'there.' It's a blank."

"A convenient blank, I might add."

Thomas took a deep breath and enlisted a tone he hadn't used in the conversation. "Mr. Churchill, it's a short time until you know whether I'm a fool who deliberately sentenced himself to death for revealing state secrets or someone who wants to be useful. Either way, I think I'm in an unrecoverable position regarding my safety."

Churchill sat down and moved some papers on his desk but was really in thought.

"Sir," Thomas said, "in any event, my well-being pales compared to the losses suffered by the people and the 1200 brave pilots that will die saving Britain."

"The total is 820, Mr. Watson. It's a number I spend considerable quiet time reviewing."

"Twelve hundred is the final total, Mr. Prime Minister. It's not over."

"It can't be denied; you're a fascinating man, Mr. Watson."

Chapter Seventy-Seven

Yuri Back at the Safe House

After his phone call, Yuri stood outside the call box and again took the time to see if he'd drawn any unwanted attention. The people who occupied the immediate area acted as though they were utterly out of touch with a war that, perhaps in a matter of days or hours, could be marching down this street. He could place a purpose on everyone he could see except a rather large man some distance down the street. He could only see his back as he walked away. Yuri's instincts frowned as the man walked with an umbrella, tapping an odd tempo. The metal tip didn't hit at the proper cadence. This rhythm was the birthright of any Brit, and the exception drew attention. "I must be getting jumpy," Yuri thought. In the distance, he heard the distinctive whine of a Spitfire.

Returning to the safe house, he thought about what was next. Margaret and Thomas weren't as safe as everyone thought. Neither was he, not while Viktor was loose. He wanted to get back to check on Mrs. Somerville and let her know about Petrie's men coming for her. Then he needed to find out where Viktor was and eliminate him. It was something Yuri seldom had to deal with directly. Other people or clever methods had always been available when such issues arose. Yuri preferred an old-fashioned setup where he tricked the target into committing a crime with informed local authorities taking action.

This time, his target wasn't a fumbling civilian, but a focused weapon intent on pursuing his agenda, and Yuri and the Watsons were in the way. It would take a more direct hand.

Yuri had just stepped onto the large common he needed to cross toward the safe house on the other side. Unlike at night, in the day, the broad green area didn't look like the edge of the world. Instead, it was filled with hedges, blossoms, and trees. The small patch of land was a calming reassurance that nature continued on its plan, despite the tortured paths of humanity.

Just as Yuri pulled open the lapel of his coat to access the key in his breast pocket, he heard a shot. The bullet pierced the open garment directly below his arm and glanced off an unused fountain directly ahead of him. Yuri immediately knew who it had to be and began running for his life, dodging in and around tree trunks, making it harder for his pursuer to take aim. He could hear his feet pounding the ground and, after a few seconds, feel his chest exploding as he ran. He thought of the stairs in the Silvertown Station and wished he'd seen them as an opportunity, not a hindrance.

For years, Yuri had visited the safe house and memorized its surroundings. Thus, he had knowledge of the area his opponent lacked. "Shooting in broad daylight," Yuri thought. "Things have gotten out of control." His feet hit the cobblestones just as he spied the opening of the walled pedestrian alley that serviced the rear of the mostly commercial tenants on the block. His escape plan was to enter and go through the kitchen door of a restaurant he frequented. He'd checked out the kitchen long ago, confirming the door was open during the day and well into the night. He would enter the rear and lock the door, warning the employees about a man with a gun on the other side. It would delay his pursuer just long enough for him to escape out the front of the business to safety. It would take too long for Viktor to run around to the front of the building in pursuit, eliminating that option.

Approaching the alley, Yuri ran awkwardly, keeping his head low, waiting for the next shot. Rounding the corner into the pedestrian alley, Yuri immediately knew he'd made a mistake. Fifty feet before him, workers were constructing a wall between the two buildings, cutting him off from his escape door on the other side. "The mistake," Yuri thought, "will cost me my life." He knew the only other door on this side of the wall was always locked.

The gunman saw Yuri duck between two buildings. He rushed to the corner, preparing to peek around but waited for the sounds of running; there weren't any. He looked up and down the street and observed people running from the gunshots and another harmless Brit too far away to matter.

Yuri spun around, knowing his only hope was to make it back out out of the alley before the shooter arrived. He would trade certain death for a slightly better chance of the gunman hitting a running target. In two steps he faced a man standing at the corner of the alley. He was trapped. The man with a complacent smile pointed a gun directly at Yuri's chest. It wasn't the man in the passport photo, but one of Viktor's men.

Yuri coughed out the words, frantically buying time. "Moscow knows you tried to kill Watson," he said in Russian.

"Moscow knows nothing," the man said, breathing heavily. "They'll only know if you live. I have my orders." The man raised the gun up, the final motion before firing.

Eyes closed, Yuri saw himself in his mother's kitchen, leaning over the table covered with flour and surrounded by the aroma of baked bread. He heard the pistol fire—Yuri felt nothing. In shock, Yuri watched his assailant arch backward, fall to his knees, then drop to the ground with the sound of dead weight.

Yuri was stunned. "Was that a shot?" He moved forward and bent over to retrieve the pistol; a second shot hit the bricks above his head. Chips of brick flew as he raised his arm for protection. "Two shooters," Yuri thought. He backed up to the other side of the alley. With the man's gun in his hand, he slid along the wall toward the street, determined to find out who else was out there. Why weren't they together per their training? He lowered himself at the corner, so he was lying on the ground. He wanted to look around the corner from an unexpectedly low angle.

From across the street, he heard, "Dacha, I hope that's you."

Mrs. Somerville, the white haired gental soul, white of hair, came into sight with an open purse and gun in her hand. She walked up and looked at Yuri lying on the ground with a most unusual look on his face.

"For heaven's sake," she said. "You're not going to do anyone any good down there."

Yuri's quizzical look turned into a small smile, knowing he hadn't the slightest idea how the world worked but was glad it did for him today.

"Sorry about the second shot," she said, holding the Derringer away from her body. "The first one really scared me. Are you all right? Is he all right?"

"Yes, I am," Yuri said, "and no, I don't think he's all right."

"Oh, God," she said. "Did I ..."

"Mrs. Somerville, I owe you my life," he said, reaching for the diminutive weapon. "Let me take this."

She handed over the weapon her husband had given her before he left for the war. "You're alive. That's all fine and good, but will I go to jail?"

Yuri looked at the man on the ground as he touched Beth's back, pushing her. "We need to get out of here. Did you see any others?"

"No, I think he was alone. I watched you both run across the common from the window in the flat. You didn't answer the question."

"Is the flat still safe?" he asked.

"Yes," she said. "I followed all your instructions."

"Then we will go there."

"No," she said, resisting the hand's pressure, "not until you tell me if I'm going to jail. I'm still unsure whose side you're on other than Margaret's."

"Then why did you shoot?"

"Because I knew you weren't very good at this stuff, and I didn't know the other man."

Yuri started to laugh while giving her a renewed push into the street. Yuri looked around and said, "We need to act normal and, no, you're not going to jail. You shot a spy. Is that clear enough?"

"Well, now," she said, "that would be true, regardless of who I would have hit."

"Did you aim?" Yuri smiled.

Beth, quite pleased, looked him in the eye. "Of course I did."

They moved quickly toward the safe house. Arriving at the rear, Yuri started up toward the flat.

"Wait," she said, "I said he was probably alone. Don't you think we should stop a second and make sure? They might see us and know where we're hiding."

"No, there will be authorities everywhere. If there's another, he won't stick around." Yuri thought of the man walking away that had caught his attention near the phone box. It bothered him that he got careless. "It wouldn't happen again."

Beth shook her head as she started up the stairs. There's a practical intelligence that comes with age, and, in Dacha's case, it was apparent it hadn't yet arrived.

Chapter Seventy-Eight

Petrie Calls Churchill

Thomas, sitting in Churchill's office, replied to the man's statement, "I don't want you to think that I'm *interesting*, I want to help."

The distinctive loud clacking of the secure phone at the end of the prime minister's desk severely interrupted the moment.

The man looked at Thomas as he said, "Unless someone is inviting me to dinner on this secure phone, I may be required to ask for a moment of privacy."

"Winston," he said into the phone.

Having returned to his office, Petrie said, "Mr. Prime Minister, Director Petrie here."

The prime minister looked up with the phone at his ear, motioning toward the door. Thomas, already standing, made his way out, shutting the door behind him. Colville, immediately catching Thomas's movement and appearance, brightened considerably, excited at the prospect of the meeting ending.

"Are we done then?" Colville said.

Thomas again touched the bump on his cheek while sitting beside the door. He smiled at Colville, moving his head from side to side.

Churchill's body visibly relaxed inside the office, "So, Mr. Director, how is the land of ghosts and shadows, over dim visions of lies and counter lies?"

"The task is getting murkier by the second," Petrie said to his longtime friend. "We could use a hand up here if you could find a spare minute."

Churchill laughed. "There is a ten-minute lull in my activities, but it would take me a full half hour to ascend the steps and report for duty. The result is that you're on your own again."

Given the events of late, Petrie was warmed at finding the man in reasonable humor. He said, "As far as decreasing the time, it might be appropriate to consult your charming wife on the issue of the day's menu."

"Oh, yes, I quite agree; it would be so easy to solve if, indeed, she was the real problem. Alas, we're meant to live life, and it's I who decided to vigorously partake of its delights. Unfortunately, the fault lies at my doorstep and mine alone. So, now that we've covered the truly secret items of State, do you have anything else that warrants ringing me up on this line and scaring the bloody hell out of me?"

"Yes, we've had a report from a series 900 agent. It lists you and me as eyes only. The agent is Yuri Stakova, the Russian we turned and used for Margaret Hatcher's security."

"Yes, yes, I remember," Churchill said, recalling the circumstances surrounding his first meeting with the agent. Three years ago, during his time as British first sea lord, he befriended a man named Yuri Stakova, who was then the liaison to his post from within the Russian Embassy. The position at the embassy was usually a cover for the NKVD station chief, reporting directly to the spy apparatus centered in Moscow. Both of them knew the silent charade that was at play. The Russian liaison was in charge of all covert surveillance and managed a group of specially trained agents operating out of the embassy. This wasn't unique to Russia, as a similar post existed at the British Embassy in Moscow. It was a known but unpublicized fact that every country's embassy performed similar duties. All members assumed their foreign intelligence was mining more gold than the effort underway in their own backyard.

As time passed, the Russian liaison and the first sea lord probed each other in a ritual dance, each searching for more information than was relinquished while conversing through a mighty list of subjects. Each meeting revealed an increasing inventory of mutual interests spawned from the minds of two well-traveled and politically astute individuals. Gingerly, they'd gained each other's confidence, with the mutual interests growing into mutual respect.

Churchill possessed a particular skill that allowed him to remain sharp to the content and continuity of conversations when others thought him vulnerable. Churchill had perceived an underlying story in their exchanges during a particularly hazy evening. The agent detested Stalin and the devastation his policies had brought to the people of his homeland. The first sea lord did not perceive a desire for sympathy or a veiled message requesting the aid of a friend. On the contrary, the agent was extraordinarily independent and very capable.

A year later, the agent was picked up by MI5 for recruiting a domestic within the Bletchley complex. Upon investigation, it was determined the domestic wasn't in contact with any secure programs and, as a result, unable to release any secrets. The domestic had broken the law but was deemed more valuable to support a larger goal. On the other hand, the Russian agent was in serious trouble, and due to their repeated contact, officials informed Churchill. Within hours, Petrie and Churchill were in a secret meeting, presenting the agent with an alternative path to the inevitable. Churchill and Petrie had suggested he work as a British double agent, offering him the only option to live out the war.

Under interrogation, the agent had revealed one of his primary assignments: to collect any information regarding a secret project. The Russians believed there was an effort to build a machine capable of calculating numbers at a high rate of speed. The agent also revealed the Russian suspicion that a successful family company, Hatcher Plc, was secretly working on the project but couldn't unearth direct evidence.

Growing impatient, Moscow decided to see if they could obtain any information from the family's daughter. To that end, Yuri had recruited a British citizen to spy on her named Thomas Watson. Watson had walked right into the embassy, asking to speak to someone of authority. The man demonstrated a complete lack of any political allegiance or knowledge but a stiletto-like focus in requesting rather ambitious amounts of money to utilize his unproven abilities. They'd arrived at an arrangement. As time went on, despite numerous meetings and demands, Watson proved to have nothing to show for the effort and money.

On the other hand, Churchill had a significant problem that several attempts had failed to solve. Since Miss Margaret Hatcher had turned down an offer from Churchill to live at Chartwell, she'd steadfastly refused protection of any kind. Knowing nothing about the family business, she was completely unaware that others might believe her to be well-informed and that her abduction would severely affect the work proceeding at Hatcher.

With her safety in mind, Churchill covertly established security details which Margaret inevitably discovered. Artfully combining tantrums and taking advantage of his obvious love for his friend's daughter, she convinced him to stop. War was hell in so many ways. He loved her dearly, but serious obligations to his country and her father were before him.

With the double agent, Churchill saw a solution to his problem. At the time, the Russians were the only party interested in, and thus a danger to, Margaret. Moreover, Yuri was in control of that danger.

Churchill had entrusted the Russian with Margaret's safety for the duration of the war.

Very aware that any leak of their secret arrangement would have put the Russian in danger and Margaret as well, Churchill had restricted access solely to the prime minister and his chief of security.

Unbeknownst to Yuri, MI5 had already infiltrated the Russian Embassy and received daily reports on diplomatic traffic. Due to this, Yuri's efforts were limited solely to reporting any threat to Margaret or his personal exposure within the embassy.

Churchill switched the phone to his other ear and asked Petrie, "Is she in danger?"

"She could be, but it's very intertwined."

"Give me the untwined version if you would be so kind."

"Remember, before working for us, Stakova hired a domestic named Watson to get into her life, establish a relationship and obtain any information on Hatcher Plc? Somehow, Watson married her and isn't as foolish as he appeared."

"Marriage?" Churchill choked out, "Margaret?"

"Yuri recruited another domestic named Somerville, who lived next door, to monitor Margaret's safety. Somerville recently contacted Yuri reporting the possible danger, and they met in person. While covering the danger to Margaret, they soon found common ground on the issue that this Watson had somehow changed."

"Changed, in what way?"

"Watson claimed amnesia and insisted he did not know about any arrangement to monitor Margaret. Yuri and Somerville are certain that he isn't the same man who married Margaret and are aware it can't be explained"

"David, of course, you know this is the fully entwined version. Is there an answer to my question of Margaret's well-being and safety somewhere?"

"Yes, we think she's at her mother's house, according to the last report."

"Thank you, now let's get Yuri Stakova. Bring him in here, and get all this straight."

"I talked to him directly, and he's not coming in. He says there's a rogue Russian agent who thinks Watson knows about the project, and the information came from Margaret. This is, of course, concerning.Yuri says it's a messy situation and that only he can address the rogue agent. Yuri indicated that it would fall on us to guarantee Margaret's safety once he did, as he would go into hiding. I said we would take care of the Russian agent. Yuri declined, indicating there wasn't time, and that it wasn't our battle. Yuri also said he's a marked man with the Russians, and his solution will solve both problems."

"This isn't making any sense," Churchill said. "It doesn't sound like she's safe at all and is in danger. I think we must bring everyone in until we can figure out what those loose ends are."

"Winston, I'm not sure how to do that. Are you still going over to Dowding's place today?"

"Yes, and since some version of Thomas Watson is outside my door, I'll have him in tow."

"Good, that takes care of Watson; we will work on ensuring Margaret is brought in or is at the Hatcher Estate and have it sealed."

"David, make sure you keep both women safe. Since we also charged Alistair with Margaret's safety, bring him up to date. This young woman has no idea what her father put in motion. Get Alistair more sentries around the perimeter and make them visible."

Petrie paused, "Who'll tell Lady Hatcher about the increased security, let alone more people on the property? She was very clear about either situation."

"Why you, of course. As prime minister and for the sake of the country, I'm not permitted to put myself in the line of fire."

"*That*, my friend, is a very sorry excuse indeed," Petrie said with dry wit.

Churchill quickly replied, "Also cowardly, I might add, but I also have a rather precious item on my agenda: surviving the war. To this end, I must engage only in items of strategy and refuse the desire to engage in the more uncertain items related to field operations. On the other hand, *you,* my friend, could go down as a war hero." Churchill laughed. "You must approach this as an opportunity."

"It's the going down part I'm worried about," Petrie replied. Both men enjoyed the humor and looked forward to their next unofficial meeting.

Chapter Seventy-Nine

Turing in Churchill Meeting

Thomas returned to the same chair after Churchill's call and was relieved the call wasn't some emergency, forcing them to continue their conversation later. Waiting for Churchill to resume the conversation, Thomas saw the office door open quickly, followed by the prime minister's secretary.

"Yes, Mr. Colville," Churchill said. "This is rather important."

"Yes, sir, I know, but Mr. Turing is here for his appointment. The day is just not following the plan. I'm deeply sorry."

Winston thought about Dr. Turing, a man he deeply admired but hadn't come close to understanding. In politics, perception was the most critical requirement. Thankfully he'd been born with the gift of reading people and using the information to further his agenda. Despite this, he was somewhat confounded as Turing, brilliant without question, appeared immune to the normal wiles of an old politician.

Churchill, trying to enter into casual conversation, found a man that appeared lost, as if studying his words and not comprehending whether they were forming thoughts. He seldom initiated contact and was reticent to a fault, although Churchill had made his project the highest priority in the war. Nevertheless, Turing never used his access and visibility to his benefit.

Today, Turing had called a driven man, exchanging his usual oblique personality for one of a parent protecting his young. He insisted on personally delivering a message of great importance that directly affected the success of his project.

On the call Turing said, "Mr. Prime Minister, we all know that given the number of variables and situations you encounter, there can't possibly be an even distribution of priority, for it absolves the word of its meaning. Thus the need for its very existence." There was a pause, "I didn't mean that your…"

As a finessed practitioner of the English language, Churchill's instincts held that anyone who could quickly eliminate a whole word without prior preparation should, if for no other consideration, have his request granted.

Thomas was pleasantly surprised, knowing Turing had expended the effort to fulfill his promise at the pub. Having the respected Turing confirm to Churchill that some of what Thomas had imparted was useful could be just the thing. Anything that would get Churchill to believe his story of Germany's upcoming failed strategy was worth it.

The prime minister looked at Thomas and said, "It would seem utterly useless to have you removed from a highly classified meeting in which you know more than the most trusted in our government."

Thomas leaned forward. "Sir, at the least, Turing might substantiate that the information I conveyed was helpful. It would help prove my sincerity and the accuracy of my claims."

"Mr. Watson, my issue isn't with the sincerity of what you believe; rather, it's the nebulous source that's most disturbing."

He looked up, waving his cigar toward Colville, and said, "Let him in if you will."

"Yes, of course," Colville said as though defeated. "It will mean turning out Mr. Anderson to keep a shred of order."

Churchill allowed him a demonstration of his frustration as a favor to a friend and a priceless asset.

Colville reached behind him and opened the door, exposing Dr. Turing's tall, ruffled, restrained figure.

Churchill rose from his chair, extending his hand. "I'm sorry, doctor, I failed to inform my colleague of our agreement, and it has led to some confusion, I'm afraid. Please sit down."

"Five minutes, Mr. Turing," Colville said through tight lips. He wasn't at all happy with what had just transpired.

Turing reached over and shook Churchill's hand. "Mr. Turing, let me introduce …"

"Well, Mr. Dunning," Turing said upon seeing Thomas, "what're you doing here? I mean, what a pleasant surprise."

Thomas's body tightened up. How could he possibly forget that Turing still knew him as Dunning?

Colville and Churchill looked at each other. In an incredulous voice, Colville said, "Everyone on God's earth, including every town constable and MI5 agent, is searching for you right now. You're considered a dangerous armed fugitive who tried to infiltrate the Bletchley site, a state secret, and escaping under a hail of gunfire. And here you are sitting in the prime minister's office."

Thomas put his hands up in self-defense, "Dunning is the name I used to get into Bletchley to meet Dr. Turing. I didn't want to use Watson because it could be tied back to my wife. I went to Bletchley to ask for the doctor's help meeting Mr. Churchill, certain I didn't stand a chance on my own. I chose the doctor because I had certain information I hoped would gain his trust. He promised to try to deliver my message, and, as we can see, he's a man of his word."

Churchill paused for a second, then said, "That appears to be the case, does it not?" Churchill looked at Colville and said, "Thank you, Jock."

Jock Colville just gave into his utter disbelief. "Sir, this man is dangerous." It was the more courteous version of what he was thinking, namely that the prime minister was being downright reckless with his security. After the earlier incident, he couldn't understand the actions and decisions he witnessed. "They deviated from everything normal. All he could say was, "Should I notify …?"

"No, and thank you again, Jock; I know you're doing your best today, but like all things connected to war … well, it's just not following the plan. Be assured. "You'll get the full story when I do, and, hopefully, all these irregularities will sort themselves out."

Colville nodded in recognition of the direct address to his issues and proceeded out of the room.

When the door closed, Turing started. "Sir, who this man might be is irrelevant. I've been trying to tell everyone I know that I must be allowed to talk to him again, and all I've gotten is a cowboy reaction of shooting him on sight. Someone must realize how much Mr. Dunning can contribute to our goals at Bletchley."

Thomas was surprised his attempt to talk to Turing had gone so wrong, and he was the target of a manhunt. After realizing it hadn't been the British who had tried to kill him, he'd figured all he had to worry about was staying clear of the Russians. He hadn't calculated on the local search for crimes against the king.

Turing turned, motioning to Colville's desk outside the door. "First of all, I'm sorry for all the fuss, but I made a solemn promise to attempt to get our Mr. Dunning a meeting with you. Also, it was important to tell you about Dunning visiting me." He looked at Thomas and continued. "He provided information that's impossible for him to have known and made vital contributions to our efforts," Turing added rather secretively.

"It's okay, Mr. Turing. I would say keeping secrets from our friend here is academic as he appears to be more informed than any of us. You may speak freely."

"Excellent. The simple fact is that Mr. Dunning has made several stunning suggestions, the nature of which only I would have or should have realized regarding the design of the machine. Recognizing the potential, every one of my people has been working frantically on the different aspects of Mr. Dunning's suggestions, knowing the pressure for a breakthrough. The curious thing, and the reason I chose to trust him, is it wasn't something classified that existed, and he secretly acquired. On the contrary, it was something that didn't exist, even in my mind, let alone on paper, and could have an exponential effect on our efforts. I'm sorry, it's just not coming out right at all. Let me try again."

"It won't be necessary, doctor. It's quite clear enough." Churchill thought for a moment. "What I mean by that is, it's as clear as anything involving our Mr. Dunning here. Everything involving him is both outsized in its importance and murky in its origin. If that's the sum of it, you've fulfilled your promise, and depending on how things transpire, I'll endeavor to make him available. Thank you for taking the time."

Turing felt he hadn't been specific enough. "But, sir, the break through, your pressure—I mean, interest, it's the process and switch speed. I mean, that's what Mr. Dunning has contributed." Turing was racing. "We could have a demonstration very quickly."

"We hope so, Mr. Turing. You certainly deserve a positive break, given your efforts. I would very much like to see a demonstration and, even more, be able to demonstrate my gratitude. Shall we now?"

"Yes, thanks again," Turing said, standing, "Mr. Dunning, my boys, are like I've never seen them. The test run should be up and running right now. The test would normally demand my presence, but there was, of course, my commitment."

Thomas was most truthful when he said, "Thank you for coming. At the least, it increases the prime minister's trust in other things we've discussed. I hope the modifications work, and in short order, you'll have, or might have, solved the input problem."

Churchill waited until Turing had stepped out. "I've heard enough that requires me to keep you in custody. So, barring any other surprises, you'll need to stay with me for a bit. I hope you can understand."

"It's perfectly understandable," Thomas said, "and, I must add, far less inconvenient than getting shot. However, I want to call Margaret and tell her where I am. She's given to worry, and my absence could create alarm."

Churchill pointed at Thomas with the same finger securing the top of his cigar. "I wouldn't count on not being shot yet, as none of this is in the least rational. Why didn't you tell me you were the notorious Dunning when we started?"

"Mr. Dunning was a wanted man by the British, so I needed to get into the building as myself."

The regular phone on Churchill's desk rang with a very different sound. Reaching over, he looked up. "Excuse me," he said. Into the phone, he mumbled a simple, "Yes?"

"My sincerest pardon, sir, it's Byron Nettleton at Number 10," said the voice on the phone. Thomas started to make a courteous exit, and Churchill waved him back into his chair.

"Yes, Byron."

"With my apologies, I find this intrusion quite out of order, sir, but a young lady at the front door called herself Miss Margaret Hatcher. She says she wants to speak to the prime minister and her husband, who's supposed to be with you. Normally, of course, I wouldn't bother you, but she says it's of prime importance, and Lady Churchill knows her, and they're, at the moment, quite chatting away. Mrs. Churchill asked me to contact you."

"Asked? Mr. Nettleton? In fact, she gave you a direct order, did she not?" He laughed.

The prime minister's head of house responded, "Well, as only you know, sir, she can be persuasive on the odd occasion she feels the need."

"Graciously presented, Mr. Nettleton. Have Miss Hatcher escorted through the passageway and to my office."

"Very well, as you wish, sir."

Churchill rang off.

"Mr. Watson, we're about to be visited by a bundle of energy that has only found its counter in the sobering directness of her wonderful mother. Then again, you don't need to be informed of something you've already experienced from both sides."

Thomas wrinkled his face. "Margaret? My Margaret?"

"God should save us all, should there be two. In a more casual moment, I shall have to tell you about the disappearance of my favorite bowler."

Thomas's puzzled look spoke first, then he said, "I'm very surprised, in fact, disturbed, to know she's here. I left her this morning at her mother's, with strict instructions to stay there. Given the events of the last few days, I thought it was the safest place."

"How long have you been married to her?"

"Sir, unfortunately, I've only really known her a short while due to the memory issue. We're still getting to know one another."

"That would verify Mr. Petrie's vague idea. "You're not the same man who originally married our exceptional and influential Margaret. You're still a young man, Mr. Watson, with much to learn about the less-than-clandestine powers women have over the likes of you and me."

"Sir, the origins of my troubling memories and my short awareness of the present appear to be under the authority of our Lady of History. I'm sure this is the power to which you refer."

"Again, an excellent bit of rhetoric," a smiling Churchill said. "However, Mr. Watson, I'm not wholly convinced that your dear Lady of History is not unlike the women who deftly mind our lives today. Each of their lovely souls is a mystery as we find ourselves at the will of an influence we cannot hope to understand."

Thomas let loose a loud and hearty laugh. "Elegantly put." He said, emphasizing his sincerity with feigned applause.

Colville put the phone down in wonder. Security had just informed him they cleared Margaret Hatcher through the passageway from Number 10. At that exact moment, he was sure he heard laughter from the PM's office.

The man moved his unlit cigar to the ashtray and back. "At some point I must eventually confront this notion that you've knowledge from the ethers." The silence hung until he followed with, "Even if your knowledge is such that it can't be explained, I must address it and determine if I have a source available to me that can help win the war. Given our somewhat grave situation, you must understand that I would welcome any source that would contribute to victory, even an over-perceptive divining rod. However, your knowledge doesn't fit into what has worked for the world since the beginning. Beliefs such as remembering the past and looking toward the future. You've managed to stand this on its head, and, as a result, it's hard to deliver the trust you're working so hard to obtain."

"Sir, I'm as confused as anyone," Thomas said, "but as you say, the stakes are high. Just give me the chance to prove myself with today's events and thus in my curious way, help shorten the war. You've everything to gain, and I have everything to lose."

"Of that, there's no doubt. As to the opportunity, at this point, you have no choice. Upon your shoulders lie two critical objectives that are mine. Those would be winning the war and fulfilling a promise made to a dear friend to keep his daughter from harm."

Colville knocked and started to announce that Margaret Hatcher, without an appointment, was here to see the prime minister who, among other things of note, was trying to save the British Empire. However, it all went terribly wrong as Margaret burst past Colville, now humbled at the loss of control.

She gave Thomas a peck on the cheek and pulled back, saying, "I just had to see you because Mrs. Somerville is missing, and the Russian who was in her house read the note with your name on it, and he had a gun and ..."

"*Margaret*," Churchill said stiffly, "if you could slow down."

Margaret literally yelled, "Uncle Winnie!" She threw both arms straight into the air as if she hadn't known he was there.

Jock Colville watched another parcel of protocols disappear as Margaret flew around the desk, gave the PM a brisk hug, and kissed him on both cheeks. All this occurred as the man remained seated, not allowed the time to rise from his chair.

In one breath, Margaret said, "I'm so sorry, Uncle Winnie, but I'm terrified something's happened that could put Thomas in danger, and I knew he had a meeting with you and figured Aunt Clementine was the only way in to see you."

"Obviously, it worked," he said, looking at Colville, who had decided that flowing with events was easier than trying to figure them out. He happily closed the door and stood looking down at his desk, wondering, only half in jest, if the events of this single day would get him fired and sent to the front. Then he thought it was very possible, in a matter of days, his desk would *be* the front.

Churchill directed Margaret to the second chair. Thomas placed his hand on her arm. "Why aren't you home? You promised you would stay there."

"I never promised such a thing. You assumed I would stay there, and it's a good thing I didn't. I was checking up on Mrs. Somerville because she didn't answer my ring last night or this morning."

Thomas leaned forward. "But how did you get there?"

Margaret's face went blank. "Why on earth would that matter? Anyway, while I was in her house, a Russian came in because I broke the back door and he found a note from her with your name on it I'd left on the table. I don't know what the Russian understood, but he must have known it was important. It ties Mrs. Somerville to both of us and, as a result, puts her in danger. It has to be that guy Yuri who accused you of spying or something and tried to kill you."

"How do you know it was a Russian?" Thomas asked.

Margaret turned and leaned toward Thomas's face and said, "He told me, okay?"

Thomas looked at her face and took a mental photograph. The face that could launch a thousand wonderful thoughts looked at him as if he was completely stupid.

"The Russians," Margaret said, "tried to kill Thomas, and the only Russian we've had contact with is that Yuri guy. He said we were in danger unless we turned over some information concerning my father's company. Also, they might be holding Mrs. Somerville hostage, in which case they're the ones in danger," she said, then hit the arm of the chair with her fist. "We need to find ..."

Churchill put up his hand in an effort to regain control. "Did you say Yuri?"

"Yes," Margaret said, "that's what he said his name was when he made us talk to him."

"You just said he tried to kill you."

Thomas shook his head, "Margaret, we don't know if it was that Russian or another. Was it Yuri in the house this morning?"

"No."

"Then there's at least more than one Russian involved. I don't think it's Viktor, the Russian who I talked to last night. When did you say you saw him?"

Margaret was growing impatient and was sure they had enough information to save Mrs. Somerville without more questions. "This morning."

"When this morning?"

"Well, it was about an hour ago. Perhaps 12:30."

"I seriously doubt it's Viktor. In fact, I know it's not. His desire for the information I promised to give him is so overwhelming, he wouldn't possibly miss an opportunity to get his hands on it."

"What do you mean?" Churchill said, "Wait -- do I really want to know?"

Thomas wasn't sure he should tell him, "Because I'm pretty sure he was killed at 11:35."

"*You* had someone kill him?" Churchill asked.

"No, I just put him in harm's way. In my memory, I've seen a black-and-white photograph of a large bomb explosion that took place this morning at exactly 11:35. The photo was taken at Richmond Hill Circle, and the time on the damaged clocktower had stopped at exactly that time."

Margaret grabbed both arms of the chair and said, "That's where you told that Viktor guy to meet you at 11:30! Oh, my God, he was bombed! Thomas, that was brilliant." She sat back and crossed her arms with a great big I-told-you-so grin.

Churchill, having never presided over any activity this much out of control, said, "Wait. We're forgetting something very inconsistent with the proper order of things. If you told him last night and the bomb dropped at 11:35 this morning, it hadn't been dropped, let alone a photograph taken when you told him. You couldn't have possibly known of the incident."

Margaret said, "He does that a lot, Uncle Winnie. It's something you have to get used to. He also predicted the bombing of Berlin the night before it appeared in the morning paper."

Churchill looked at them both. "Well, I think all this has distilled down to whether Thomas is a spy."

"What?" Margaret said. "You don't understand."

"Indeed I do. Either I've been presented with the most significant secret weapon in history, or I must try the husband of my ward for treason. Both are fraught with their problems. The only way to determine this is for me to see this flexing the rules of time for myself. If it's as Thomas says and this afternoon's attacks are unprecedented, it will prove beyond a doubt the integrity of his … dreams or something. At that point, I'll have an entirely different problem.

"Also, given we have dangerous spies wandering about, assassination plots, and God only knows what else, I can't have either of you exposed to danger. Therefore, you'll *both*," he said, looking at Margaret, "follow my orders until I release you."

Still looking at Margaret, he said, "As to you, young lady, you're to promise me," his finger tapping for emphasis on the following two words, "right now—on your father's grave, you'll do exactly as directed until then."

Margaret was taken aback by his harsh tone. No one had ever talked to her in that manner. "Besides," she thought, "I can follow the rules as well as anybody, and all he had to do was ask normally." Nevertheless, she was stunned at the reference to her father.

"Yes," was the only word she uttered. The statement wasn't followed by an explanation, opinion, or any sign of the heretofore required negotiation or discussion. It was indeed one of those rare moments in her brief history.

Churchill was still leaning over his desk looking at Margaret when his eyebrows rose, and his facial features slowly rearranged into a look of surprise. "I believe the earth just moved."

"Mr. Churchill, sir," Margaret said formally, "it's not that big a deal."

He paused and continued staring. Margaret finally said, "Yes, I promised, didn't I?"

"As our Mr. Watson, wizard of things forthcoming, has indicated, I'm scheduled for a much-delayed visit to the Kenley operations centre at Uxbridge. I'm most interested in seeing firsthand the wonderful procedure that Dowding has implemented. That's the problem with being in this position. What becomes a routine quest for knowledge duly expands into a visit from God himself. Such an event means that the floor is polished, and all the lights on the dispatch board, which I've not yet seen, must be removed and dusted.

"The both of you'll accompany me until time sorts this all out. You'll return to my residence right now, and Byron will find you something to eat. You'll wait for further instructions."

Chapter Eighty

Lonnie and the Sergeant

Lonnie Garrah walked into the circular hall entrance, mindlessly adjusting the jacket of her uniform, pulling it taut from below the belt at her waist. She was sure the designer was the same bozo who had created Army field tents. In mid-motion, she felt the sensation before looking up and seeing the sergeant avert his eyes. The Royal marine was again at his post in full parade dress, with his holstered gun and bright red stripe down his trousers. It was all mostly for show for the visiting brass. "Simple, but he did it with such colour and," she thought, "with handsome flair." The girls all thought he should pose for a recruiting poster, joking how easy it would be to get women to sign up if he did.

Lonnie stopped her tugging and said, "Sergeant, is there a problem?"

His hand flew to his cap in a military reaction. "No, sir—ah, ma'am, there's most certainly not a problem." Still at attention he added, "It couldn't be further from the truth, ma'am." He said it a bit stiffly but with a definite note of comfort and confidence.

As a warrant officer, she was just above a sergeant in the Army, but she felt the sensation despite her formal demeanor, like two people making contact but only at the end of a single finger, the tingle of the energy forced through the narrow point. She liked this game of flirting from a position of power although it was against the rules. It wasn't often that a girl found herself in this position, and so she decided to play it for what it was worth, just to draw his reaction.

"You realize, sergeant, this isn't the first time I've had to deal with this issue on my way to the control room. Although I might add, I've had the presence of mind to act with proper discretion," she said, returning the salute. "I trust you've been fully briefed as to the issue of fraternization."

Still at attention, he threw his arm to his side. After a pause, with a face masking an internal smile, he said, "Ma'am, military regulations don't cover every possible contingency."

"I'm very impressed. "This implies you've read the entire collection front to back?"

Still looking straight ahead at the opposite wall, his tone changed to a very formal, soft voice as he said, "May I speak freely, ma'am?"

"Go ahead, sergeant; I can't wait to hear what's next."

"Ma'am, fraternizing doesn't directly address the 'issue,' as you refer to it."

"Well, then, how would you put it, sergeant?"

"Freely, ma'am?" he said.

Lonnie nodded.

He turned and looked directly at Lonnie and said, "Admiration, ma'am.... Sincere admiration."

It caught Lonnie off guard. He said it without even a hint of male sarcasm or bravado, key elements of a man on the make. He said it as if he meant it. Lonnie stood there, knowing the situation had existed for some time. It was different, though, once it was into the open. Now there was no mistake. On many occasions, her body language included a smile. She hadn't discouraged the 'issue' and she knew it. Still, there was the war and the awful restrictions it imposed on people in every corner of their lives. In the space of a few seconds, a complete novel had been written in mostly silent, invisible words. Frankly, she wasn't sure what to do. There was certainly the military option, and that was to report him. However, she had actually given him permission. Then, in a fleeting vision, she saw herself invisibly touching the side of his face. She felt the energy.

She chose the middle path.

In a steady conversational tone, Lonnie said, "Your thoughts," she swallowed, "are duly noted, sergeant." She paused long enough to perceive his muscles unconsciously relax. He was still looking at her, and it was her play. "He was right," she thought. The hell with it; she'd screwed up once already.

She placed her cap under her arm and said, "That will be all, sergeant," as she stepped toward the door leading to the ops room, ten feet away.

"Yes, ma'am," he said, as he once again went rigid.

Lonnie took five or six steps. A quick look over her shoulder caught his stare as she walked away. "That was supposed to be all, sergeant," she said through a smile he couldn't see but unmistakably could hear.

"As you wish, ma'am."

Deliberately, Lonnie stopped with her hand on the ops room door and, without turning around, very clearly said, "That's Andersen, sergeant, Warrant Officer Andersen. I trust you'll remember that."

"I certainly will," he said, "Warrant Officer Andersen." Though his forward stare had returned, there was no mistaking the tone in his voice.

Chapter Eighty-One

Drive to Uxbridge

Thomas and Margaret were in the back seat and could see Churchill's car just ahead. Behind them was a car full of men specializing in jackets that didn't fit. As appropriate to the travels of a prime minister, local police blocked all side roads corresponding with this route, making possible the shortest travel time to Uxbridge. It was an hour ride that should have taken over two hours.

Thomas looked across at Margaret and smiled. "What a catch," he thought. Margaret moved over and put her head on his shoulder.

"There's something I've been meaning to ask you," she said. Sitting up, she pulled her chin in, pushed her chest forward, and started speaking in a deep voice, mocking the prime minister's distinctive delivery. "What happens when," she started, "time sorts this whole thing out?" Then she giggled, sounding normal again. "Do we get to have a normal life?"

"Let's make sure of what we have today before we start venturing into things that might occur tomorrow." Thomas knew exactly where she was going with the line of thought, and she knew he knew, so he waited for her predictable response.

"That's rubbish, and you know it. It's inconceivable for anyone to live without thinking about tomorrow. It's the anticipation of a better day on top of a good day and a great day following a bad day. Who raised you anyway?"

Thomas looked at her, his eyes in thought, saying, "I'm not sure."

She nudged him with her elbow. "Why don't you ever answer any of my questions?"

"I believe sheer volume is the probable cause. Also, I believe that response qualified as an answer to your question."

"Thomas, I'm losing my patience with you and your verbal dancing."

"Patience, pray tell, where and when? I rather think it's a subject you shouldn't have brought up."

Margaret took a deep breath as she crossed her legs. Unaware of the silent statement her mother perfected, she started arranging the folds in her dress, completely ignoring him. It was vintage Margaret.

"Okay," he said. "You wanted to know when we would have a normal life. Well, right now is a good time to start but without any of your illogical rules and barriers. Are you with me on this?"

"Oh, Thomas, till death do us part," she said as she put a hand up to the side of his face. "You might be starting to get romantic."

With that, he reached over, grabbed a piece of her dress, and pulled it back, exposing a good portion of her knee. She slapped his hand. At the sound, the driver instinctively flinched, glancing into the rearview mirror.

"I beg your pardon, that was hardly the action of a gentleman. Besides, a couple of brief diversions don't give you the world."

"Diversions? Well, I must admit it's the first time I've heard it described that way. By the way, when exchanging vows, did you say 'to honor and serve'?"

"I did not! As far as you're concerned, you'll have to take my word that we're even married. Further, you haven't the faintest idea of what you might have said. I remember your complete compliance at honoring my every wish."

"Now that, my dear lady, I believe."

She was reaching for her purse, and when she came back to face him, she was beaming. "Thomas Watson, you're impossible."

"Excuse me," the driver said, waving for their attention. "We're coming up on the Uxbridge depot. Mr. Churchill has business at the Group Headquarters and wanted me to take you directly to the Operations Centre. He'll catch you up shortly." They saw the auto up front turn right as they turned left into the car park.

"What an interesting building," Margaret said. "Is all that dirt on the side for protection?"

"Yes, it's not perfect, but considerably better than not doing anything. It would be a sweet target for any German to knock out. I think they've also reinforced the roof, even though it's several stories underground."

"That's a big hole. Are we going all the way down?"

"I'm afraid that's going to be the case. It's why we're here."

Chapter Eighty-Two

Paddy on the Ground

Paddy had landed after a very boring patrol, checking out a reported German submarine sighting. They didn't fly many patrols, as the system dictated all available planes to be on hand to scramble at any moment. He was sitting in the open air outside the dispersal shack. All but two aircraft were topped off, ready to go. He watched his crew working to refuel his plane. He hoped they were checking out the intermittent restriction in a flight cable he encountered when turning hard left. Of course, it never did it when the crew checked it out. They thought him a bit fussy.

The pilots waited for the call to action, in various states of activity and consciousness at the airfields. Some were napping in chairs, writing letters home, or reading. Paddy was thinking about what he'd said the night before to Edith. She appeared sincerely happy, which hadn't been guaranteed, as most women were sure pilots only truly married the part of the sky they happened to occupy at the time. He thought about how she looked, her slow, confident manner, the smell of her hair, the feel of her in his arms. He'd 'gone and done it,' as the boys would say— committed himself, and, to his surprise, it felt wonderful. He drifted back to his last year at upper school and Annette, his first love, to retrieve the intensity of the dreamy passion that gripped his soul when holding her close.

The pilots were waiting for the phone to ring in the small wooden dispersal shack. With its clamor, everyone's ears would stand at attention, waiting to see if it was a flight update or a scramble. On a scramble, the men, already dressed in flight suits, would charge to their planes. Everyone was locked into the same system, and with it, an assigned responsibility

The daily grind produced a certain informality among the pilots when they were not in the air. To that end, Auggie gently kicked Paddy's chair, "You look very suspicious today, mate. There you sit with a sappy grin cross your face as you stare into the blue. Recalling a fond memory, are we?" Auggie looked the other way, "Gordon, what do ya think, lad?"

Gordon leaned forward in his chair and, in jest, stared hard at Paddy. "Yup, Auggie, I shouldn't have missed it. You're dead on. So that's why he has been walking around here like he forgot we were fightin' a war. Or perhaps our dear friend might have seen the inside of some knickers."

Gordon moved closer, leaning over Paddy and looking into his eyes. Paddy put a hand on the side of Gordon's face, shoving him away.

"Bugger off, the both of ya," Paddy said.

"Yup, that's it all right," "Gordon yelled all around. "Paddy has gotten himself laid; *worse,* he shows signs of being in love. Be warned lads. Stay out of the way of Number 6 as he might be a daydreamin' up there."

Everyone cheered, raising non-existent pints over their head, shouting, "Only the virile will survive. We want pictures and not the ones ya send yer mum."

Paddy stood up, waving his arms, and shouted, "I'll have all you ladies contain your fantasies. It's not like that at all. This happens to be the real deal, and I want to enjoy the biggest, most important thing in my life."

"Here, here," another pilot shouted. "Here's to Paddy's biggest, most important thing in his life. And may he find a pair of britches bigger than a parachute to keep it."

Paddy looked over in mock anger, pointed his finger at his fellow pilot, and pulled the trigger, rendering him dead on the spot. He blew off the tip of his finger and sat back down in his chair.

Chapter Eighty-Three

Arrival at Uxbridge

The agent pulled up, exited the car, and opened Margaret's door. Before swinging out, she looked back at Thomas with a giggle and said, "Lookie here, a gentleman," as if Thomas wasn't, and then blew him a kiss with her hand hanging in the air just a second longer than expected.

"Lucky you," Thomas said. "Only two gentlemen are left, and you have us both; imagine that." It was late, around 4:00 pm, and the sky started to change as if preparing for what was to be a long night. Usually, white contrails would appear and then disappear in the blue between the intermittent clouds. It was unusual not to hear any planes.

They followed the driver, entering what appeared to be a steel door that ended up in front of officer Templeton of security. He was head of the unit assigned to the complex and took his job very seriously. Thomas remembered that he didn't have any identification. The driver held up his street ID and said, "My name is Handraddy; I understand Mr. Colville has called ahead about two guests."

"These two?" the officer said.

Handraddy nodded.

"Their names?"

"Mr. and Mrs. Thomas Watson," the driver said.

Margaret looked over at Thomas, very pleased with the sound of the man's response. The sentry ran his finger down a page and looked up. "There aren't any names for any of you. I'm sorry, I'll need something more than your good looks, sir, as this isn't the dining hall."

The driver reached into his coat pocket and pulled out his MI5 identity card. Officer Templeton scrutinized it carefully. He started to write down the details when the driver reached over, placing a finger over the box where the officer was to fill in the identification number. "I'm sorry, it's *Agent* Handraddy, and the credentials are for eyes only."

"I'm supposed to rely on that? I'll get shot."

"Perhaps not, I think," Handraddy said in a monotone voice, "but I fully understand your concern. You may call Director Petrie, the prime minister, or Mr. Colville. It's your option, and no offense is taken. We can wait." He backed up, motioning for Thomas and Margaret to sit on an old wooden bench along the wall directly behind them.

Thomas didn't immediately move, and Margaret said, "What?" Having grown unrealistically accustomed to being on the inside of security protocol, she didn't like her credibility questioned. When these inconvenient matters arose, she merely called the prime minister's wife or someone else, and that was that.

Templeton, clearly frustrated, was looking for some modicum of control. He said, "Do you mind if I at least perform a search?"

"Not at all," the driver said, standing back up and allowing the still-standing Margaret and Thomas to move forward. "You'll find I'm authorized to be armed in a level three security area, as noted on the credentials."

Margaret had her arms crossed, growing impatient at the back and forth. "You'll also find I'm female."

"Margaret," Thomas said sternly.

"On an appointment without names, a single identification I can't record, I'm supposed to allow an armed man and two unknown civilians into the prime minister's presence?"

The agent, maintaining a consistent voice with a complete lack of emotion, said, "You may call Director Petrie or the ..."

"Okay, I get it; wait here." Still holding the agent's MI5 identification, the man stepped toward the hall.

Handraddy reached out to Templeton, bringing him to a stop. Handraddy said, "Excuse me, but that must remain in my sight. Memorize the number if you must."

Obviously put out, the officer looked at the badge and handed it back. Quickly descending two flights of stairs, he arrived at George's desk and picked up the phone. "I'll need this," he said rudely and started to dial.

Due to the poor acoustics, Margaret could hear talking, but nothing she could understand.

"Yes, sir," Templeton said before putting the phone down. As he walked back up the stairs, he wrote notes of the conversation on paper. After signing a slip of paper and handing it to the agent, he said, "We're all set. Sorry for the delay. I was just doing my job."

The agent put his hand up. "No need. We all are, and I would expect nothing less."

Margaret was surprised at the comment, having taken the officer as nothing more than a mechanical robot. Handraddy addressed both Margaret and Thomas with an after-you gesture.

Thomas followed Margaret as they moved forward, nodding to the guard as they passed into the passageway and made their way down the stairs. Margaret looked around. She thought it looked like a giant machine with bolts, wires, tubes, and rust everywhere. Perhaps the icy agent following her was part of the building. After two long flights of stairs, they came upon a table on the landing where an older man sat next to the phone used by Templeton. The man discreetly stared at Margaret but having had to deal with it most of her life, she knew when to be flattered and when it should be ignored. The sparkle in his eyes conveyed female admiration, and she saw the man almost jump to his feet, lifting his hat. "Evenin', Miss. Just what this place needed, a bright flower like you."

"And you, sir, with that smile, you could illuminate a train station," Margaret said.

"Oh, thank you, Miss." He looked at Thomas and back to Margaret as he sat back down and nodded his head slightly, unconsciously placing his hat over his heart.

"Aren't you a sweetie," she said, leaning over the desk and kissing his cheek. "You could conquer half the world with an attitude like that."

George said, "Templeton gave you the go-ahead, so nothing for me here."

With a purposeful glance, Margaret reached out to Thomas and Handraddy and said, "Looks like we've some work to do, gentlemen." Then, delighted with herself, she walked them arm in arm farther down the hall.

"Sorry," Thomas said to the agent. "All this enlightenment has gone a bit too far."

Margaret noticed the first expression of humor on the agent's face. "I saw that," she said. "I definitely saw that, Agent Handraddy. I just wanted you to know."

"Yes, madam, can I get the door for you?" he said in the dark, monotone manner of a highly trained agent of death.

"Why, yes," she said, "*Agent* Handraddy, you may, and how kind of you."

Thomas said, "All right, you two, enough of the tit for tat."

They stepped into the connecting ring corridor. A short flight of steps led to the glass-enclosed viewing room to the right. The room could also be accessed from inside the Ops room. Standing rigid in front of the VIP steps was a guard in parade uniform.

Margaret noticed the guard was standing still as a statue—but a very attractive statue. She wondered what she would get if she put the gallantly charming personality of the previous guard into the masculine picture that stood before her. Trouble, she decided, lots of trouble.

The agent presented the paper to the guard, who glanced at it and said, "Mr. Colville's authority, yes, sir." His hand offered the stairs, and the group proceeded up.

"Two pence for every stair in this place would buy Windsor and then some," Margaret said.

Again, the agent held the door open, and Margaret entered a room. Addressing Thomas, the agent said, "This is 11 Group Operations Room. I understand the prime minister will be with you shortly."

The room was electric with activity; most everyone was engaged in some way. The agent walked over to a junior RAF officer who rose after they entered the room. They conversed briefly, below ear level, in a manner that conveyed an understanding.

That concluded, Handraddy reached out to shake Thomas's hand and said, "I'll take my leave but," glancing at Margaret, he produced a slight but genuine smile, "I wanted to offer the best of luck in your efforts toward the very charming, albeit unique, burden you must bear."

Thomas laughed as they shook hands. "In a friendly gesture, he placed his other hand on the man's shoulder. "Well, Agent Handraddy, someone must step up in these trying times."

"That's enough, you two," Margaret said. "As for you, Mr. Secret Agent, that was a genuine attempt at humor, and you should be reported. Wait, I'll do it myself. What's your real name anyway?"

The agent broke out the first broad grin they'd seen, touched his hat toward Margaret, and silently left the room.

"Cheeky, at the least," she said.

Thomas responded, "Perceptive, at the *very* least. You had it coming."

Their entry had drawn the attention of those in the glass-enclosed room.

One of the senior officers was standing while talking on the phone. He rang off, saying to the man sitting at a control desk, "Two thirty-six is at readiness, 12 Group is getting hit hard." The man was a New Zealander by birth, and with over twenty kills in the First World War, he was highly respected, especially by Hugh Dowding. The junior standing officer said, "This is the Colville party, sir: Thomas and Margaret

Watson. May I introduce Air Vice Marshal Keith Park, Commander of 11 Group? Sir, they're here waiting for Mr. Churchill."

"Yes, I see, of course. Sorry, we're a bit busy at the moment. Please find a place anywhere but here if you don't mind." Park said, waving his finger in a circle toward the desks behind him. "Not sure what the PM has in mind, but I understand he is but moments away."

"Most kind of you, and please pay us no mind," Thomas said.

"Splendid then," Park said as he was already focused back on the task.

"Big isn't it," Margaret said. "And all a hundred feet underground."

"Not quite," Thomas said, procuring a look from Margaret requiring a response. "Okay, it doesn't matter," he said. He waited a few moments and said, "It's fifty feet."

The response was a stern, "Thomas!" Margaret was fascinated; it wasn't as if she'd some previous concept of what she was supposed to see. She hadn't even given it a thought. "Nevertheless, before her was something that did not resemble anything she'd ever encountered.

Almost in wonder, Thomas also surveyed the room below as the different elements came together in his mind. Walking down the tunnel entrance, he wondered if he would recognize the Centre. To his surprise, it was more than just recognition. He generally understood the workings, as well as what was going to occur in the hours to come. He wondered what it meant. Until now, everything was like educated guesswork, far from the certainty whose presence he could now feel. What did this mean for the future, especially his future with Margaret? It was a concern that was growing stronger. Churchill would know he was right and thus as dangerous as valuable. It would conflict with a normal life, and that *is* what he'd promised Margaret.

Thomas reached for Margaret's arm. "Amazing, isn't it? It wouldn't work without the British inventing radar and untold numbers of spotters on the ground. Remember, back at the house, I said radar would eventually cook your food?"

"That's all I need," she said, "to be cooking a roast and have it tell me where some wayward bomber is flying. I don't think so. Not in this lifetime."

Margaret thought she'd been quite clever and was expecting a humorous acknowledgment. Thomas continued to view the activity below. Then, without expression, he said, "Lifetime? On that, you might be right."

"Thomas, did you hit your head again, just a little bit?" She held two fingers very close together in front of him, so he could see them. Thomas concentrated on the activity below.

"Thomas, do you know what's going on down there?"

"Yes."

"There's no way you could know that, Thomas. You're the one who said it was top secret, which means you've never heard of it, let alone seen it. How does that happen?"

"I wasn't sure I was right back then, but my ability and confidence have grown in the last few days."

Margaret recalled that tear-filled morning when she realized something was very wrong. She looked at him silently. "Do you know what's going to happen in the meeting?"

"No, well, not completely; I mean, I know one of several possible conclusions."

"Did you have any influence on the outcome?"

He took a long, loving look into her eyes as he smiled.

"Thomas?" she said.

"I believe we might never know," he said.

"So why are you here? Why the mystery? Why appear in my life? Not that I'm not happy you did."

"To save you from that mess you got yourself into with the other Thomas. You have to admit I'm a *little* more reliable."

It was her turn not to acknowledge a comment begging for a witty reply.

Thomas continued, "I really don't understand the mystery of my being here, but just because we don't know how or why doesn't mean there isn't a significant reason it occurred."

Chapter Eighty-Four

Control Room

Thomas continued observing the personnel and equipment. He knew that 11 Group Operations room was but one component of an incredibly integrated, totally secret system whose sole purpose was to deploy precious air resources where they could be most effective. It did this by keeping the planes out of the sky until needed, providing the maximum amount of rest, and using a minimum amount of petrol. It required vectoring British fighters to meet a German attack at precisely the right time and position. It was a brilliant system designed by Dowding.

Dowding had divided the extensive coastline into sectors, each consisting of its radar stations, ground observers, sector headquarters, and airfields. Thomas knew that even some of the pilots weren't fully aware of the comprehensive nature of the system. During times of battle, it was a hectic atmosphere with analyzed messages distributed, senior officers changing directives, and somehow they managed it all despite the dire consequences of any error. It took about 200 people from the various services to get one Spitfire into the air and return to base.

Even though the Germans were working on radar at the time, they'd never fully appreciate the integrated quality of the system responsible for their defeat.

Thomas looked down at the Sector Station Operations room. The ceiling was very high, with the room divided into two levels, one where they stood and the one below. The upper level contained Park and his senior officers who, looking down upon the room below, could observe the battle unfold in striking detail. Through the curved glass panes, they peered over the plotting room floor. In the center of the floor was a large map of southern England on an irregular table. Their sector was one of the most important as it covered the routes into and out of greater London.

***

Dowding's system had started with the radar stations along the coast. One of those was the installation that sat in the coastal town of Thruleigh. Being posted at the Thruleigh radar station wasn't something you fought for, though some others were worse. It was far enough away from London that a twenty-four-hour leave left little time to play. The local offerings were limited to the Horse Guards pub, frequented by farmers. It made the post enjoyable if you were a grandmother.

Thurleigh station wasn't underground or protected at all. It was a non-descript weathered building where the four girls staffed the station. The second shift supervisor, prone to being late everywhere, hadn't arrived yet, and they were quietly talking during their duties, which was against regulations.

Audry was barely twenty, slightly built with stunning large brown eyes, and had spent her short life being completely anonymous at school. She was holding a cup of tea just under her nose, making continuous odd noises while taking tiny sips. It was her first day back after a two-day furlough, and she had delicious stories that couldn't be recounted in confession. Her biggest claim was never having spent a *dime* the whole weekend, but she wouldn't admit what she had to give up to make the claim.

"I was doing my duty to God and country comforting those poor boys," she said between noises.

Corporal Nancy Hillsend was sitting at her console, wiping the round glass surface of the cathode ray tube. "I don't think God appreciates your efforts, dearie. Anyway, it's *King* and country," she said. Nancy was one of the specially trained WAAFs who peered at the screen of the radar receiver by the hour, waiting for the telltale signs of a raid. Dowding's miracle started here, deep within the Thurleigh and other coastal radar stations. Nancy and hundreds of WAAFs like her were at the front lines of the war, as the radar towers were a constant target of the Luftwaffe.

"Come on, Nance, when did you last have a little fun?" Audry said.

Despite being only a year apart, Nancy looked at life from a different angle. She turned in her chair. "Audry, that's not the point. Eventually your …" she stopped talking as Craig bounded into the small building, closing the door behind him with one hand, still fastening buttons on his shirt with the other.

"Nancy?" was his first word.

"Nothing to report, sir. It's all clear," she replied.

"Good, my ride was late again," he said.

No one bothered to listen to what was his overused excuse for what could be a serious violation. He knew Nancy would be there on time, which comforted his supposedly tight schedule. To the annoyance of Audry, Nancy was clearly his favorite.

Nancy started filling out the shift paperwork as a flicker from the screen caught her eye. She stared intently at the straight green line with a small blip on the left side representing the outgoing signal—nothing.

"That's curious," she thought. Seconds later, she saw the slightest blip on the other side, representing the signal bouncing back. Under the line were marks calibrating the distance between the two. Something was wrong as the line extended past the calibration on the far right of screen. She'd never seen the radar pick up anything that far away.

"I have a distant contact bearing 125," she said.

"And ..." her supervisor said as he came over.

"Too early to tell the distance, but I've never seen something like this."

The supervisor looked at the empty screen and said, "Am I missing something?"

"Wait, there, there it is again."

"Oh, I see what you mean. How long has it been there?"

"Less than a minute," she said.

"I'll call Beachy Head Station. They're a little closer in that direction." He returned to his desk, and Nancy said, "Sir, I think you should see this."

"What?" he said, coming over again.

Nancy adjusted the vector, barely moving the knob, trying to bracket the echo signal. The system was so new that manuals didn't exist, and practical interpretation was a matter of playing the machine like a violin. Experience proved women were far better at the art than men. She turned one of the attenuation adjustments, which meant nothing to her, but she knew it would steady the line, helping to reveal the blip.

"It's the size, sir. The reason we haven't seen anything that far away before is due to the group size. It's bouncing back more of our signal from farther away, meaning it's unusually large."

"Magnificent, Nance. I think you're spot on. Like I've always said, that head of yours is more than just pretty."

"Beg your pardon, sir? When did you say that?"

Nancy said to Audry, "Contact designated T917-1." It defined the station, month, date, and contact on that date. It was Audry's job to document what Nancy found, regardless of whether it amounted to anything.

Craig smiled at Nancy with the phone at his ear and gave her a thumbs-up.

Nancy wasn't happy. She knew she was smart but didn't like being toyed with by someone with half her wits. He had the job because he was a man.

"Stanton," Craig said, "we have a contact at 125 that's very faint. Can you cross-vector it for distance? What do you mean? My operator has it on her screen; what're you chaps doing over there? Nancy, why? We're telling you exactly where to look, for heaven's sake. This'll cost you a pint, dear boy; get back when you see something." he said as he hung up.

She frowned. "Sir, I can definitely say the contact at 125 is 40+ at 60 miles. I think you should ..."

"Call it in...," he said, finishing her sentence. He called Observer Corp. headquarters to report a new raid.

Chapter Eighty-Five

Churchill Arrives

Margaret and Thomas moved aside as the prime minister entered the room, passing directly before them. He nodded at them, saying, "I'm glad you both could make it." He added a single word, "Margaret." She knew what he meant. He was acknowledging his surprise at her following his instructions.

Churchill looked around and, addressing the junior officer, said, "Is there a place we can sit where we won't affect anything? We don't want to be a distraction."

"Yes, Mr. Prime Minister, we have a separate VIP room up here, and there's a rumor that you qualify." The smile disappeared. "Ah, sir, sorry, sir."

"Relax, my boy; there's an easily discerned difference between a sense of humor and a lack of respect. Can we manage another chair so we can all squeeze in here?" he said, motioning to Thomas and Margaret.

With an unusually discreet and lingering glance at Margaret, he said, "That I can do easily. No problem, sir," he added and stepped out of the room.

Thomas and Churchill looked at each other with half smiles.

"By the way, my dear," Churchill said, putting an arm around Margaret, "could you make yourself available the next time I must address the house of commons? Your duties would consist merely of sitting next to me holding my notes?"

"That's silly; of what possible use could that be to either of us, more importantly, you?"

Churchill replied with his famously dry humor, "Since the vast majority are men, they'd be somewhat distracted, preoccupied, and inattentive to the task at hand. At which point I could, and would, pass any agenda. A tactical move of deception, I admit, but wholly justified for the greater good."

"Winnie, stop that; you're making fun of me."

Thomas burst out laughing. "I will, sir, only in the country's interest, volunteer my wife as your assistant in just such a situation."

"You're both looking to get me riled, and I'll have none of it," she said.

The junior officer returned with the chair and placed it directly behind Margaret, nervously holding it as she sat down. "Will that be all, sir?"

"Quite indeed, soldier. You've not only provided us with comfort but perhaps brought to light a heretofore overlooked political strategy."

"Sir?"

"Thank you very much," Margaret said. "Your manners are commendable and will be made known to your superior officer. Isn't that what you said, Mr. Prime Minister?"

Churchill, face aglow, nodded to the man.

"Yes, ma'am," the soldier said as he carefully left the room.

"An incorrigible moment, the both of you," she said. "Don't we have a war to fight?"

"Yes, my dear," Churchill said with a glow. "Indeed, you're right."

Chapter Eighty-Six

Birling Gap and Flight Control

The Birling Gap observation post was part of 11 Group's sector and situated atop the cliffs right on the sea. The post was one of the hundreds of Observer Corps outposts scattered to the South and East of England. When the chaps at Home Chain picked up a raid, their equipment could only follow it up to the coast, as the radar only pointed out toward France. Once the raiders flew over the beach and anyplace inland, it was the job of the Observer Corps to keep track of the raids visually.

Birling Gap's high location provided excellent visibility but exposed it to the elements. Constantly buffeted by cold sea winds, the only escape for the men was to duck down inside the circle of sandbags that came up to their chest, drink a large amount of hot tea, or both.

Andrew Tembly, thinking he was partially frozen, had had enough. "Cappy," he said, "stop nick nacking with the pot. It's clean enough, for God's sake. Put the bloody thing on the hot plate, or I'm gonna die out here."

Cappy Barns looked at his fellow volunteer, sitting on the dirt floor with his arms tucked between his drawn-up knees and chest. "Be nothing short of drop-down funny, Andy boy, if you survived combat and died of poisoning from a tainted pot."

"Cappy, Cappy, Cappy, me bones they ache, me nose is frozen, an' I would like a surprising' quiet day to end with a cup, but it has to get here sometime 'fore the bloody war ends."

"Such an ornery cuss. Tis a reason why no one hasn't marry ya. And, at this rate, you're destined ta spend the rest of yer life in a pub, gawkin' at the rest of the world." As Cappy spoke, he held the teapot just above the hotplate, adding to his friend's anxiety.

"God demm it. Put it down," Andy said.

Just then, the Headquarters phone rang and, finally putting the pot in its place, Cappy picked up the handset. Andy grabbed the logbook, and tried to wrap his fingers around the pencil.

"Yes, sir. Ready, sir." Cappy looked at Andy and said, "Bearin' 125 at 60+ at twenty-five miles." Andy wrote this down in big, jerky letters while Cappy said, "Roger, sir. Will report back upon our sightin', sir."

"That was jus' too many 'sirs' for me," Andy said. "You don't even know who he is."

"Well, old boy, tis the reason I'm the important one runnin' this station, and you're jus' a cog in the big wheel at me beckon command."

"Rubbish, stinking rubbish. How long ago were they sighted?"

"Fifteen minutes, so we best be on it." They actually had only another ten minutes or so, as twenty-five miles went fast at 200 miles per hour.

"Yeah, yeah," came the reply. Andy was now standing, his elbows on the top of the sand bags, holding up a pair of high-powered binoculars. He turned to look at the pot.

Cappy gave him a scowl. "Ya gotta give it time, man."

Back to scanning the sky, Andy said, "Bit late for the Jerries, don't ya think? Wait."

"Got something?" Cappy said as he moved to the sextant, preparing to map out the details.

"I'm not sure," Andy said slowly, looking at the usual altitude. "Bet it's a false run just to …" Andy went silent. He raised his view to the sky and said, "Bloody hell at Christmas."

It was their job to identify the planes as friendly or hostile and estimate their altitude and direction and provide a count. What Andy saw in the distance was a sight he'd never seen before. He silently handed over the glasses, giving in to his more experienced partner. Cappy took the position, not seeing anything. He dropped the glasses down with a moan. He was surprised Andy was still at his shoulder, as the pot had reached a boil but was no longer on his mind.

"Look higher, man," Andy said impatiently.

Cappy retook the position. Starting again at the horizon, Cappy moved the glasses higher, going past something. Coming back down while adjusting the focus revealed more planes than he'd ever seen in a single formation. They were spread across the clear sky like black stars. "Mother of God," he said, wheeling around to a sextant like-device to calculate the direction and height. "Mark," he called out, and Andy studied the markings, listing them on the confirming side of the log. Cappy was now cranking on the phone to the filtering rooms at Bentley Priory.

"This is Birling Gap reporting," he said, haste in his voice. "We've hostiles thirty-plus, I repeat thirty-plus bearing...," Cappy waited for the answer.

"127," Andy said.

"127," Cappy barked into the phone. He turned to Andy. "What's the height? Gimmie the altitude," he said nervously.

"Fifteen thousand," Andy said, having never seen his mate in such a state.

Cappy almost shouted into the telephone. "Bearing 127 at angels 15. Wait for update, do you copy?"

"Why only thirty?" Andy said.

Cappy hung up the phone and returned to the glasses. "Because," he said, "we need more time to count. Get the other glasses. We need to compare our count and phone in again."

***

Things were moving frantically as Cappy's sightings came into Bentley Priory in Stanmore. Additional reports from other spotting and radar stations were coming in. To combine and filter the information down to the clearest possible picture, the threat was assigned to the proper Group's headquarters, which had complete responsibility for oversight and defensive measures.

In this case, the call went out to 11 Fighter Group HQ, based in Hillingdon House at Uxbridge. 11 Group's assignment was to protect London from anything approaching from a south or southeasterly direction. Headquarters dictated to their seven Section Stations the number of planes to put into the air and at what coordinates. By this time, it was looking to be a massive attack.

11 Group Kenley Field was Edith's Section Station and was the only one also located at Uxbridge. The other six were scattered within their sector. She was one of several WAAFs seated around the edge of the plotting table. They'd been waiting for action longer into the day than expected and were curious at the delay. Once it started, each plotter was assigned a hostile squadron, and it was her job to track them on the plotting table. The controllers directing the attack and the senior officers in the upper level depended on the constantly updated plots on the table.

Edith was busy recounting her materials when she heard the slight gasp as her friend Roxanne finally noticed the ring on finger.

"Oh, my God, lady," she said. Roxanne looked up at the smile on Edith's face. "Well, that certainly explains the unusually quiet manner attached to that silly arse grin on your face. Let me see that gorgeous hunk ah commitment."

Edith extended her hand. "We'll have to wait to resize it," she said.

Roxanne bent over and, with two hands, brought the ring up closer. "Well, aren't you just the cheeky one? Resized? Listen, lady, it could be square, and are you gonna give a damn? Is it that flyboy of yours?"

"Paddy," she said.

"Oh, no. We warned you, girl, in the strongest terms to protect your heart from those air jockeys." Roxanne moved closer, "But mostly it's jealousy, because we don't have one of our own." Roxy held up Edith's hand and said, "Lay-dees, looky here! Edith's gone and thrown her life away on a flyboy."

"No," said Clair, one of the other WAAFs. "Edith, you're the smart one, the pretty one; you have your choice of guys."

"Yeah," said another, "you can have a banker or anyone on the ground. Why did you settle for…"

"She didn't settle for nothing," Roxy interrupted. "She's in love, and that's a tad better than what any of us have goin.'"

"Can't argue with that," Clair said. "Congrats, Edith, we're all just jealous."

"Edith, come over here. Let me see."

Instead, Edith put her hand up to her headset as it began to crackle and looked around the table. The headset came to life with a voice assigning her Hostile G26, the code assigned to a specific group of planes in a raiding formation. Edith was senior plotter and was the first to receive any information. After a raid started, the rules dictated no talking except the minimum required to communicate with the controllers. Roxy, next to her, was also listening to the voice in her ear. She moved to her position on the table, and the action was underway. The plotting room came to life as if hit by lightning, with everyone now engaged. The Germans were very organized, which created patterns, and everyone knew this wasn't a typical day's attack.

"G26 30+ angels 15, heading 127," the voice said. Edith selected the proper numbers and letters from a tray in front of her. She then slid them into groves on a triangular wooden block called a marker. 30+ was the number of planes sighted; angels 15 was the altitude expressed in thousands of feet; and the heading in degrees. On top, she placed a small flag showing the raid number and, with a long pole, pushed the marker into position per the grid coordinates. Next to it, she placed an arrow indicating the direction the raid was traveling. G26 would be traced and pursued as a target all the way in from France until it was heading back across the Channel.

"G26 update, now 40+ heading 135."

Edith pulled the marker back and noticed Roxy and Janet were doing the same with their groups. Edith changed the numbers and looked up. All the girls around the table were exchanging glances as they knew that the average number in a hostile group was 15 or 20. Roxy started to update her G27 marker and hesitated. Roxy then gathered new numbers, changing them yet again. Edith and everyone else, including the controllers, noticed the 50+ on the marker when she pushed it out.

Edith also got the call to increase to 50+. Since each was a different group, it meant just she and Roxy were tracking more than 100 planes. The planes were all heading for London, right through her sector.

She looked up at her flight controller. His face was long with concern as he stood to better look at the rest of the table. He glanced up at the tote board behind Edith that provided the planes' status from readiness to engagement with the enemy. The panel provided the officer with the number of aircraft available and on what field. The board was kept up to date by another team of WAAFs.

Edith could see the increased activity and hurried motions around the room. This is what they'd practiced for, and they were good at it.

The highly trained flight controllers were adept at matching British squadrons to every incoming group of hostile aircraft. Britain was the world leader in detecting, plotting, and vectoring defensive measures against an air attack. None of the other adversaries Germany faced possessed this skill. However, it was becoming evident this day was going to be particularly challenging.

Park turned to Stephen next to him. "Winston would pick a day like this to come for a visit. 12 Group is reporting the same level of incoming hostiles. Their portion split off the main group and is making landfall now."

Park hung up the first phone. Into the other phone, he said, "Yes, thank you for holding. Can you tell me if there are any convoys scheduled through the Channel? Yes, I will. Nothing for this afternoon? Thank you." Park rang off.

"It doesn't make bloody sense."

"Let me guess: no convoys," Stephen said.

"Not until early morning, so that's not the reason for the increased activity. I think we better increase the squadrons on standby. Looks like a major run on the factories."

"Notify all fields. Put the first line on twenty-minute alert, engines running."

"Yes, sir," Stephen called the switchboard and issued the blanket message, which reached each dispersal shack in minutes.

The Headquarters phone rang. Park looked at Stephen, picking it up. "Park here. Yes, sir, copy that. We'll get to it at once."

Stephen was waiting as Park paused for just a moment in thought. "12 Group reports they're targeting just the airfields and not going inland as usual. They already have three fields out of action. Well, at least we know what they're after. Stephen, get the ready planes in the air. We will vector in flight," Park said. "And have each airfield sound an air alert: attack eminent. No, I'll do that; you tend to the planes."

Stephen was already on the phone with his controllers.

Park rang up the field manager's line. "This is Park," he said hurriedly to the man who controlled all airfield operations. "Sound air alert: attack eminent. I repeat, they're targeting the airfields—end message."

The Headquarters phone rang again.

"Damn, don't they know we're a tad bit busy?" He picked it up mid-ring, "Park here. Yes, sir, we've given the alert. How many? Good God, right away."

Stephen stopped talking. He put his hand over the phone and gave Park a curious look. He had to wait but a second.

"Headquarters reports more formations fifty miles out, 100+." It was the number they used when there were too many to count.

"Tangmere and Biggin Hill are out, sir," Stephen said. "7 and 20 squadrons made it up at Tangmere and 260 at Biggin Hill, but 137 took it on the ground. Towers two and five are hit and out, making current reports sketchy."

At this point, no one fully understood the gravity of the situation, as everyone was executing specific individual duties associated with their sector. Soon over the Channel a formation of more than a thousand fighters and medium bombers flew, occupying 800 square miles of space one and a half miles high.

Chapter Eighty-Seven

Birling Gap and Flight Control

Margaret heard it all unfold and was stunned. Thomas focused on every detail, saying to Margaret, "It's just the beginning."

Overhearing the comment, the prime minister looked at Thomas.

"Speaking of the war, Mr. Watson, what do you think of Hugh Dowding's little organization?" Churchill said, motioning toward the room below.

"It's well ahead of its time."

"An interesting description, I must say. Soon, we will see on what side of history you reside. As for myself, I came to see Dowding's system in action, resulting in our ability at getting planes into the air to meet the raids."

"Mr. Prime Minister, if I may, this day will test Mr. Dowding's design to its limit and the resources it controls. I understand you're in no position to believe anything I have to say, but it's a fact that England barely survives this day."

"As you have, in no small measure, imparted in your most interesting manner." Churchill, holding his cigar, stared at this man who had no taste for the usual bounds of reality.

Thomas felt an urge, needing to add, "Sir, it's not this wave that will be the problem."

The prime minister looked at Thomas in silence, providing approval to continue despite his reluctance to verbalize it officially.

Thomas knew he was way out of line, but he didn't see another choice. "Sir, we, I mean you, need to order all inland reserves to start for the coast. They can't help now, but they can for the next coming wave."

"On its face,' Churchill replied, "authority is a wonderful tool in the right situation. It's of little use when applied to these men, who understand what they're doing far better than I. Mr. Watson, you might not know our strategic objective is …"

"I know, sir. It's not our intent to defeat the Germans but to stay in the game. By default, it's a victory if we can't be beaten. However, right now the Luftwaffe is assembling their entire force in the western theatre. It's a final attempt to destroy the airfields and bring us to our knees. It's vital they realize we can withstand the second and third waves."

"Third?"

"That's what I said. Wave two will come from Norway in the east and three from France in the south. I'm sorry, but it's true. It all feeds into the cabinet meeting later tonight."

Churchill put his finger up to Thomas as he saw Major Dowding walk quickly into the room. "How does it look, Major?"

Dowding's colour and rigid motions belied a man who was pressed on many fronts. However, composure wasn't something a British soldier misplaced; it was sewn into his being. In steady monotones, he said, "Mr. Prime Minister, it appears to be our largest engagement, with about a thousand hostiles at the moment. They're concentrating on the airfields and doing a bang-up job catching our planes on the ground during refueling. But our boys will give them bloody hell; we can count on that." He quickly glanced at Margaret and before he could make amends, her smile eliminated the need.

"Do we have everything up?" Churchill asked.

"Yes, sir, the lot."

"Reserves?"

"The lot, sir. Every local plane that has a pilot is in the air on the way to the coast. Some will be engaging shortly."

"Well done, major. It's up to our boys then."

Churchill and Thomas exchanged looks. Neither had a comment that would clarify or explain what was occurring before them.

Chapter Eighty-Eight

Paddy Scrambles

Connor had just pulled open a drawer inside the dispersal shack to stow away extra stuff on the top of the desk. "What a mess," he thought. The watch before didn't clean up anything.

RING RING—RING RING.

The clamoring sound drove into his ears. Everyone within earshot of the shack tensed. Paddy opened his eyes and, from a fully inclined position in the upright chair, instinctively pulled his feet back underneath himself and pushed down on the arms to stand up.

Connor stuck his head out of the open window where everyone was sitting and yelled, "Two Section Scramble, vector airborne 50+." He then made his way to the large bell hanging just outside the door, where he made as much noise as possible.

"Let's go, lads—*now*," Paddy said. He looked for everyone in his squadron as they all stood and bolted for the flight line. The flight crews using Coffman starters were igniting the engines coughing black smoke. Chief mechanics climbed out of the cockpits as the pilots approached in full stride.

"Devin!" Paddy yelled over the top of the Merlin's pounding noise and choking exhaust. The fresh pilot stopped and turned. Paddy took three running strides, closing the distance, shouting, "If you stick close to me, you're going to be fine. If you don't, you're not coming back. Am I clear?"

"Yes, sir, I understand."

"Good luck."

Paddy stepped up onto the wing and dropped into the seat on top of his parachute, putting his arms through the harness. He grabbed the chest strap of the chute harness, pulling it tight while scanning his gauges; oil pressure and petrol were all that mattered. He plugged in the radio telephone connector and pulled down on his leather helmet. A thumbs-up amidst the din of the engine noise was the signal for the mechanic to close the side door with a bang no one could hear.

Paddy looked up from his cockpit at ten o'clock in the deafening roar unleashed by the mighty engines. There the flight crew director held his arms out straight as he stared at the boys under the plane, pulling the chocks away from the wheels. He waited until they were clear, then looked up and locked eyes with Paddy, signaling to increase engine speed by rotating his finger around in the air. Paddy gently shoved forward on the throttle, feeling the plane start to taxi. He listened to the mighty engine smooth out into the familiar harmonic sound of a finely tuned warrior ready to go to war.

The flight director dropped one arm, raising the other toward the taxi lane. Paddy saluted him as his other hand pushed harder on the throttle. Soon he was rolling into position. Reaching back for the canopy, it rolled down its track and dropped into its final position. Paddy pulled back on the locking levers on both sides. He scanned the flight line to see if everyone in his squadron was in position.

Verey lights, shooting into the air from the control tower and dispersal hut, warned other planes that a squadron was scrambling. It was best not to be in the way.

A minute later, Red squadron was dashing across the grass airfield, four abreast, increasing speed as they bounced along on the uneven surface. Paddy pulled back on the stick, as did the others in unison, the nose of each plane rotating upwards toward the sky. The second, third, and fourth sections of his squadron followed. Each pilot threw the lever just in front of the throttle, causing first the right, then the left under-gear to raise, finishing flush with the underside of the wing. These ordinary people, who happened to know how to fly, climbed upward to meet the enemy. England hadn't yet, but would soon, fully appreciate their contribution to the future of their nation and the world.

The entire sequence occurred in less than three minutes.

Their course heading had them flying directly for the channel, although that wasn't necessarily their final bearing. Squadron and control designations changed once they were in the air to keep the Germans from obtaining the order of battle information by monitoring the voice traffic. Rabbit squadron today was Fox squadron the next.

"Top Hat control, this is Foxtrot leader," Paddy said. "Squadron airborne and awaiting vector information, over."

"Foxtrot leader, this is Top Hat control, Intercept 50+, angels 15, vector 135."

Paddy brought his plane to the new heading with every airplane in lockstep.

"Copy, Top Hat control, 127 angels 15."

Park was leaning with both hands on the desk in front of him, looking down at the room below. He turned and looked directly at Thomas. He took a few long strides toward his guests.

Churchill addressed him on approach. "Splendid job, Marshal Park. You and your group have indeed made us, yet again, proud."

"I'm not sure we can make any conclusions yet, Mr. Prime Minister, as there are indications it's not over."

He looked up at Thomas. "I heard what you said earlier about bringing up the inland reserves early in the fight. Dowding has indeed authorized the very unusual step, but it leads to an interesting question. Why would someone who I think is unfamiliar with even the basics of our system suggest such an unlikely and perhaps an even unknown option?"

Addressing Churchill next, he said, "Mind you, it's an issue of curiosity more than being a prime issue for treason." Park followed with the type of laugh that put light on the comment but didn't hide his inner concerns.

Thomas wasn't ready for the question.

Churchill responded, "Our dear friend, Mr. Watson, has a unique ability to foretell the future, a skill perfected while being a gypsy in a former existence. At least that's what he told me." Turning to Thomas, he said, "Unless you've another story today."

"No, sir," Thomas said. "I'll stick with that one, as it's the most believable." Thomas also followed with a laugh, but one composed of nervousness and uncertainty.

"Good then, I wouldn't want my Margaret involved with any shady types." Churchill then looked back to Park. "Does that do it then?"

Park, receiving the clear message to let it drop, replied, "Most certainly, Mr. Prime Minister. Is there anything we can get you?"

"There's nothing better that you could provide this citizen than what you and your people are demonstrating today. It's most impressive."

Stephen poked his head into the room, "Sir, HQ is reporting new formations and a probable new wave."

"Well, then," Park said, smiling and addressing Margaret directly. "I'm needed, but should you need anything, we can get right to it."

Churchill, always inclined to subtle observation, addressed Thomas, saying, "Another bit of evidence demonstrating the attention our Miss Margaret has over those who appreciate the ... let's say ..."

Thomas smiled. "The finer things crafted by our Creator?"

Margaret silently but theatrically crossed her arms. She then made a point of looking down at the Operations floor, ignoring them both.

"Well said, Mr. Watson. But I feel if you've any further musings on the subject of the task below us, you offer them to me alone."

Sheepishly, Thomas said, "My apologies. My convictions blurted out the information before I prepared for the consequences."

Chapter Eighty-Nine

Paddy in the Air

Paddy heard the voice in his headset. "Foxtrot leader, this is Top Hat control confirming your status vector to 135 at twenty miles, hold at angels 15."

"Roger, Top Hat control. This is Foxtrot leader, out," Paddy replied.

He then switched the frequency on his radio to talk directly to his group. "Foxtrot squadron, come to 135 on my turn." Sixteen planes all made their way to the spot in the sky that dozens of people in various ways indicated was the best place for this squadron to inflict damage on the enemy. Paddy monitored the planes as they drew together in formation. Something was wrong,

Paddy spun his head side to side, looking through the canopy. "Blue 4, Devin, where the hell are you?"

"Down on your six, just to your port side."

"Bring it in closer, man, so I can see you and stay there."

"Yes, sir, err roger." The young Canadian pilot had had just 35 of the expected 100 training hours in a Spit, and it was his first time in combat. Paddy had taken him up, chased him around, and even fired at him a few times to scare the hell out of him. Three months ago, he'd left the family home on the sound in Vancouver to much fanfare and, he had to admit, with a bit of swagger. Foolish swagger, he now knew, as he increased speed to close the gap as he was instructed. It was hard putting all the training to use, as it didn't duplicate the deep fear that locked up your body and mind in combat. The apprehension interfered with maintaining group position, watching the airspeed, listening for instructions, and staying in formation. This was all to be done while scanning the sky, looking for a surprise ME 109 before he starts blasting away at your plane.

"Paulson, pull up; Devin, where are you?" Paddy sounded like an impatient mother trying to herd her ducklings across a busy path.

"Blue 4 in position. Out."

"Keep her steady and close, son."

Paddy was the Foxtrot Squadron flight leader and one of the four section leaders with four planes each. His was Blue section. He was Blue 1, and the pilot with the least experience was Blue 4. If they paired off, 1 would go with 4, and 2 would pair with 3.

They continued climbing to altitude, staying in formation. The flight controllers would provide additional changes to the vector headings if necessary. With Foxtrot and the raiding Germans heading toward one another, it didn't take long to close the gap. The idea was to get to the contact point and be in the best position to execute an attack. That's why a speedy take-off was critical. Getting to the point of attack too late would put valuable assets in the open air, and a battle missed.

"Foxtrot leader to Top Hat control, approaching position. Over."

"Foxtrot leader, this is Top Hat control. They should be at angels 15 with 50+ to your Southwest. Can you see them?"

"Negative, Top Hat. Out." Paddy pressed the button to talk. "Keep a keen look out, boys. We should be on top of them any second."

Moments later, Eric, Red section flight leader, yelled, "I see them, 4:00 o'clock low. Henkel's without an escort. Bloody hell, there are a million of them."

"No escorts, hallelujah," someone said.

"Top Hat control, this is Foxtrot leader. We have bomber formation in sight."

"Roger, Foxtrot leader."

"This is Foxtrot leader to Red flight leader. Stay up here and look for that escort. They're here; we just haven't seen them yet. The rest on me, executing a dive run through the bomber formation. After we break through, everyone to the west comes around for another run. Just follow me. Everyone turn west in formation, or you'll end up alone."

Whether a bomber or fighter, it was almost suicide to be a straggler, losing the protection of your group. Staying with your formation was the best way to stay alive, even in a dogfight. A bomber with engine problems would fall behind and almost certainly be picked off.

"Foxtrot leader, this is Top Hat control. Look for fighter escort trailing main body at angels 14."

"This is Foxtrot leader. I see them. Out."

"The escort doesn't know we're here," Paddy thought.

"Red flight, this is Foxtrot leader. Climb to angels 17, and wait for the escort. That should put you coming down out of the sun."

On the ground, Park spoke without looking over. "Who's making first contact for us?"

Stephen looked down at the board. "Squadron 125, out of Kenley, sir," he said. "Call sign Foxtrot."

"Put it up on the speaker."

"Yes, sir." Stephen called the switchboard and gave the order.

The sector controllers talked directly to their flight leaders, and it came over the speakers. The control room could also hear the individual pilots, as once the battle commenced they were all on the same open channel.

Edith never got used to it. It was Paddy's voice. And it wasn't the first time, as she'd heard him going into combat numerous times but could never breathe a word of it. She had wanted to tell him last night, but it would have ended their romance, what with her being shot for treason and all.

The gunners in the German bombers had now located them in the sky and tried to fill all available space with as much metal as possible.

"Mayday, mayday. Red 1 to flight leader. Red 4 is hit and flipped over. I think he's out."

A tumbling speck in the sky fell unnoticed until it blossomed into a big white cloud, "Ferris is okay."

They continued their run through the formation of bombers. Pulling up on the other side, they gathered into formation for another run and the inevitable retaliation of the bomber's close support. The ME 109s in the fighter escort wasted no time. The defenders close to the bombers were on them quickly. The tactic of having Red squadron occupy the higher trailing patrol did not work, as on contact, Red found themselves outnumbered three to one.

Paddy lowered his seat so the red dot on this gun sight was in the center of the circle. The German escorts were now well inside the British formation, where individual battles were the order of business. Down and to his right, Paddy saw one ME make a pass at Devin, who was on his own. Paddy threw the stick forward and came in from behind. He lined up the sight.

"Blue 4, this is Blue leader. I'm behind you, pull up *now*."

Paddy saw Devin's plane pull up as Paddy's tracers tore into the rear of the German plane, missing Devin who would have been directly in the line of fire. The bullets went through the fuselage and tail, tearing off the plane's elevators. A plane was able to fly with a lot of damage, but even the best pilot was helpless without being able to maintain level flight. The ME's nose went down, and Paddy saw the pilot release the canopy and jump over the side into the air. He would be picked up by British patrols and spend the rest of the war in a secret POW camp.

A violent swerve to the left brought him behind an ME. It started a circular chase he knew he would win if the German pilot stuck with it. At maximum Gs, the Spitfire could turn a tighter circle, eventually bringing the enemy into his sights.

"Foxtrot leader, this is Top Hat control. New formation 30+ angels 16."

"Roger, Top Hat. We have a visual. Out."

Paddy's group fought their way through the escort and circled back, and regrouped for the next run on the new enemy formation.

"Foxtrot to Top Hat control. Attacking now," Paddy said in a voice that didn't anticipate the mayhem that would follow.

The air war against a stronger foe continued. The squadrons attacked the formations on their way in and again on their way back to France. 12 Group met the enemy planes getting through to the southwest and then the process started over. Only after the last threat was heading back was it time to determine if their airfield was in good enough condition to land.

"This is Foxtrot leader. Bang up job, boys. Let's break it off and refuel."

It wasn't going to be that easy. The Chain Home had already spotted another group forming over the French countryside. Momentarily, they'd split apart, starting for the channel, yet another wave in the first attack. It continued that way for most of the day in the most significant effort by the Germans to date.

"Foxtrot, this is Top Hat control. You're cleared for return to Kenley. Mind the restrictions."

The ground personnel had been busy surveying the landing areas and had placed orange indicators marking out the only straight path through the bomb craters that was wide enough for the returning planes to use. It wasn't great, but it allowed pilots to land back at their original field where the crews assigned to each aircraft and pilot were stationed. The alternative was a patchwork of backups that worked but weren't anyone's first choice.

The battle dragged on into the late afternoon. Some of the planes went up for the third time. The sheer number of hours in the air alone would warranted concern, but the real toll on the pilots was in constant combat. A pilot performing at the top of his game for too long was a recipe for trouble.

Later in the day, a note containing the current numerical status of the battle reached Churchill.

"One hundred and eighty-three enemy planes downed, with our losses under forty," Churchill said. "So far, it's a more than a respectable day."

"Sir," Thomas said, "history will find those casualty numbers will be far different on both sides. However, it was a sterling effort but serious enough to create tonight's meeting. Göring will also get incorrect information, which proves the British have far more planes than his sources were reporting. Two weeks ago, Göring informed his flight commanders the British had fewer than ninety fighters. To his annoyance, the number will become a point of humor, as his pilots will jokingly claim shooting down the same ninety fighters."

Churchill was presented with another note, and he read it carefully. He gave Thomas a curious look and said, "Mr. Halifax is requesting a call to discuss a meeting to be held as soon as possible." Churchill called an aid, asking him to get Mr. Halifax on the phone. "Preferably that one," he said, pointing to one on the table just a few feet away.

"Yes, sir," the aid said.

The PM looked up at Thomas and, in a voice fully recognizing the turn of events, said, "It appears, Mr. Watson, tomorrow's meeting is to be this evening after all."

Thomas, sensing the moment, replied quietly, "Apparently so, sir."

The prime minister directed his attention to the floor below and said, "Disturbing to the core is my growing comfort with your 'memories' of things to come that are proving critical but equally outside my control."

Within seconds the phone rang. Popping back in, the aid looked at Churchill and pointed at the ringing telephone as Churchill said, "Thank you, young man." Churchill picked up the receiver and said, "Lord Halifax, I received your note."

Churchill noted the slight pause of his constant opponent as though he was gathering energy for a fight or trying to constrain an abundance of anger to avoid one. "Mr. Prime Minister, we have a set of circumstances requiring the attention of the war cabinet, sooner than later. I'm requesting we meet this evening to address the faltering state of our defenses."

Churchill calmly said, "I would venture you're informally with a group of the war cabinet at this time?"

Halifax looked around the room and said, "Well, yes, I am."

"Trying to save the country, as we all are, I'm sure." Churchill said. "It would please me greatly if you could convince the members to meet here at Kenley as soon as the group can assemble. I'm sure we can secure the group conference room at Hillhouse. My duties should allow me to be there at 1700 hours. Bring your version of today's losses and the plan you wish to see fulfilled."

"Well, yes, I'll do my best, as they're obviously still coming in. Winston, we need to face the escalating losses and our ability to mount a viable defense squarely."

The prime minister replied, "I can assure you, all points that warrant consideration will be met head-on. I look forward to discussing our nation's proper posture as we move forward. You'll be there then?"

Thomas was, of course, delighted that the meeting would take place, as he predicted. The more significant event was witnessing a master politician completely take the initiative away from Halifax and make it his meeting, and Halifax knew it.

Halifax could barely get the words out. "Yes, Mr. Prime Minister, at 1700 hours."

Margaret looked at Thomas, but not for the reason he thought. She looked at him almost in wonder. "Thomas is right again," she thought, "proving that a normal life wasn't in the near future, if at all."

Thomas said, "Pardon if I'm out of line, but well done, sir, extremely well done."

"Mr. Watson, I've survived being shot at, being held prisoner, the Dardanelles fiasco, and, not the least, being married for forty-three years. I've acquired a few skills I deploy from time to time."

"Winnie, being married hardly compares to the rigors of which you speak. I know that you and Aunt Clemmie are mad about each other."

"Of course, my dear, of course, you're right," he nodded his head toward Margaret.

"That's the meeting I was talking about," Thomas said. "It's somewhat gratifying that it's going to occur, proving that I'm not altogether crazy."

"True, Mr. Watson, but this particular meeting with Lord Halifax doesn't come as a complete surprise, as our paths have been on a trajectory to cross for some time, not regarding discussion of the day-to-day aspects of the war but regarding the much larger question of the manner in which I'm waging war. Tonight will no doubt include whether *I should* be waging war?"

Thomas nervously put his hands in his pockets. "It will be a moment far exceeding anything that those in attendance could conceive."

"Have you lost faith? If your version of history has any credence, we're facing a problem that has already been solved."

"If you can prevail," Thomas said.

"Given your track record, it would appear in some far corner of the universe, I already have."

Thomas wasn't ready for the man to grant him any credibility. Churchill still had his hand on the receiver, still cradled on the phone. He picked it up and dialed. "Mr. Colville, there's to be a war cabinet meeting at Hillhouse. Please secure the use of the largest conference room for 1700 hours. In addition, I'll need you here as quickly as possible. Please bring any numbers that apply to today's attacks, if you would. Yes, that's correct. I'll see you shortly."

Meanwhile, as the discussion about the meeting took place, Margaret listened to the radio speaker and its portrayal of the ongoing battle. It was starting to bother her, but she didn't know why. She figured she didn't really want to participate in such detail.

She blurted out, "Thomas, can we turn the speaker off?"

"I'm not sure. I'll see."

Churchill put his hand up as Thomas started out of the room. "Now isn't the time to distract them due to our discomfort. We have boys in the air."

"Of course," Thomas said. "That should have been obvious."

"No, I'm sorry, that's not really the problem." Now standing, she leaned forward, bracing herself by placing her hands on the glass. She looked down at the room below, feeling something foreign and out of place. A chill ran through her body. She could see the supervisor briskly walking around the table, checking positions and talking to the plotters.

Thomas previously had second thoughts about Margaret as a bystander in the actual environment of a battle. Now he was sure. "He shouldn't have exposed her to this much reality. However, it didn't change the necessity of his needing to be here, and she'd insisted on not letting him come alone.

He put a hand on her elbow to turn her around. It was stiff, and she didn't move. "I could take you out into the other room if you like," he said. She didn't move.

"Margaret, are you okay?" Thomas asked.

As if in slow motion, she looked directly at Thomas with an expression that wasn't her own. He'd never seen her face convey what it was expressing right now.

She said, "Thomas, I'm scared."

Chapter Ninety

The War Goes On

Paddy's group had made it through the day, losing the one plane and Ferris for the afternoon. Ferris would be back tomorrow morning after being rescued. They were again up in the air, headed for another vector and another effort at defending the island.

Paddy peered through the front of the cockpit at the tiny bits of danger growing ever larger. His group again pulled off the strategic position. They were coming down on the bomber group in attack formation. Paddy looked for his target and a space between the German planes. Given his diving speed, he needed to know exactly his path through the formation after the strafing run.

Paddy's thumb moved to the firing button and pressed. He felt the vibration as a burst of 20mm cannon fire erupted from the plane. The stream was purposely ahead of the target, and Paddy watched the bomber fly into the line of fire. It was always easier to shoot ahead of the target and let it fly into the deadly path than to try to hit it directly. A pilot needed to do this while keeping in mind the moving space that was his pass-through.

As planned, the shells ripped through the air and found their mark. The Henkel's wing first caught fire, then broke off completely at the wing root next to the pilot. It made the bomber skew in the air like a paper plane. Paddy knew the remaining wing would put the plane into a tight spin, creating a force that would pin the crew against the insides of the plane, unable to escape. As always, he thought, "What a waste."

Once through the enemy formation, they reformed for another attack while the rest of the squadron tried to fend off the escort. Paddy refocused, swinging his head side to side, and found Devin to his rear on the right. He'd completed the run doing exactly what Paddy had done. They locked eyes.

Again, both pilots were heavy in the seat as they pulled up from the dive to engage as they came around. Paddy encountered a single 109 flying level. He figured it was another boy thrown into a cockpit without proper training. Any pilot with experience knew to never, ever, fly in a straight line while under attack. Paddy tried to overtake him, coming around. He knew staying the course would shortly put the plane within range.

"Blue 4, are you with me?"

Devin could smell something that wasn't normal. He looked down at his gauges. "Right here, Blue 1. I'm running hot."

"Stay here. It's almost over."

The 109 saw Paddy and put his plane in a tight turn, moving from Paddy's left to his right.

"Bank right," Paddy said. He felt an uneven force on the stick as it swung over to the stop, creating a tight turn. Paddy took short, quick breaths, tightening the muscles in his midsection. This drove the blood to his head that gravity was pulling away, avoiding a blackout. He fired just as the ME entered his gun sight. He knew he hit it, but with no visible effect. "Lucky day for the rookie," he thought.

Both maneuvers caused him and Devin to lose altitude, and he had to return to the bombers. He could see them directly above as they were coming over land. Paddy deduced they were heading straight for Kenley field. "This is Foxtrot leader. All planes break and head for the bombers. We need to break this up, lads, if we want a place to set down."

"Foxtrot squadron, I repeat, all units make a run at the bombers."

Once they cleared the formation, it would put them very close to the deck as they pulled out. "Blue 4, mind the pull-up or get wet."

"Blue 1," Devin shouted, "109 coming in high. Break left. I'm on him."

Dead ahead, Paddy saw the stream of tracers coming from the diving plane above. He calculated the distance to their impact and then desperately threw his plane to the left. The move would put him closer to the deck, increasing his vulnerably, but that was why he had a wingman. Paddy kept his eye on the tracers. They were getting close. The plane wasn't responding, or he'd miscalculated. The stick was dead over, but it felt wrong. He looked down and saw it stopped, not on the restraint but a few inches short. Paddy took his right hand off the throttle and hit the stick as hard as he could. He felt it break free, but it was too late. He was vertical in his turn, with one wing pointed up to the sky. In slow motion, he saw the holes appear at the tip of the wing as they marched right toward him.

Paddy felt the pressure of the impact and thought his eyes were open, but he wasn't sure. His smeared goggles made it dark. It got darker as the pain set in. He felt sluggish, which was never good in a dogfight. He needed to pull up but wasn't sure if he was upside down. He decided to pull up, and nothing moved. He tried to reach for the canopy, and searing pain through his chest and shoulders hindered any movement. The pain was quickly replaced by the unfathomable emptiness of being alone as his mind realized he wasn't going home. "Bloody war," he thought, "took her away from me."

"Edith," he said.

"Blue 1, *BAIL! BAIL*! Paddy, get the hell out," Devin yelled. "Can you hear me? Pull the canopy *now*. Paddy! Paddy!"

In the cockpit of Blue 1, the headphones dutifully responded, delivering the message. However, a sound not heard is but vibrating air.

Edith looked at the speaker mounted on the ceiling. She'd heard her name, spoken into a hopeless void, but right after her name, the speaker went silent for an eternity. Edith waited for the words that would define the rest of her life. The background static played the dirge feared by all, and then it came. Devins's young voice struggled, "Top hat control. "This is Blue 4." Then, in hushed, reverent tones, the voice said, "*No chute. I repeat, no chu…*" The last word was truncated, a victim of emotion.

"Blue 4, 109 behind you. Break left; break left."

From the speaker came a grunt as Blue 4 slammed the stick over, and gravity slammed him into the flight seat, dimming his sight and crushing his lungs. "Bloody hell," he thought. "Follow your training or die." His midsection went solid as he struggled to keep his head clear. Short breaths, he said to himself, short breaths.

The war went on.

Chapter Ninety-One

Uxbridge—Plotting Area

Before Devin struggled to deliver the news about Paddy, Thomas had listened to the chatter over the speaker as the pilots' voices shouted positions and the leader's instructions. Back then, he'd marveled at how calm everyone was in the plotting area. Pushing their marks, the girls continued to keep track of the battle. It was almost surreal. Then Margaret stood up beside Thomas, looking very uncomfortable. She crossed and uncrossed her arms while looking around. He looked into the eyes of the woman he loved, but, given the look on her face, she was different from the woman he'd met.

Then they all heard the words: "*No chute,*" emanating from the tiny speaker in the control booth. Thomas immediately saw the differing body language of the women in the room below. One of the plotters leaned forward for support against the table, her head bowed.

Margaret reached out, grabbing a fistful of Thomas's coat.

The room below spoke volumes in its lack of movement. Thomas sensed something was very different with Margaret. This wasn't the first pilot to go down today, but the new recruits were unknown to most. However, many personally knew those who had extended duties. He was immediately aware this was the case.

"Thomas?" Margaret said in an elevated voice.

Edith Bristo hadn't heard the words as much as felt them hit her with brute force. It turned the anxiety and tension at listening to Paddy in combat into quiet incoherence. She felt her eyes drop from looking up at the speaker down to the plotting table. Instinctively, she reached out onto the table to brace herself when her knees started to give. Her arms weren't strong enough. "Paddy," she thought.

Margaret heard those same words from the speaker and was still holding Thomas's coat. She'd known deep inside that something awful was to unfold, and to see it come true shook her. It was just like an emotional bomb had shaken the place, and time paused inside the room. Everyone's body language first shouted shock, then horror. Each person within the confines focused on the woman leaning on the plotting table. Margaret could almost feel the woman's agony flow through her own body. She watched from above as the young woman tried to remain upright.

"Thomas!" Margaret said again but much louder than she realized. Churchill's head snapped, surprised at the volume. Pointing down with a finger, she said, "That's her—she was the one in the restaurant last night. He proposed, remember?"

Thomas looked again and agreed. It wasn't as if they'd met, but it made the moment more personal. "I think you're right."

"I know I'm right," she said, turning and heading for the door.

"Where are you going?"

He'd said it, never expecting an answer.

She was gone.

Margaret flew down the stairs to the central corridor, running toward the entrance she'd seen coming in. The guard noticed the hurried pace, sensing something was unusual—but what kind of unusual? Was it something that needed his attention or someone in a hurry? The fact she'd been upstairs with the prime minister was significant, but he remembered the paperwork and knew she wasn't just an average observer. However, the Operations room *was* 'authorized personal only.'

Margaret burst through the control room door. Making her way into the room, she collided with a WAAF officer. The officer's face was pained and distant. Margaret grabbed both of the woman's shoulders, making sure she hadn't knocked her off balance.

Lonnie wasn't sure what she was doing when she heard the words from the speaker. They made Lonnie's heart disappear within her. She couldn't believe it. "Paddy," she'd said reverently through the fingers at her lips. "Paddy," she thought, the love of her life and center for so many years, was now gone. Her legs were weak. She moved both arms across her chest as if trying to hold the emotion inside. Hours appeared to pass; she realized she was breathing rapidly, still staring at the speaker.

"Edith," Roxy called out. She approached Edith and grabbed her at the waist, keeping her on her feet. Roxy looked to the floor supervisor.

He nodded, and she walked Edith to one of the benches used during the down times between attacks. Through the incoherence, Edith fell onto the bench and part of the wall simultaneously. She felt her body move oddly, but it seemed an outer experience. Edith leaned forward, holding her head up with her hands, her elbows on her knees. She tried to compose herself, but she really didn't care.

Annette, the plotter closest to the supervisor, leaned over, saying, "Paddy asked her to marry him last night."

Lonnie was on the other side of the room when she saw the woman almost collapse. Lonnie started over to help as she had no assignment at the table, but nothing moved. "Edith?" she thought. "Did they say, Edith?" Ten feet away, the fleeting glint hit her eye, and she instantly knew. It was on the woman's finger, half covered in cascading hair. Conflicted, Lonnie forced herself to take a step, finally covering the distance. She hesitantly placed her hand on the woman's shoulder and said, "Edith…" and stopped. Lonnie could see her fingers touching the dress's fabric, but they were devoid of sensation. All the old wonderful images and emotions flew through her mind instantly, flashes of events with Paddy that were once hers alone.

Lonnie almost silently said, "I'm so sorry," and she moved her hand up and away.

Lonnie knew Edith didn't know about her and Paddy. She remembered Paddy explaining at the field how much he loved this woman. It was deep and sincere, and it hurt. There were too many divided emotions. Given the gossip line, Lonnie didn't know who in the room knew what. A gripping thought took her over: regardless of her sincere sympathy for Edith and the bond all women felt at this time, she didn't belong. Knowing she also wasn't going to be able to maintain control, she wanted to avoid any misconceptions. She urgently needed to leave the room and quickly made her way to the exit, hoping all eyes were on Edith. Rushing, the closer she got to the door, the higher the feeling in her body. Her face was flushed; she needed to be strong, just another few feet.

When the two bodies collided, it interrupted Lonnie's daze. The woman grabbed Lonnie and said something.

Margaret said, "I'm so sorry. Are you alright?"

The woman in the uniform she was holding didn't respond. Margaret looked toward Edith, sitting on the bench and back to the WAAF. Margaret was trying to decide what to do when a tall guard outside the door appeared right next to them. Margaret was about to ask if he could help her when the guard wrapped his arm around the woman, holding her up. He looked at Margaret and nodded. With that, Margaret took off for the other side of the room.

The supervisor had been through it before. Why did this one appear different? "Bloody war," he muttered. "Who was that woman flying by?" he thought. She wasn't in uniform, and he didn't recognize her. He looked up at the room above and saw Winston Churchill standing and looking down.

Parks nodded his apparent approval, and the supervisor returned to the moment at hand. He clapped his hands once and almost yelled, "All right, people, we have planes in the air."

He put down the report he'd been carrying, picked up Edith's stick, and pointed a finger directly at Roxy, who was still holding Edith.

"Clair, help Roxy cover Edith's squadrons," he said. They both left Edith and returned to the table. The supervisor handed Roxy the position stick, saying, "Janet, fetch another plotter in here on the double."

The switchboard operator reached for a clipboard, plugged in a connection, and started dialing.

Margaret kneeled in front of Edith just as the two other women left. "My name is Margaret, and I can help. What's your name?"

"Edith." She didn't look up.

"Edith, I was in the restaurant last night and saw you and Paddy having dinner. I know he was taken away, and it's such a tragedy. It was all too obvious he adored you, and I'm sorry I was watching, but I know he proposed. Edith, I know this is a tough time, but you must know that other people, like your family and friends, also adore you. This tragedy will never go away, but knowing that he came into your life for however long, made your life richer. Do you believe that?"

Edith looked up at Margaret through reddened eyes flooded with tears. She nodded.

"Your man will always love you from somewhere. I know that. You need to start supporting that love and see yourself through this, and I would like to help."

Edith was confused. Who was this person? Where was Roxy? She started to drift. In her mind, she saw Paddy underwater, separated from the plane, just suspended there.

Startled, she heard Margaret say, "Do you live alone?"

"What? No, I have a flatmate."

"Is she there now?"

"No."

"Well," Margaret said, "it's not my decision, but I think it's best you not be alone, and you certainly shouldn't stay here. If it's okay, I can arrange to have you taken to my house by car and driver. Is that all right? It's my mother's house. I'll be there shortly after that, and we will take care of you. I think it's best right now unless you have other ideas or someone to call."

Edith didn't respond. Paddy was fading from view as the water grew darker.

"So, I'll call her with instructions to take you in and wait for me. Will you let me do that?"

"Yes, but why are you trying …?"

"It's okay. There doesn't have to be a reason."

Edith looked around and found Roxy, who understood Edith's confused and questioning look. She'd heard the full conversation being only a few feet away. Roxy had seen Margaret standing next to Churchill as the man put his arm around her. It's as good a personal reference as one could have, and she said, "Go, Edith, she's right. You need to be with someone and not alone. It's okay." Roxy pointed up at the balcony. "She knows Churchill; I saw it."

Edith looked up at the balcony and saw the prime minister looking down. Their eyes connected as the prime minister stared down at Edith with concern. He said something to the man next to him.

Margaret noticed the exchange. She turned to Edith. "I call him Uncle Winnie. He has known me since I was a child. That's my husband next to him. You'll be very safe."

"But I'm on duty," Edith said.

"Leave that to me; I can take care of that. Churchill bows to no man, but I can make him do almost anything within reason, and if it's not reasonable, I just cry."

Edith looked at Margaret. She reached forward, putting her hand on Margaret's arm in gratitude.

"Besides," Margaret said, "we're going to be friends."

The remaining pilots in the air were thankful they'd made it through the last wave. They were equally grateful their only problem now was figuring out how to get back on the ground. Here and there, sometimes using questionable and dangerous creativity, they found places to land. A Hawker Hurricane landed in a mature cornfield, harvesting a swath wing-span wide until coming to a rest in an older field directly next to it. The pilot happily jumped off the wing to the ground when heat from the oil cooler started the dry harvested stalks on fire. In the end, the plane and the field were lost. After acquiring a few minor burns, the pilot helped the gathered farmers fight the fire. He would be back in the air tomorrow.

Kenley field was destroyed. One of the pilots ditched into the Channel and came to a stop right next to a Navy rescue ship. The plane sank, but the young, inexperienced pilot was very grateful to be feeling anything, including the terrible pain in his head from hitting the instrument panel. In addition to releasing the canopy, he'd also undone his cockpit straps before coming down so he could get out of the plane if it flipped over. He thought it was a good idea at the time.

Someone pressed a gauze bandage on his head, saying, "Hold this, son."

Higher up, a more experienced pilot purposely turned his Spitfire upside down. He then fell harmlessly out of the cockpit, into a full chute, just as his plane's engine sputtered and died while waiting for his turn to land.

Everywhere, smoke billowed from the airfields. Ground crews frantically tried to save anything useful while locating comrades and fighting fires. They tried to stay clear of the ordnance cooking off from burning planes, destroyed ammo dumps, and the arming carts on the tarmac. In all, six airfields had suffered severe damage and would require at least three days' repair before returning to active flight operations. Three airfields were lost for five days or more. Two satellite airfields would be serviceable by dawn.

Margaret had taken Edith off the floor and into a room. She called home and talked to Alistair, clarifying that she wanted Edith picked up and explaining all the details. Alistair could hear the personal nature of her concern. In the same tone he'd been using her entire life, he assured Margaret that he would take care of everything, including bringing the woman safely back to the estate.

Together, Margaret and Edith made their way back upstairs to the entrance. Edith held a tissue at her nose as the guard motioned for her to sign out. Without a word but with a stare to slay a dragon, Margaret quickly dispensed with the bother.

Margaret turned to Edith. "You're going to my house where a man named Alistair will see to your every need. Don't be shy; you can ask for anything. My husband and I'll be there later today. I'm very sorry we can't go with you now. There's something important that requires we stay a little longer."

Margaret grabbed Edith's hands and said, "I trust Alistair with my life. I know this is all very quick, so I want to know if you feel comfortable."

Edith, having gathered herself by this time, was far from being blindly led. "Margaret, I'm deeply grateful, but why are you doing this?"

Margaret was still holding her hands. "Because I can, and if I can, I should. Besides, there was a connection at the restaurant, and sometimes things happen. Really, it's like they come out of the air."

At that moment, a car pulled up with two men inside. Margaret was confused and a little wary. It was too quick, and she wasn't sure the car was for them. Margaret looked at the man exiting the passenger door. He reached into his inside coat pocket, ready to pull out his identification, but stopped when he saw Margaret.

Margaret's worries faded. "Mr. Handraddy, what're you doing here?"

"I'm under orders to escort an Edith Bristo back to the Hatcher Estate."

"Why you?" she asked.

"Good question. Someone called someone, and here I am. It was flagged a priority and *way* above my pay grade."

"Edith, this man is a government agent or something. Anyway, I know him. I have to get back inside, as critical things will occur. It's impossible for me to go with you right now."

Edith hugged Margaret and said, "I can't thank you enough."

"Good. Now, remember, you have friends and family who love you."

Edith got into the back of the car. The agent closed the rear door behind her and said to Margaret, "Don't worry; we will get her there safely."

Margaret looked at Handraddy, saying, "I hope so, Mr. Agent. I can be a handful when displeased."

With a smile, Mr. Handraddy, one of the prime minister's elite bodyguards, said, "Ma'am, of this, there's little doubt."

Chapter Ninety-Two

Uxbridge—Flight Control

Margaret returned to the perch above the room after caring for Edith. The three continued watching as the afternoon wore on. Churchill knew he had, for better or worse, witnessed firsthand the heaviest attack on his country and knew his nation was in grave danger. In his hand, unread, were the day's figures, handwritten on the pieces of paper. He didn't need the details to know that his country faced a dire situation.

Security had already informed him that the group had arrived, so Halifax walking in the door wasn't a surprise. The surprise was his doing so in an energetic huff.

Halifax held up a neatly bound set of papers next to Churchill's head. "Are you aware of what has occurred today?"

Churchill looked at the bundle of handwritten notes in his lap and found the difference in presentation representative of the two men's differing approaches to life. Churchill was never one for structure. "He was comfortable in a changing environment, using his skill in connecting with people to forge a path, whereupon his associate lived in a world dictated by the logic of numbers, the carefully thought-out path, the proper choice.

He looked up at Halifax and decided to start with a left jab. "Yes, I make every effort to keep up with the efforts of those who wish to destroy our little empire."

"Winston, this is no time for your rhetorical sarcasm."

It had worked. Halifax never acquired the skill of moving his overexposed jaw, leaving it vulnerable to those who wished to marginalize his considerable intellect and sully his usually impeccable manner.

"Truly, sir, it wasn't sarcasm," Churchill responded.

"Winston, the friction between you and me is of little consequence and furthest from my mind. We meet with great concern and fear for our people to discuss our options in ending this ill-fated carnage."

"Tell me, Mr. Halifax, do you mean the ill-fated condition of the Germans? Or of the men still fighting, defending so tenaciously what you find nearly gone? The invaders have also suffered, to an extent exceeding our loss of equipment. In history, an invincible force, even one given to overconfidence, must consider carefully its inability to be invincible. But I'll join you shortly, and we shall sort this out."

Halifax, beside himself, spat out, "Winston, there shall be no sorting if you see what's in plain sight. It should be obvious even to a child."

With a calm manner, the inverted equal of the energy before him, Churchill addressed the distressed man, saying, "I've been called worse."

Halifax huffed a curious sound and stormed out with a death grip on the folders and papers under his arm, heading down the stairs.

Thomas watched the exchange, fading away from the dialog to a specific notion that entered his mind. The notion brought together the combined and considerable weight of all the experiences within his memory. "Of course," he thought. For some reason, it now all made sense. He must tell the prime minister before he goes into the meeting. There can be no other chances.

"Sir, could I have a minute alone?"

"Son, I don't have a minute. A fighter pilot I'm not, but currently, I have a ME109 on my tail that wishes me harm. Besides, you had considerable latitude earlier today. I listened to your theory. What more could you add?"

With his cane in hand, he reached for his bowler, starting out of the room.

Turning to Park, Churchill said, "I couldn't be more impressed with what I've seen today, and I extend the gratitude of the English people. Mr. Park, dawn and dusk have an eerily familiar look about them, save for one is the absence of darkness, and the other the absence of light. Be there no mistake, Mr. Park, at this moment, what may appear to be darkness before us is most assuredly giving way to the ascending light of justice."

Park looked at the man before him. "Thank you," was all he could say.

Thomas turned to Margaret quietly and said, "We need to talk to him now, alone, " before he steps into that room. It means everything. It's why we're here."

"We?" Margaret said.

"That's right. Exactly right. I've always known England needed to avoid surrendering at this critical time, and Churchill argued to continue. What I didn't know was why, in the short term, it was the correct choice. That's now very clear, and I need to tell him."

She looked into Thomas's eyes and saw power, confidence, and certainty. He wasn't searching for clarity as in many previous conversations. Without turning away from Thomas's face, she said, "Winnie?"

The man said, "Yes, my dear," in acknowledgment as he exited their small room.

"Thomas needs to tell you something new before you go into the meeting. I'm aware of the pressure you're under, and I'm not sure I've the right to ask this, but can you give him a minute before leaving?"

To Churchill, the tone was as unmistakable as it was wholly unrecognized. Gone was the little girl who had played the great man like a willing violin. Gone was the young woman who could coerce the smallest favor and generate the largest laugh with the twinkle of an eye. This woman sounded an awful lot like—her father.

He looked at Margaret, and in his gaze was respect. The young woman prone to defending contrary positions to prove a point was giving way to issues on a larger canvas.

"Please be brief," he said.

Thomas felt the pressure of the moment, but he also felt the disparate pieces coming together like a puzzle floating in the air. Could the following few seconds be the reason he'd mysteriously appeared? He was certain the moment was suspended in time, and Nature's laws dictated that the time would be brief.

"Sir, you're right about the Germans having also been damaged and having to reconsider their options. Upon the return of their planes, their combat assessment numbers, although inaccurate, will show they shot down more planes than we had in our total inventory. That means their plan of attacking the factories to stop the production of new planes has failed."

Churchill kept to his word, letting him talk.

"After the first attack," Thomas continued, "Göring and Hitler were unaware of the damage they've inflicted on the airfields and airplanes. The RAF is at its weakest point in the war, unable to defend against the planned second wave. Instead of sending the second wave, Hitler, thinking more robust measures were needed, made the biggest blunder of the war. Still enraged from the bombing of Berlin, Hitler redirected *all* bombing from factory and military targets to bombing civilians in

London, hoping the extensive loss of life and property would destroy the people's will.

"I'm sorry, Sir," Thomas said. "I know this takes more than a leap of faith, as I'm not sure the exact time he makes the decision. It could be just hours." Thomas took a breath that caused an unintended dramatic pause, "However, I'm absolutely certain this is a pivotal point—beyond imagine, for the entire world."

Churchill's face tightened. "I'm saddened at the thought of civilians bearing yet a greater burden. However, if what you say is true, while grievous, not bombing the airfields will provide time for the RAF to recover. It would take but a short time before they could be back to decent strength to defend the island."

"Yes, you have it," Thomas said. "Upon this realization, Hitler faces an irreversible situation and a fundamental equation. If he couldn't deliver a knockout blow to a staggering foe today, how could he defeat the same force he gave the opportunity to become stronger tomorrow?"

Churchill, prime minister of a staggering England, fully understood how the pieces fit. "It's an amazing failure," he said, "as it could well cost Hitler the war."

"Sir, it *does* cost him the war, as the island provides a platform for our invading Europe. Something that would be impossible from the shores of America."

Winston idly tapped the brim of his hat against his thigh. "If that decision is made based on the results of today's damage, this information isn't yet compiled and not known. We must conclude the decision has, in fact, not been made. Given simple logic, one must again ask how you could know this to be forthcoming?"

"That, sir, I can't explain."

"You mean you won't, again," Churchill said.

"No, sir, I can't. My best explanation is the information isn't mine; it belongs to history."

"I'm afraid, Mr. Watson, that history isn't the owner of anything but the keeper of the past and ..."

"...the steward of tomorrow," Thomas said.

The prime minister eyed the man before him. "Either way, young man, I must move those in attendance to persevere, for they're good men. Yet, to save King and country, they're determined to strike a deal with the devil at the expense of freedom."

"I can assure you," Thomas said, "God saves the King but employs your unique qualities to manage the mortals."

"Mr. Watson, what I know is you've been right more than you've been wrong. However, I've decided quite recently to fight and in any light persevere." The prime minister placed a hand on the side of Thomas's shoulder. With the slightest smile, he said, "Although, I might now fight a little harder."

Margaret threw herself at Churchill, wrapping her arms around his neck and giving him a peck on the cheek. "Winnie, thank you. Thank you for listening because I'm certain that once you have all the information, you always make the right decision."

Churchill's mind took him back to when he was first sea lord, to a critical discussion with a close confidant and friend. Now wrapped around him was little Margaret Hatcher, every bit his own daughter, having unknowingly quoted her own father.

The war cabinet members crowded into the conference room, each one making do without comment. The prime minister began.

"Distinguished gentleman, we have before us an issue of such gravity; never in the 1700 years of the British Empire could it have been imagined to even be upon us. In the following days, perhaps hours, our island nation and the commonwealth face a pivotal moment in history that will rearrange all the roads that lead to the future. It has come upon each of us in this room, all mortals to the core, to summon what Godlike manner we may possess as we determine the fate of our people.

"In a conflict mired in disastrous engagements, today has proven particularly eventful, as the enemy has administered a heavy blow. Lord Halifax, in his wisdom, has called a meeting of this cabinet to assess how it has affected our ability to protect our citizenry. At the outset, it's a position I wish to proclaim in the affirmative."

Halifax flew bolt upright from where he sat and, in a voice filled with insistence, said, "Mr. Prime Minister, given the losses sustained in today's engagements and the resulting inadequate readiness reports, how can you even entertain a positive position? Upon what scenario do you propose as to the future independence of the British Empire, except to needlessly sacrifice her people?"

Halifax held up the bound papers. "The briefest look at today's losses forces one to consider our pursuit of the best possible peace terms to save the monarchy and a civilization. England in this state can't defeat what's certainly an imminent invasion with massive loss of life."

Churchill responded, "I agree to your damaging list of our inadequacies but differ as to your dramatic and irreversible solution."

He looked at the members gathered at the table. "Regarding the items provided by my colleague, I wish to make a few points of my own. I must draw your attention to the fact that on this day, the Luftwaffe was dealt a bitter experience, and their losses parallel if not exceed ours. While it's true we can't sustain the loss rate that they appear to be adequately equipped to endure, they don't know this to be a fact. This places them quite literally in the dark as to our actual defensive position.

"In addition, I might add, our services have shown an extraordinary ability to recover from what might well be characterized as hopeless situations.

"Please add that we've confounded the German attempt to destroy the RAF at every turn and countered every tactic. I can assure you the mood in the Reichstag is most certainly a review of their plans. They're sure to include a change in some form, which we will counter again."

"Counter?" Halifax all but shouted. "Counter with what?"

Churchill, still standing, moved a closed fist pulling back his coat, and placed it on his hip. Leaning forward, he placed a finger on the table before him. He looked Halifax right in the eye, saying, "Counter with the spirit of a free people who've endured such circumstances that they should be given a further opportunity to defend their liberties. Privileges that have been their birthright, paid in sorrow and blood by their ancestors on virtually every continent. Privileges they've accepted the task of defending, as caretakers of their century, ensuring their children can continue to call this island free. That, my dear sir, is the counterweight to the heavy burden you so eloquently present at this hour.

"Lord Halifax, if we were to have processed your figures and fed them to logic, we would have ceased resisting at the fall of France, at the seemingly impossible effort before us at Dunkirk.

"What do we tell those boys who've fallen in a foreign land? That we bargained away the nation they defended with the ultimate sacrifice? At the very least, when it comes to our time to face the keeper of courage, they should insist on an effort proportionate to theirs. They should *insist* we show ourselves their equal. The mothers of those should equally insist, such that they'll have avenged their loss, and carry their heads high for the rest of their years.

"That gentlemen is what's right—not *easy*—but right."

Churchill paused, taking a breath. "Are we to *appease* yet again, before we have absolute proof of the intentions of the enemy? I say not! We must wait until Hitler makes his next move. It's not, as it has been suggested, ours to make, but most certainly his. I ask but for time, to let the enemy play their hand, before considering any form of capitulation."

Churchill looked at the faces around the table. In the silent countenances there was the fear of making the wrong decision, fear that the minute-by-minute account of the war surely to follow might place them on the wrong side of history. In the extreme, they faced a choice between holding out for freedom with the possible slaughter of a nation, or risking their survival under the subjugation of a race set to dominate the world.

With skills unequaled in the precise expression of thought, Churchill extended the dramatic moment. "Gentlemen, destiny is at a crossing point with the time behind yesterday on one side and the past of tomorrow on the other. A point where the sand in the hourglass is drawn tight, fused into a moment of neither. A singular moment in time, when a few able souls will, with the grace of God, write a history as benefits our land." He raised his voice as the words came to his lips. "You should not in your hearts consider that people shall be killed but that *freedom* shall die."

The men of the nation's war cabinet shifted in their chairs. Halifax could sense the change in the room, with Winston again using his gift of knowing exactly what to say, with an unequaled ability to say it. He knew he had to rebut the shift if he were to save a people who had endured great tragedy from yet more suffering. Halifax slammed closed the portfolio directly before him, the motion a preamble to his retaking the initiative.

As Halifax's actions changed the atmosphere of the room, Churchill sensed the moment to strike. He placed both hands flat on the tabletop and leaned forward from his position at the end of the long silent table. "Who then be ye? Who shall provide freedom to your children's children, as our grandfathers rendered liberty from lands afar? Let's come forth and be counted." With a master's touch, he'd changed the agenda at precisely the proper moment from continued debate to an immediate vote.

Churchill raised his voice slightly and increased the tempo. "Who's for waiting on the enemy to make their next move and, with steady hand, reacting to the new reality? *Which*, gentlemen, might well include the proposals presented by our distinguished Lord Halifax."

Halifax knew it was over; he hadn't carried the day, his disappointment matched only by the begrudging admiration of a master's skill. Churchill had worked the meeting into a delay. The man had also done so without directly confronting another cabinet member or eliminating the critical part of the opposing agenda.

There was little movement. After an eternity, Secretary Bragdon raised his hand, saying, "I'm for waiting a short bit, but no longer."

Bidden followed, saying "As am I."

Then there was an infinite moment of silence as not a cabinet member moved. Churchill looked at Shawston who owed his position to commitments made by Churchill concerning issues vital to the labor party.

Finally Shawston said, "I, too, am for waiting, as I can't go to the hospital and tell my son, who's alive and thus by proxy those who are not, we have surrendered without exhausting every possible angle."

That was four of seven and a simple majority was the rule. Halifax sat back in his chair. Churchill could feel the silent conflict inside the man as the full-blooded aristocrat faced yet another defeat from the poorly educated son of a minor politician.

The prime minister turned to the War Cabinet Secretary, seated against the wall away from the table. "As prime minister and, as such, chairman of the War Cabinet, I formally request Mr. Collins to notarize the vote and draw up the minutes with the appropriate copies."

Mr. Collins, schooled as an exacting solicitor, formally replied, "As per the vote herein, and directions of the prime minister of England, the preceding vote, authorizing an unspecified delay in peace negotiations with those that engage in war upon this nation, shall be entered into the record."

Churchill took in the moment from a mental space outside the room. He believed firmly in the course he proposed, but there where the conversations with Watson that gave him the innermost confidence to argue against the logic that was Halifax's case. If Watson was right, the next few hours would offer in a complete parcel: a devastating day for the population and redemption for the nation.

Chapter Ninety-Three

Turing Arrives

With the meeting still in progress, a spirited scene was evolving just outside the Cabinet room door, as Turing had arrived out of breath and in obvious stress.

"I have," he stopped to take a deeper breath, "just come from Bletchley and, thanks to Mr. Watson here, we've decoded a message almost as it arrived. It must be given to the prime minister immediately as the information isn't only timely but astronomic in its value."

Turing handed the note to Thomas. "It's all due to you, old man," Turing said, with a smile.

Thomas read the note.

Turing continued, "We were able to reset the machine quickly with the new patch cords installed. By the time we converted the message to the ticker tape, we were ready to go. The old girl took barely twenty minutes to spit out the gold. This will change everything."

Turing was obviously highly relieved at the result but equally concerned at the message. Thomas looked up from the note, also concerned.

Approaching the group, John Colville grabbed the note from Thomas, saying, "Give me that! This is a security breach, and I'll see you both to jail."

"Really," Turing said, pulling out his pipe. "How so, Mr. Colville? Without Watson here, there would be no message at all."

Thomas said, "Mr. Colville, you must interrupt the meeting without question. We must make sure Churchill is aware of all the facts. There's no other conceivable choice."

"I'll do no such thing, as I need an important signature to cause such a serious disruption. It's my job to make this call." Thrusting his arm outward and pointing directly down the hall, he shouted in a stage whisper, "Any more of this nonsense, and I'll have you both removed."

Thomas grew impatient, painfully aware that the meeting could conclude at any time. He wasn't sure why or how, but this was the moment it all came together. It was clear now: the meeting with Turing that generated the message, witnessing the day's battle, and his eventual success talking to Churchill before the meeting. It was, up to now, confusion in his brain, the unwanted thoughts, and un-remembered memories. The pain it had created for Margaret, let alone exposing her to danger.

Thomas's focus returned from a distance. Despite the current situation, he couldn't be positive about the meeting's outcome. With the context of the war's eventuality and knowing the price Margaret had paid, he turned to Churchill's trusted aide, saying, "Colville, don't be a bloody fool. Rome is burning, and you're majoring in minor things. Read the bloody message, for Christ's sake. If you don't take it in, I will."

Colville looked down at the message, saying, "If you do, you won't see the morning."

Thomas reached for the note and, as Colville felt it starting to slip from his fingers, tightened his grip, then let it go. Colville was stunned.

Turing, a step behind Thomas, moved forward. "Or, Mr. Colville, I will."

Colville looked past Thomas and saw Turing moving forward, looking straight into his eyes. He'd never seen the Turing before him.

"Jock, I mean it," Thomas said.

Colville was surprised at the informality. He noted the change of events in his mind since Watson had been lying on the floor next to his desk. He could call the security guards, causing a frantic reaction outside the door of a Cabinet meeting. He had the authority, but he would have to explain the consequences, and it would all come down to the message's contents.

"Mr. Colville," Margaret's much-needed calming voice said, "I can hardly believe that a man of your experience and responsibility would put regulations over what's surely critical information. The type that, I might add, could very well change the decisions behind that door. We all feel strongly; you must present it before the vote."

"What vote?" Colville said.

"Halifax wants to sue for peace," Margaret said.

Thomas was surprised at her being so confident. He felt she'd never really accepted the notion of his being here.

"That's it then," Colville thought. Whatever magical power little Miss Margaret had over the prime minister would be his protective cover. Without a word and almost relieved at his choice, he put his hand on the doorknob and slowly turned it while tapping ever so slightly on the door.

Inside the Cabinet room, with the vote finished, Churchill was still taking in the position he'd carved for himself, a path for which there was neither return nor one desired. At that moment, he heard a faint, reluctant tap on the door behind him.

Halifax's frustration had been looking for a target, and it found one.

"Good God, Mr. Prime Minister, it appears you're managing your staff with the same competence you employ running this war." He stood up theatrically, gathering his briefing material.

The prime minister turned to the noise and saw an extended hand holding a note and half Colville's face obscured by the door. The man whispered his sincere apologies. As soon as Churchill grabbed the message, Colville disappeared.

Colville was still holding onto the knob of the closed door; he spit out, "You, or we, could all hang for this."

Thomas, now far more relaxed, offered, "Surely, given what's occurring behind those doors, you've completely missed the irony of that statement. Without that information, we may hang anyway."

Churchill let the message fall to his side in much the same way he had when he received the message of the bombing in Amersham. It was again a stunning turn of events.

Churchill faced the group. "Gentlemen, may I have a moment."

Lord Halifax, and his fellow cabinet members, sat as Churchill read the words from the pasted strips of stock printing paper.

Führer Headquarters
17 September 1940

TOP SECRET

The Führer
OKW/WFSt/Op.No. 662552/43 g.K. Chefs

To Reich Marshal Goering,

Operation Sea Lion was to commence upon establishing control of the airspace over the channel and southern coastline. This hasn't

occurred, nor does it appear imminent. Therefore, Operation Sea Lion is postponed until after the Eastern campaign. Hereby you're ordered to immediately redirect the full fury of the forces, at your command, directly upon the civilian population of England.

Adolf Hitler

Prime Minister Winston Churchill folded the note and placed it in his pocket. It wouldn't take long to determine if the message was real and not subterfuge.

"Gentlemen, history has seen to it our humble souls shall remain in her graces. With this order, Hitler has abandoned the invasion and will concentrate on conquering the will of our people. There's no need, I'm sure, to point out the RAF will take full advantage of such valuable, and in human terms, costly, time it has been given."

A cabinet member removed his glasses, and wiped them with his handkerchief. Halifax was still standing by his chair with his notebooks under his arm. Mr. Shawston was holding back a certain tear in the silence, as the weight of the moment was indeed the same as the world.

Churchill was the first from the room. As the door closed, he could hear the voice of an agitated Halifax arguing about the veracity of the message.

The prime minister addressed the group gathered just outside the door, locking eyes with Thomas. "The cabinet," Churchill said, "had voted to persevere just as the message arrived. Had they not, I'm sure the message would have changed their minds."

"It might be the message wasn't needed after all," Thomas said with a smile. "It would appear the result rested on a dominant figure with a particular set of skills laying out a plan for victory, and skillfully selling it to those who had accepted defeat. It is, however, my personal opinion that throughout the war your tenacious grip on the idea of victory virtually pulls it from the nether realm into existence. I believe they call this an important moment in history, certainly in the twentieth century."

"A moment—indeed," Churchill said. They looked at each other, having reached a mutual understanding. Churchill said, "We've much to talk about, Mr. Watson."

Margaret looked at the prime minister addressing her Thomas with a smile.

"Mr. Watson, it has been a long day for all. I believe you need to take this precious lass home for some rest."

"I'm so very proud of you," Margaret said. She followed with "Mr. Prime Minister."

Winston thought of the work the Hatcher companies had done for the country and, in particular, Turing's indispensable project. He held up the note. "It's not like you didn't have a role, my dear, regardless of the size or its effect." Puzzled by the comment, Margaret's face drew a confused frown, but she decided to stay quiet.

He continued, "Mr. Colville shall arrange a security detail to take you directly back to your mother's, where you'll be safe, as there are still a few things that need to be straightened out." Churchill was thinking of Petrie's report on the rogue Russian agent and Yuri's declining to come in for protection.

"Look, Muffy," Churchill called out; it had been his pet name for Margaret since she was a child.

"Oh, no," Margaret said at hearing the name. "There's never good to come out of this."

"That's all the excitement I'll be allowing you today. Your safety is heavy on my mind."

Margaret wasn't convinced, "Is it my beauty sleep or my safety that concerns you—you can't have both."

He returned a stern "do as you're told" look, and drifted off to look at the end of his cigar.

"I don't think a caravan is necessary," Watson said, "but I would appreciate you getting us back to your office, where my car can take us back."

"Why is it that I've managed a great empire in times of war but can't control the two of you? No, straight back to safety, and your car will be there shortly after you arrive. Now off with you two." He looked at Thomas and said, "Mr. Colville? Our Mr. Watson will call tomorrow morning for an appointment, as we've many things to discuss. Let's see if we can fit him in."

"Yes, sir," Colville said, thinking appointments were becoming a waste of time, as once formalized, they were subject to the whims of anyone.

Churchill then addressed Colville directly. "And knowing you struggled with the decision to interrupt the meeting, let me say you did the right thing. It took a lot of internal fortitude to make the right decision, and that's why you're so valuable. Now, please take these two and get them home."

"Mr. Colville, I believe all's well that ends well," Margaret said with a smirk.

"Yes, Miss Hatcher," he said through tense lips as he passed her. "Please follow me so we can get you going."

Margaret, very pleased with the situation, slapped Thomas on the back and pointed her nose in the air as she grabbed his arm.

Chapter Ninety-Four

Going Home

The sun was low as Margaret and Thomas drove through the town. As instructed, the driver took the most direct route back to the Hatcher Estate. They were well outside the Uxbridge compound as they passed through a peaceful residential area—small town, not on any target list, that appeared little bothered by a world in turmoil. As shopkeepers pulled shades and locked doors, Margaret noticed the almost complete absence of damage or evidence of war. It all could have been a picture taken any time in the last fifty years. From the backseat, Margaret made a note of the large man in the passenger seat, concluding that all the men detailed to the security service were large. She also decided they needed bigger cars, as he definitely looked uncomfortable.

Thomas was thinking of the other problems he'd created, having accomplished his primary objective at the Cabinet meeting. Viktor was out of the picture, but that Yuri person was still out there. In addition, they'd have to get Mrs. Somerville somewhere safe until all this was clear. He thought of Margaret's narrow escape in her house—their house.

Thomas held Margaret's hand during the contemplative silence. "Thanks for your help back there with Uncle Winnie. It was really important."

"Of course, it was, although I didn't know it then. Did you know all along?"

"Heavens no, but in the last two days, things have been getting clearer, then just before the meeting, it all came together. Why we're together, and what was going to happen. I don't think I'll ever be able to explain it, and that's what he'll ask me tomorrow. Hopefully, it's not with a bunch of generals sitting around."

Margaret laughed. "Oh, Thomas, I can see them now. Harrumphing with nervous coughs with the crossing and uncrossing of polished boots. God, that's going to be funny. What's not so funny is it will need to be addressed."

Thomas looked up. "While you were talking, I had a thought. Churchill could wave his wand, make me a state secret, and not have to deal with me at all."

"You were thinking while I was talking?"

"Well, not really," he said. "The thought was riding on your thoughts, which I wouldn't have had without your talking."

"You're so full of your own nonsense; you're not sure of anything."

"No, that's not true. I *am* sure of one thing," Thomas said.

"Penny, for your riding thoughts," she said with a great big grin that barely fit on her face.

"That's easy." He squeezed her hand and said, "I love you. Please promise you'll *never* leave me."

"Oh, Thomas, you can be such a romantic, and girls eat it up, but I'm worried about you. Besides, given your unstable memory, and questionable knowledge that shouldn't exist, I'm not sure what promise I'm making. So *never* is a situation that really can't be..."

Thomas placed a hand on either side of her face, pulled her close, and kissed her until she started to push him away. With her mouth pressed against Thomas's lips, she mumbled, "Ahawwright" and pulled away. "This is the back seat of a car, and I'm not that kind of..."

Glass exploded into the car from the back window. Margaret could feel it hit her hair and face as she felt Thomas grab her violently. A second explosion got the driver's side and front windscreen. Thomas threw Margaret down on the floor between the seats, hearing her make a noise.

"Are you alright?" he said.

"Yes," she said. "Thomas, what's happening?"

"I don't know."

Thomas raised his head just above the seats and saw the driver slumped forward onto the steering wheel. The car veered to the left with a severe jolt and went over the curb, crashing through a front display window. The car stopped well into a clothing shop located on a corner. Additional glass cascaded over the car's hood and firmly implanted into the car's front grill, as was the window's display dress. Margaret felt blood drip onto her hand from her head as she lie on the floor.

The agent on the passenger side yelled for them to stay down as he tried to open the door on his side. Heaving his weight, he pushed aside a small display case jammed against the door. Accessing his weapon, he half rolled out the opening, keeping low, and close to the car. Thomas heard another series of shots, followed by the metallic sound of the agent's gun hitting the shop floor. Thomas could hear the agent cry out in pain.

Thomas opened his reverse rear door. The front door partially shielded the agent. Keeping it fully open with his right hand, Thomas reached down with his left to pull the agent closer to the car while trying to stay below the window level.

"*Thomas*," Margaret yelled, reaching out to him from the floor inside the car.

Thomas tried to discern the location of the shooter, or shooters, to determine where they could take cover. Another shot rang out. He felt the force on the door he was holding open. He looked back out the rear window and saw two men crouched low, running up the other side of the street. Thomas reached over and picked up the agent's gun. The driver hadn't moved, and the agent at his feet were not responsive. Thomas looked at the weapon, recognizing it as a Walther PPK. "Light and small," he thought. "Exactly why the agents carry them." He looked around, listened, and reviewed his options.

Surely outnumbered and remembering the incident in the park, he made his decision. He grabbed Margaret's still outstretched hand, saying, "Stay right here. Don't run or move; do you hear me? I'm the one they want. I can get them to follow me away from here. You call security on the car radio or phone when they come after me. Tell them to get here fast."

"No," Margaret said.

Thomas continued, "When I lose them, I'll come back to here or call in from somewhere to let you know where I am. It's going to be alright if you do as I say."

In forceful tones, Margaret looked up with her standard determined look and said, "Thomas Watson, there's no way in bloody hell you're leaving me. We're staying together. You can't fight those men. You're a schoolteacher, a professor."

Thomas reached down. Margaret was dumbfounded as he gently put his finger on her lips, making a hissing sound to be quiet. Something only her father had ever done after having heard quite enough from his daughter. Until now, he'd been the only one who dared try.

"You're whip bright, Hatcher. Now be sensible. This is the only way." Thomas set the safety on the PPK and dropped the clip on the handgun into his hand. "Full," he thought. Eight in the clip and one in the chamber if he remembered right. Seating the clip back up, he heard its click. He turned the safety off and placed it in his outside coat pocket. He saw the stunned look on Margaret's face.

"Look, I know what I'm doing," Thomas said. "I can't explain now, but I'm positive it's the only way."

Another shot hit his door. "Look, everything is going to be all right. I'm not going to lose you after finally *finding* you." Then with a smile, he said, "After all, I love you, and that's all we need."

In addition to being scared, Margaret was now confused. "Thomas was looking for *me*?" She thought.

A car coming down the street slowed, thinking it was an accident. The driver ducked down in the seat, stopping right behind the crashed vehicle in the store. Thomas bolted from behind the door and, using the new car for protection, ran toward the corner just twenty feet away.

Margaret saw the four men running and yelling in what she thought was Russian. She couldn't believe Thomas was gone. Her hand wiped her brow of blood. Slowly, she looked out the open rear window, now deprived of glass. Thomas was right; she was helpless and hated it.

Having turned the corner, Thomas could feel the gun bounce against his side as he ran. He sprinted as fast as he could, knowing he would be a target as soon as they turned the corner.

Seeing the shooters run past, the driver in the new car looked into the store. He saw Margaret looking out the rear of the disabled vehicle.

He shouted, "I'm sure they're gone, but stay down," his hand motioning his directions." Noticing the blood on her forehead, he quickly added, "Are you all right?"

Margaret Hatcher was dumbfounded to silence as she nodded at the man.

Standing in a covered entry, Thomas waited for the men to round the corner. He pulled the gun out of his jacket and waited. It took a second or two longer than he estimated, and for a moment, he wondered if they'd stayed with Margaret. Soon enough, a figure appeared, and then another, and Thomas, lying in wait, pointed the gun upward and squeezed the trigger. At the sound of the shot, the men retreated out of sight. Thomas set the safety. Knowing he had them in tow, he raced for the next corner. There were four of them, and one obvious voice of authority was yelling in Russian. Oddly, the man in charge wore several bandages and limped slightly when trying to run. Thomas thought he recognized the voice, but at this point, it didn't matter who was chasing him. Instinctively, he knew they couldn't get off an accurate shot while running. The solution, of course, was one of them would stop and take aim while the others continued the chase, and they'd rotate. Another strange piece of information appearing when the circumstance presented itself. He was hoping the pack chasing him wouldn't figure it out.

Thomas knew the pursuer was at a disadvantage in a chase like this. They must defensively advance, wary of places for the victim to hide along the way. On the other hand, the pursued had the advantage, as their only concern was where they were going. In this case, Thomas stayed in sight to draw them away from Margaret. The tactic kept him from increasing the distance, but he had no choice. The chase continued for several blocks into a residential area, and the exertion became a factor. Down yet another street, he knew the tension in his chest would restrict his air intake, and he consciously tried to breathe deeply.

Now a safe distance away from Margaret, Thomas knew his tactics had to change. He stopped behind a parked car on the street, reached into his pocket, and released the safety. Thomas leaned on the bonnet, placed his hand down on the flat surface, and placed the gun's handle in his palm. He took aim at the opposite corner, drew a long breath, and slowly let it out. He took a shot at the first thing that appeared. One of the men grabbed his thigh, shouting. The others had to scurry for cover. With that, Thomas was off onto the street at the end of the alley. It was now three to one.

Thomas arrived at a series of shops. Several had taken deliveries, which sat on the sidewalk. In front of one were several large wooden crates stacked one on top of another, about three feet square. They were about six feet high in front of the store, offering solid cover and an advantageous angle of fire. He quickly concluded it was the best place for the next hit-and-run.

Thomas took cover behind the boxes. Out of sight, he could hear the men as they turned, coming down the street from his right. He then heard more orders shouted from up the street. In a gamble, they'd split up and guessed right. There was no way he could have known, and now they were two approaching from the left and one from the right, with nowhere for him to go. He couldn't move without coming into the sight of three guns. Soon they'd start the search. The options were few, and little time remained.

The Russian issuing commands shouted at one man, motioning for him to come closer. In a moment of confusion, Thomas recognized the distinctive sound of Viktor's voice, and his heart dropped. Viktor wasn't a thug.

Thomas thought, "If the Russians want me out of the way, getting me out of the country would be impossible." That meant they'd have to kill him.

Leaning against the crates, Thomas noticed three large windowpanes across the front of the shop right behind him. For an instant, his movements reflected in the glass and caught his eye. He was crouched down low, balancing on his toes, and put his hand on the glass to steady himself. He realized his reflection in the glass might have betrayed his position. It worsened a bad situation, but it would have to do for now, as he was stuck with his choice.

The shooters were converging on his position. He realized that this was, in one way, a welcome sight. It meant, hopefully, Margaret ran safely in the other direction. He looked at the gun in his hand, knowing it was useless. You can only shoot one or two before the third person reacts. He thought of Margaret and that he would die not seeing her again. His heart dropped at the thought. He'd promised to meet her later, but he knew things were about to end. What *was* clear was dying wasn't as important as losing the love of his life.

Thomas moved slightly, trying to stay out of direct sight of each of the three men, but it was becoming impossible.

He heard Viktor say, "Find him, you fools. He has to be close and hiding."

He moved again, and Viktor pointed, yelling, "He's behind the boxes, those boxes," he said, pointing. "Don't shoot. He's mine."

Viktor was only fifty feet away now, running in the open without regard to his safety. Thomas saw Viktor approach with a reddened face and heavy breathing. Now only twenty feet away, Viktor was momentarily distracted by the reflection in the window.

Viktor pulled the trigger, and Thomas heard the sound of glass shattering; then there was another shot, and Thomas saw Viktor's knees buckle. Viktor's gun hand went limp, dropping the pistol, and his other hand grabbed the sacred place above his heart. He fell to the ground, heavily, with the additional burden of his evil history. Thomas hurried, trying to stand, losing his footing and falling backward.

The other Russian agents saw Viktor fall. Running up, one of the agents nervously looked down at Viktor, lying in the street, moments from dying.

He said to the other agent, "Viktor was an idiot bent on death and finally succeeded. That doesn't mean we have to die here."

The sounds of sirens were close, and a patrol car appeared up the street.

The agent said, "We have to get out of here now. We can still do Moscow's bidding, but this situation has grown too dangerous."

The other agent said, "You're right. Let's get out of here."

Lying face down on the street, Viktor knew the direction of the shot. He managed to lift his head and locked eyes with the shooter. He realized the flaw in his plans.

Behind a small mountain of debris, Yuri Ivanovich Stakova looked over the barrel of Pavel's pistol and into the soul of a man who had played the game and lost. Viktor, for a brief second, as time slowed before the moment of death, would know who brought him to his end. Viktor fought to maintain his hate-filled stare as long as he could. It was the last thing that lit his mind; the slow descent of his head measured his life drifting away. Fighting to the last inch, Viktor's face finally touched the paving stones, and his body went limp.

Yuri exhaled, saying, "Grant to no one but what you wish."

Yuri saw Viktor's agents running the other way. He didn't recognize them, but that wasn't a surprise. He'd patiently followed Margaret and Thomas, knowing Viktor wouldn't be far behind and would eventually show his hand. Yuri had fulfilled his promise to ensure the couple's safety by protecting his own. It's what a professional would do. Sadly, Thomas and Margaret would spend the rest of their lives thinking he was the enemy. With a half-smile, Yuri thought of the irony.

For a brief second, Yuri thought about running to see if Thomas was OK, but the local officials were exiting the car. Yuri had his own set of problems now. If arrested, the local officials could inform Moscow, and he would be a dead man.

It was time to set in motion his plan of escape. A private plane would meet him at an airfield and take him far out over the Atlantic to Portugal. He would then transfer to a commercial flight to Morocco, where a neutral freighter would take him to a safe destination for the remainder of the war. "American food," Yuri thought. He objected to the two words used together as he curled his lip in a snobbish flair. Yuri had made many contacts during his long career and had called in favors. The United States was warm and out of harm's way, but it wouldn't erase the unusual story he would leave behind. The very curious Thomas Watson would haunt his thoughts for a long time.

Chapter Ninety-Five

December 31, 1989
Caribbean Sea
Voyager of the Sea Cruise Liner
New Year's Eve

Something didn't feel right. Thomas grabbed the rail of the cruise liner to steady himself, feeling a little light-headed. He looked down at the fast, powerful water flowing past the ship's sides. It appeared to him that the boat wasn't moving, but the water was rushing to unknown places. The wind hit the left side of his face, a gentle touch of reality. He knew his mind wasn't right and wondered if the moving water disoriented his thinking. Standing out here wasn't the way the evening was supposed to end.

He thought, "Wasn't he supposed to meet someone?"

He felt a profound and utter sense of deep loss. A story that shouldn't end. His distracted mind could hear the muffled laughter and music from the New Year's Eve party inside.

Gripping the rail harder, he tried to make sense of the remorse that sat heavily in the pit of his stomach. It felt like the most significant gift imaginable was missing, and a giant unfilled space remained in the middle of his heart. Unconnected images were flying through his mind like an exploding building, heat against his face, and a beautiful room with sunshine and flowers. Thomas almost felt he was holding his life's love in his arms under a large tree. The thoughts and feelings were real but beyond his current reality.

The uncertain and surreal thoughts made him think it was a dream. Thomas squeezed his eyes shut, trying to focus his mind.

Then, from behind, he heard a woman's voice say, "Hey, are you the good Thomas or the bad Thomas?"

He turned to the sound and saw the woman with the flowing dress on the dance floor. He remembered the feelings of disappointment at her going away. Thomas wanted to ask where she'd gone. What was her name?

He thought, "Wait, her name was Margaret."

Thomas saw Margaret walk out onto the ship's deck, crossing her arms against the cool air. Her hair and that magical dress were swaying with the random breezes. She was the essence of absolute beauty, but he felt he'd lost her.

Although unsure of his thoughts, Thomas felt drawn to where she stood. What was he going to say?

Thomas said, "Well, I think I'm the good Thomas."

She said, "That's the right answer because that's who I was looking for."

At that moment, Thomas felt himself being drawn back to visions of being chased, hearing gunshots, and running. He thought he heard Margaret say, "Thomas can you hear me?" But she didn't say it.

Was he now hearing things? He shook his head as if nothing was making sense

Thomas had closed the distance; they were now standing very close. He couldn't explain the changed feelings since she floated away on the dance floor. Sometime between then and now, they'd gone from a flirting attraction to absolute desire and love.

She moved even closer. She placed her hand on Thomas's coat, on the space above his heart. Pulling her in, he felt them both drawn back to…an unclear somewhere.

"Did I lose you?" He asked.

She giggled, "No, you didn't; you wouldn't be that lucky.

He said, "Then what's happening?"

She smiled, "It could be a dream."

Thomas said, Well, one thing is certain, we'll have a future together; I just don't know where or when?

She looked up again with delight and said, "Well, in that case, big boy, the rest is history."

THE END

"The farther backward you can look,
The farther forward you're likely to see."
– Sir Winston Churchill

Follow Margaret and Thomas and their London
adventures in the next book, including the
characters you've enjoyed. A brief description
follows.

TARGET LONDON

A New German Secret Weapon
A High Stakes Battle For Survival

In the WWII sequel to Behind Yesterday, Thomas Watson, gifted with a unique memory of the future, helps discover the existence of a new German secret weapon. This new science dramatically increases the accuracy of the already deadly German bombing campaign.

Winston Churchill urgently assigns Watson and a team of scientists to develop a countermeasure to save the only factory building Spitfires and even greater damage to London. The high-stakes effort involves some of the brightest minds in the empire and an impossible timeline.

Failure to meet this challenge gives the Germans air superiority and will result in Hitler's immediate order to invade England.

You'll love this story if you like plot twists, suspense, and mystery.

Re-released 3-28-2023 Re-Edited by Kelli McMaster.

I live with my family in the Bay Area in Northern California, and writing came to me late in life. It's now something I look forward to doing every day. The comments I receive make it a labor of love. I would be very interested in what you think of this story, and thank you for supporting my writing. You can find more information on my other books and a contact form on my website.

FOLLOW THIS LINK TO MY WEBSITE

https://richardDtaylor.com

Sign up for my newsletter for news and upcoming release dates on my upcoming books.

FOLLOW THIS LINK TO SUBSCRIBE.

https://landing.mailerlite.com/webforms/landing/n0o5d3

Please let your friends know and consider writing an online review or star rating if you enjoyed reading this book. Writers live by reviews as they help us evaluate the writing from the readers' comments, and we get to see what you enjoyed in the story. The market for books is very competitive, so the opinions shared by people are very important. If you would like to write a review or leave a rating, you can select the link below, and it'll take you directly to Amazon and a review form for this book.

FOLLOW THIS LINK TO SUBMIT A RATING

https://www.amazon.com/review/createreview?&asin=%20B09C3ZWNQN

ADDITIONAL BOOKS BY
RICHARD D TAYLOR

Enjoy a sample of Geneva Intrusion.

GENEVA INTRUSION
A Kate Adler Book # 1

**IRAN WANTS TO START A WAR HIJACKING TANKERS. KATE
ADLER ESCAPES AN ASSASSINATION ATTEMPT AND IS
RUNNING FOR HER LIFE TOWARDS A BIG SURPRISE.**

CHAPTER—1

BOARDING THE *MONTCLAIR STAR* — THURSDAY PM

Panama-flagged oil tanker *Montclair Star*
Location: The Persian Gulf, 25 miles off the coast of Iran.
US Fifth Fleet in the area

"Pirates, pirates on port side," Juarez, a deck hand, breathlessly shouted as he careened up the stairs to the bridge.

Captain Carlino Bertucci, standing on the tanker *Montclair Star*'s bridge wing, was aware of the situation. A man with twenty-four years' experience, he was tracking the pirates on radar and concentrating on the small boat through his binoculars. He lowered the glasses, walked into the wheelhouse, and quickly radioed the US Maritime Administration emergency group.

"Mayday. Mayday. Mayday. This is the *Montclair Star*. Hijacking in progress. Request any aid. Coordinates 26 degrees 30 minutes by 53 degrees 15 minutes, course 135, speed 19 knots."

"*Montclair Star*, this is the warship *USS Connolly*. We copy your transmission," said the young ensign on the Arleigh Burke-class destroyer. "Relaying your information to coalition channels now."

"They're on approach, situation is critical, *Montclair* out," Bertucci said, leaving the channel open.

Five men in a small, sea-worn skiff violently attacked the choppy waves fighting their way towards the massive oil tanker in the Strait of Hormuz. The leader, a large man, stood at the front with knees bent, absorbing the powerful surges of the bow as it dove deep into the water then thrust upward. He studied the distance as they approached the plodding behemoth. It required his total concentration to maintain his balance atop the erratically battered boat. Drawing his forearm across his face once again failed to wipe away the saltwater stinging his eyes. A fatigued AK-47, whose violent history would never be known, lay at his feet covered in the spray that filled the air.

"Faster," the leader shouted, "faster." The skiff suddenly shifted starboard under his feet, causing him to slam his foot against the outboard rail to stay aboard. He looked disdainfully at the frail young man soaked to the core, trying to control the screaming outboard motor. "Keep her steady, or we lose speed," he yelled with a wave of his arm. Eyes fixed on the tanker, he waited until the last moment to pick up the semi-automatic rifle.

Bertucci walked over to the wall speaker and pushed the ship's PA button. "This is the captain, pirates alongside, this is not a drill, repeat this is not a drill." With the ship's phone in his hand, he selected the engine room and said, "Banoy, you heard the announcement, pirates will attempt to board. Give me all the speed you have."

Banoy said, "Do you authorize full ahead?"

"Yes," the captain yelled to his chief engineer, "do it *now*."

The radio speaker came alive. "This is the warship *USS Connolly* to the *Montclair Star*; what is your status, over?"

Bertucci looked over the port side wing and saw a man on the skiff below with a gun pointed directly at the bridge. "Everyone down," he shouted, taking an awkward dive for the floor as bullets pinged off the outside of the bridge.

On the *Connolly*, the ensign turned to his captain. "No response, sir, but I heard automatic gunfire."

The *Connolly*'s captain turned to the executive officer and said, "Get a helo in the air, and you," he pointed at another ensign, "turns for flank speed and, navigator, get me to their position."

"Yes, sir," was the reply from each of the crewmen.

The craft was still trying to gain on the tanker as it fought against the dangerous waves generated off the enormous ship's bow. The leader put down the AK-47 and picked up a Soviet-made grenade launcher. Holding it up to his eye, he observed the larger ship move in and out of the weapon's sight and fired.

The unstable platform on which he stood caused the grenade to errantly head for the upper corner of the superstructure, where it entered the side window of the bridge and went out the front without an explosion. Glass rained down on the *Montclair*'s bridge crew.

Captain Bertucci commanded the helmsman, "Hard-a-port," attempting to run into the smaller craft, making it more difficult to board.

Bertucci's voice was tense as he turned to his first mate. "Let's get those jets on." The man moved swiftly to the control panel and threw the master switch. "Jets on," he shouted as the four-inch water jets around the ship created a non-lethal means of making it more difficult for the pirates to make it to the ladder from their small craft.

Just then, automatic gunfire came in the open door. The captain watched as the overhead exploded in a sequential pattern of bullets above him. He looked at his crew face down on the deck.

"Change that order," he said to the first mate. "Get your men to the citadel. Leave the jets on."

The first mate rushed everyone off the bridge and into the companionway.

"All hands to the citadel — *now*," Bertucci said over the PA. He then picked up the telephone. "Banoy," he said, "shut down the engines and electrical power and get your guys to the safe room."

"Aye, sir," Banoy responded.

Another cartridge-full of ammunition came up from below, pinging off the outside hull and taking out more glass. Bertucci, on his knees, could feel his heart pounding as he turned the dial on the ship's safe. He pulled at the door and grabbed the ship's log. Bent over, he exited the bridge descending five flights of stairs into a room designed to deny the pirates the leverage of hostages. They knew untrained pirates could not start the engines, and short of an explosive charge applied to the hatch, they were reasonably safe. They expected the pirates to leave once they realized time was short, help was on the way, and that they could not navigate the ship to a friendly port.

Bathed in the water from the jets, the leader motioned for a crewmember to throw up the ladder. The third try caught the tanker's bulwark. He and his four men ascended the ladder, all barefoot and dressed in the typical Somali pirates' threadbare clothing. Clearing the bulwark, the men took cover behind a raised oil tank access hatch and, from the duffel bag, unwrapped four KL-7.62 semi-automatic assault rifles from their waterproof covers, several flash/smoke grenades, extra ammunition, and a medical backpack. The lead man felt the engine's muted vibration under his feet come to a stop, and the noise generated by the defensive water jets fade as they shut down. The five men moved quickly towards the main superstructure in practiced precision. The trailing two men concentrated on the superstructure's gangways, with the rest looking for any threat at deck level. Silently and methodically making their way to their destination.

Seconds later, the five men stood on the port bridge wing just outside the pilot house. The group leader, gun at his shoulder, nodded as one of his men pulled open the hatch to the wheelhouse. A second man rolled a flash/smoke grenade into the room. Their backs were against the outside bulkhead as it went off. The leader entered, quickly swinging his gun's barrel into the space, ready to open fire. Two men who covered the right and left sides of the area immediately followed him. It was unoccupied. Not surprised, the leader knew the crew would be locked away but was trained not to take any chances. The smoke that hung in the air streamed towards the broken windows and outside as if needed elsewhere.

Silently he pointed at one of the men who went over to the helmsman's console. Looking at the dark gauges, which showed no sign of damage, the man nodded his head, indicating everything seemed okay. The leader turned to another man also at the console, looking at a sheet with the new coordinates. He motioned for them to stay. Both men pulled on latex gloves before they touched anything. He nodded for the other two men to follow him.

Having previously studied the ship's layout, they proceeded directly down to the engine room, guns raised around every corner, expecting the unexpected. As they approached the engine room, one of the men had another flash-bang grenade ready. The group leader looked through the round window in the hatch and found the room empty. He waved his hand at the grenade, and the man put it away. As the door opened, they all entered the dimly lit, pale green engine control room. There was a shadowy quiet and the thick and stale air smelled of diesel. Large windows overlooked the massive silent engines in the dark room two decks below as the start team technician stood at the engineering console. With an assistant, his job was to start the engines. He surveyed the panel and nodded to the group leader with thumbs-up.

Finally, alone, the group leader turned to the start team and spoke aloud in a Persian dialect. "Time for you to do your job. Let me know when you're ready." The start team put their guns down, and the still-armed leader moved to the entrance door to protect their position.

The assistant pulled on his latex medical gloves as he approached the thirty-foot-long gray control panel that resembled a lineup of ten tall refrigerators, each with a withering array of gauges and dials. He came to a stop in front of the electrical generator module. He pulled open his vest and extracted two plastic-covered sheets of instructions. As he looked at the papers, he flipped the breaker switches in the proper sequence and watched the red status lights turn green. He pulled down on the master handle and heard the generators restart. Their eyes adjusted as the regular lights took over from the dim battery-powered lights.

"Electrical on," the assistant said.

"Check," said the tech as he stared at the control console indicator lights.

More switches set by the assistant started to bring up the hydraulic and lube oil pressure.

"Check again," the tech said, monitoring the pressure gauges.

Moving down the control panel, throwing another multi-breaker switch sequence started the air compressor. The tech watched the indicator on the control panel rise to 128 PSI. He checked the fuel flow indicator and several other gauges and said, "Check, starting main engine one." He held down the large red button labeled "M/E One Start" until the green light above it came on. The deck vibrated beneath their feet as the room filled with the groans and deep moans of a powerful giant awakened. The same sequence was employed to the "M/E Two Start" button and so on until all three engines were idling.

"Normal idle in three minutes," he said to the group leader at the door.

"Good," the group leader said. "Full ahead when you're ready. Lock the door behind me. I will be on the bridge. Don't forget, nothing is to be left behind when you leave. Wipe down any questionable areas."

"Yes, Captain," both men said. The tech looked at his assistant and then put his hand on the maneuvering handle that engaged the propeller shafts and looked at the maneuvering chart that said Max 105, Full 95, half 65. After four minutes and with full green indicators, he moved the handle slowly, first to 65 RPM. The tech felt the additional vibration on the console and in the room, as the noise level rose significantly. The immense vessel was now ready for its new heading.

GET YOUR COPY OF GENEVA INTRUSTION TODAY.
https://www.amazon.com/dp/B09C3ZWNQN

Enjoy a sample of Primary Protocol.

PRIMARY PROTOCOL

A Kate Adler Book # 2

WITH 70,000 LIVES AT STAKE, KATE ADLER AND THE CARTEL RUSH TO STOP AN ATTACK ON THE FRENCH NATIONAL STADIUM

A page-turning suspense terrorist thriller that delivers constant surprises.

CHAPTER—1

Vianden Castle Luxembourg

The confidential referral was from *Tangent Day,* the code name for Martin Alejandro Perez, President of the United States. Brad Danner sat at his desk in Vianden Castle in Luxembourg, headquarters of the secretive Cartel, waiting for a call from the French ambassador to Mali. A unique referral was required before anyone could directly contact the Cartel, and *Tangent Day* was about as unique as it got.

The ambassador's call would almost certainly involve a problematic issue needing a somewhat unconventional solution. The kind of solution where a national power would find their options limited due to the restrictions of law or convention. For the past two years, Brad managed the outside world's contacts for the organization and contributed as a special advisor to Kate Adler, the acting chair. Out of college, he joined the military for action, but his computer skills landed him in an intelligence tent at Bagram Air Base. The experience qualified him later to be a bodyguard to Kate in what was supposed to be an NSA intelligence center in Munich. The problem was Kate didn't know about the arrangement, which resulted in a rocky start to their relationship. Kate was his boss, having taken over the Cartel two years ago, fulfilling her late father's wish to further the group's agenda into the future. She was flying in today from New York. She would undoubtedly want an update on the ambassador's call.

The phone vibrated on the hard surface spinning on its axis as its bright screen lit the dark lampshade above it. He picked it up and entered the "one-time" code into the touchscreen.

"Hello, this is agent 2810. Can I help you?" Brad said in a balanced voice.

"This is Renee Magnant, French Ambassador to the Mali Republic."

"Madam Ambassador, I want to thank you for your call, and I must tell you this conversation will be recorded and available only to those in the Cartel."

"I would hope so because if it gets out, I'm dead. Who is this I'm calling? Who is the Cartel?"

"We are someone your referral thought could help in some way."

"Well, that was evasive enough," she said. "I will get right to it. I have information regarding a probable terrorist attack and have not been able to convince anyone it's real. I guess you are my last chance at avoiding a disaster."

"We will certainly do what we can to help."

"I don't need help. I need a miracle. As you know, at the request of the Mali government, the French military came in, confronted, and defeated a terrorist group named Ansar Dine. They killed all the leaders except a man named Mokhtar Belmokhtar. I have it on good authority that Mokhtar's group, and several other offshoots located in Southern Libya, Tunisia, and the northern parts of Niger, have formed an alliance."

"What sort of an alliance?"

"An alliance to finance a vindictive response to Ansar Dine's humiliating defeat and a warning to the French to stay out of their area of operation."

"Did they say what form this response would take?"

"That I don't have. I just know, as a group, they have raised over thirty million euros, and revenge is their goal. I can guarantee it's going to be big, and many French people are going to die somewhere."

"Why do you want us involved? Shouldn't you go to the French government?"

"Really, Mr. 2810? I have been in this business for a long time; don't you think that was my first thought? I called DGSI (French for General

Directorate for Internal Security), and they could not find any chatter or Intel to support my alarm. All I got was they would investigate it, which means they didn't believe me. I called French President Maurice Jossart, who agreed to make some calls and also found DGSI didn't have anything to substantiate the claim. I know my sources here on the ground, and this is real. Mokhtar and his band of lowlifes are being very quiet about it. I insisted to Jossart that someone needed to do something, or the prospect of dying Frenchmen would land in his lap. In confidence, he provided the information to contact US President Perez, who I have known for some time.

"Perez was very gracious but came to the same conclusion after checking with his people. I'm not exactly shy and probably pursued this a little aggressively with the President. I also hung on him the prospect of thousands of lives on his shoulders. He finally gave in, providing me with the method of contacting you people. By the way, who are you, and what's with the writing letters and this funny phone I have?"

Brad, who had been taking notes, replied, "I can assure you we have the same goals regarding your concerns. Innocent people should not have to suffer at the hands of a few who are radical in their beliefs. To my knowledge, we have not picked up any information regarding an attack on French soil. Who were your sources?"

"That's another problem I had with the DGSI. It's from previously used anonymous informants that I trust, having used them for years. Their information once saved my life during an assassination attempt. However, it's not the kind of information that the formalized institutions of my wonderful country consider the last word."

"Who did you talk to at DGSI?"

"I was given to a man named Durand. I was told he was high up, had access to all the information that would be available, and could make decisions. He was polite but didn't believe a word I said."

"Madam Ambassador, I want to thank you for providing this information. We have certain capabilities that we will incorporate to see if we can discover more information concerning your suspicions of an attack. I can assure you we will follow up on this. Please keep this phone in a safe place and tell no one of our conversations. I will get back to you with whatever we find. I will send you a meaningless text with a new code and a time on your mobile when we need to have an encrypted conversation. You will then repeat the procedures you used to make this call. Meanwhile, keep listening to your sources. If they have any updates, use the text feature of the G9 phone to get back."

"Well, Mr. 2810, this has been an interesting conversation. First, how do you know my mobile number? Second, I'm not used to sharing this kind of information with someone I don't trust or, in fact, know yet. Even if you find out what they're going to do, what can *you* do about it but wave another unnoticed flag?"

"As to your mobile number, well, as I said, we have our capabilities. Second, we don't publicly wave flags. If we find something vital that's not addressed by the traditional authorities, we are capable of handling it."

With a challenge in her voice, she added, "A well-funded group bent on killing as many as possible somewhere in France?"

"Anywhere."

"As I said, this has been an interesting conversation. I will wait for your text."

Brad put the phone down and started filling out the call log on the screen. He could understand the ambassador's skepticism due to the unusual secrecy involved in her eventually making contact. He didn't take the time to explain that the Cartel determines where to apply its resources in two ways. One is from a POC (Pattern of Concern) generated by Geneva9, also known as Mom, the Cartel's massive intelligence and surveillance asset. The other is information received from a secure phone conversation after receiving a written request for contact. All requests came in through letters re-posted several times to new addresses before arriving at the Cartel's headquarters and onto Brad's desk. In the age of computers, it turns out regular mail is the safest way to transfer information anonymously around the world without any digital trail. Each country's mail privacy laws and the sheer volume of mail within any country inhibited regular scrutiny. A letter is old fashioned and uncomplicated, but it is foolproof.

GET YOUR COPY OF PRIMARY PROTOCOL TODAY.

https://www.amazon.com/dp/B09CG9RBLQ

Enjoy a sample of Islands of Peace

ISLANDS OF PEACE
A Kate Adler Book # 3

**WILL ONE MAN, AVENGING HIS BROTHER'S DEATH, USE
RISING TENSIONS BETWEEN THE USA AND RUSSIA TO START
A WAR? CAN KATE ADLER AND THE CARTEL STOP HIS
DEADLY PLAN IN TIME?**

A mystery/thriller series full of unexpected twists and turns
delivers nonstop action.

CHAPTER 1
MOSCOW

Kate Adler entered her penthouse suite in Moscow's Ararat hotel and surveyed the utter chaos. Someone had ransacked her room while she attended a state dinner. Moving farther into the suite revealed a man ripping cushions apart. He looked back at her.

"What the hell are you doing here?" she asked, frozen.

Turning to escape, someone grabbed her from behind. She instinctively resisted but felt the grip tighten. Hearing heavy breathing and becoming overpowered, her body tensed. Angry at being accosted, she felt her high heel give way upon stabbing the man's foot.

"Bitch!" he yelled, reacting to the pain and violently throwing her to the floor.

Kate glanced off a couch and fell hard against the coffee table. An upward glare revealed a 9mm Glock held by a furious bald man with hollow eyes. Pumped on adrenalin from the struggle, he shouted in a thick Russian accent. "Where is the information from Tonkov?"

Kate frowned. "I can't help you and probably wouldn't even if I could. I'm sure you know by now whatever you want isn't here."

The other man pulled the purse from Kate's hands and dumped the contents onto the carpet. Looking down, he sifted the items with his shoe. The bald man put a finger to his earpiece; receiving instructions, he said, "We can't stay any longer; we need to leave now." Still holding the gun, he looked intensely at Kate on the floor, the stare threatening and unmistakable. Both men turned and left.

In her thirty-five years, she had been shot at several times and survived a bombing but never experienced a physical assault. She thought briefly about calling hotel security but then mused; This is Moscow. Instead, she reached for a specially designed secure phone lying on the carpet, along with the remains of her purse. Seconds after she hit the button, she heard Brad Danner's voice, a friend and associate.

"Hi, Kate," Brad said. "How was the dinner? Boring? I have you on speaker in the operations center. The team says hi."

"Hi, Brad, hi everyone; I have bigger concerns than the dinner at the moment. I came back to my room and look at what I found." She held the phone up to show a video of the disarray the men had left behind. Everyone in the center could see the images on one of the many large display screens on the walls.

"As I walked into the room, someone grabbed me and threw me to the floor, but I'm fine. I don't know what the men wanted, but I think it has something to do with Russian President Kozloff and my friend Aleksis. Tonight, after the dinner, Aleksis received a troubling phone call, and he told me to leave the country right away. I need the team to safely get me out of the hotel before someone else arrives."

Brad didn't need any more information, as this was as important as it got. His voice tightened, "Are you safe right now?"

"Yes, I have both entrances to the suite locked, and I have closed the curtains."

"Good, we will work on it and be right back." Three years ago, Kate had inherited her father's industrial empire, placing her high on the world's multi-billionaires list. High society knew Kate as the very public face of the Helmut Adler Children's Fund, named in memory of her father. Only a handful knew she had also inherited her father's powerful covert organization called the Cartel.

Everyone in the Cartel's operations center heard her request, and in practiced precision, each addressed their specific assignments.

Elena and Lauren, the two with direct access to the Cartel's supercomputer affectionately known as Mom, queried for any Moscow police or security notifications out of the ordinary. In charge of field operations, Penn Hauer sent an alert to the Cartel's special operations group. He then brought up his contact list, looking for someone from his past. Another agent in the room placed the status of the Cartel's small fleet of private planes on a second screen.

Penn looked up. "We can't use her plane sitting at Moscow International airport. Whoever did this will already have it under surveillance. Someone call Captain Silanos on the plane and tell him to take off ASAP before they impound him and the plane, or worse. We will give him coordinates in the air."

A voice in the room answered, "I'm on that."

Penn found the name and reached for a secure phone. He heard a voice asking, "Hello, who is this?"

"Freddy, it's Penn Hauer. Where are you right now?"

"On my way to meet a few friends for a beer. Oh, by the way, it's nice to hear from you, too," the man said, outright laughing.

Freddy Faraday was more than just an old-time friend; he was a man of many talents, not all reputable. These talents made him extremely resourceful, depending on the need.

"Hold on a sec," Penn said to Freddy.

"Lauren," he began, "I need a small airport well outside of Moscow that can take Captain Silanos and the Gulf Stream 650."

"Yes, I'm ahead of you. Kaluga is two hours or so outside of Moscow by car via the E101." Lauren queried the keyboard. "It has a 7,000-foot runway. The Gulf stream only needs 5,600 fully loaded."

"Great, get those coordinates to the Captain. Freddy, are you still there?"

"I'm here; where else would I be?"

"My principal could be in danger, and I need to quietly get her out of Moscow. Can I count on you?"

"You always have; why stop believing now, brother?" Did you know I had dinner with Ms. Adler tonight?"

"No, I didn't, and don't know why you would. Hold on."

"Brad," Penn said, "can you get to Kate and tell her a Freddy Faraday will call to escort her out of the hotel?"

"On it," Brad said.

"Freddy, I need you to pick up Ms. Adler at the Ararat Park hotel. I need you to go to her room and stay with her through the lobby and outside.

Then I need you to drive her south toward an airport in Kaluga. Do you know where it is?"

"Hell no, I only live here—I was born in Cincinnati, remember? Send the directions to my phone. There went my beer and poker game with a few heavy rollers. You're going to owe me big time, my friend."

"Really, Freddy?" Penn had to crack a smile. "This is a hardship? When was the last time you had a beer?"

Freddy chuckled. "At lunch."

"That's what I thought. Freddy, take this seriously."

"You have that tone in your voice again. I know this is serious. I'm a highly respected psychologist in my spare time."

"What do you mean, my tone?"

"Every time you mention her name, you get all wobbly on me. You were going to introduce me to her sometime, but that never happened."

"Not in a million years would I introduce her to the likes of you," he said, laughing. "Besides, being concerned for her is my job, Freddy. She's a high-value target wherever she goes."

"Yeah, thanks for the company line. What's Ms. Adler's status? Is she ready? Do I go now?"

"How far away are you? More importantly, do you have a car more reliable than the one you had on my last trip out?"

"How about an Audi R8, their big guy? It's the baddest vehicle Audi makes. This thing is a rocket and chick magnet."

"How in the world …?"

"Some people just shouldn't play poker," Freddy laughed. "You declined last time here, smart man. I was already downtown, so I'm perhaps eight blocks away. I just hung a U-turn, and I'm on my way. Hey, Penn?"

"Yes."

"Not that it matters, but just how serious? It's a tactical question. What are we facing?"

"She attended a Kozloff state dinner, and when she got back to her room, someone had tossed it. Two thug types attacked her at gunpoint. Do you have a sidearm in the car?"

"In Moscow, it's not good when thugs come out of the woodwork, especially brandishing guns. That means it's serious. To answer your question, I always have one installed in a fake door panel, and the Audi is no different."

GET YOUR COPY OF ISLANDS OF PEACE TODAY.

https://www.amazon.com/gp/product/B09KTFGVQN

Enjoy a sample of Brimstone Offensive

THE BRIMSTONE OFFENSIVE
NEVER UNDERESTIMATE YOUR ENEMIES

CHAPTER 1
Marseilles, France

In every direction, monolithic walls of shipping containers slept, and loading cranes reached into the dark sky. The area was traditionally the driest region in France, but heavy rain fell, and rushing water searched for drains.

Four men sat in a van in front of an office at the massive Marseilles-Fox Port 2 terminal. The largest container port in France. Havel Vanek, head of special operations at TerraDyne Industries, was inside. Vanek's job was to do whatever Milosh Petrovic, founder, and owner, directed. That included everything from leaning on someone to get their cooperation to blowing up part of a competitor's business

Vanek looked through the rain-spotted window then down to the picture on his phone to visually confirm the address. "What do you see up there?" he asked the driver.

"Nothing from up here, all clear." the driver said, looking out the front and side windows of the van.

His team had gone over the details of the operation many times. But Vanek's knack for survival depended on never assuming anything. His obsession with details kept him alive to tell the stories of his previous assignments.

He nodded and said to his team, "OK, let's do this."

He pulled the balaclava down, and the others followed.

One man opened the rolling side door of the vehicle. The three of them left the driver behind and rushed to the front door of an office. All of them were grateful for the protection of the overhang.

Vanek looked up and pointed. "Get that," he said.

One of the men ripped at a surveillance camera covering the front door.

Vanek tried the key, and it didn't work. He said, "Why am I not surprised that our inside man gave us the wrong key. I want his name." Disgusted, he pointed to another man and moved back.

"Take care of this lock. I don't want to be standing out here without an excuse."

The man pulled out a spray can of compressed air used to dust off electronics. With thick insulated gloves, he began spraying the metal lock on the heavy wooden door as frost began to form outside the can. As he emptied the can, the metal got icy cold and became more and more brittle. He hit the lock with a hammer and watched the shattered pieces fall out from the door to the ground.

"Alright, move over," Vanek said as he walked past, making his way to the alarm panel. He thought of the wrong key, "This better work."

He entered the number code given to him by the same employee— someone whose family had been threatened and forced to cooperate. Vanek saw the green light and let out a sigh of relief.

Vanek reached up and sprayed black paint on the lens of a security camera just inside the door. "Take the place apart, boys," he said. They proceeded to reduce the ordinarily sedate office into something resembling the aftermath of a typhoon. They overturned desks, chairs, and emptied drawers onto the floor.

"Pull that bookshelf down, and someone destroy the glass partitions," Vanek said. Compared to some operations he had directed, this was a frivolous activity, but it would send the required message. The computers were on, and Vanek sat at one, trying to use the password from the inside man to no avail. He cursed and slammed his hand onto the keyboard. Vanek looked at the safe but knew it was never a target. He walked down a hallway to the manager's office, trying that computer with similar results. After looking at some papers in a basket, he reached down and over-turned the desk, ignoring its noise. Vanek pulled a printed message from a pocket and left it on the manager's office floor. Vanek turned to look directly into the one security camera they'd left in place. The prolonged look made it a defiant gesture and challenge to anyone monitoring the footage.

Vanek had lived a tumultuous childhood in and out of foster homes and a life of crime. During that time, he fought with anyone and everyone.

For Vanek, violence protected him from the dark internal forces and his anger about the failed efforts to help him

After a series of standardized tests, one of his schools told his foster guardians of his inability to perceive others' emotions and physical pain. His extraordinary life and mental state qualified him for this position. Petrovic had harnessed Vanek's "defense" mechanism. It resulted in Vanek finally feeling he had found a place where he belonged.

A voice spoke in his earpiece. It was the driver outside. "Boss, we have two harbor security vehicles approaching. Something or someone tipped them off."

"Are they driving by?"

"Hold on. No, they have stopped a hundred feet away and are blocking the road. One is getting out."

"Are they blocking the only way out of here?

"No, but it's the best way. I've another option."

Vanek thought for a moment. "Disable the vehicles with the M130. Make sure they can't follow us. While you're doing that, we'll run for the van."

"Got it." The driver reached between the seats and pulled up an M130 assault rifle. He stepped out and sprayed the front tires and radiators of the two cars from behind the door.

Vanek and his men bolted from the front, running to the van.

"Get us out of here," Vanek said, looking at his watch. "I've got a plane to catch. I need to be in Tanzania tomorrow."

The driver circled, taking the van up and over a sidewalk, destroyed the sign for the office next door. The driver pressed hard on the accelerator, and everyone felt the van surge forward as they pulled away and into the damp night. Behind them, above the open door of the destroyed office, the sign read, "Morton Roth Shipping and Maritime Services Company. A division of Adler Industries."

THANK YOU FOR SUPPORTING MY WRITING

Printed in Great Britain
by Amazon